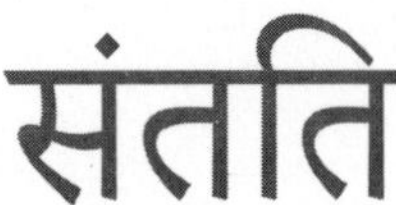

MAHATMA GANDHI

THEN. NOW. NEXT

Celebrating 150 years of the legend, the life, the legacy

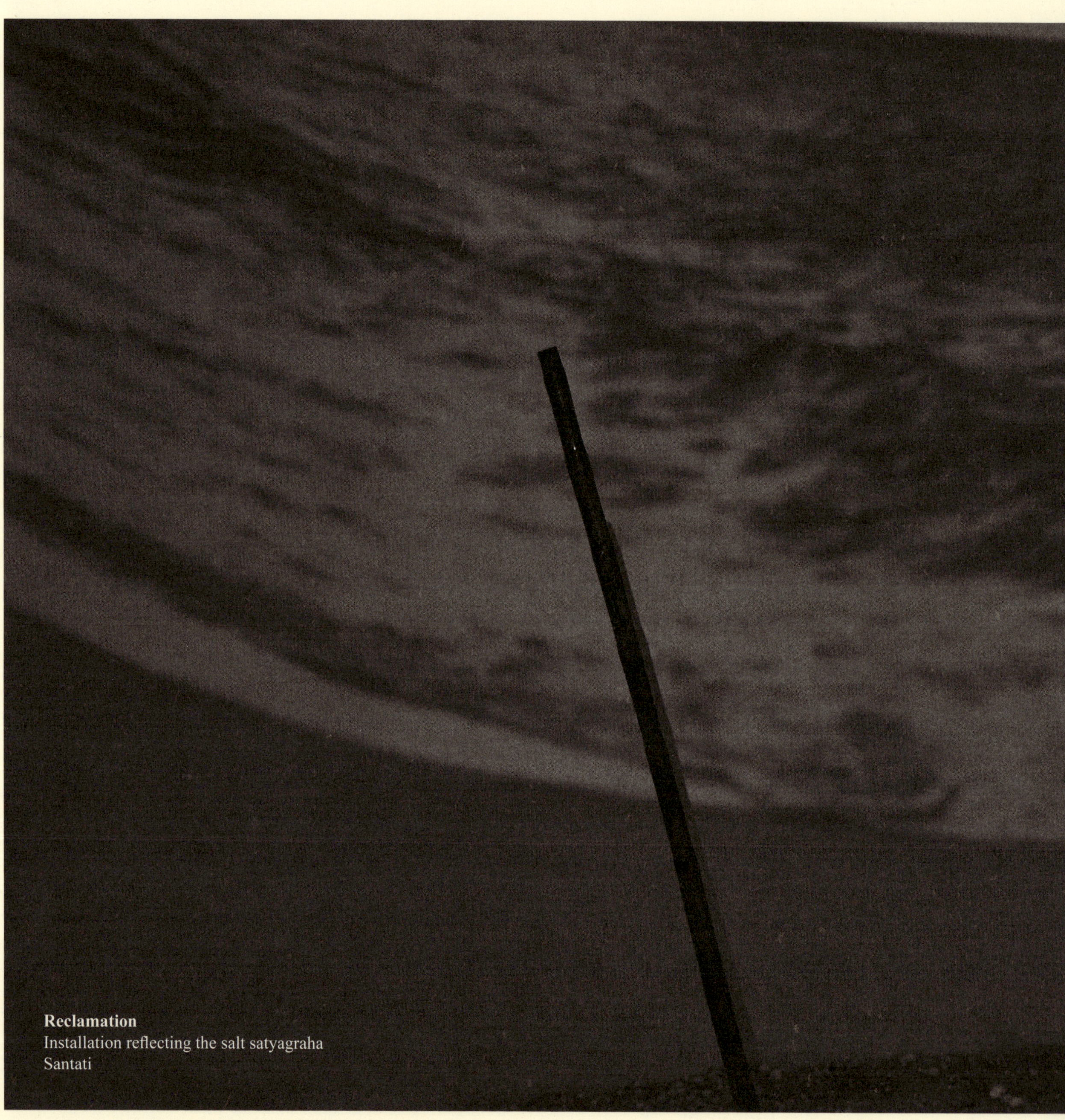

Reclamation
Installation reflecting the salt satyagraha
Santati

Each act performed
For myself alone
Each journey that marks
My progress
Solo
Each possession gathered
To further my comfort
Will dry up
Drop by drop
The ocean that once held
Water for all

हर कर्म जिसका ध्येय स्वहित हो
हर कदम
जिसका लक्ष्य मेरा आरोहण हो
हर धन
जिसका उपयोग मेरा भोग हो
बूंद बूंद कर देगा लुप्त
वह सागर, जो हर करता था तृप्त

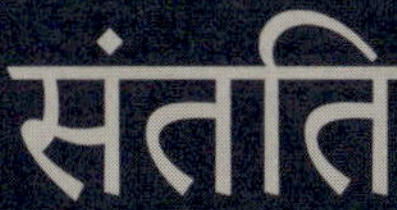

MAHATMA GANDHI

THEN. NOW. NEXT

Celebrating 150 years of the legend, the life, the legacy

Author
Navkirat Sodhi

Exposition Curation // Hindi Translation
Lavina Baldota

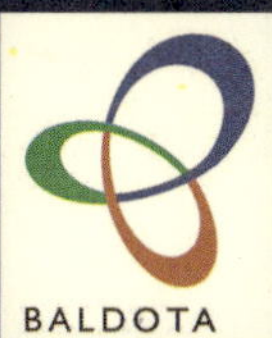

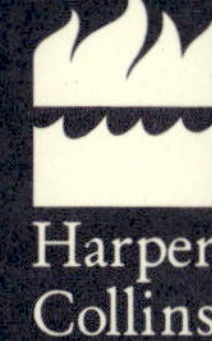

First published in India by
HarperCollins Publishers in 2020
A-75, Sector 57, Noida, Uttar Pradesh 201301, India
www.harpercollins.co.in

2 4 6 8 10 9 7 5 3 1

Cover image: National Gandhi Museum Archives

P-ISBN: 978-93-9032-795-9

Typeset in Times New Roman by Vijendra Bhardwaj

Printed and bound at
Thomson Press (India) Ltd

Rooted in the philosophy of Mahatma Gandhi's findings lies the backbone of the Abheraj Baldota Foundation. Deploying wealth to nurture growth, realizing the power of indigenous resources as a people, as a country and enabling sustainable living have been pivotal working principles of the Foundation.

Santati is a natural extension of our long-standing relationship and homage to Mahatma Gandhi and his messages. Through this coming together of art, artisans and India's prosperous heritage, let's begin a subtle journey of finding the Gandhi within.

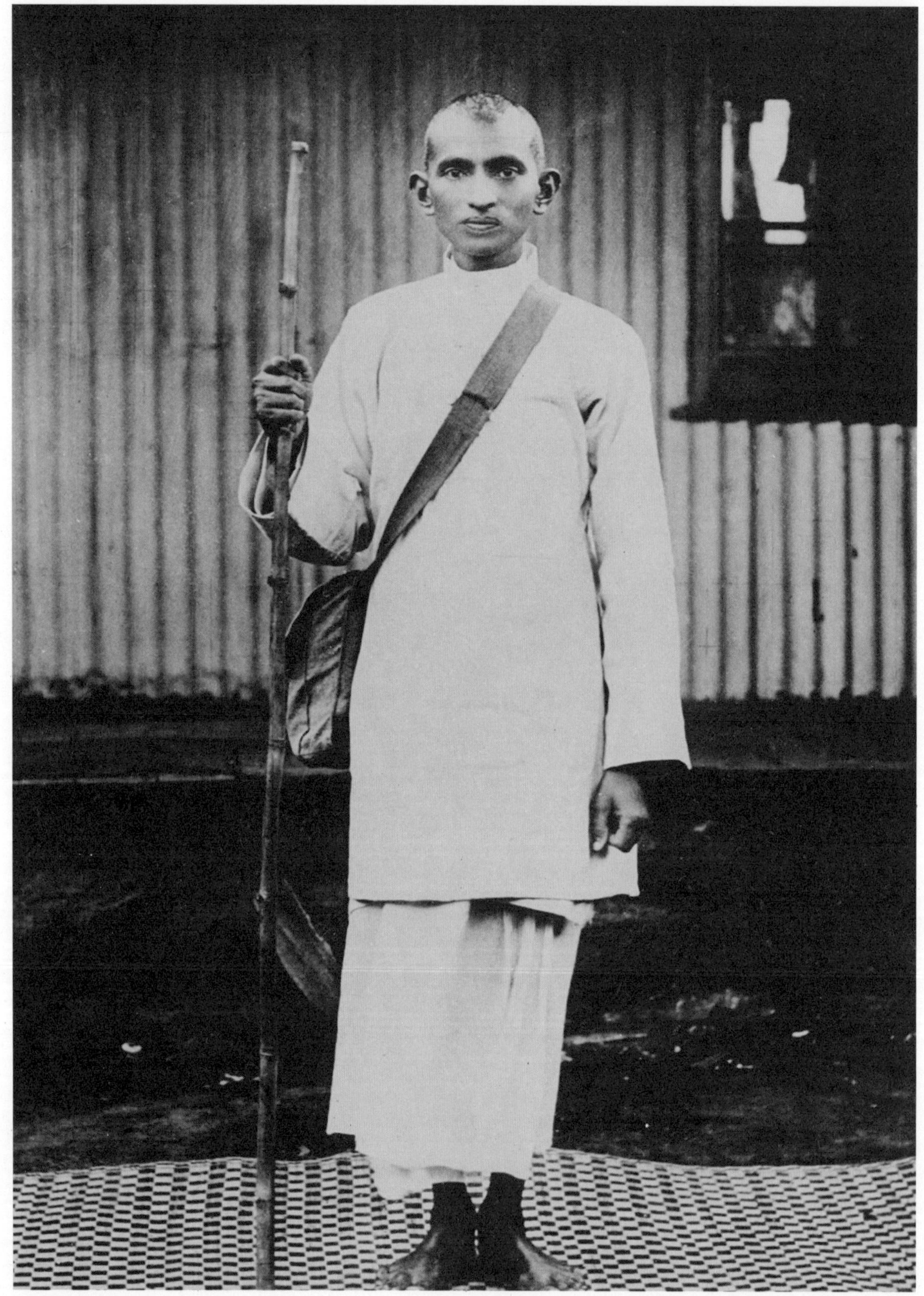

CONTENTS

संतति

PARTICIPANTS

Gaurang Shah
Textile Designer

Gaurang Shah interprets iconic paintings by artist Raja Ravi Varma as handwoven visuals on saris, hand spun in khadi. The focus of his work revolves around the *swadeshi* movement.

Klove Studio (Prateek Jain and Gautam Seth)
Light Designers

Klove Studio translates the philosophy of *ahimsa* through architectural light design. Their work celebrates the simplicity and poignancy of Gandhi's life.

Gaurav Gupta
Couturier

Gaurav Gupta's installation is an ode to Mahatma Gandhi inspired by his heartbeat, his search for Truth and the infinite quality of his message.

Rajesh Pratap Singh
Designer

Rajesh Pratap Singh's work is a study in how Gandhi has been observed by the world, told through metal and indigo.

Ashiesh Shah
Architect

Ashiesh Shah combines through the idea of less is more, designs that are modern and minimal in their aesthetic while deep-rooted in traditional practices of Indian artisans.

Jean François Lesage
Couture Embroiderer

Lesage transfers handwritten letters of Mahatma Gandhi and the route of the march to Dandi on to khadi through couture embroidery.

Navkirat Sodhi
Poet

Navkirat Sodhi pays her tribute with experiential poetry written around the spiritual and philosophical significance of Mahatma Gandhi's messages.

Kishore Jhunjhunwala
Collector, Philatelist, Numismatist

An avid collector of all objects and documentation related to Gandhi and deeply influenced by the life of the Mahatma, Kishore Jhunjhunwala contributes to Santati with his extensive collection of over fifty years.

National Gallery of Modern Art (NGMA)

Apart from artworks revolving around Gandhian themes created between 1940–60, the NGMA also shares paintings from artist Raja Ravi Varma's landmark collection.

Raja Ravi Varma Heritage Foundation

The Foundation showcases works from artist Raja Ravi Varma's repertoire. The visuals of these paintings transferred on to pallus of khadi saris by textile designer Gaurang Shah have been inspired by the same.

Sir JJ School of Art

The works included are by students of the Sir JJ School of Art, many of whom went on to become widely known artists of their time. Created between 1940–60, these works reflect the deep connection of art with the freedom struggle and depict various scenes from Mahatma Gandhi's life and his dream for a perfect India.

Indira Gandhi National Centre for the Arts

The Centre lends to Santati, rare and unseen works of photographers Henri Cartier-Bresson, DRD Wadia and Sunil Janah and painter Elizabeth Brunner.

Museum of Art and Photography (MAP)

The Museum of Art and Photography (MAP), Bengaluru, lends from its collection, works in painting and chromolithography, depicting Mahatma Gandhi, his journey and how he was observed by artists like Jamini Roy, Kishan Duriseti and Jagadeesh Thammineni.

From the Author

In the few months leading up to the opening of *Santati*, the Gandhi Museum and library in Delhi became my studio and second home. I wanted not merely to read Gandhi but to be able to immerse in and taste his mind, his message and meaning and soak in the light of his philosophy.

To bind this most unique exhibition through poetry called for some deep diving, a submission and a letting go – of all superficial learning hitherto and of the web of bias that appears every time Gandhi is brought up. It's hard for poetry to find a place in a room crowded with solid perception and yet that is its purpose.

In and around this tranquil, unadorned building, through its vibrant, vacant corridors or perhaps arising from the dust settled peacefully on rare books, for the tiniest fraction of time, I think I caught a whiff of the man. He appeared like a mercurial mirage. His eyes, his skin and his gaze shone like the sharp reflection of light bouncing off a newly brandished sword – singing a song of mettle, over-prepared to conquer. He appeared marching around in the pages of his collected works, nimbly, hurriedly, steering time with his own wheel. The museum, the library, his works and works about him, Mani Bhawan (Gandhi's abode in Mumbai) and delving into the works of the participating artists added to the process, becoming sublime. Effortlessly the pieces started coming together and, in a few translucent moments, his figure stood before me, fluid in form, stark in its resolve. He said, wrote, worked, walked and inspired so much that the path he treaded became a mark on the timeline of time. It divided history into a world before Gandhi and a world after him.

Often shunned, violently questioned, mocked for his beliefs and finally made prey to cold bullets, Mahatma Gandhi's journey is akin to that of truth. He held up a mirror for us to see who we could be and what we did not do to get there.

Santati, the exhibition and the book celebrate this piercing vision and his fired-up dynamism urging us to look for a moment, somewhere along the way, at the Gandhi *within*.

Cover me with the gospel
Of the truth
Without religion

When Lavina Baldota first expressed her vision of Santati, I was drawn in without an instant of hesitation – by the purity of her enthusiasm and the singularity of her idea for this first-of-its-kind interpretation and story.

Her relationship to art, artists, artisans and poetry revealed itself as a curious dichotomy between extremely refined and absolutely untouched. She has a distilled way of looking at life and I've often observed her peering into not the form but that which informs it.

Throughout the process she remained true to her belief and made the whole journey as subtle and seamless as it had first appeared to her ten years ago – in meditation. She saw the figure of Mahatma Gandhi while in deep contemplation and it became a vague but firm chapter in her bright, elegant mind. A decade later, it shaped up as *Santati, Mahatma Gandhi – Then. Now. Next.*

Navkirat Sodhi

I wish not
To be a hero
Dare I leave
A cult behind
All I wish is for you
To wake up
And claim your mind

चाह नहीं मैं कहलाऊं
कोई संत महान
या कोई पंथ छोड़ जाऊं
जो बने मेरी पहचान
स्वयं से आपको अभिन्न कर पाऊं
यही मेरा अभियान

"All cults are wrong. They make of a man or a woman, a demi-god, placing him or her beyond the touch of human association. To turn a person into a deity and ideas into an ism is to consign them to stony lifelessness. Gandhi himself said, 'There is no such thing as Gandhism and I do not want to leave a cult after me.'"

Gandhi – Essential Writings by Gopalkrishna Gandhi

From the Curator

Nandalal Bose, a contemporary of Mahatma Gandhi and a prolific artist, expressed, "Mahatmaji may not be an artist in the same sense that we professional artists are, nevertheless I cannot but consider him to be a true artist. All his life he has spent in creating his own personality and in fashioning others after his high ideals. His mission is to make Gods out of men of clay. I am sure his ideal will inspire the artists of the world."

Santati for me is a limitless canvas of introspection and self-discovery woven by yarns of ethos derived from Gandhian influence, rendered with the hues of my most intrinsic emotions, especially love and pride for my roots, my country, its leaders, artists, artisans, aesthetics and its rich heritage.

To me, Mahatma Gandhi is a symbol of perfect balance, the balance between doing and being. The process of putting together Santati, the Mahatma's life and ideals have inspired me to move from thinking to doing, from becoming to being. Like the Mahatma's ascetic life, Santati is austere. It does not distract. Instead, it compels the viewers to look inward and find the Mahatma within.

Lavina Baldota

संतति *// Santati was conceptualized by Lavina Baldota as a tribute to the father of the nation. A cherished patron and mentor to the arts, curator Lavina Baldota spearheads the corporate social role of the Abheraj Baldota Foundation whose founder chairman Shri Abheraj H. Baldota was closely associated with Mahatma Gandhi during the freedom struggle. The Foundation has as its backbone, Gandhi's message on wealth – "You are not the owner of your wealth but a privileged trustee to serve the community with it"*

Santati is a sequence that does not break, an infinite loop, a continuum. Through his seamless, sleepless journey from Gandhi to Mahatma, this visionary radiated, imbibed and left behind messages in mindful living, messages bare in their truth, messages that move in the concentric rings of time, holding within them the power to gently overturn the world.

From uniting a diverse country through non-violence to inspiring global leaders and instilling the resolve of tireless, detached action, he entered the veritable spirit of generations. Ablaze with a dream, charged with an electric intellect, carrying a mind and body deeply willing to suffer for Truth, Mahatma Gandhi is no more just a person, a philosophy, an idea. After 150 years of his birth, he has merged with the soil to become a state of mind.

To permeate this state of mind, exceptional artists and minds from their walks come together for *Santati* to interpret *their* Gandhi.

इस संक्रमण काल में 'संतति' एक ऐसी अटूट श्रंखला है जो कि एक असीमित अपरिमित निरंतरता लिए हुए वृत्त के सदृश्य है। अपनी व्यापक विचारधारा जिसमें समग्रता एवं समरसता का समावेश हो, लिए हुए "मोहन से महात्मा" की कालजयी यात्रा ने एक ऐसा अनूठा संदेश मानवता के लिए रख छोड़ा है जो कि सत्य और केवल सत्य पर ही आधारित था और जिसके केन्द्र बिन्दु में मानवता के लिए बस निरपेक्ष, शावत एवं व्यापक मूल्य ही था।

गांधी न केवल स्वदेशी बल्कि विदेशी कई पीढ़ियों के मानस पटल पर एक अटूट छवि हैं, जिन्होंने केवल अहिंसा के माध्यम से एक अकल्पनीय विविधता वाले देश को अपने असीम पौरुष, अनन्त वीरवृत्ति तथा अपराजय पराक्रम के द्वारा सूत्रबध्द किया। सत्य की खोज में उनकी प्रतिबद्धता का कठोर तप में परिवर्तित होना, जिसे एक दर्शन, एक विचारधारा के रूप में देश की मिट्टी मिट्टी में व्याप्त हो जाना, आज भी कितना प्रासंगिक है।

इस विचारधारा को व्यापकता प्रदान करने के उद्देश्य से कुछ चुनिंदे कलाकार महात्मा गांधी पर मानसमंथन करने के लिए 'संतति' पर एकत्रित हुए हैं। यही बापू की १५० वीं वर्षगाँठ पर हृदयपूर्वक श्रद्धांजली है।

"In my opinion, true art consists in learning from nature without struggling against it."

Mahatma Gandhi

THEN

These eyes can walk
Beyond our feet
Way further than barricades of time
Tread above the patterns of past
Clear the path for a new dawn
In a blink
With their lashes
They can draw us
Out of the well
Of submission imposed, created
Foreign, native
And show us another way
To demand what is ours
They can look from above
And behind and ahead and within
And convince our soul
To rise from the floor
Show us the infinite
We hold within
These are seats of true power
Lent to us to uncover our force
When open

When closed they become receptors
That can hear
The detailed plans of time

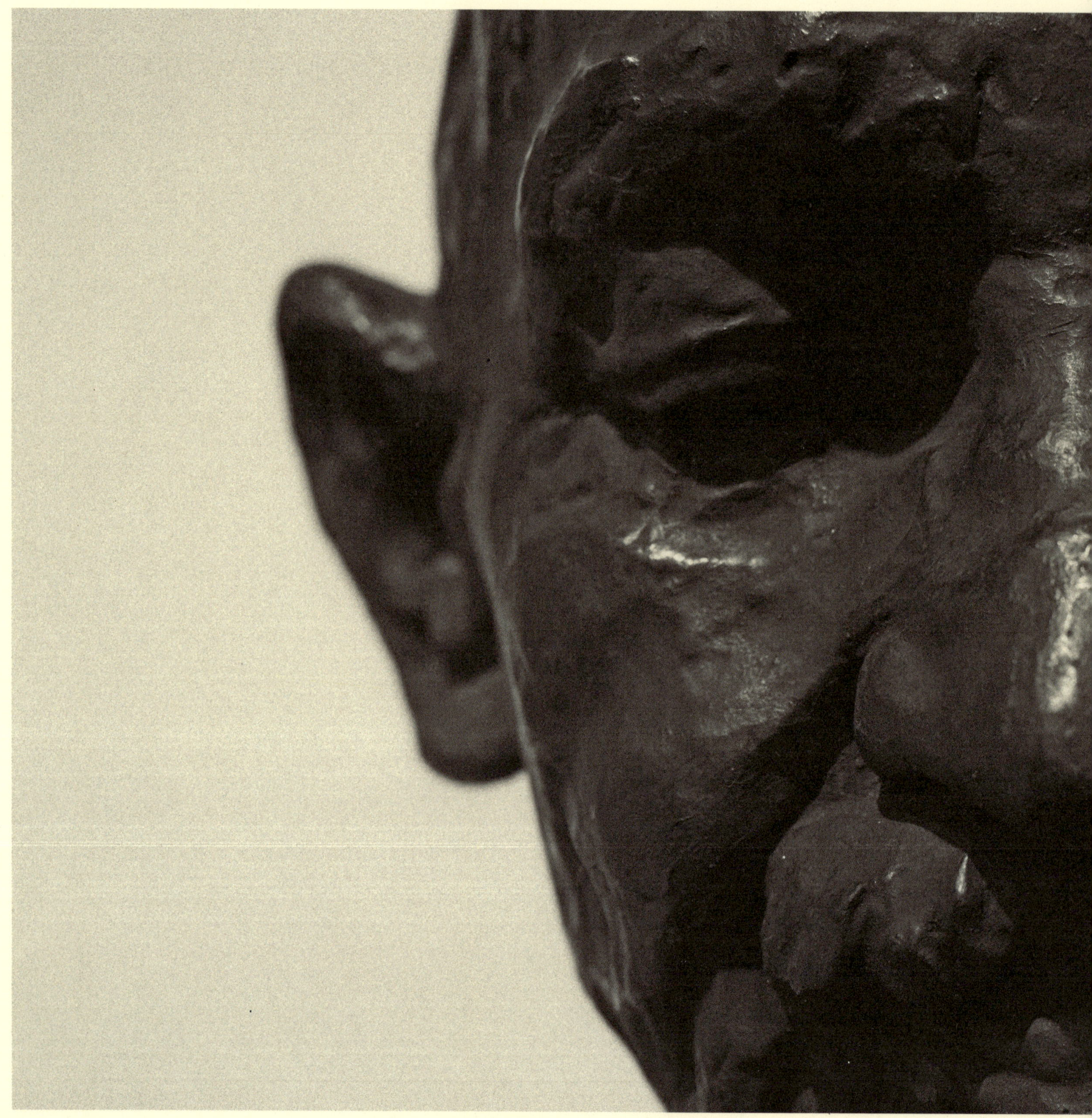

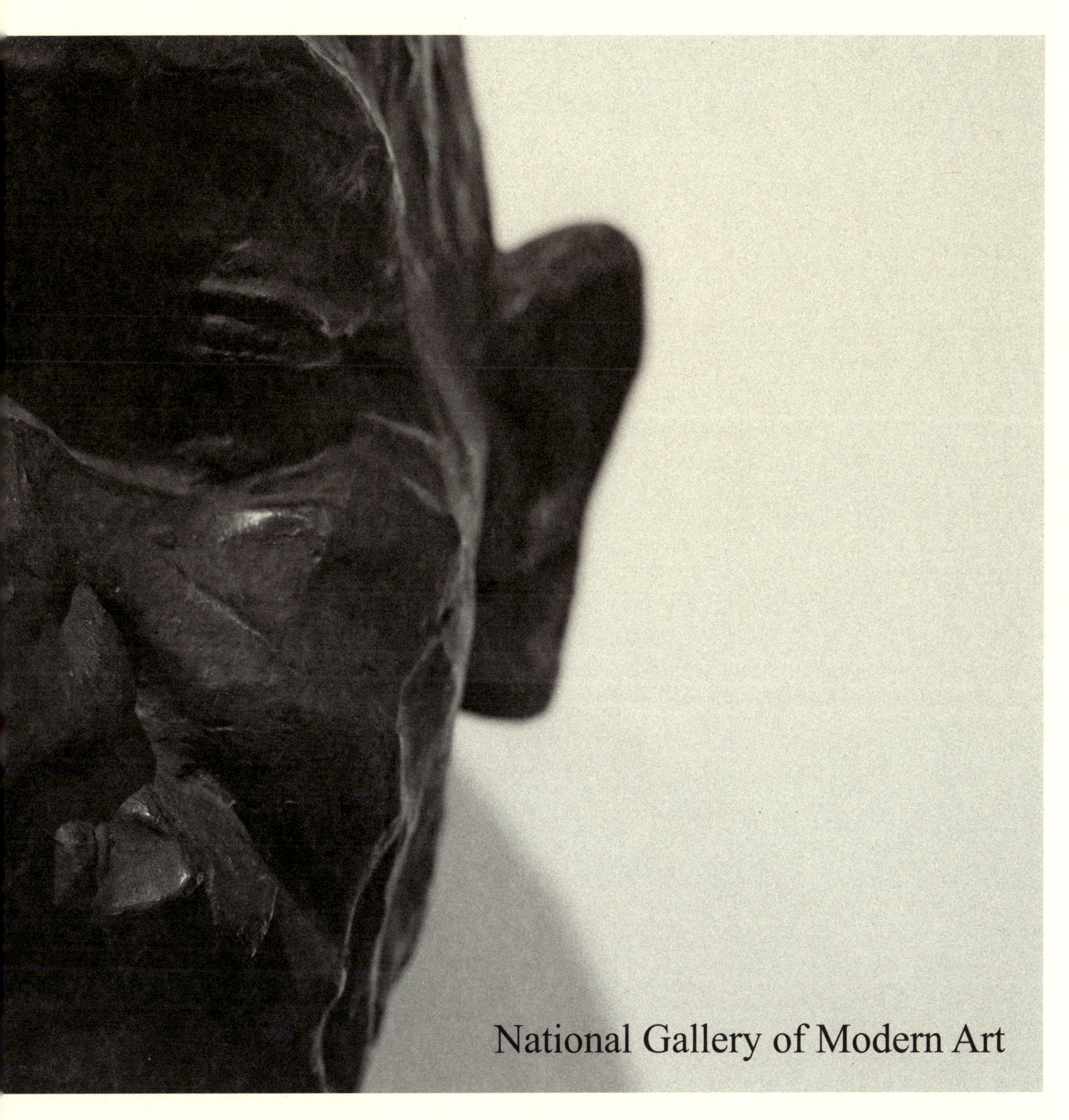
National Gallery of Modern Art

ART HAS, THROUGHOUT HISTORY, been a channel for the human consciousness to express its churning. Evoking, reflecting, questioning, projecting, it essays to illuminate the complex lattice of life. Mahatma Gandhi was a champion of high thinking and emphasized on the role of art as being an aid for the soul to realize its inner self. He maintained that anything which is a hindrance to the flight of the soul is nothing but a trap. His work in the socio-political spheres during India's struggle for freedom became a pivotal inspiration for many artists and thinkers of the time and continues to impact movements in philosophy, art and politics.

The unique works of artists featured in this rare, exclusive collection from the National Gallery of Modern Art are a glimpse into their impressions of Gandhi.

"I hold that so long as I live, I must have a student's inquiring mind and thirst for learning."

Mahatma Gandhi

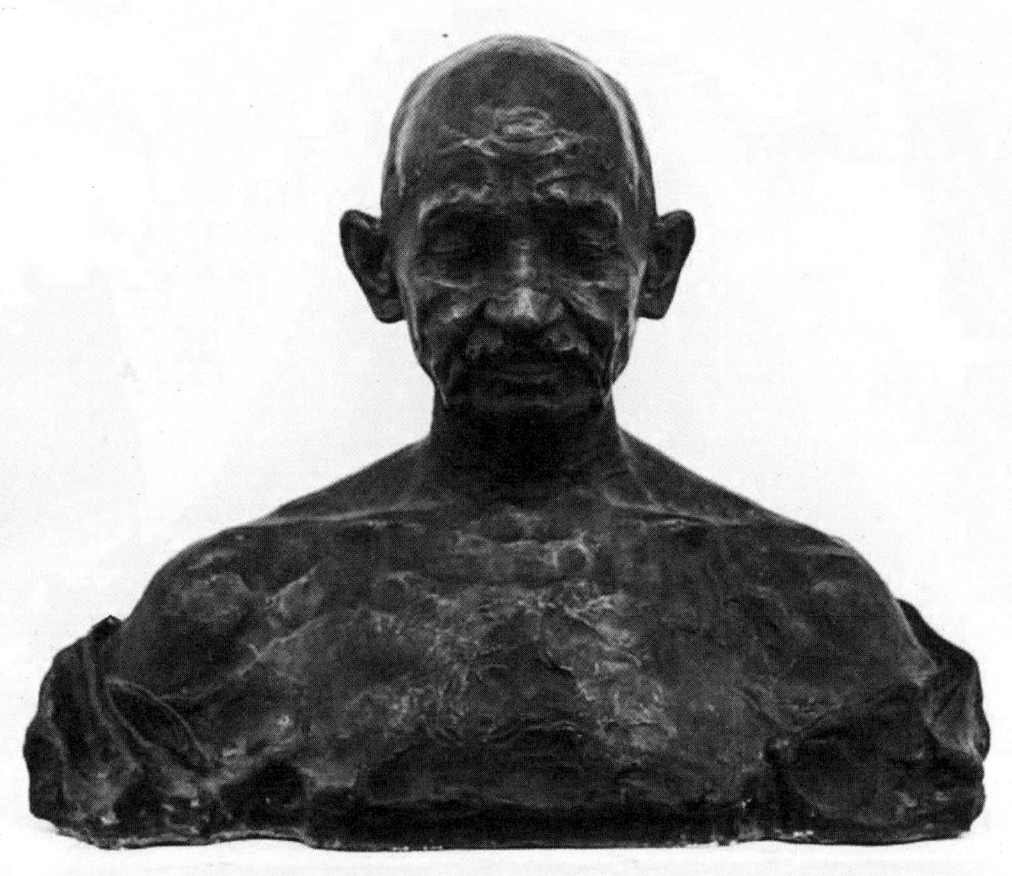

Mahatma Gandhi
Ram V. Sutar
Bronze // NGMA Collection

Subtle as vapour
Sharper than time
The difference between
Truth and Reality

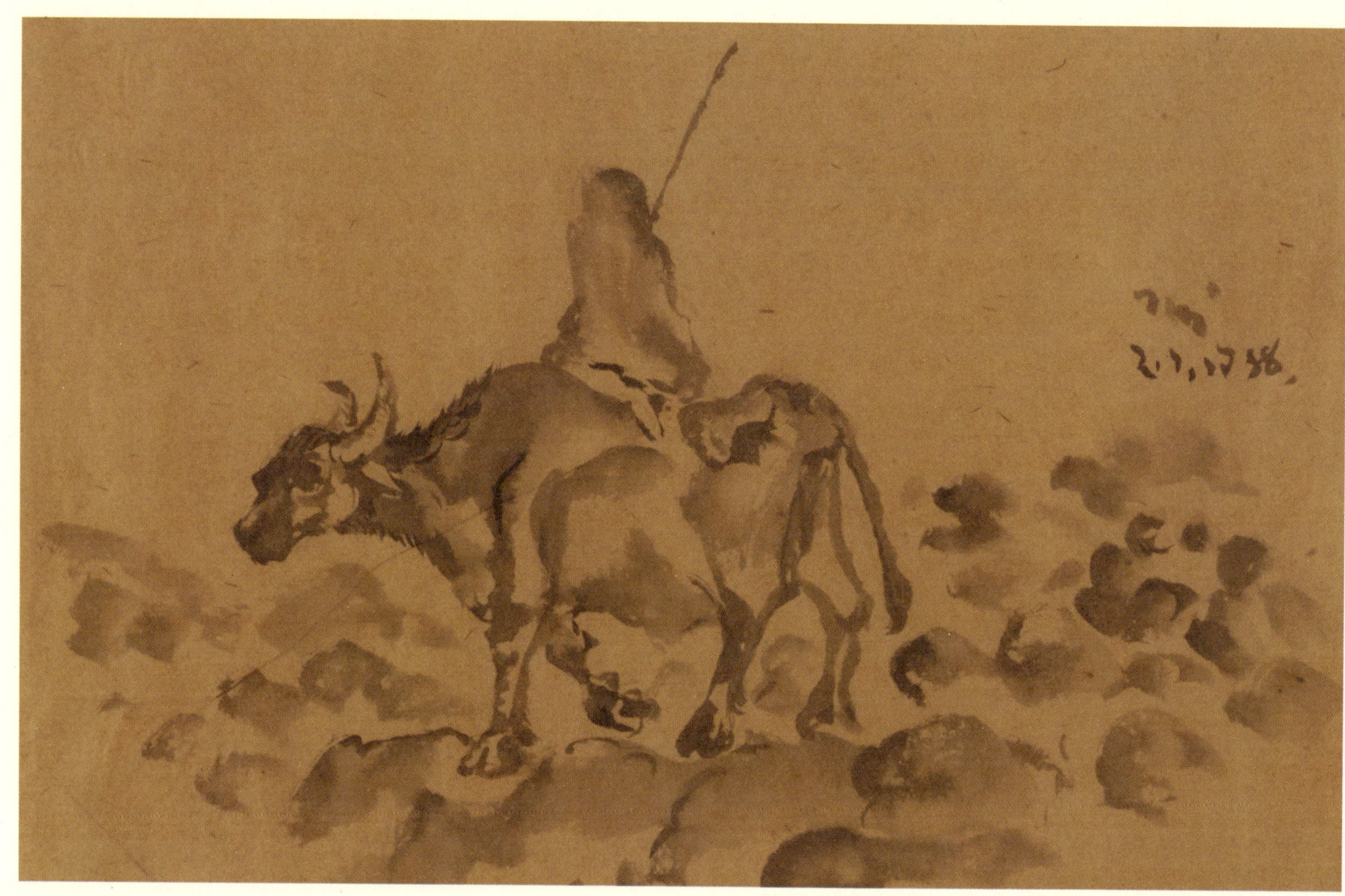

Buffalo rider
Nandalal Bose
Watercolour on paper // NGMA Collection

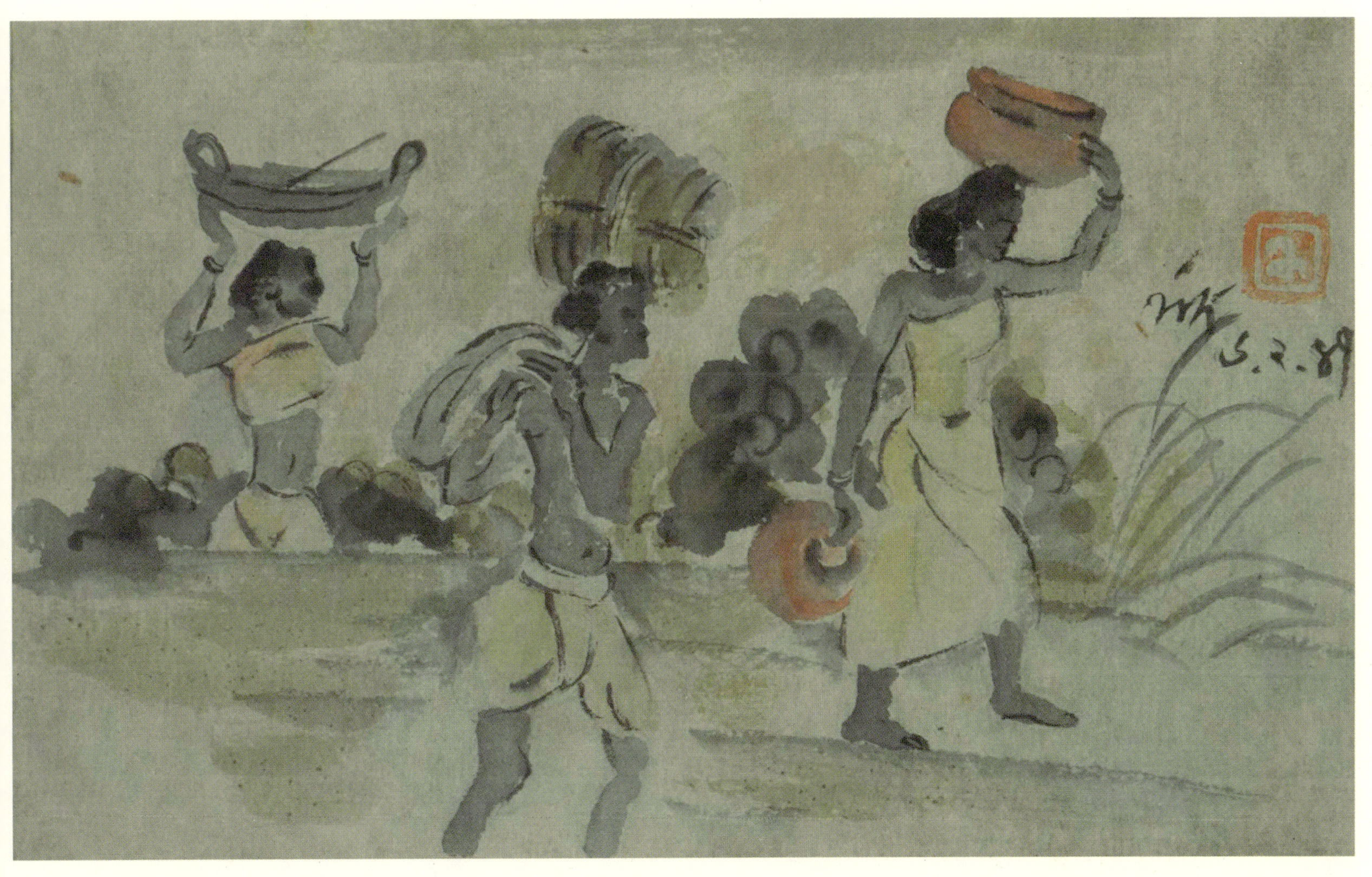

After the mela
Nandalal Bose
Watercolour on paper // NGMA Collection

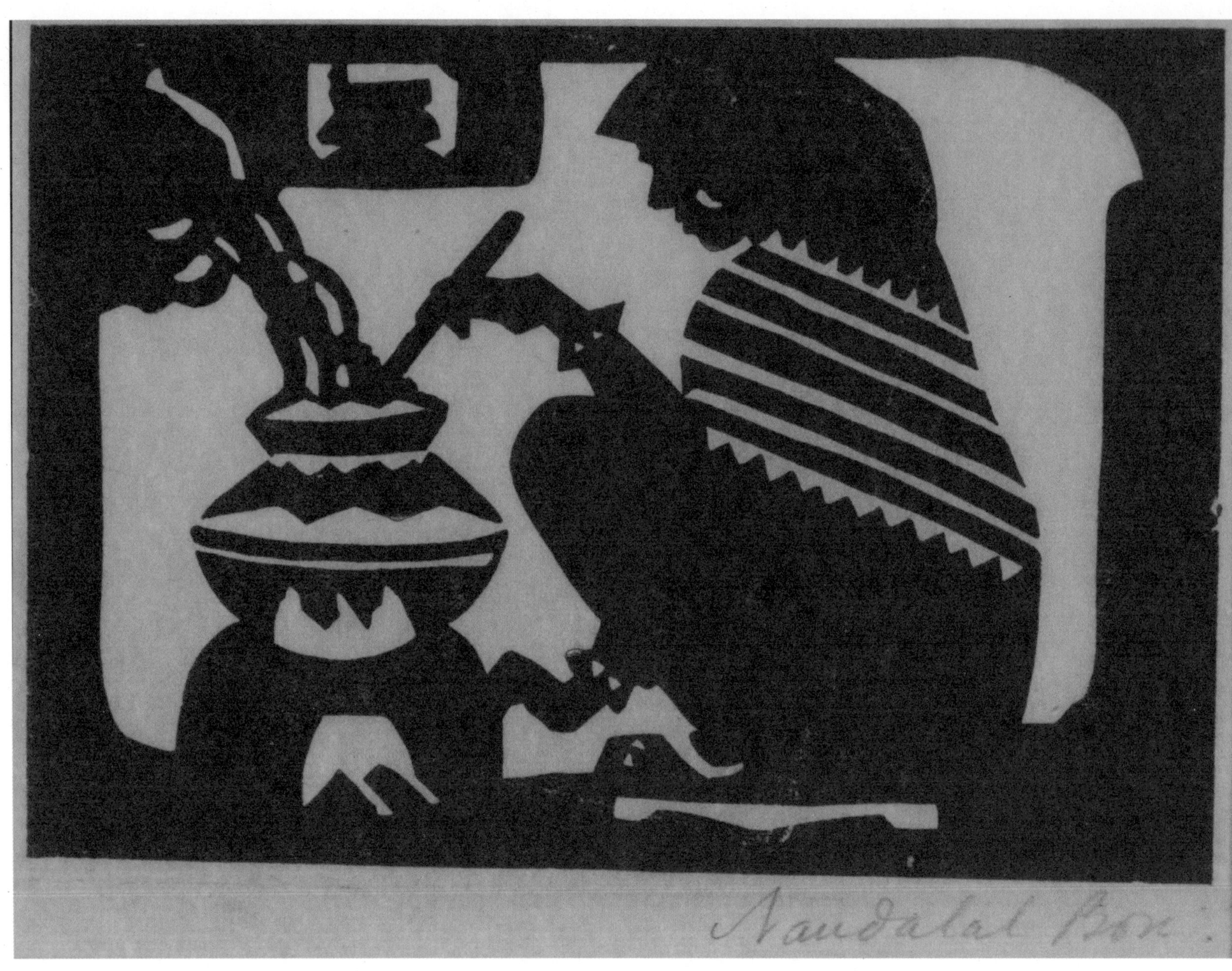

Woman cooking
Nandalal Bose
Linocut // NGMA Collection

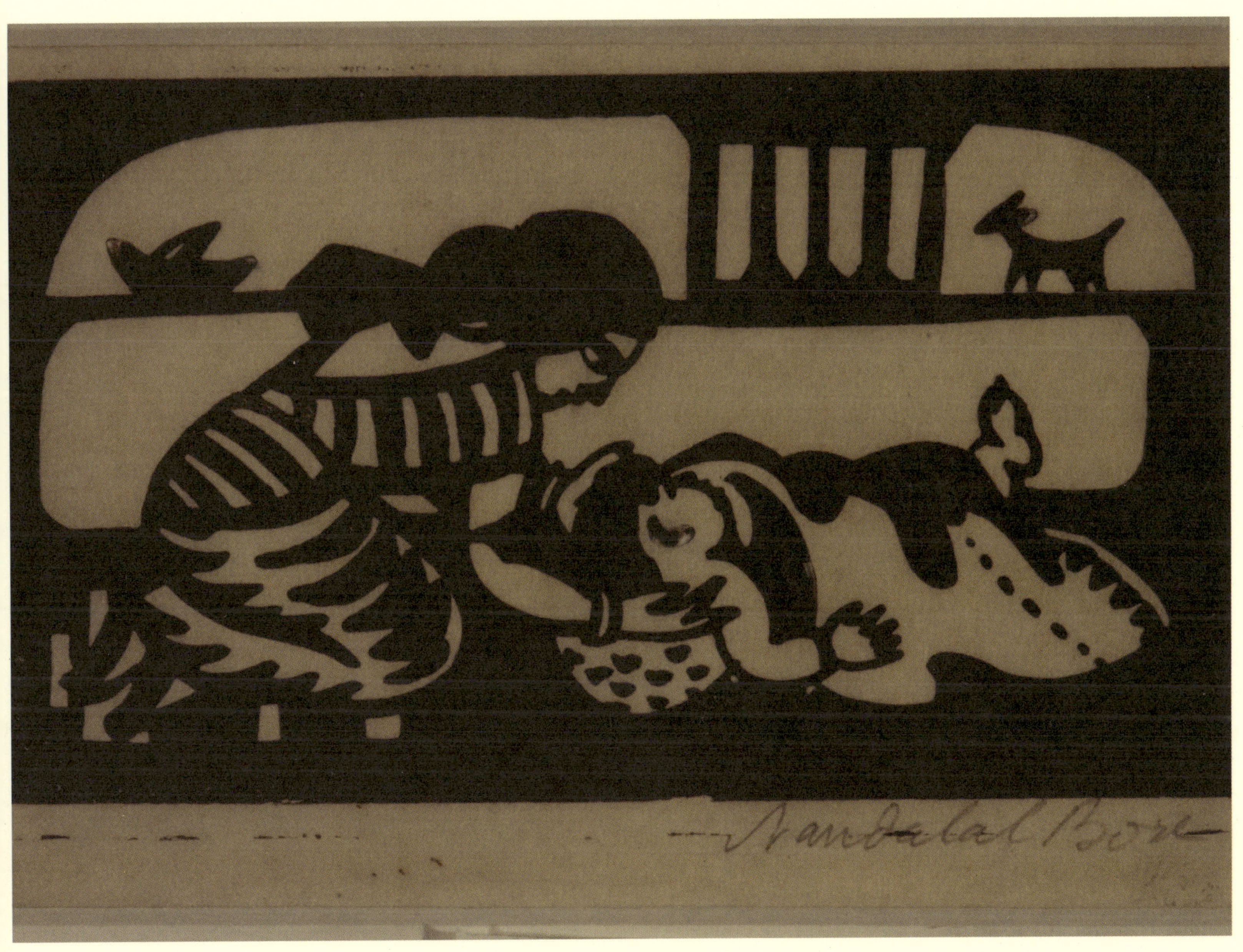

Mother and child

Nandalal Bose

Linocut // NGMA Collection

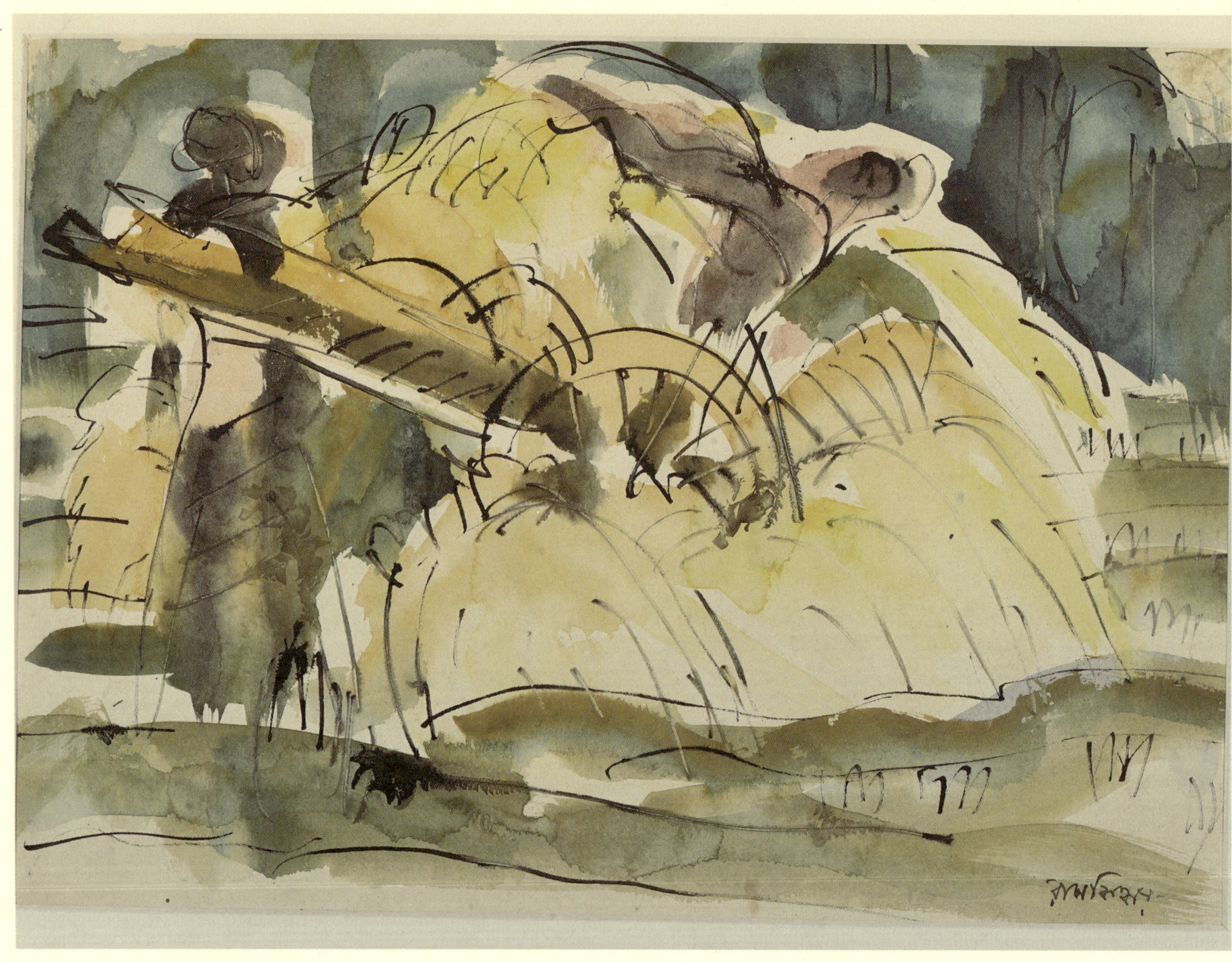

Loading the crop
Ramkinkar Baij
Watercolour on paper // NGMA Collection

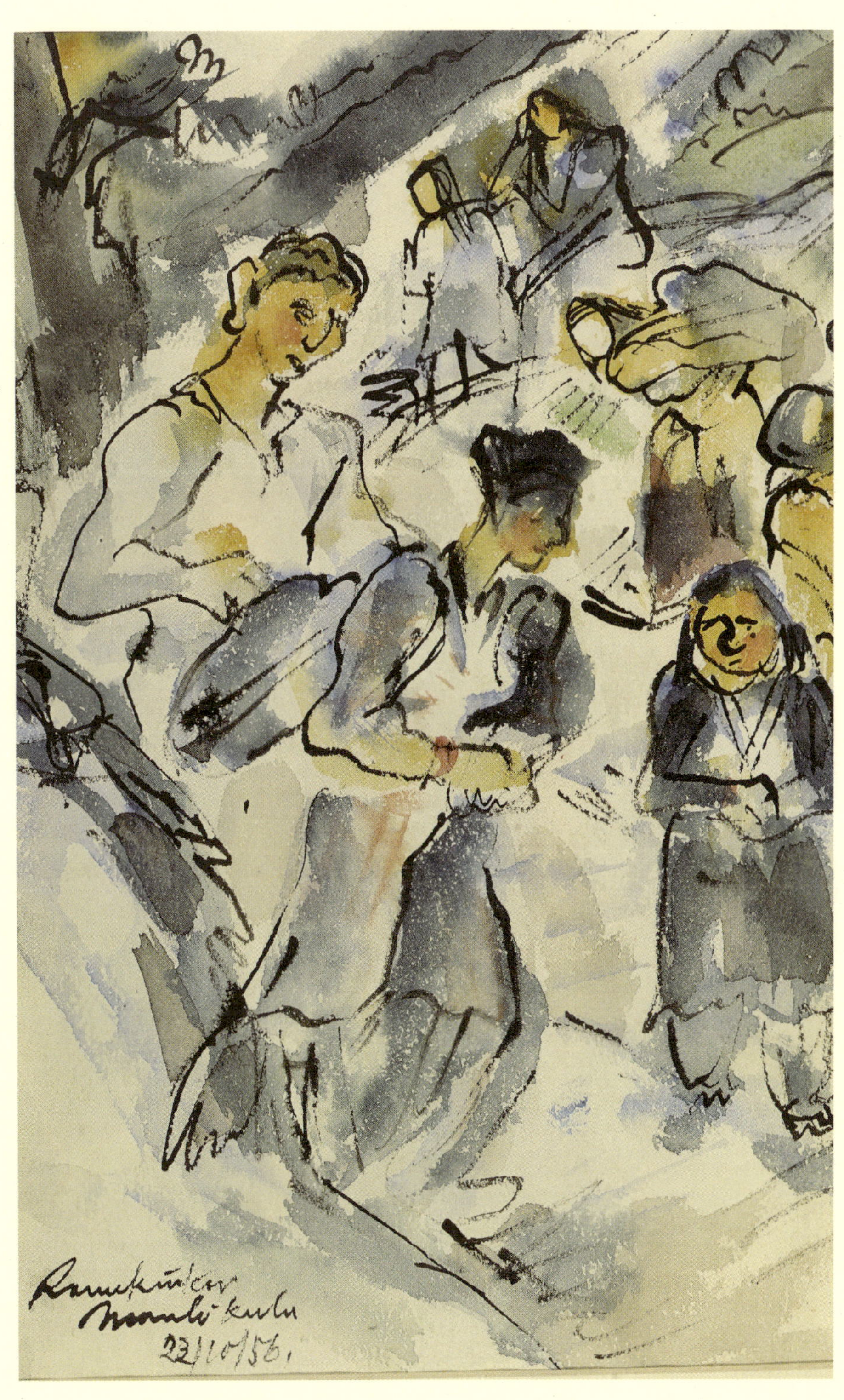

A Village Scene, Mandi, Kulu, 1956
Ramkinkar Baij
Watercolour on paper // NGMA Collection

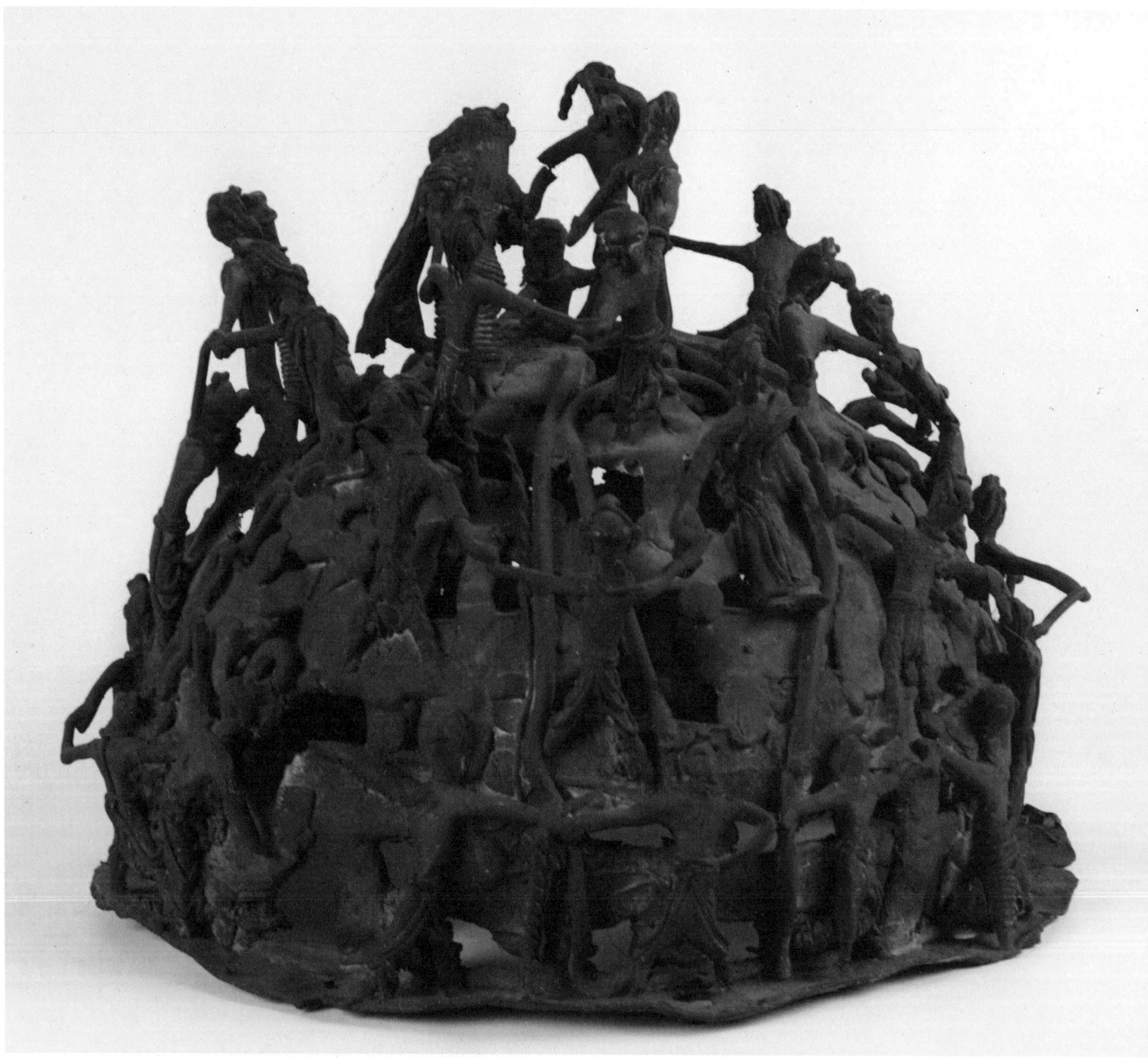

Untitled
Meera Mukherjee
Brass // NGMA Collection

"When our reform becomes part of our nature, we shall cease to discuss it."

Mahatma Gandhi

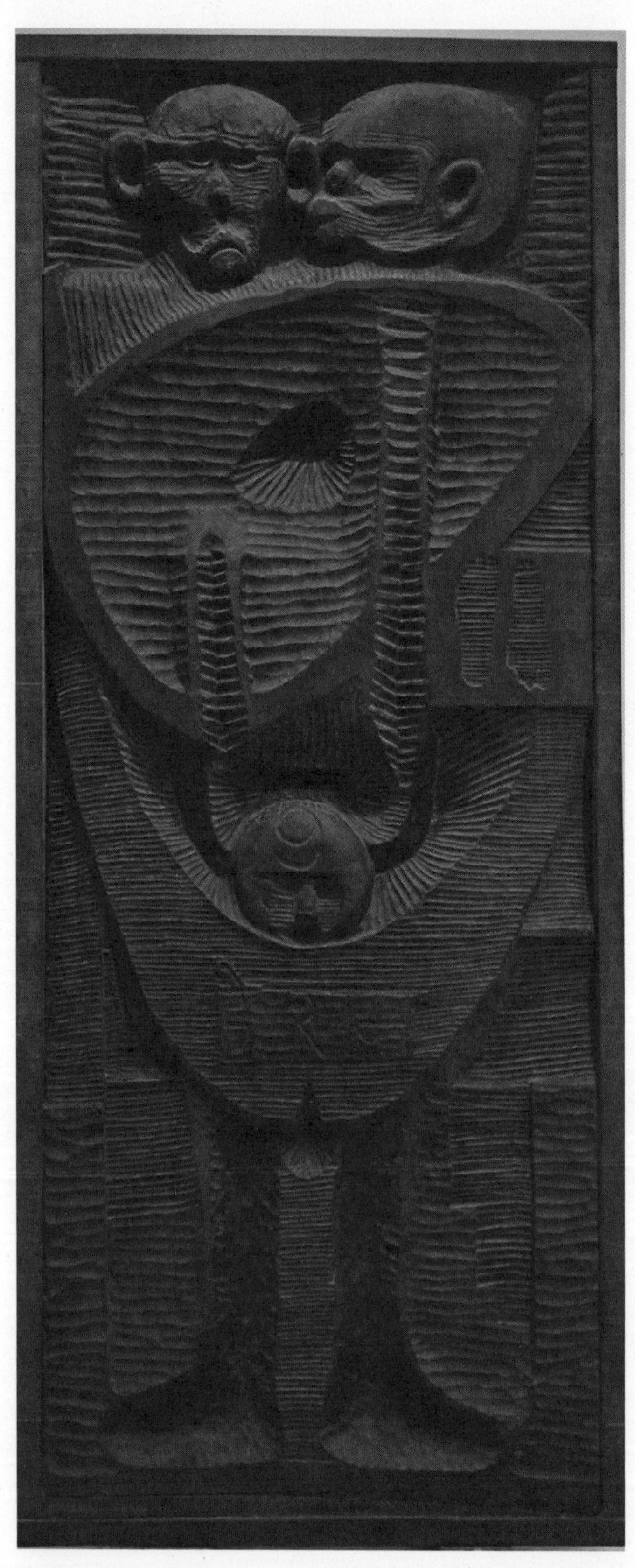

Yatra
M.S. Rawat
Wood // NGMA Collection

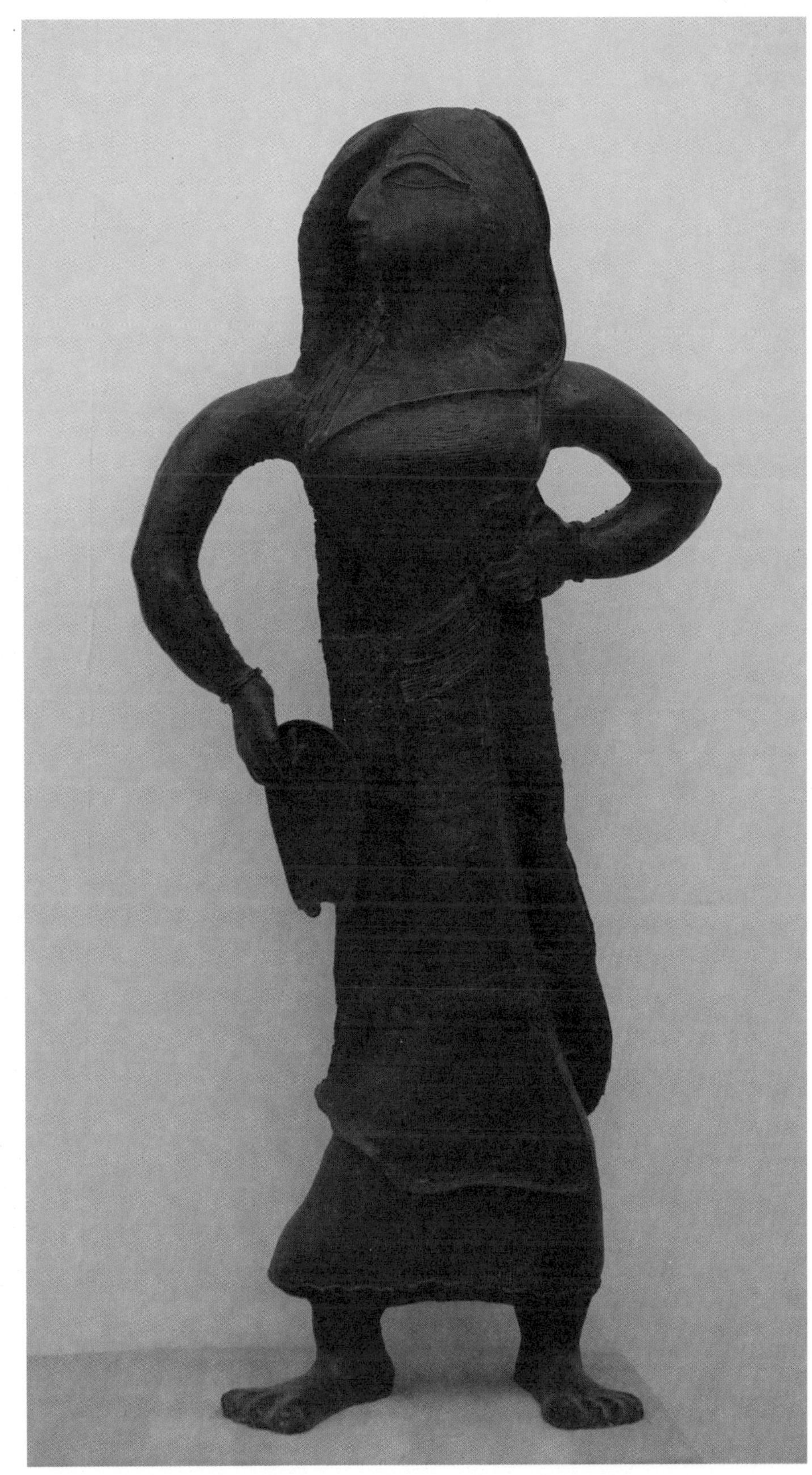

Spirit of daily work
Meera Mukherjee
Bronze // NGMA Collection

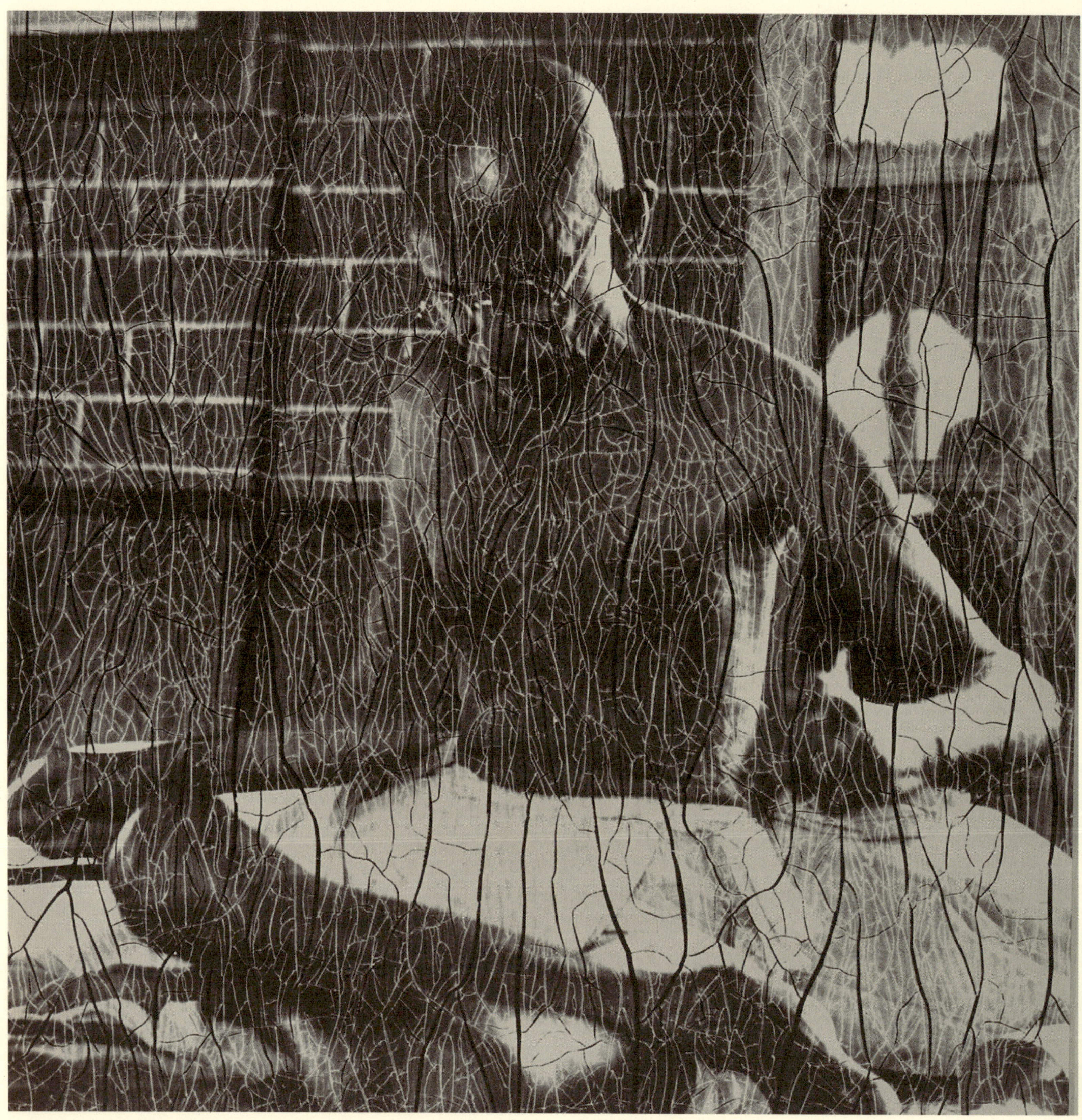

Kulwant Roy

In a time when photojournalism had just made inroads to India, Kulwant Roy after completing his duties in the Royal Indian Air Force, along with the support of the Gopal Brothers, took the camera out of the studio to capture images of the events that were shaping the future of India. His lens has frozen some of the most iconic and important moments from the pre- and post-Independence era. A dynamic and pioneering figure in photojournalism, Kulwant Roy followed the movement around Mahatma Gandhi, recording various crucial events in the fight for freedom.

His rediscovered broken negatives form a continuous thread in the *Santati* narrative and a part of NGMA's rare archives.

Opposite:
Mahatma Gandhi at his spinning wheel
New Delhi // 1940
Broken negative // NGMA Archives

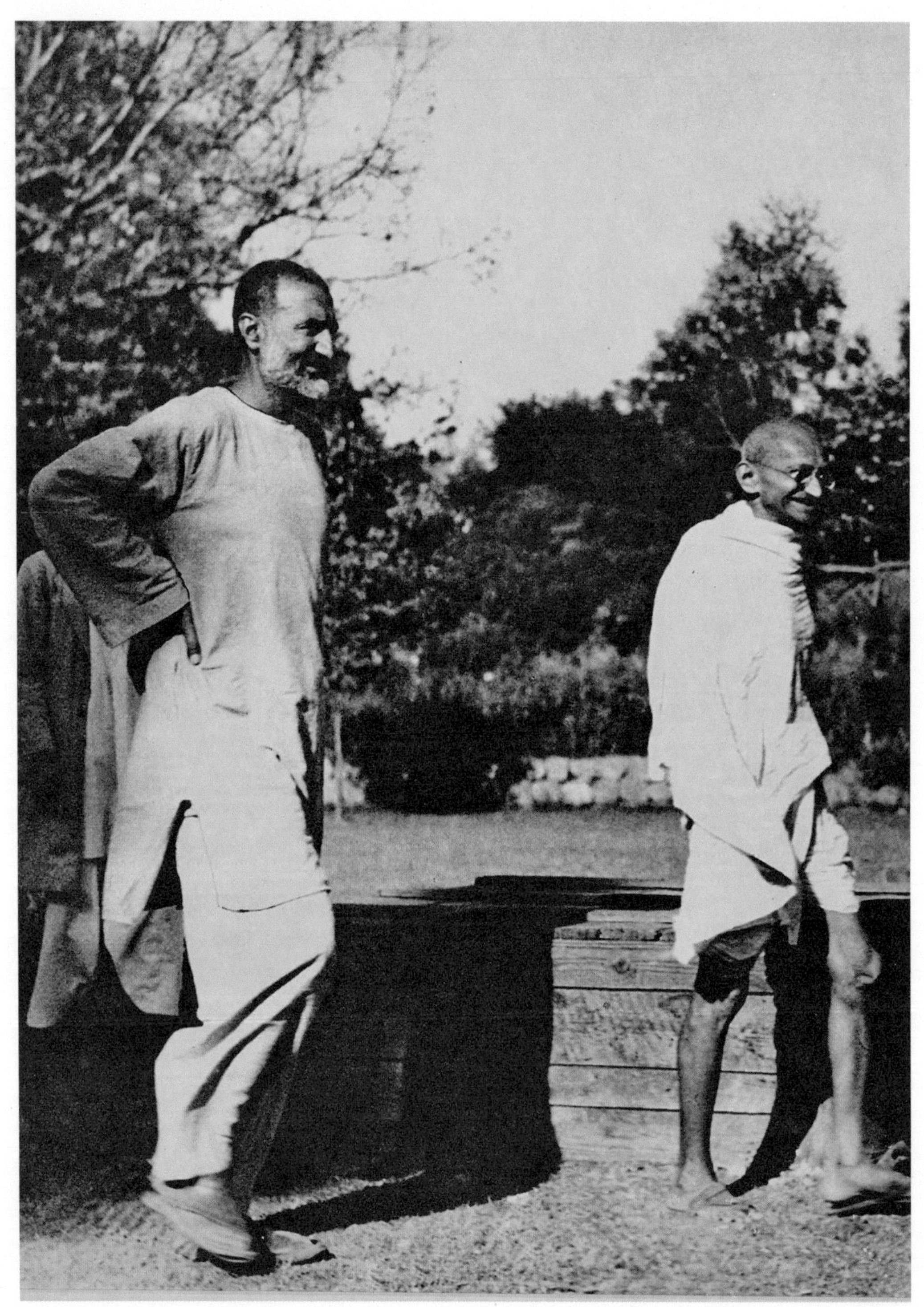

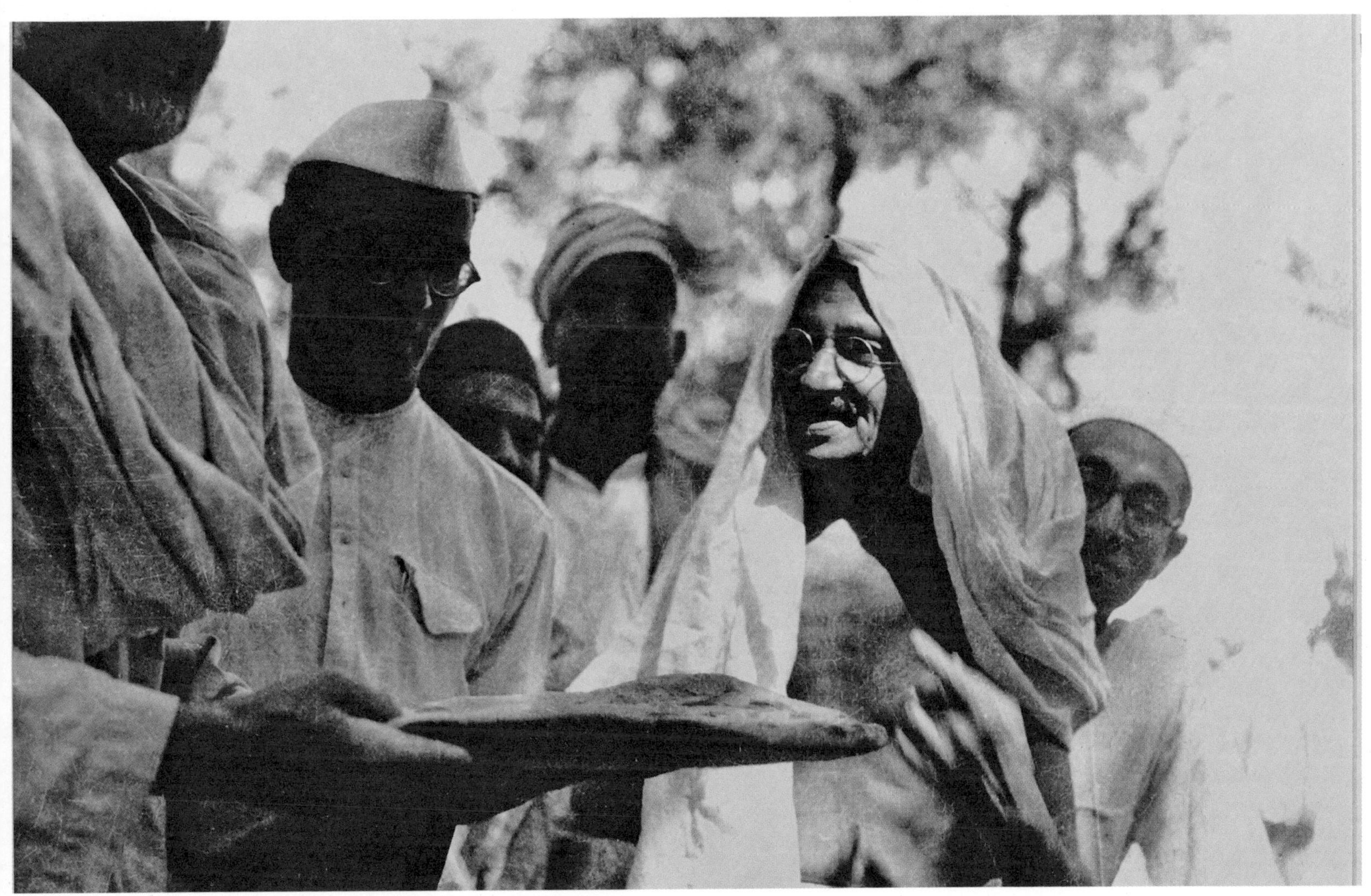

Opposite:

Mahatma Gandhi with Khan Abdul Gaffar Khan in Peshawar during his visit to North Western Frontier Province (NWFP)

Peshawar // 1938

Above:

Mahatma Gandhi at Utmanzai (NWFP), the native village of Khan Abdul Gaffar Khan

Peshawar // 1938

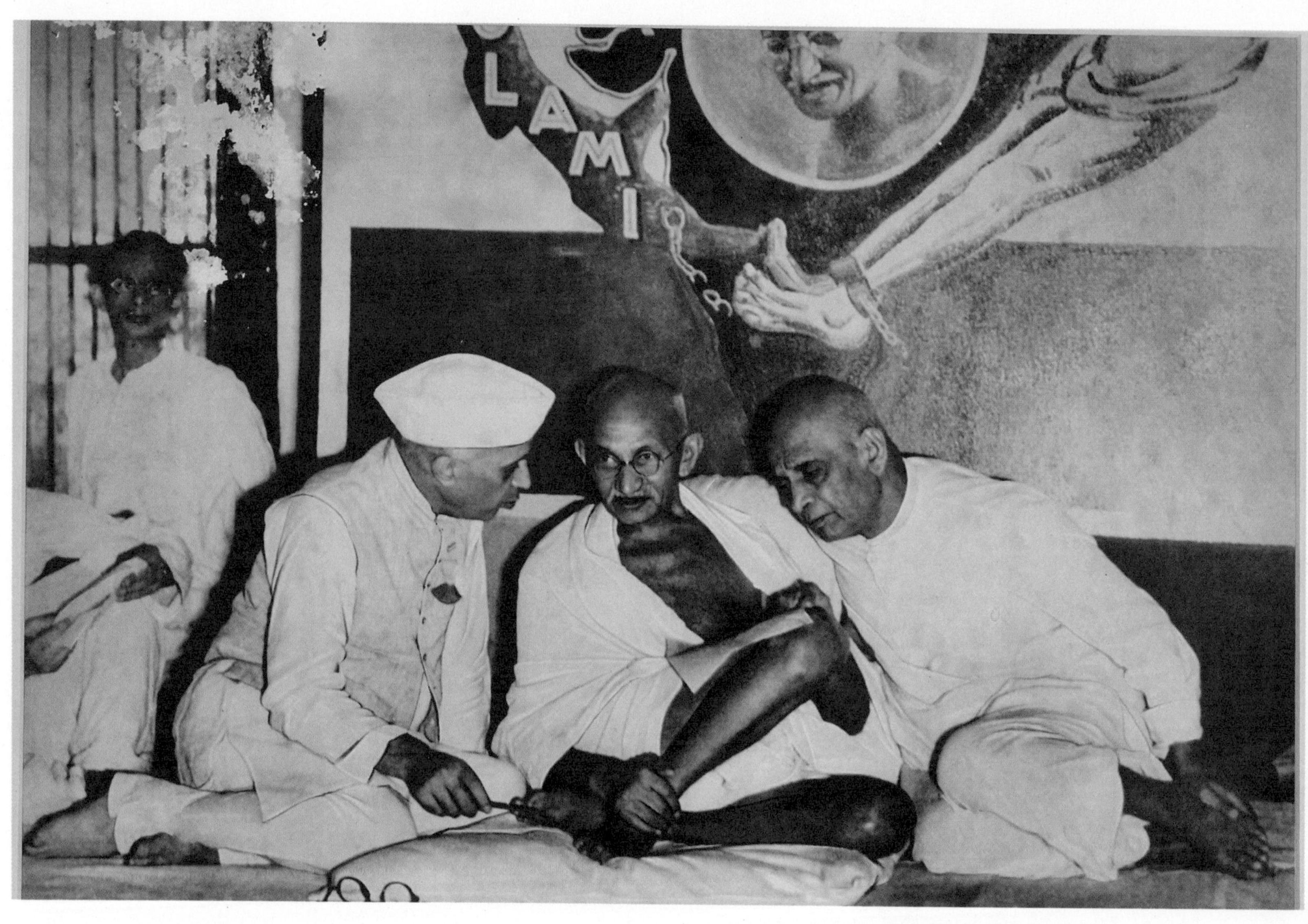

Mahatma Gandhi with Jawaharlal Nehru and Sardar Patel
1946

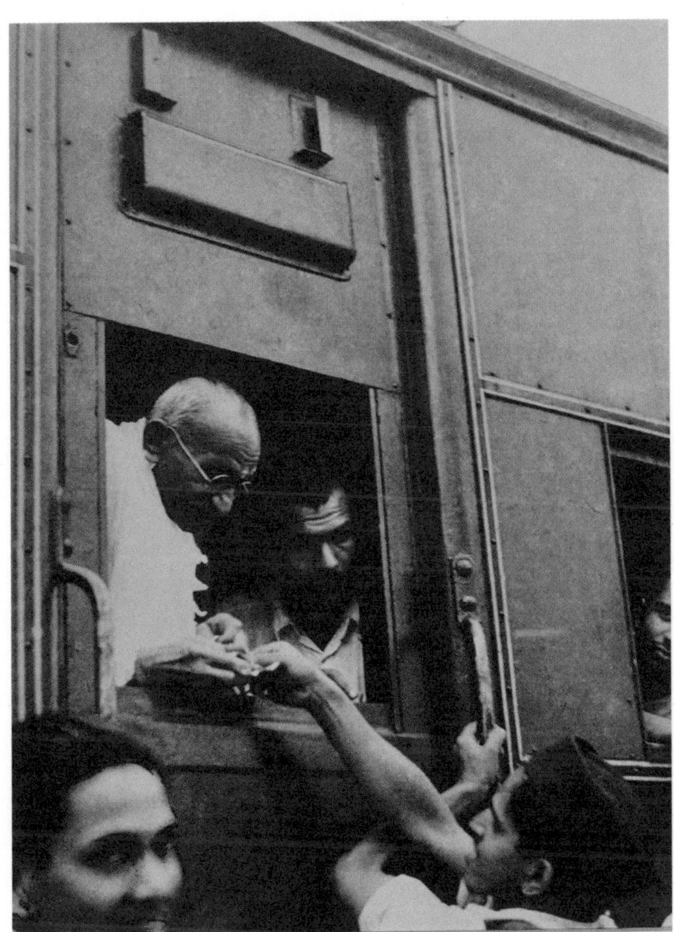

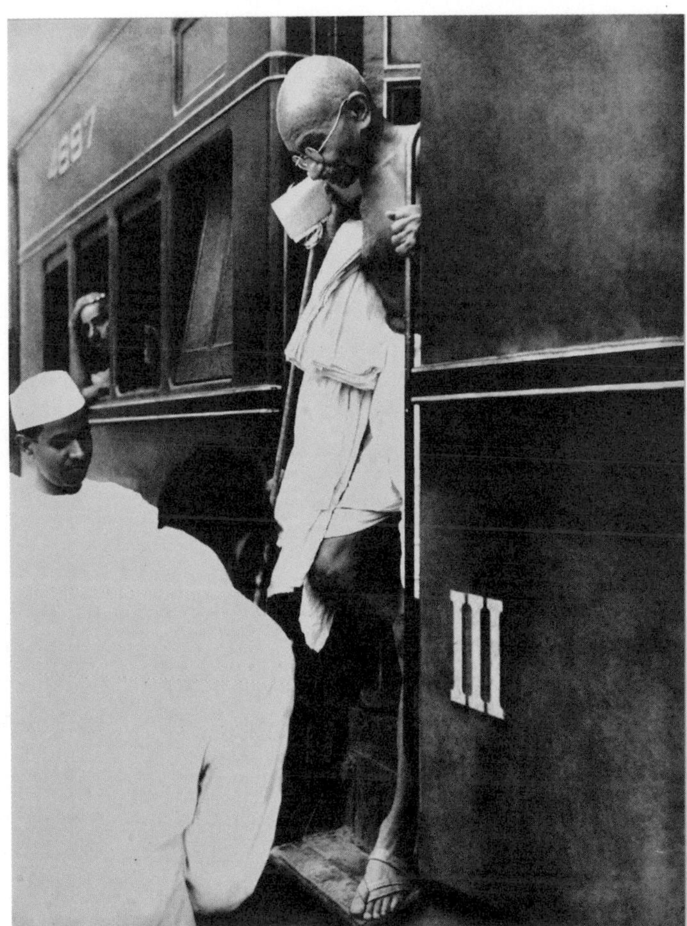

Above left:
Undated

Right:
Alighting from the train
New Delhi // 1940s

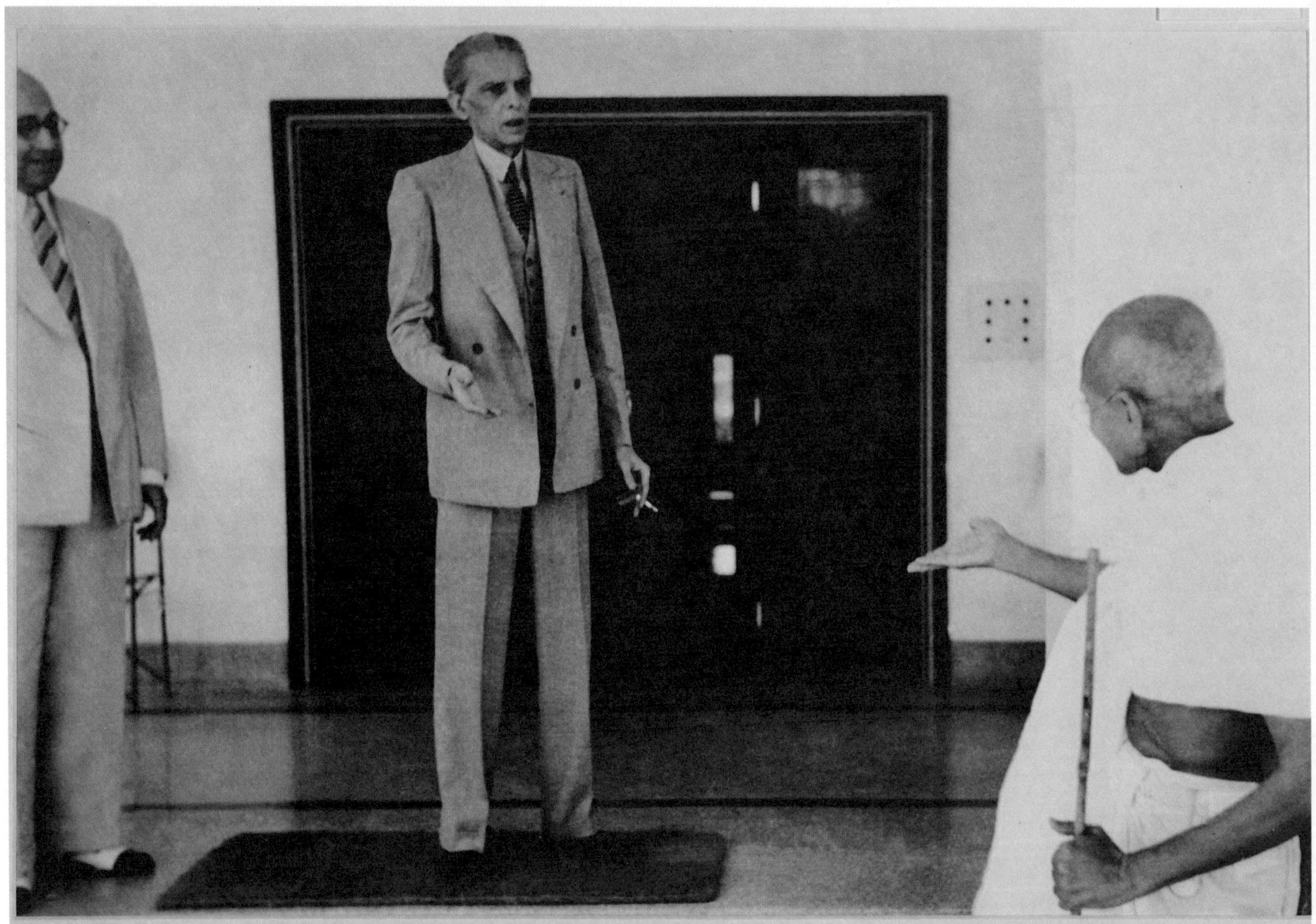

Above:
Meeting Muhammad Ali Jinnah at his Delhi residence. Shaukat Ali is also present
Undated

Opposite:
With the Mountbattens
Government House // 1947
Broken Negative

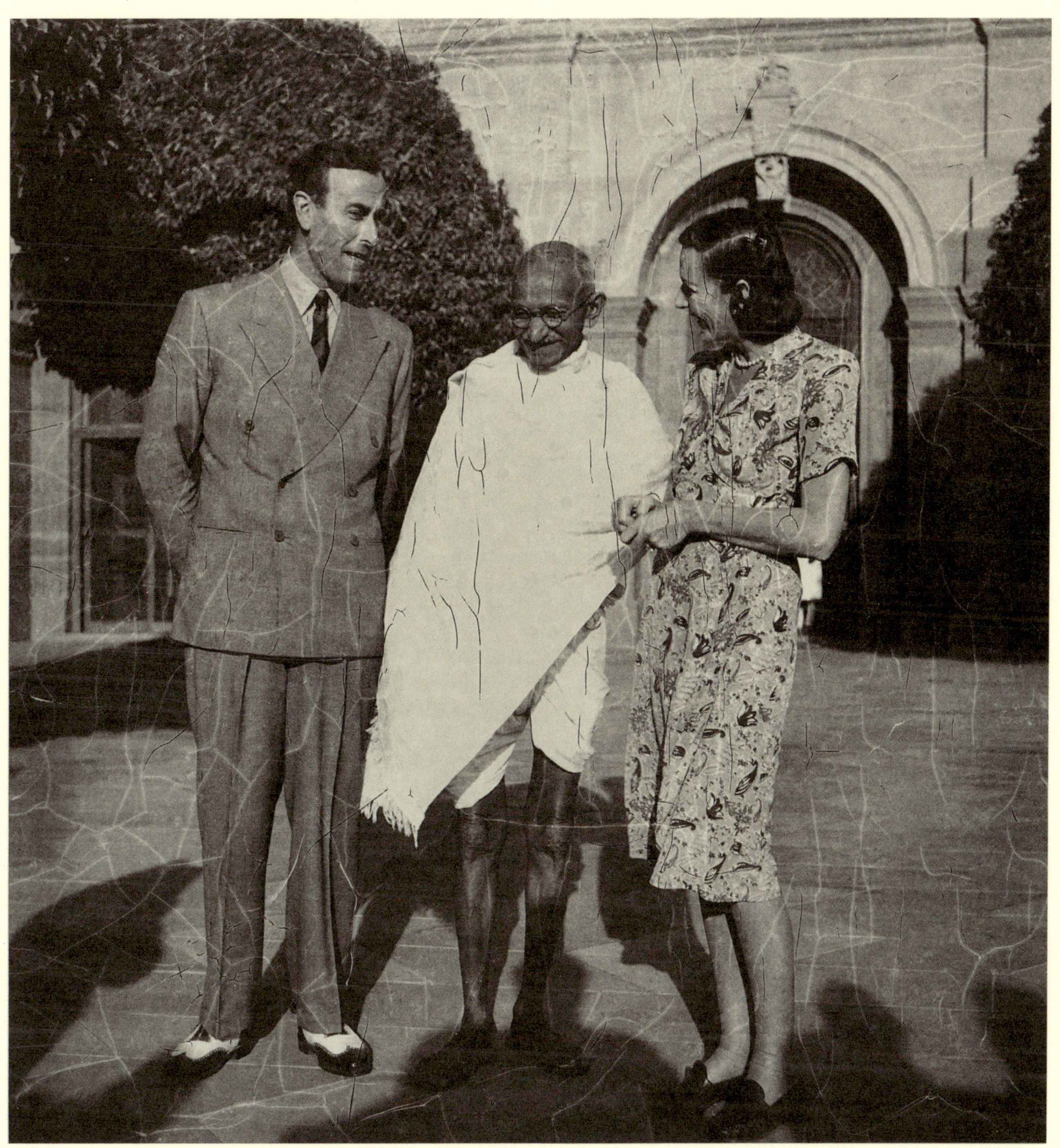

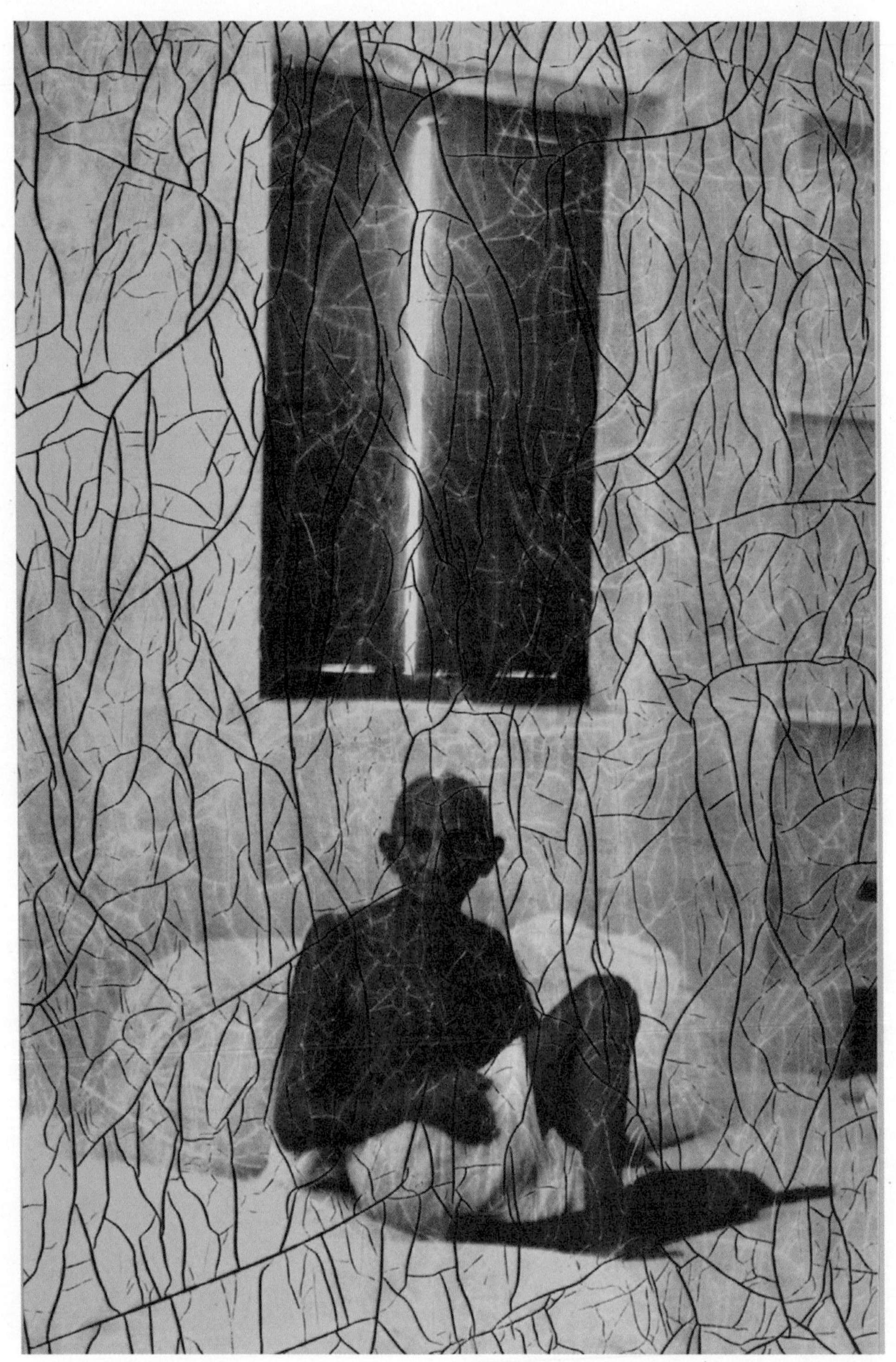

In lies we go on
Floating together
In truth we must
Swim alone

Opposite:
Mahatma Gandhi
Undated
Broken negative // NGMA Collection

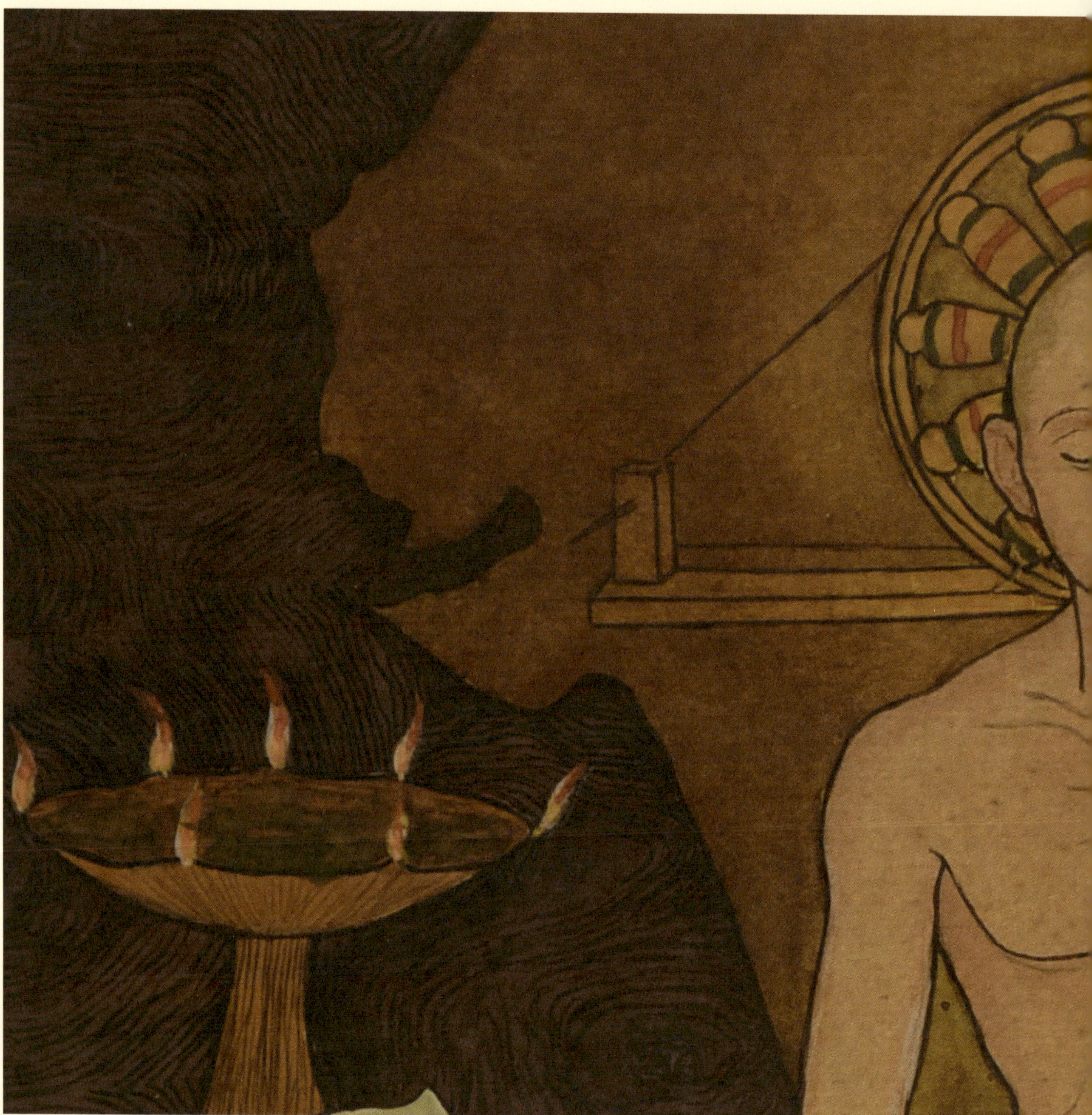

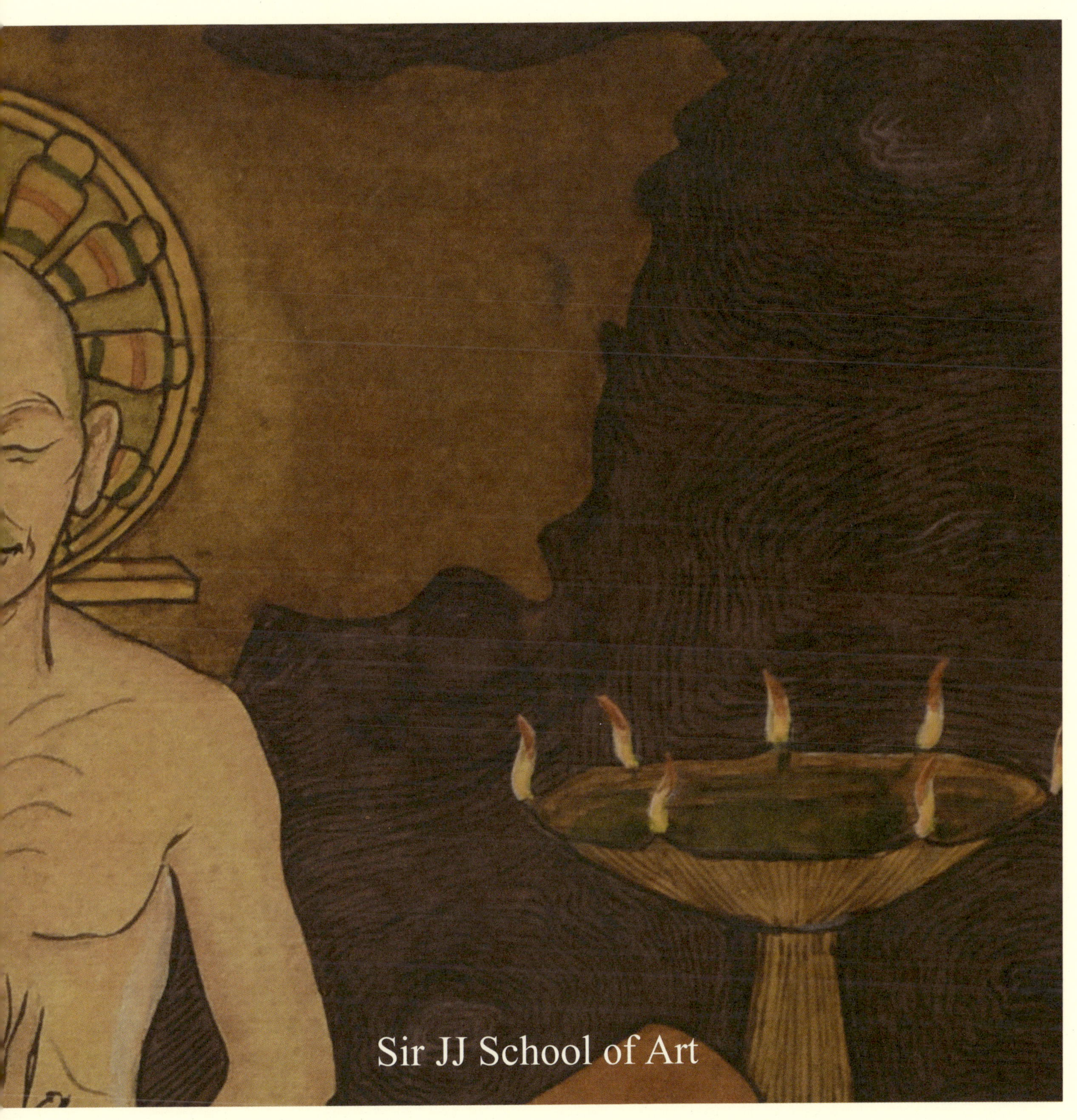
Sir JJ School of Art

ACHIEVED BETWEEN 1940 TO 1960, these works by the Sir JJ School of Art, Mumbai, reflect directly or abstractly, the inevitable bond between art and the freedom struggle. They are works of the school's students who tapped into the manifold layers of Mahatma Gandhi – the man, the message, the messenger. And while many of these works remain anonymous and untitled, they are tied by the common thread of Gandhi's vision of that divine world which inhabits simplicity.

"Dharma lies in doing one's duty, not in making no mistake at all."

Mahatma Gandhi

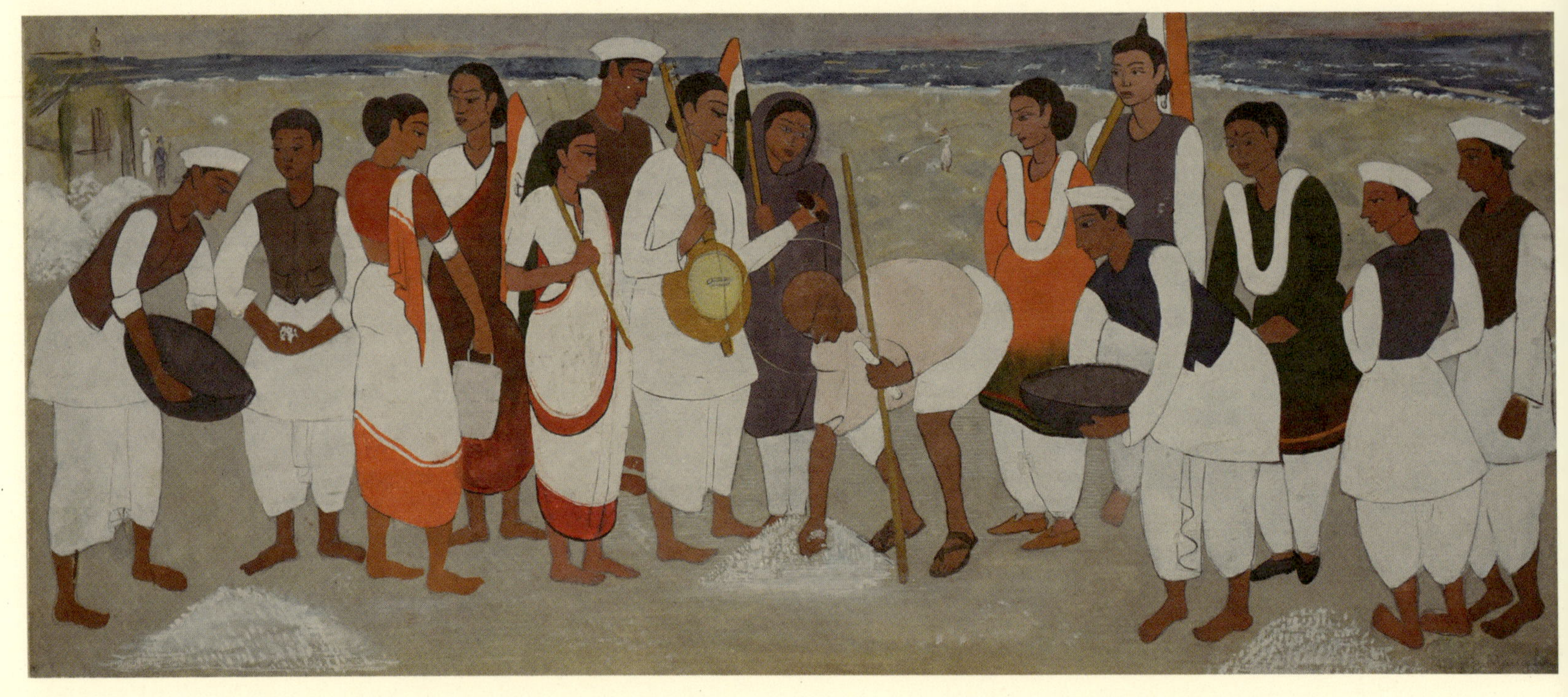

Sourced from the archives of the School, these paintings are essentially studio assignments for the subject Pictorial Design.

The paintings about Gandhiji's life and scenes from India's freedom struggle borrow profusely from the language of Indian miniatures, particularly the elements of spatial composition, landscape and architecture and the preference for human figures in profile. The artists effectively create a gamut of emotions and situations such as the spirit of the *swadeshi* movement in the Dandi march and salt s*atyagraha*, the ruthlessness and violence of the Noakhali riots and the spartan lifestyle of the charkha-spinning individuals of the Sabarmati Ashram with equal ease.

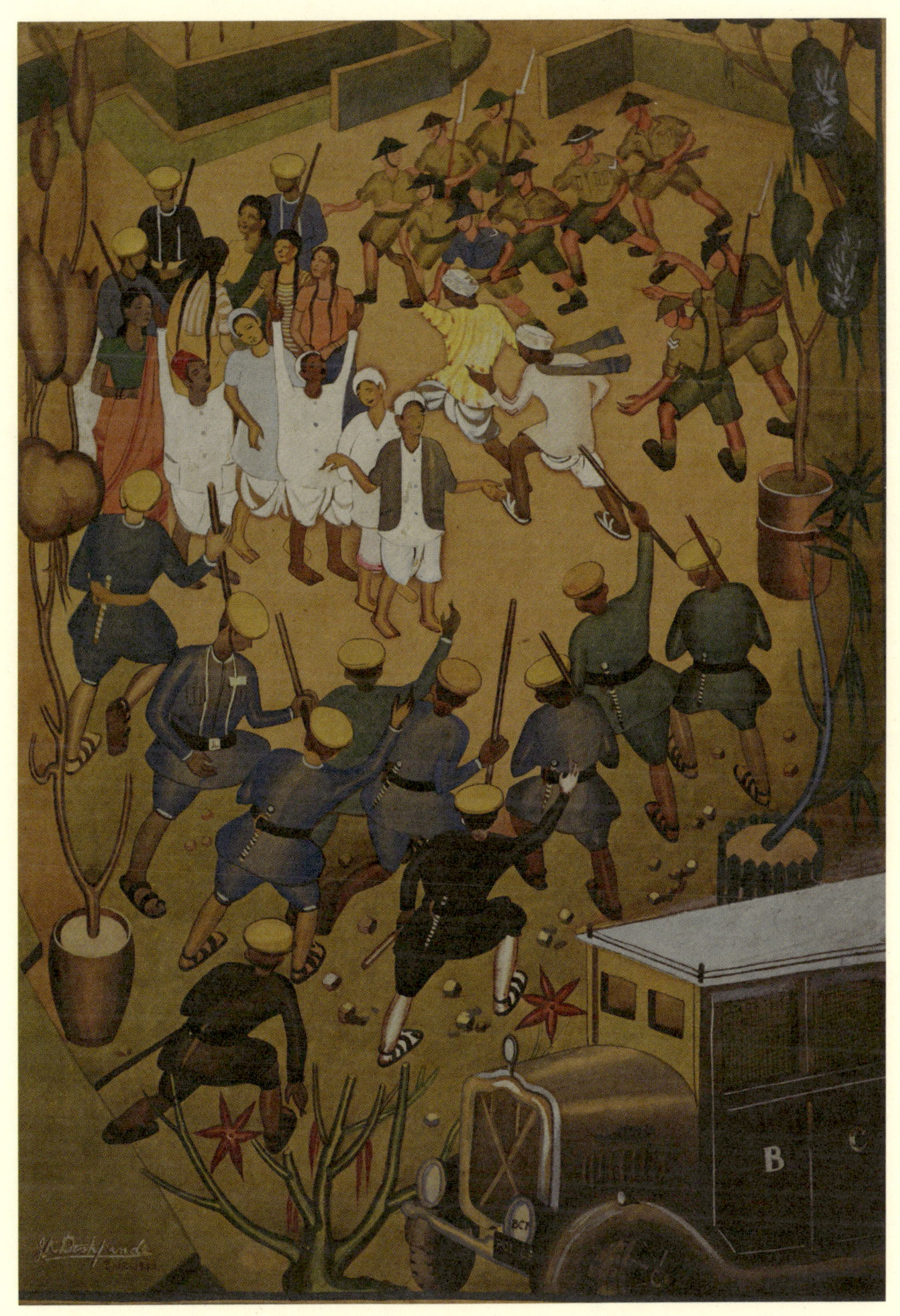

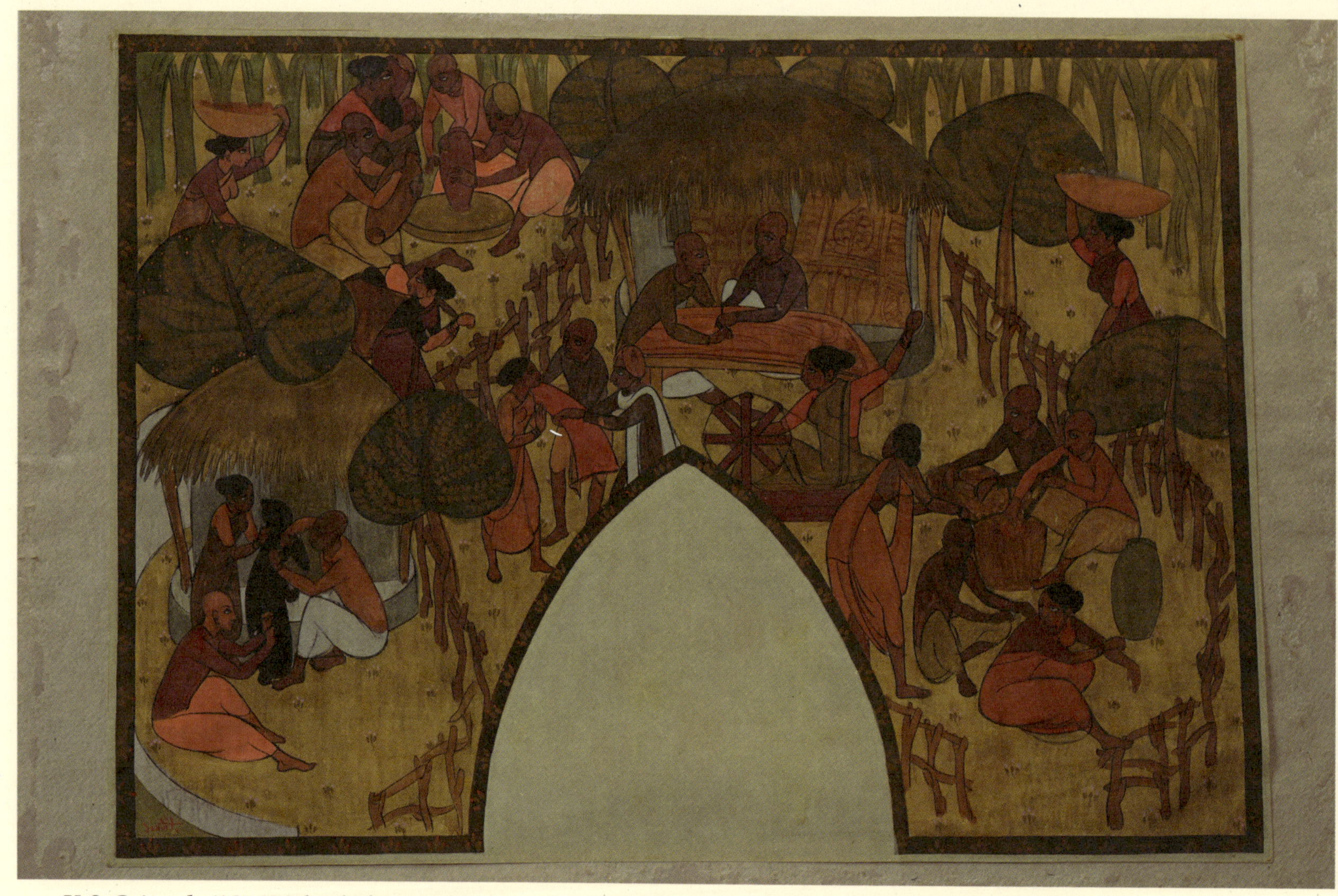

V. S. Gaitonde // Sir JJ School of Art Archives

The collection also includes a painting by eminent abstract painter, Vasudeo Gaitonde. A proficient figurative painter and follower of Ahiwasi in his student years, Gaitonde transports the "Gandhi" theme to a rural setting, simplifying the figures of men and women engaged in tasks such as spinning the charkha and making pottery.

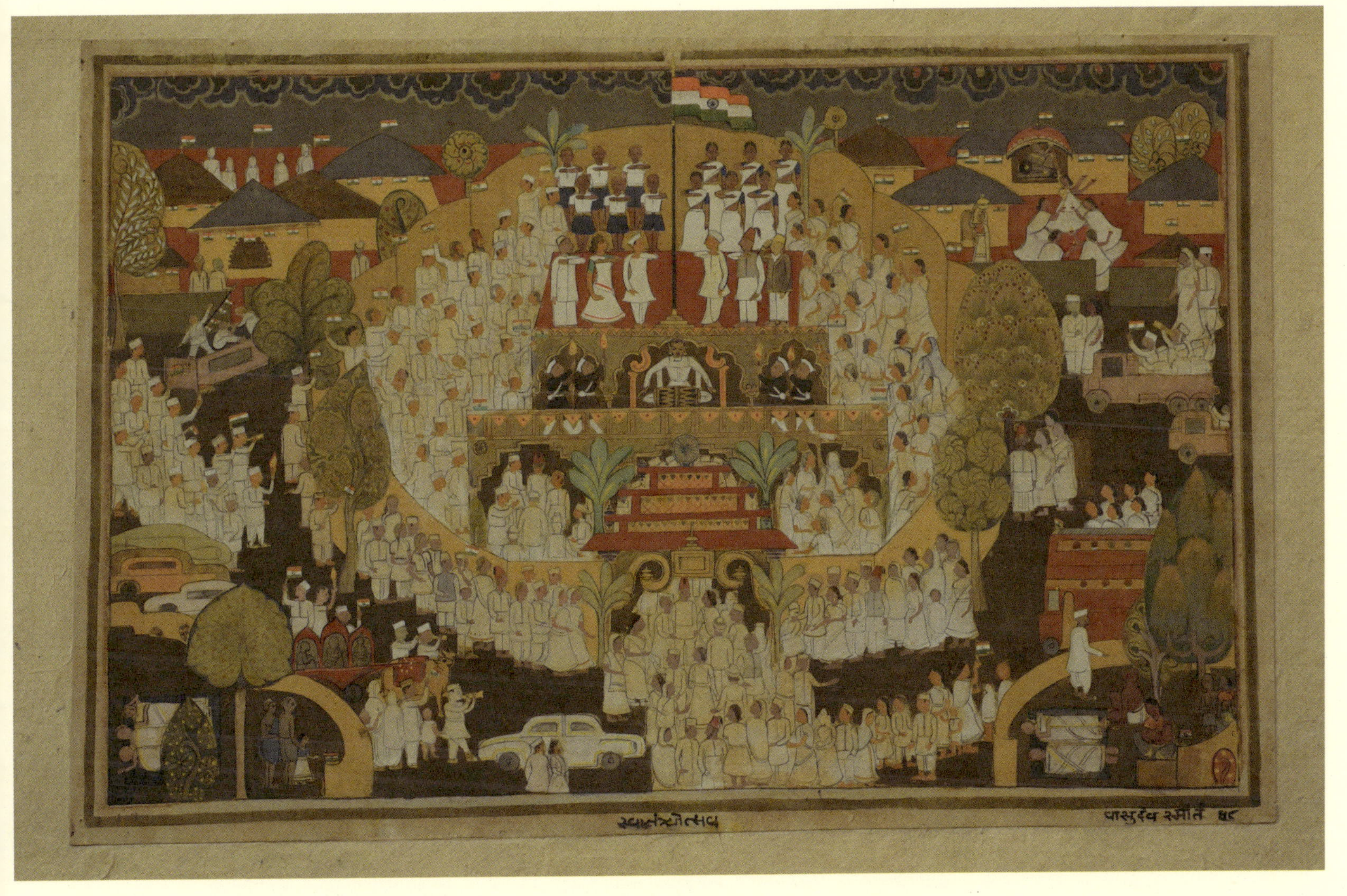

A painting by the Surat-born artist, Vasudeo Smart, recalls a Rajasthani miniature, and celebrates the event of India's independence.

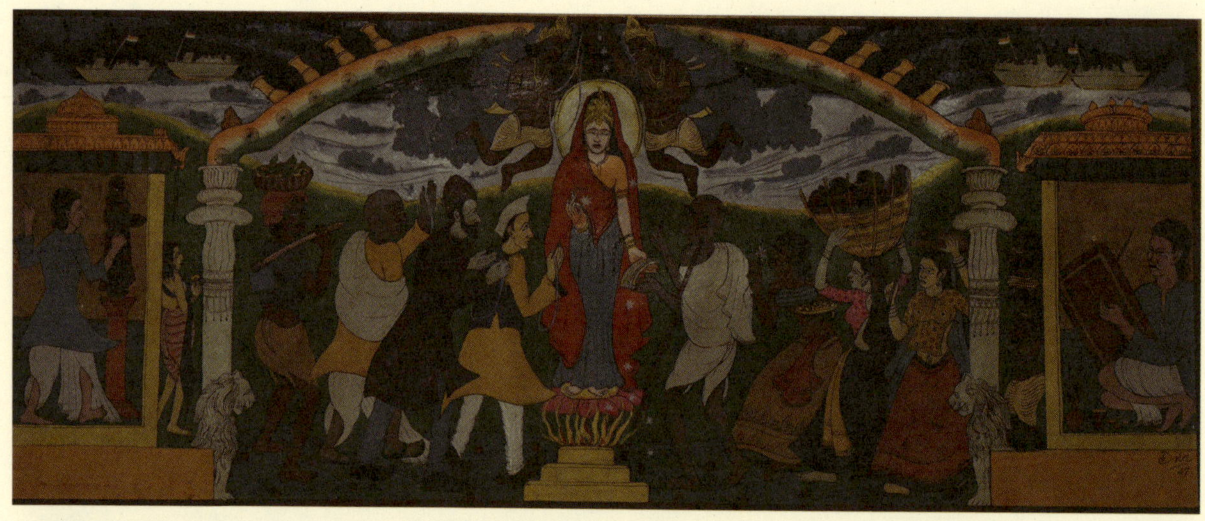

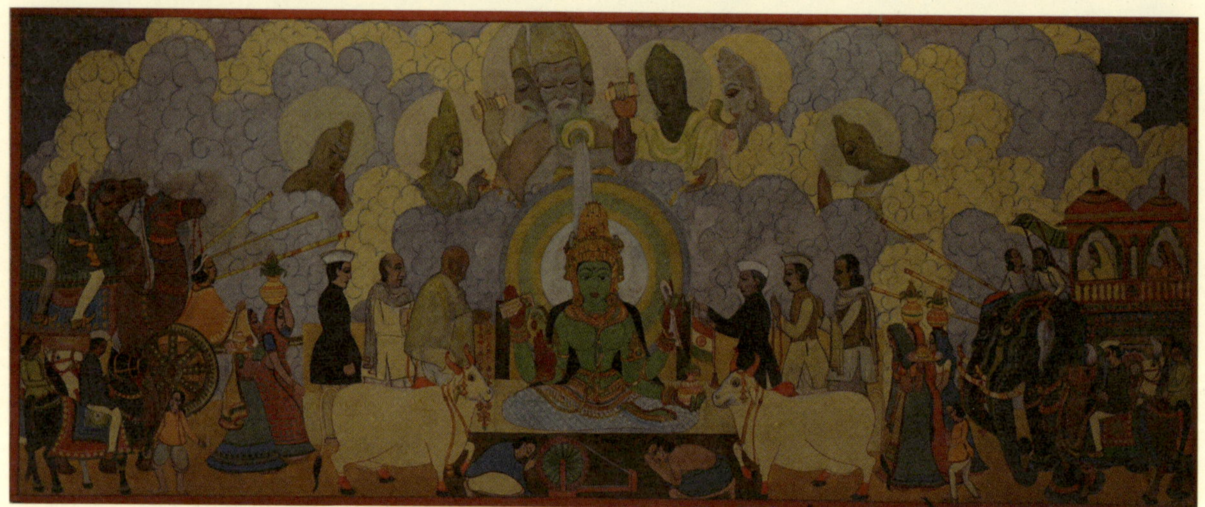

A couple of paintings delineate the mythic figure of Bharat Mata, whose image was popularized in the public domain through calendar art at the turn of the twentieth century. In one, Gandhi and Nehru, along with other khadi-clad political leaders congregate to worship Bharat Mata, shown seated in this case, and receiving the blessings of a multitude of gods. Another crowded composition features Gandhi and Nehru venerating the standing goddess. Bharat Mata, in this case has other trappings such as the Ashokan pillars on the sides and the tricolour which morphs into an arch above her.

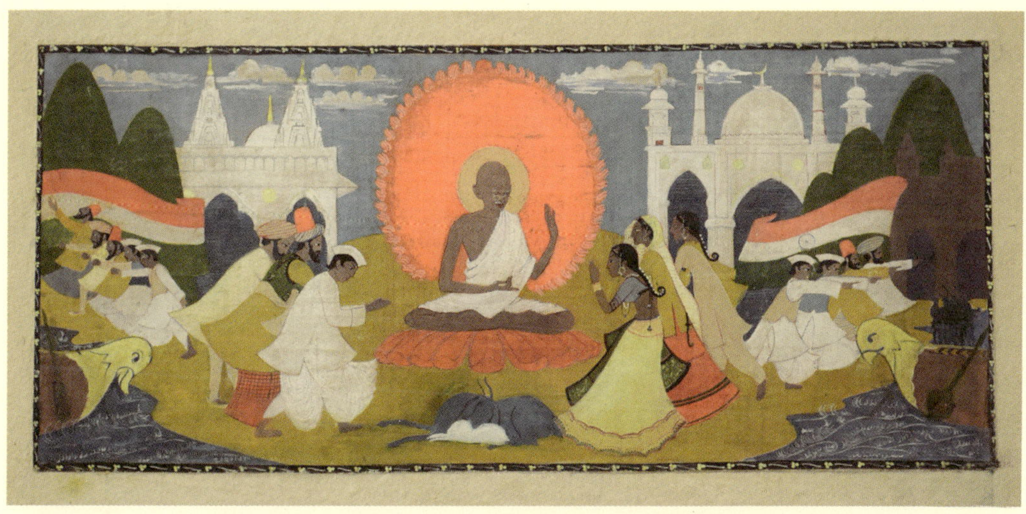

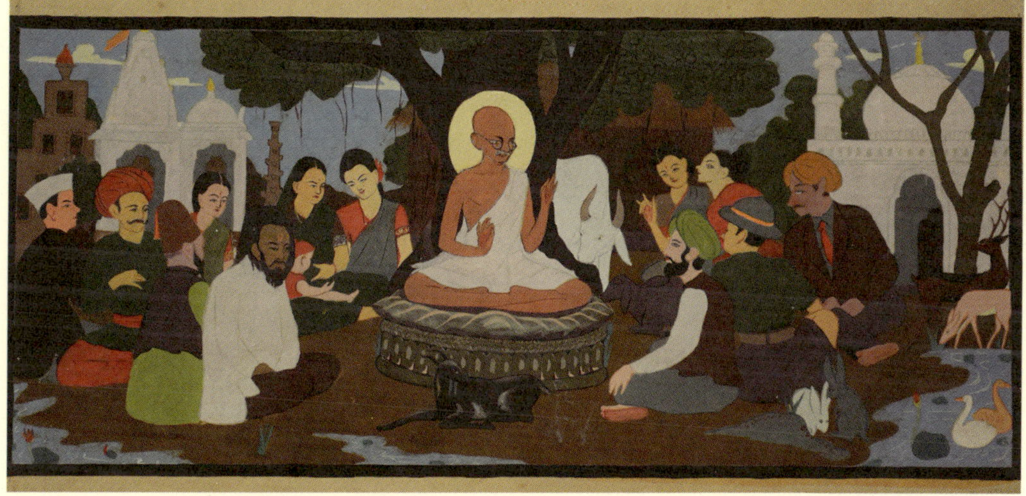

Envisaged as Buddha with a halo and preaching mudra, or as a Jain monk venerated by his disciples, the Mahatma's presence appears magnetic. Mahatma Gandhi and his ideals pervade village scenes and town sequences, processional marches of men in khadi and a bustle of ashram activities, flag-hoisting ceremonies and marchers confronting uniformed policemen.

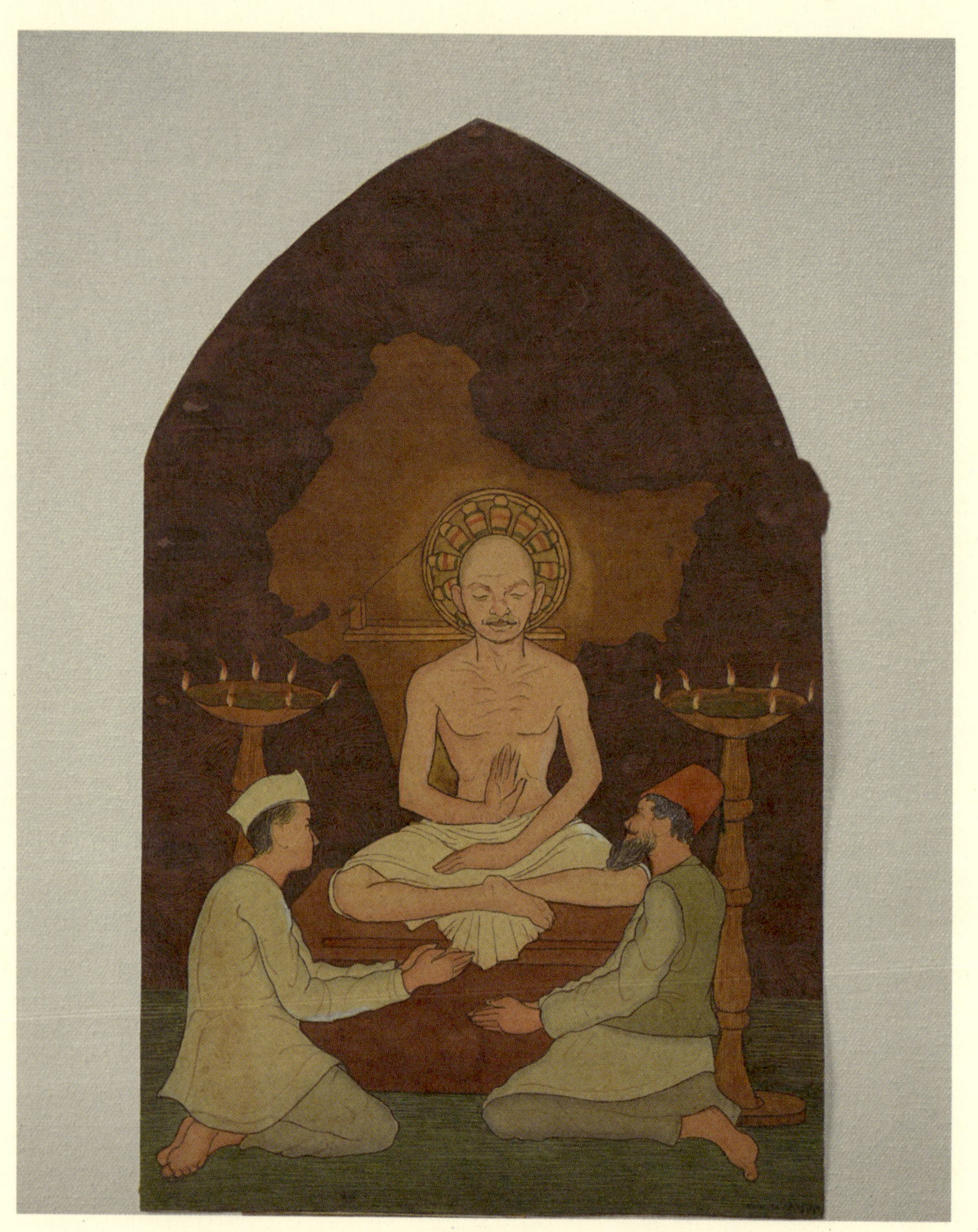

Religion is
All the moments
Where the heart
Is at home

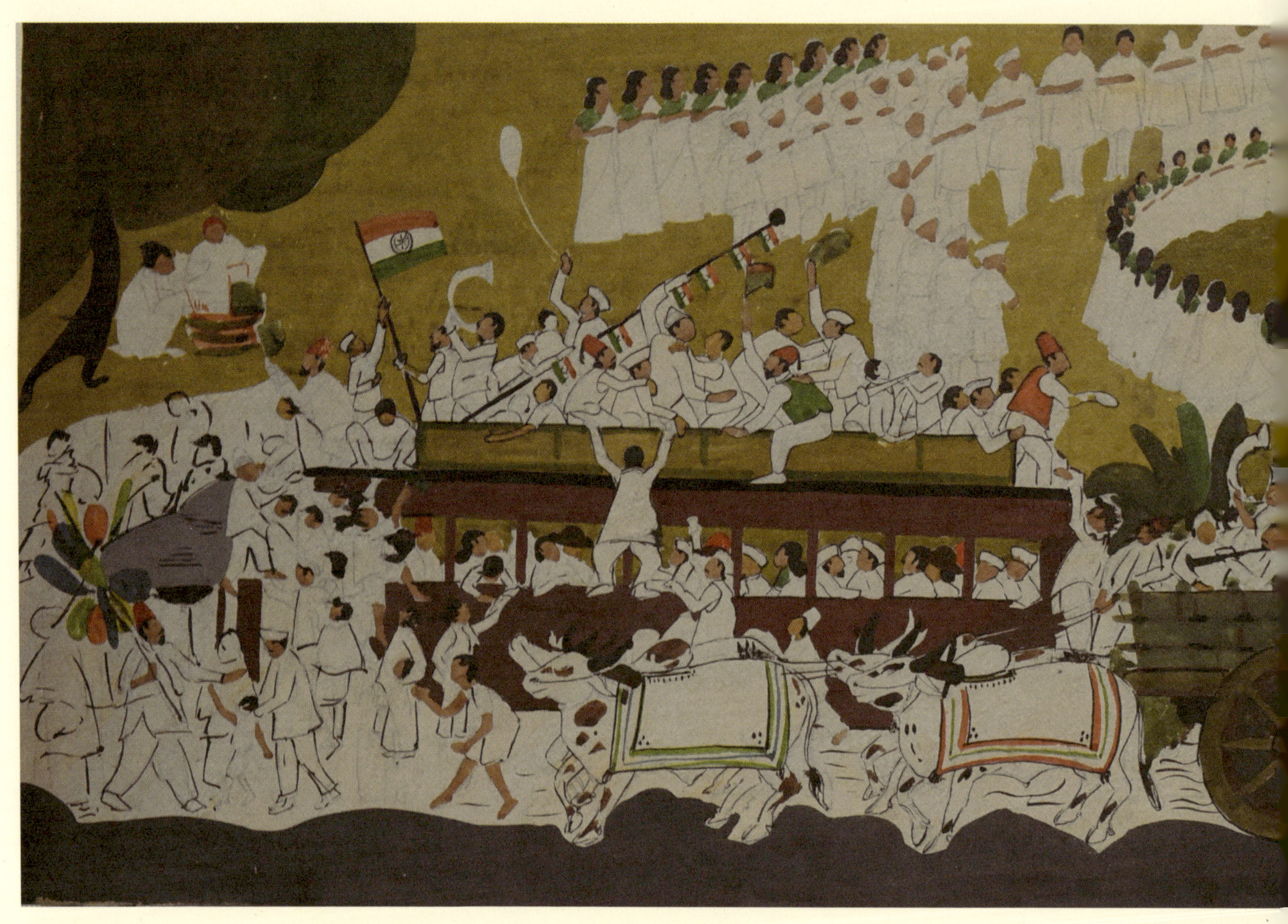

Prabhat Pheri // Sir JJ School of Art Archives

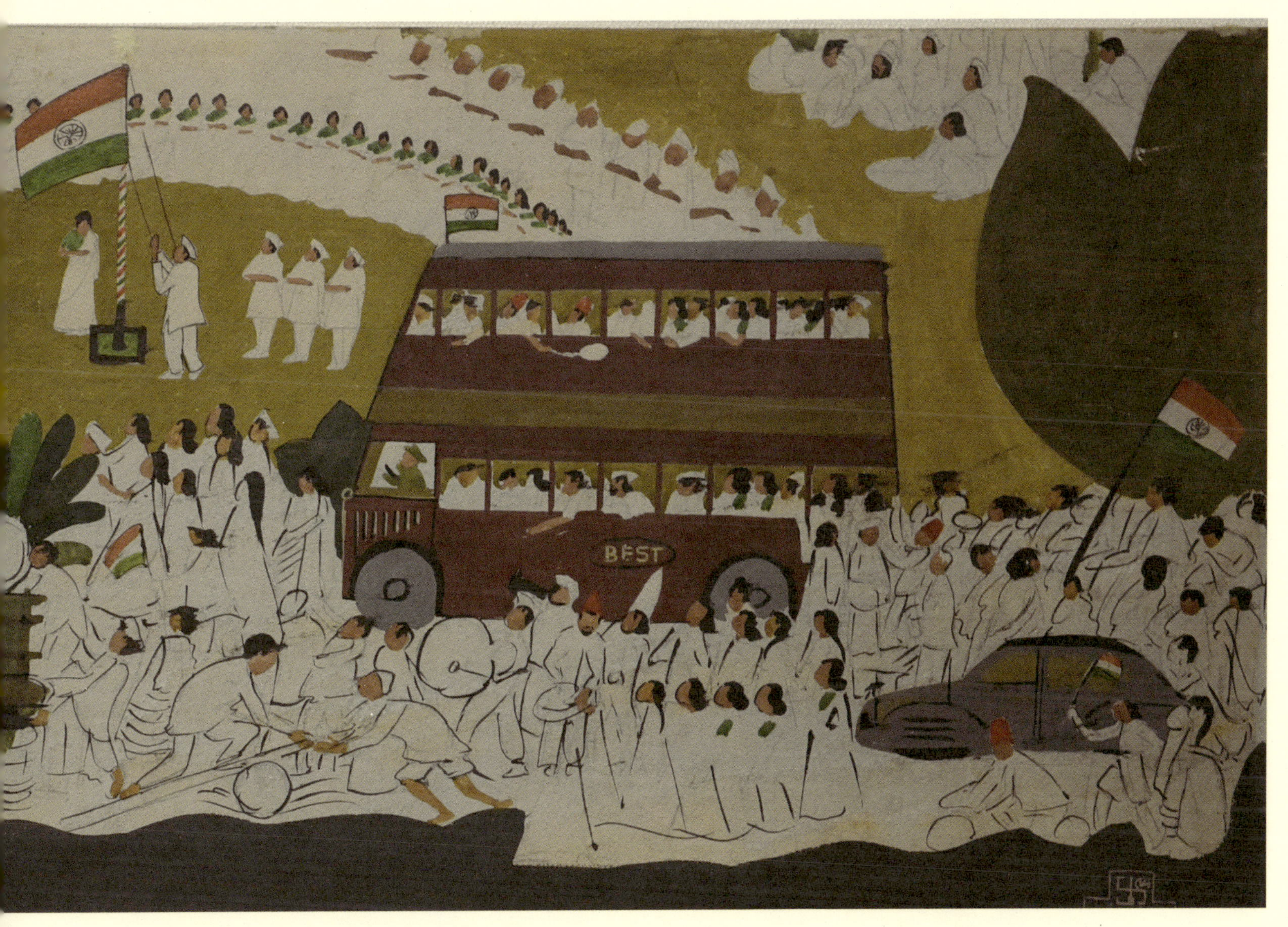
BEST

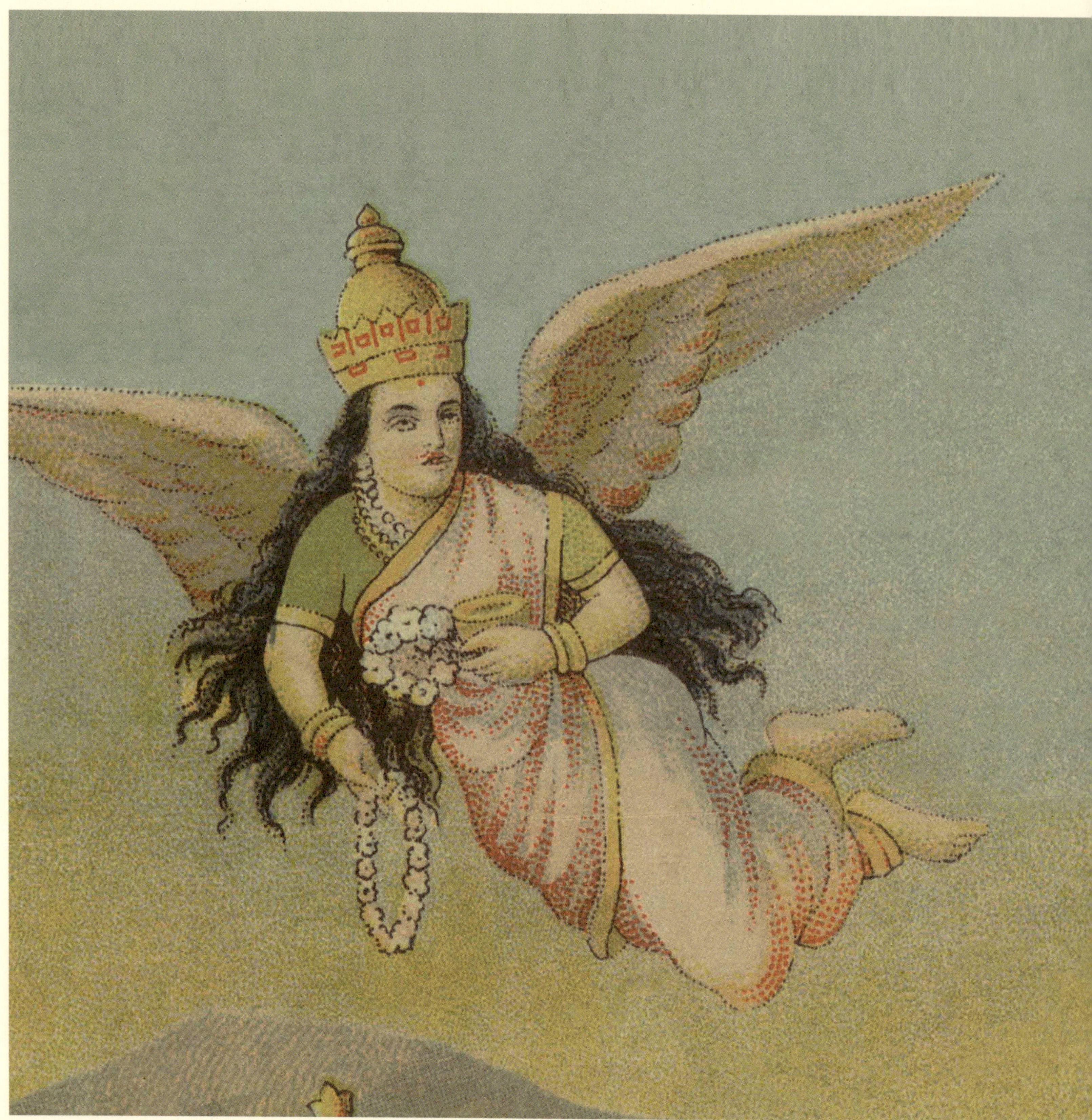

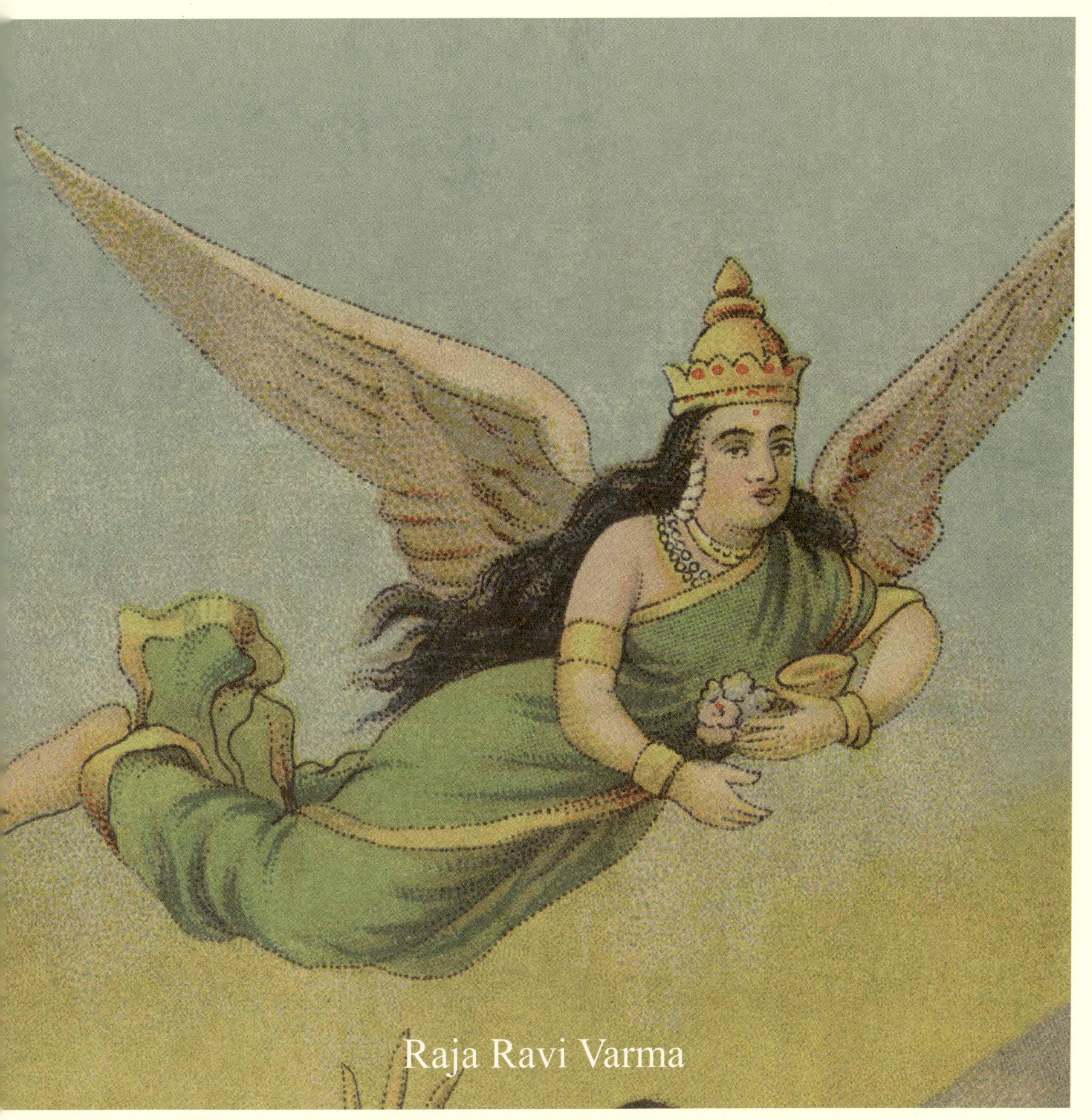

Raja Ravi Varma

ARTIST RAJA RAVI VARMA'S WORK CELEBRATES BEAUTY, freedom, love and the complex liberation that thus ensues. With his imagination and strokes, his work enhances the realms of possibility, mythology and romance. He has a way of viewing mythology and characters with a distinctly personal, almost voyeuristic peek, claiming his signature and then as if releasing them to the other side of the fence of space and time. His nymphs carry us on a flight, his musicians and dancers play us and with us, his depiction of scenes from scriptural tales tell a story yet leave that perfect silence intact which turns words into a song.

Much like Mahatma Gandhi, he brought fine art to the masses and like him, his work contributed to India being established on the world map. Perhaps it is mere coincidence that they both shared the date of the last day of their lives, perhaps there are deeper yarns that connect them.

For the exposition, the Raja Ravi Varma Heritage Foundation lends lithographs from the visionary artist's repertoire. He often painted on canvases of jute and it is his work that gets meticulously translated on to the pallus of khadi saris by textile designer Gaurang Shah in the next section.

"Nothing is beyond the power of love."

Mahatma Gandhi

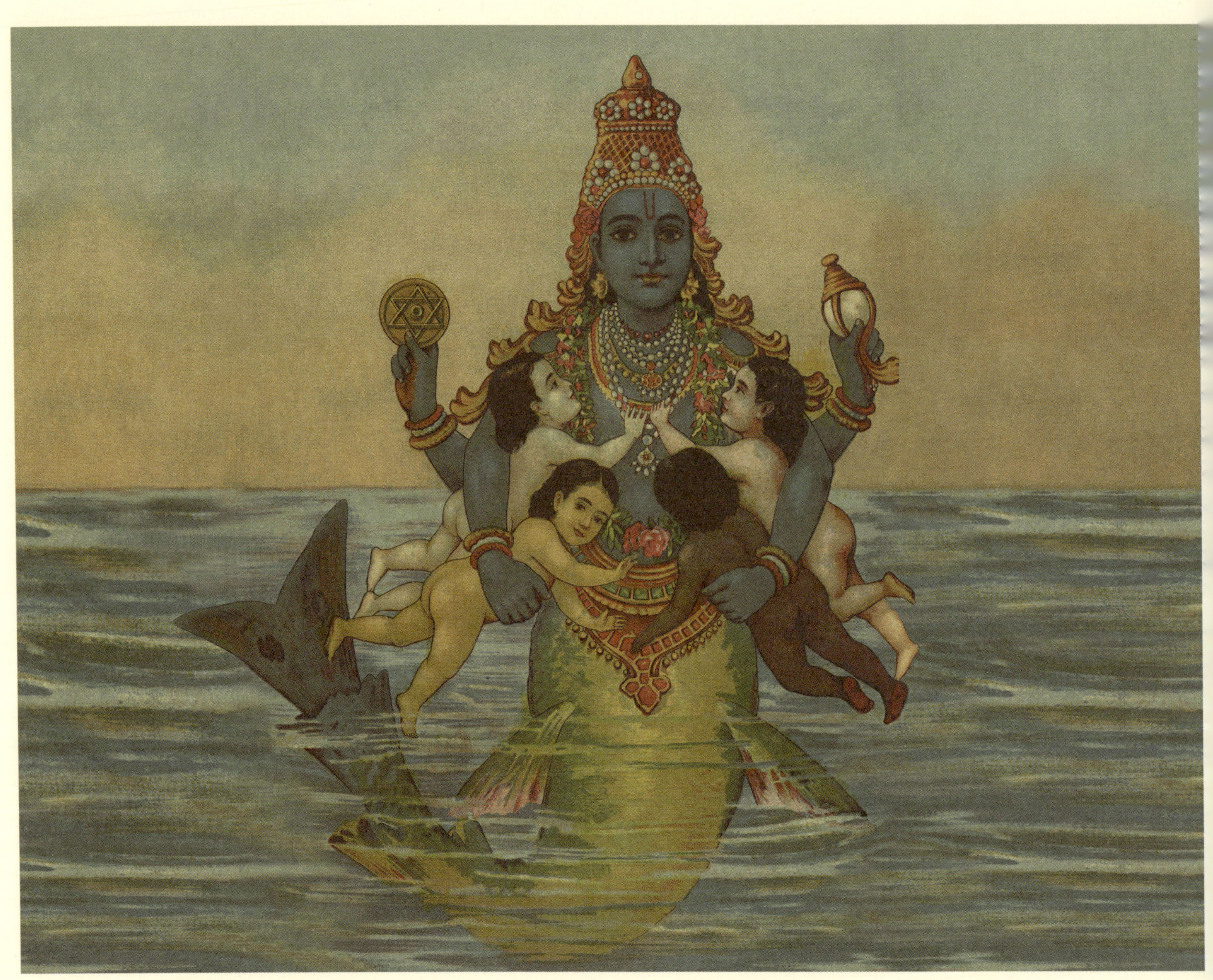

I am the reflection of the mirror in me.
I show all.
I reveal nothing.

Matsya Avatar

Matsya Avatar is the first of the Dashavatars of Lord Vishnu. In this half-man half-fish form, he is believed to have saved the world from *pralaya*, the final deluge. Growing from a tiny fish in Manu's hands into something bigger and bigger, from a pot, to a tank and finally to the ocean, the Matsya Avatar holds safe four infants who could be alluded to the four Vedas, the fountainheads of all existence.

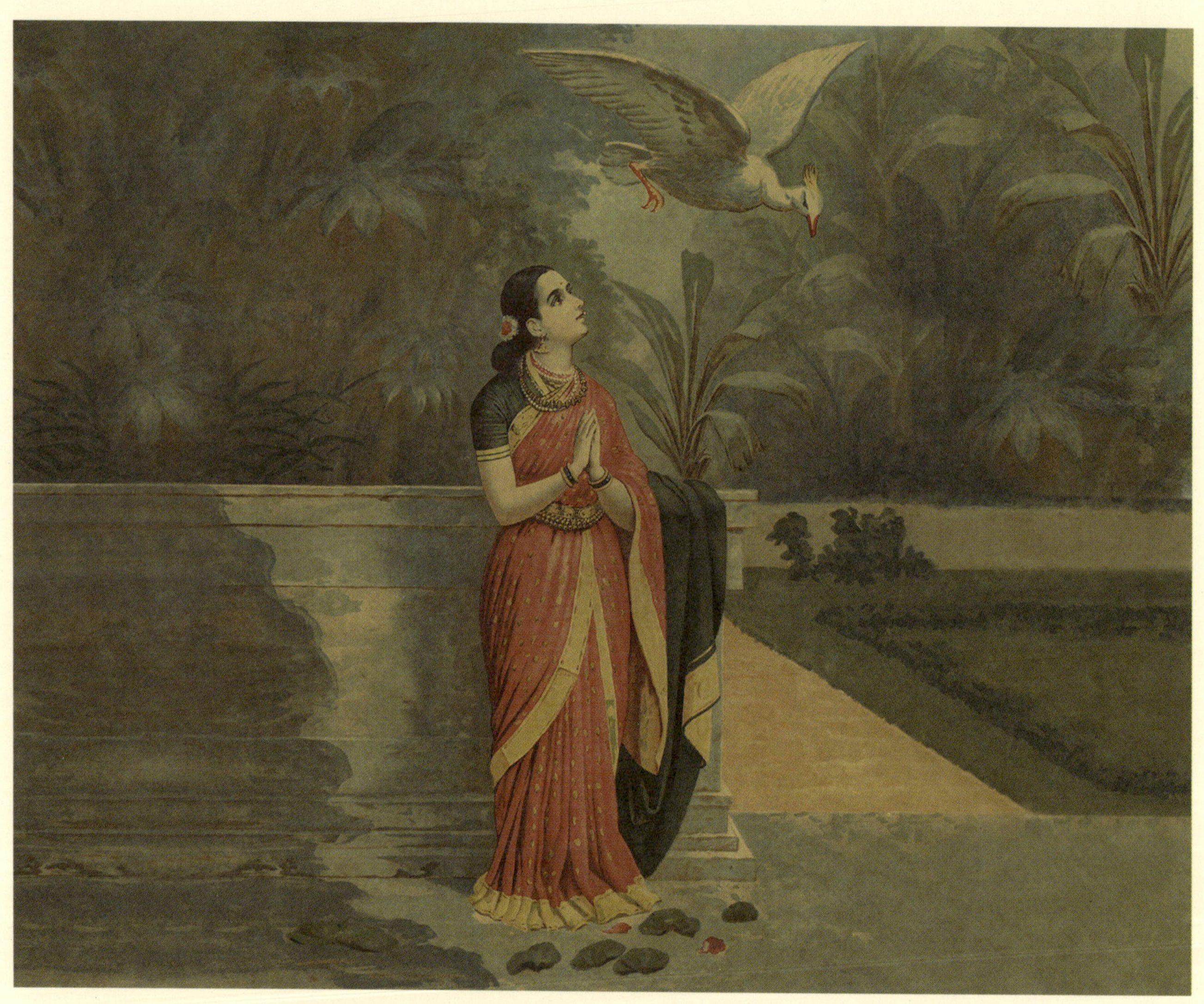

We breathe to inject
Vacant dreams
With stories
To keep us awake

Hamsa Damayanti Samvad

With a gentle swoop of its flight, the swan takes over Princess Damyanti's heart and mind, coating them with tales of the glorious virtues of Prince Nala. In a trance, Damyanti listens to this flying messenger, the gaze of her heart fixed on a lover miles away, a lover she is yet to meet. The swan becomes a veritable thread joining two souls, apart only in body. This tale is told in the Mahabharat.

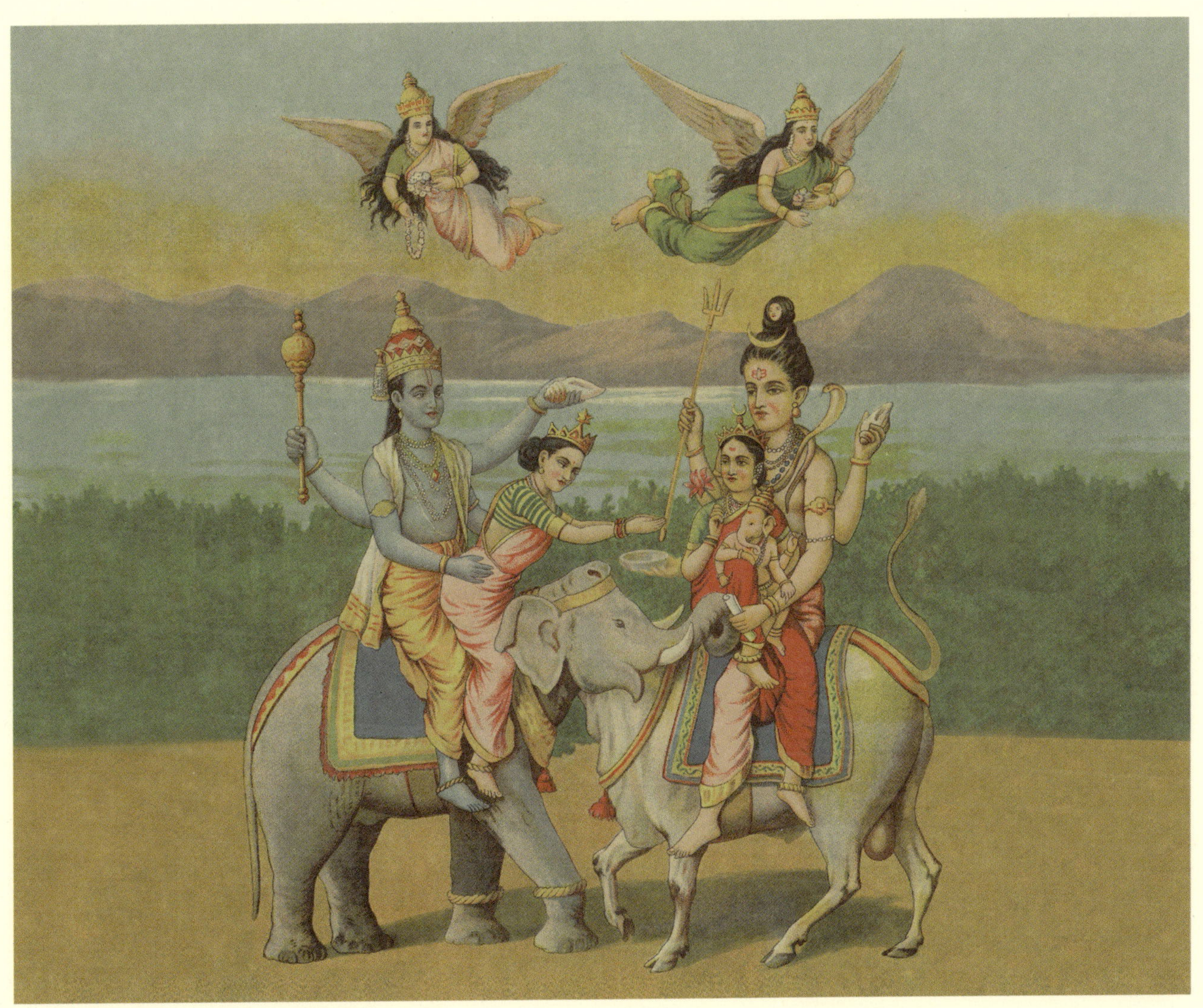

Your elbow bends
My universe
Is framed

Hari Har Bhet

A meeting or *bhet* between Hari (Lord Vishnu) and Har (Lord Shiva) as they arrive with their consorts Lakshmi and Parvati. Lord Vishnu and Lakshmi astride the elephant offer their blessings to Ganapathi, Lord Shiva and Parvati's young son. With playful optical depth and divine celebration, this scene nurtures further the unity of two of the three Supreme Beings in Hindu mythology – Brahma, Vishnu, Shiva.

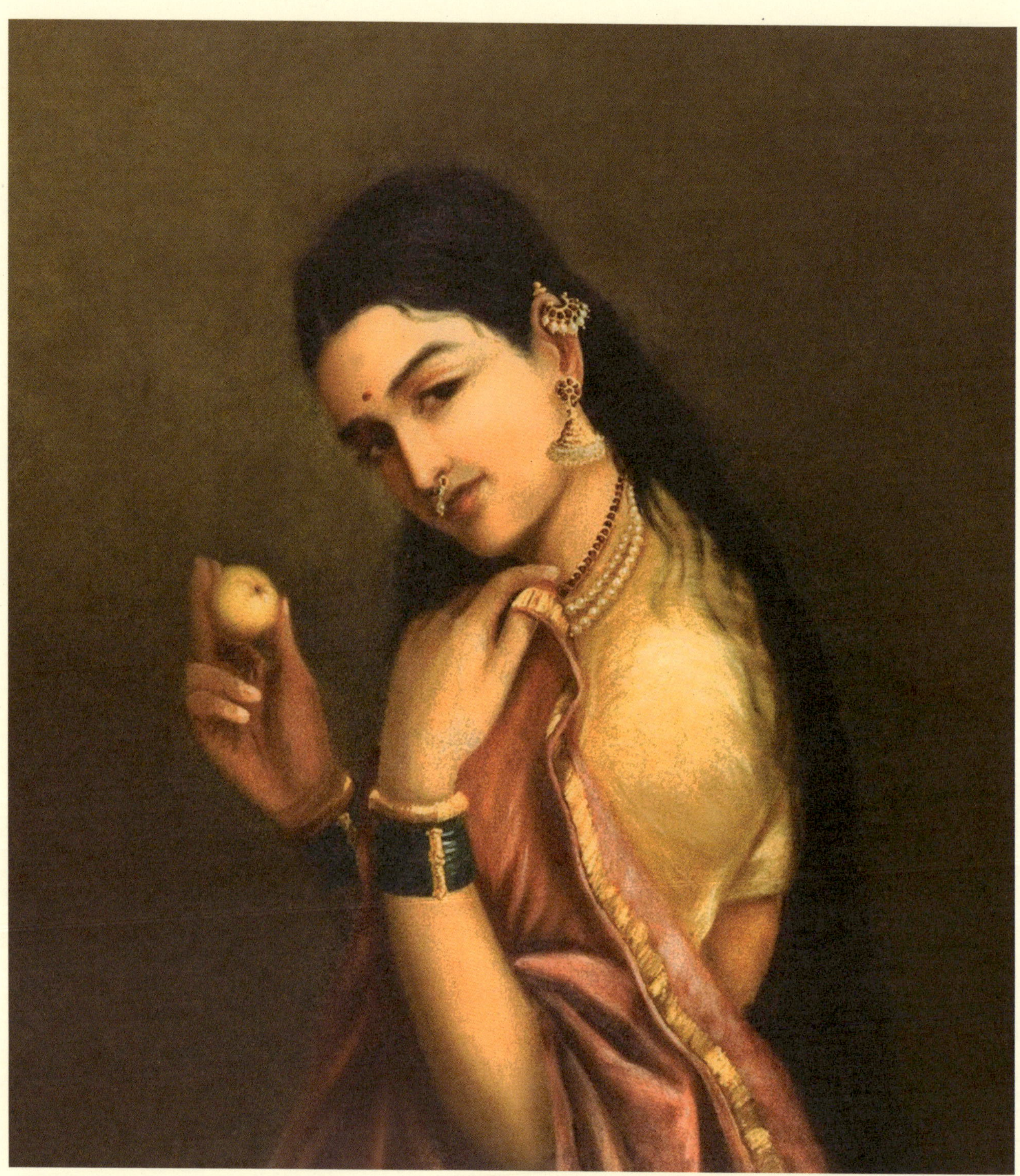

The image I saw
Gets darker now
Brighter than your lips
With your love
You erase me

Woman Holding a Fruit

A classic in a series of Raja Ravi Varma's distinctive style in portraiture, the "Woman holding a fruit" also holds mischief in her eyes and a resplendent innocence hard to miss.

Opposite:
Woman Holding a Fruit
Raja Ravi Varma
Oil on canvas // NGMA Collection

All tornadoes can be predicted
Except the ones
Arising in man
Without a warning they rise and each time
Destroy more than they had planned
If we were
To devise a device
That pre learns the trajectory
Of the collective mind
Would we still
Willingly steer
Ourselves into the heart of storms

Krishna Shishtai

In a last attempt to avoid the war between the Kauravas and Pandavas, Shri Krishna visits King Duryodhana's court on the insistence of King Yudhishthira. Here, however, he encounters deep contempt and the Kauravas try to take him captive. Enraged, Satyaki, one of his ardent devotees, lashes out with his sword. Shri Krishna then arrests Satyaki's arm to forbid him from this violence and goes on to reveal his Vishwaroopam, his omniscient, omnipresent, majestic form. Shishtai translates as mediation, reflecting that anxious, uncertain moment which can lead to pure calm or vast chaos.

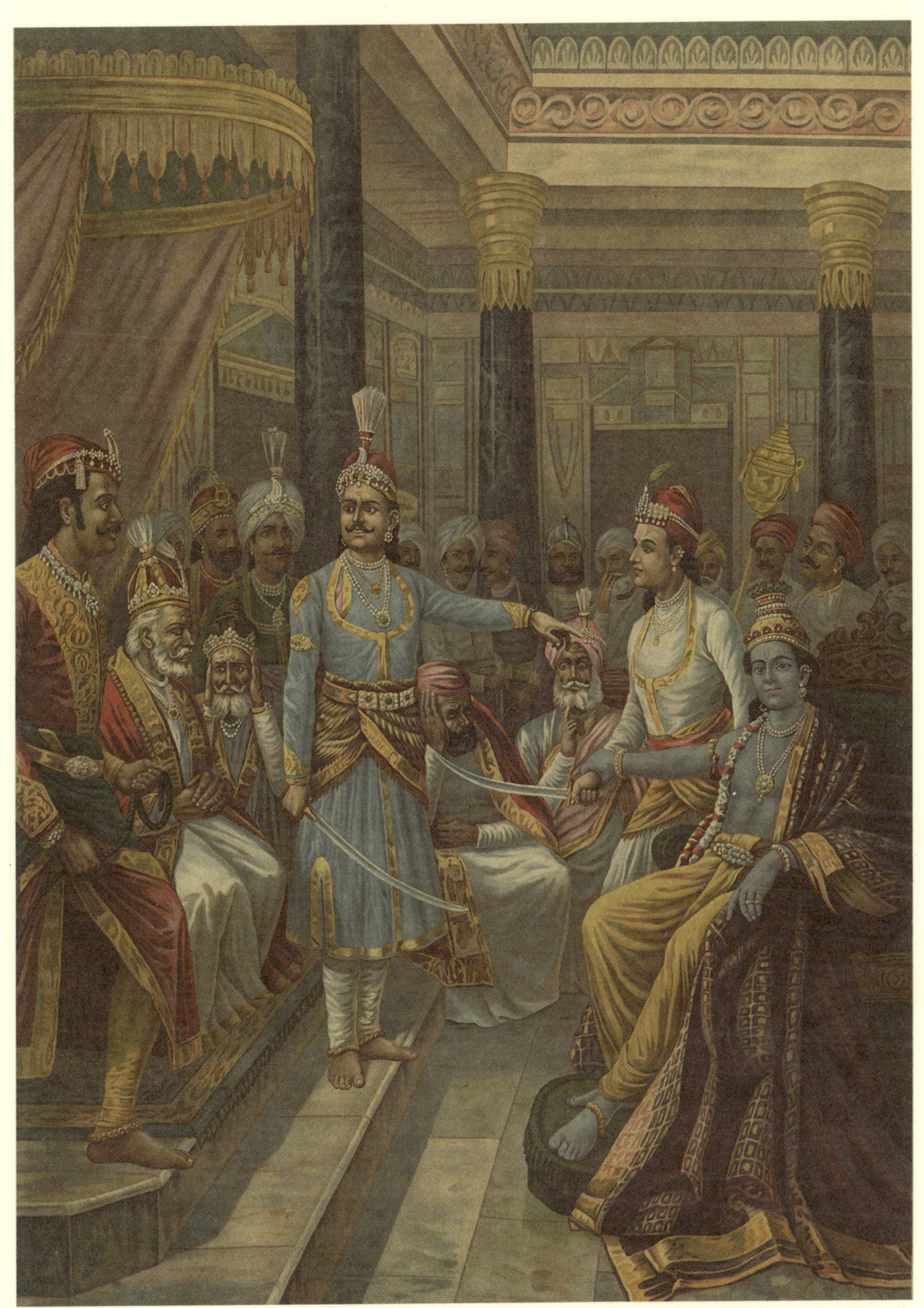

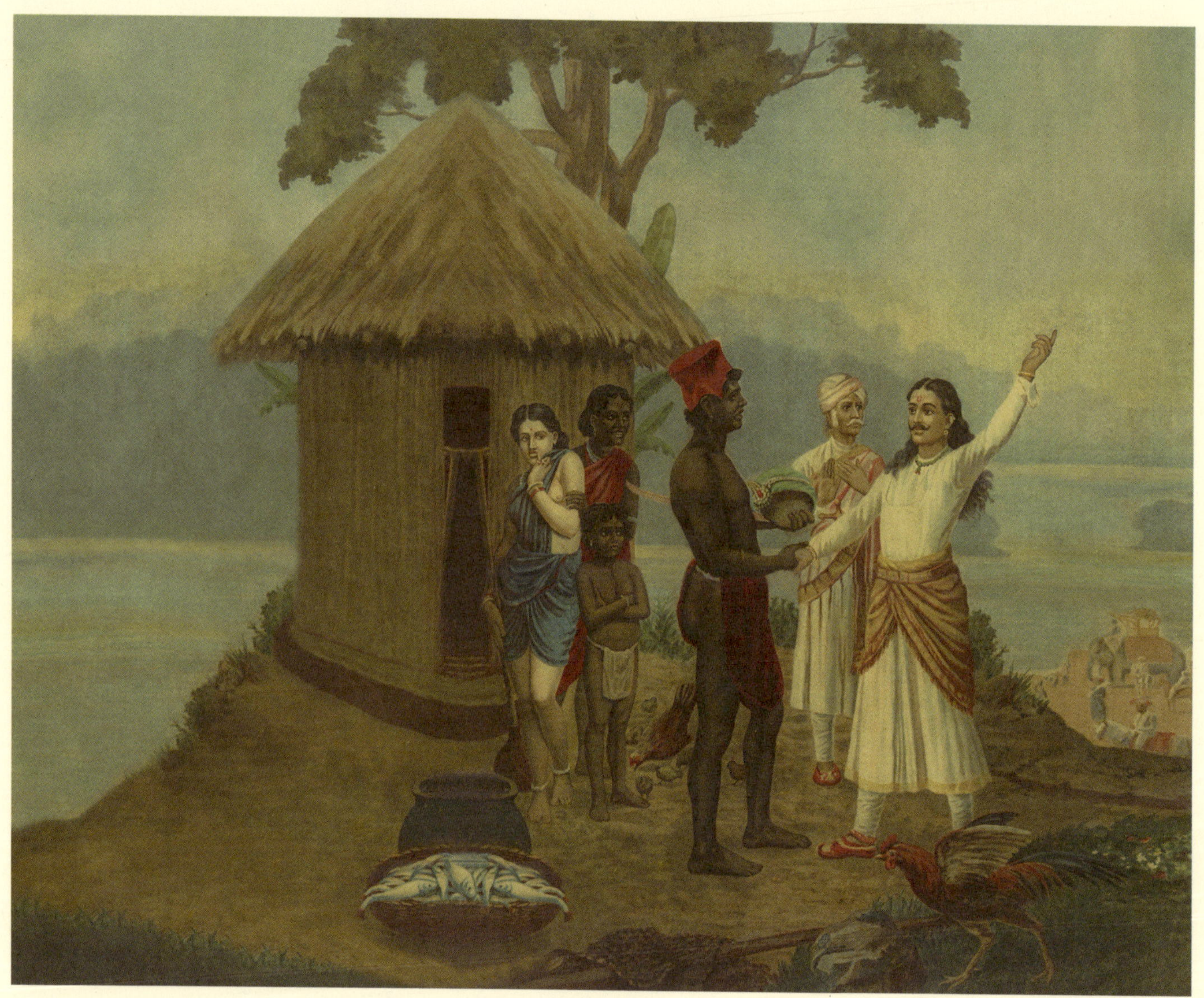

Be a volcano
Of resolve
Watch fate change
As you erupt

Bhishma's Promise

This setting reveals the moment that turned Devavrat to Bhishma, laying the foundation to what would consequently unfold as the complex story of the Mahabharata. Also famed as the Bhishma pratigya or oath, this is the episode where Devavrat abdicates his right to the throne and vows lifelong celibacy. He makes this promise to Dusharaj, the fisherman whose daughter is Satyavati or Matsyagandha. He does this in order for his father King Shantanu to marry Satyavati, whom the King has fallen in love with. This is a part of a tale of bold sacrifice, the prelude to a storm.

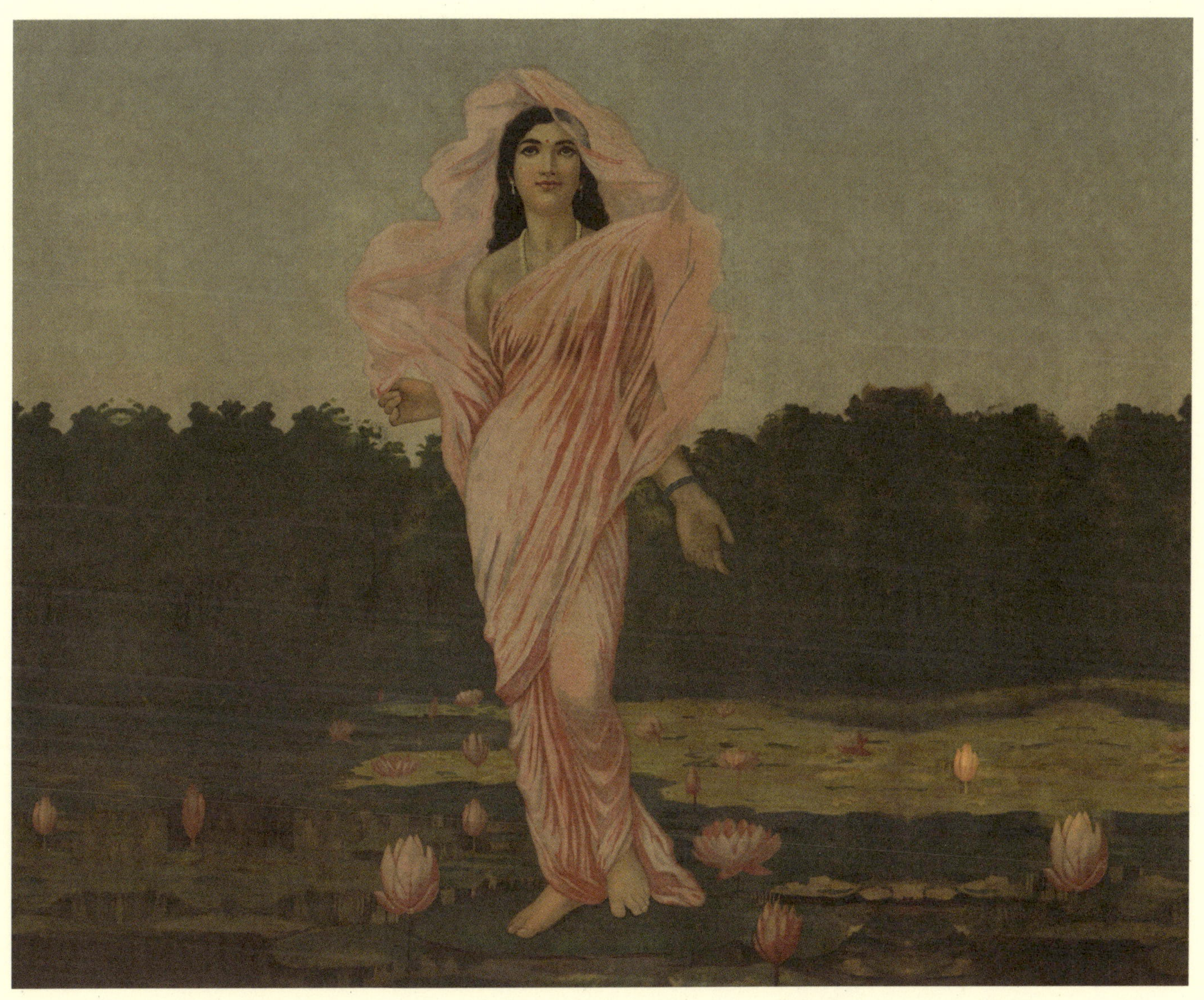

Where do you
Keep your words
When I look at you

Padminii

With the lightness of her spirit she seems to rise above all that is around her, akin to the lotuses and sheer like the fabric swirling about her form. Padminii is second in a series of three portraits of nymphs, fluid in their gesture, ethereal in their strokes.

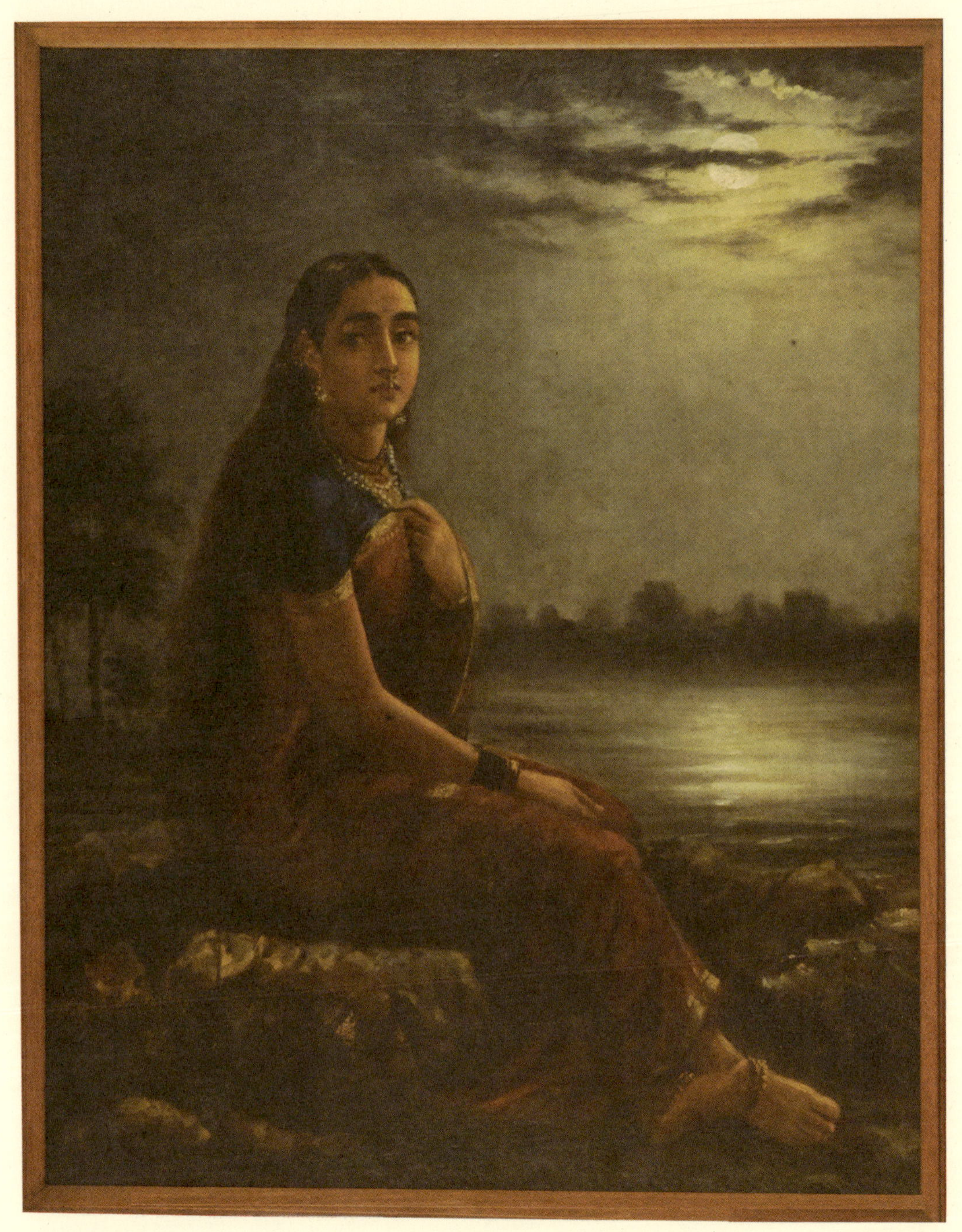

Lady in moonlight
Oil on canvas // NGMA Collection

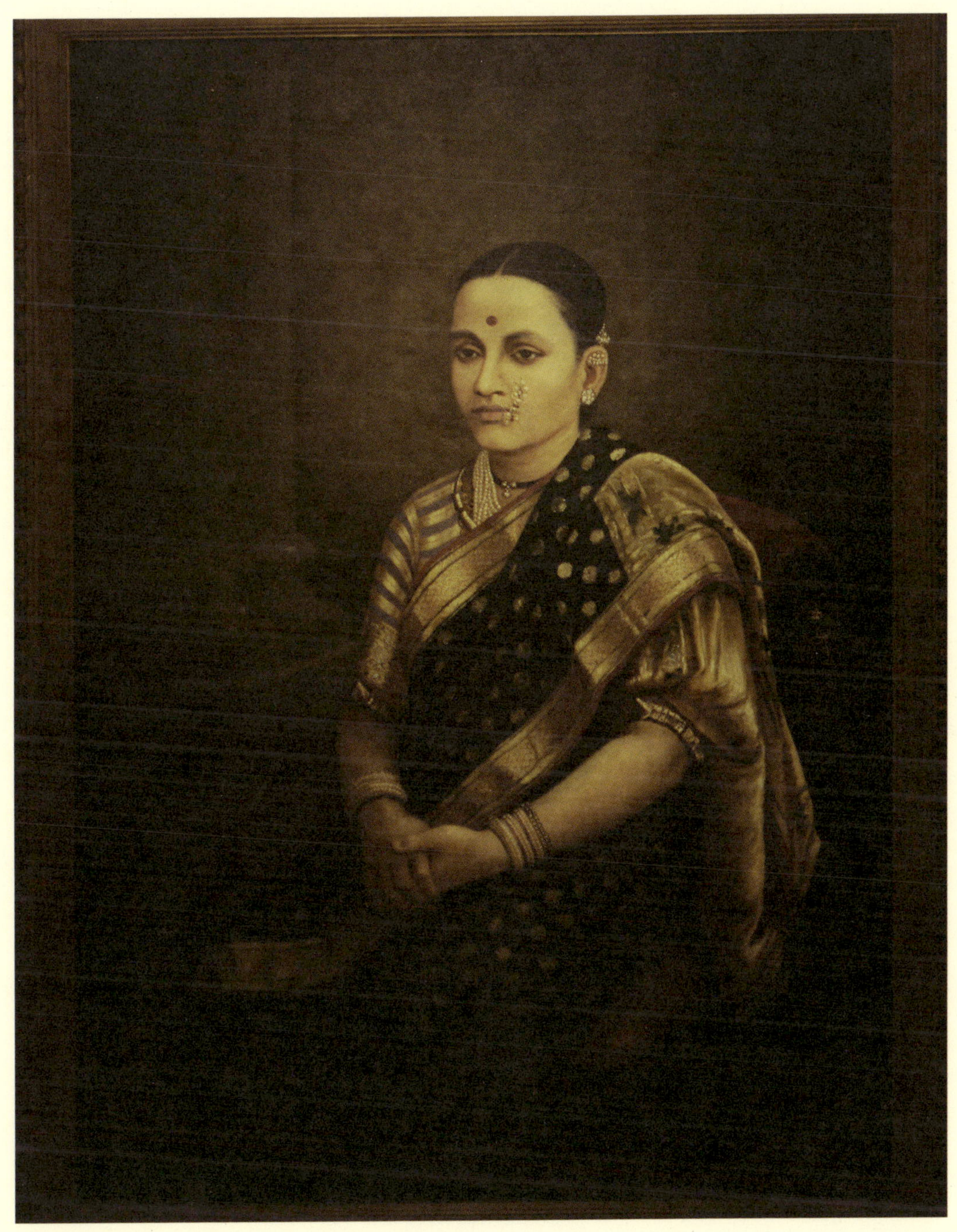

Portrait of a lady
Oil on canvas // NGMA Collection

To ride the bat of time
I travel
He knows of secret caves
Where we often lie and unravel
Puzzles on light
Riddles on waves

Vishnu Garuda Vaahan

The place of a *vaahan* or vehicle in Indian mythology is pivotal. It is synonymous with mystical travel, the main axis of every tale. Garuda, the mythical king of birds is the *vaahan* of Lord Vishnu and in this widely familiar scene he carries Vishnu along with his consorts Sridevi and Bhudevi, forever protecting them from venom of which the clawed serpent is a symbol. Through his strokes and perspective, Raja Ravi Varma breathes into this static painting a sense of flight, of constant kinesis towards belief.

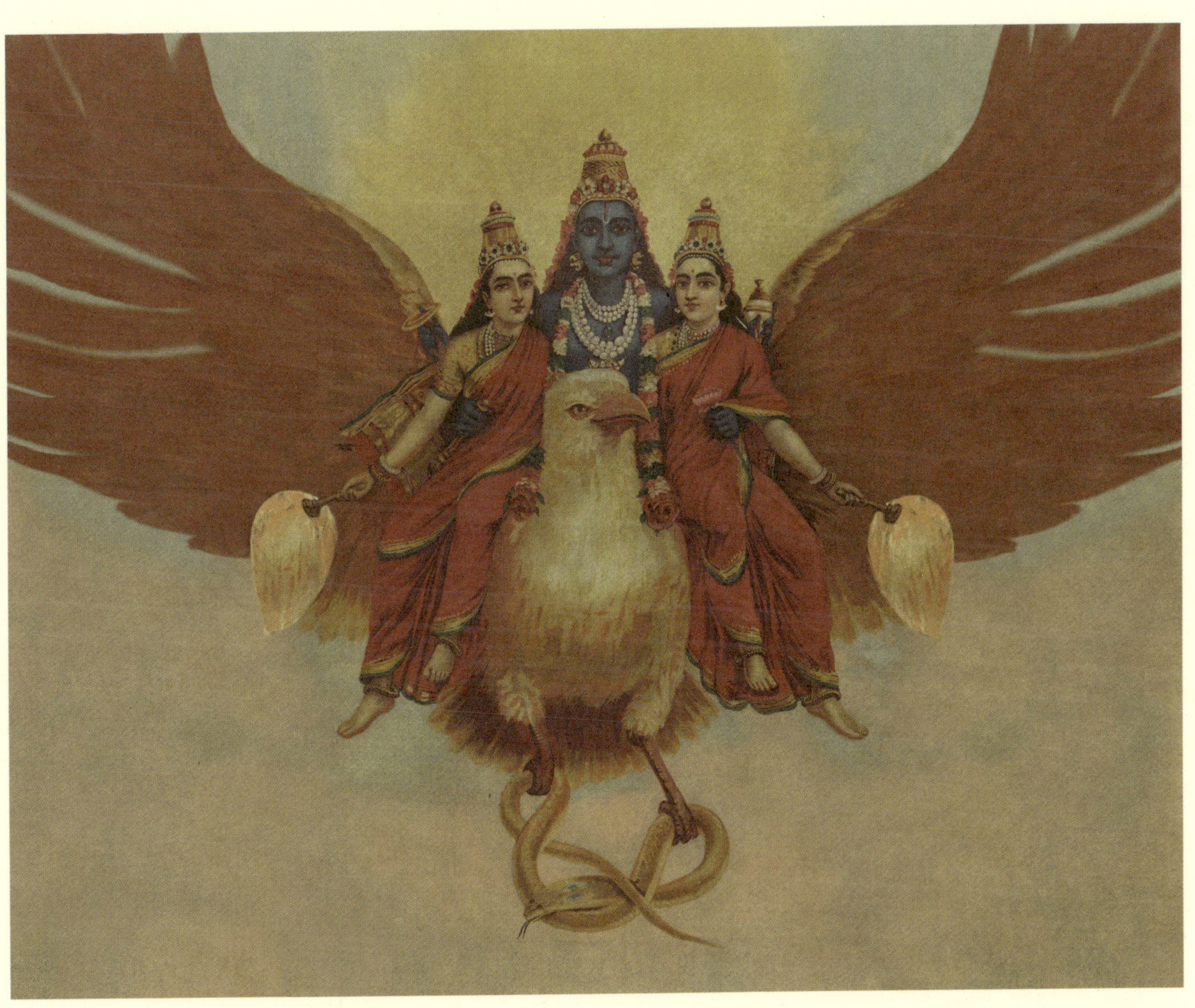

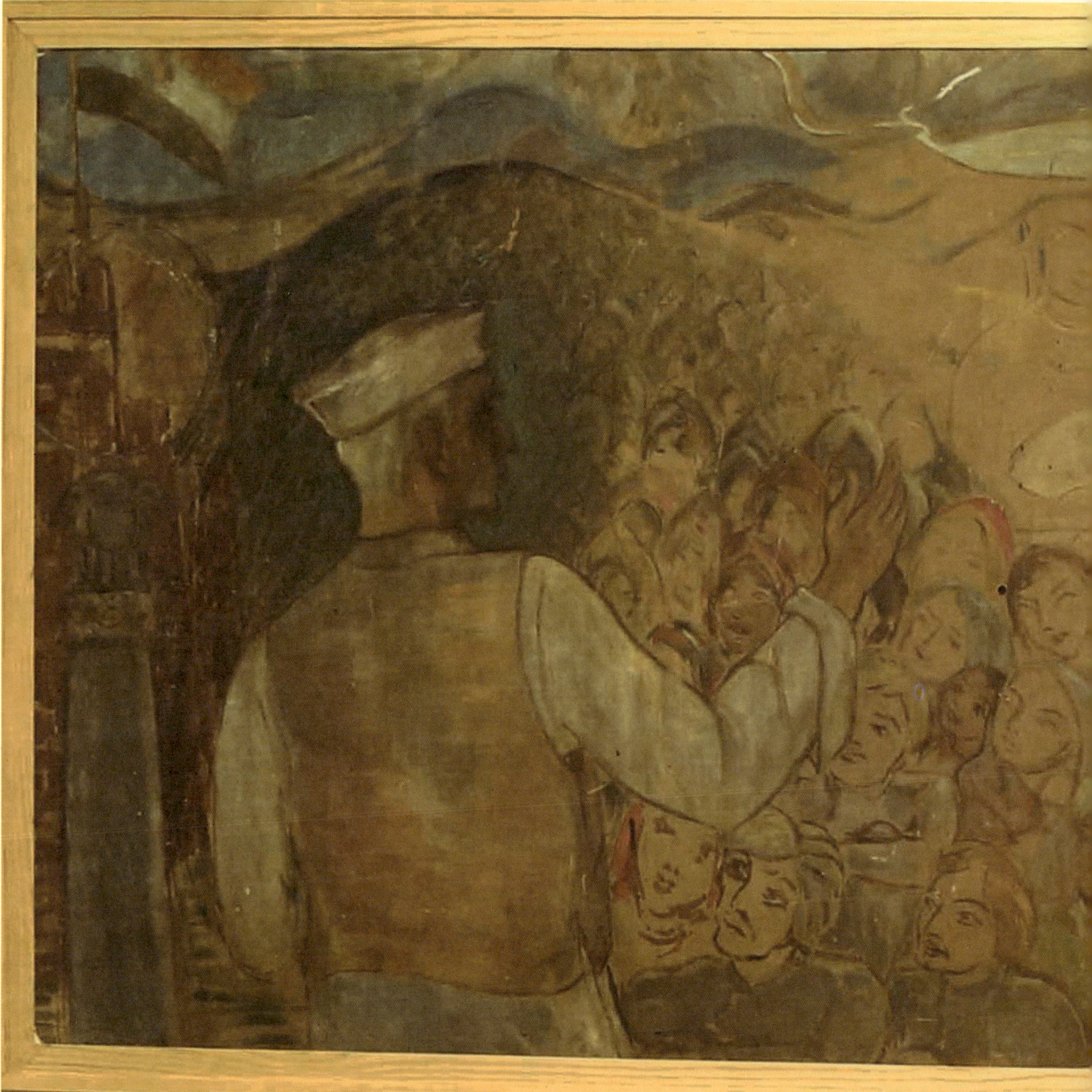

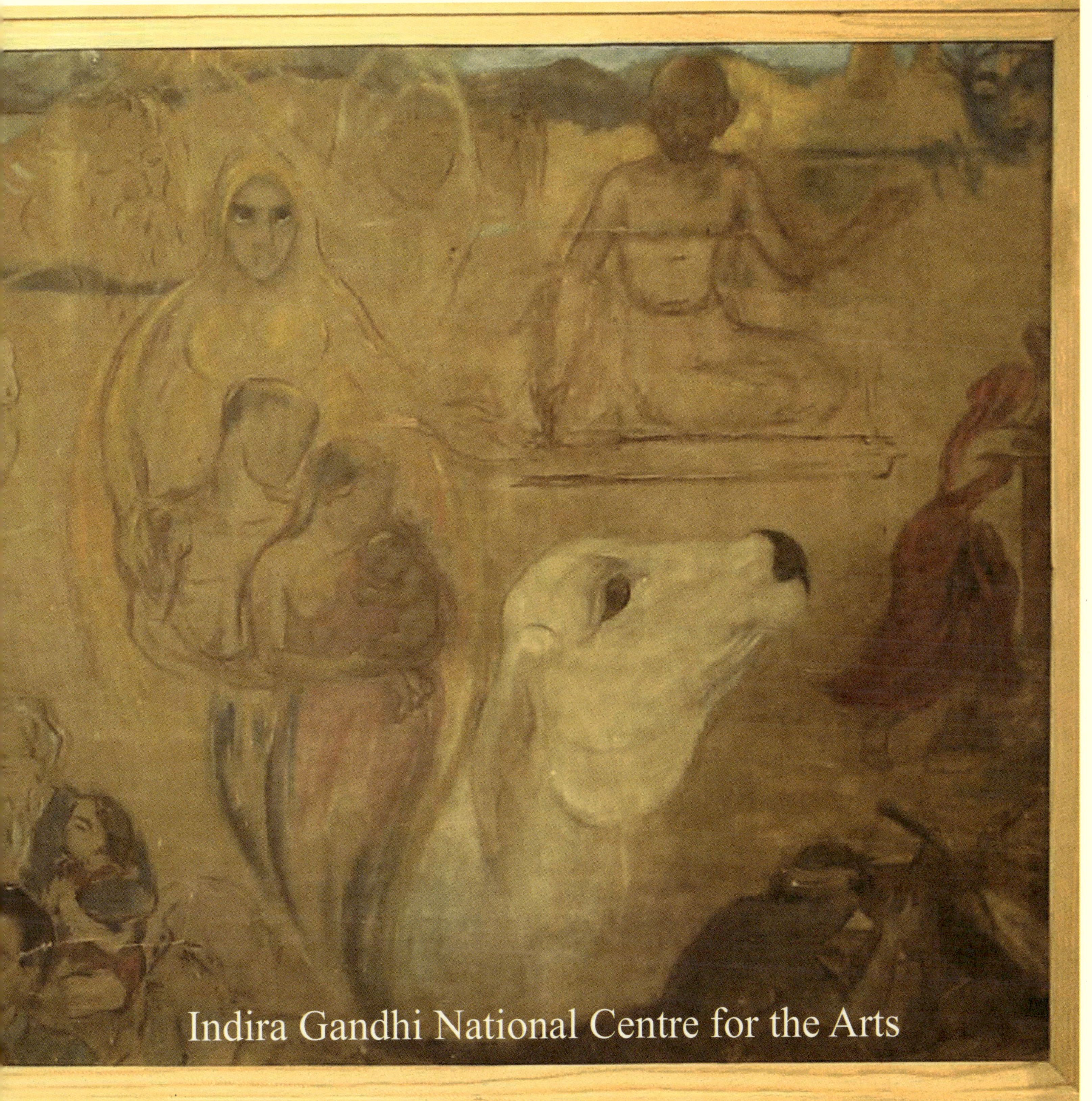
Indira Gandhi National Centre for the Arts

THE SCOPE OF ART FOR THE IGNCA IS A VAST UMBRELLA that includes facets of various disciplines like creative and critical literature (written and oral), visual arts, architecture, sculpture, painting, photography and performing arts comprising dance, music, theatre and beyond.

The Centre lends to *Santati*, rare and unseen works of photographers Henri Cartier-Bresson, DRD Wadia and Sunil Janah and painter Elizabeth Brunner.

"I am a man possessed by an idea. If such a man cannot get an organization, he becomes an organization."

Mahatma Gandhi

Shambhu Shaha

Shambhu Shaha was responsible for capturing some very rare moments that Mahatma Gandhi and Kasturba spent with Rabindranath Tagore at Santiniketan. His work taps into the dichotomous relationship between Gandhi and Tagore where they might have differed in their views of the world but essentially drew from the same idea that art must enable self-realization and that the whole world is one.

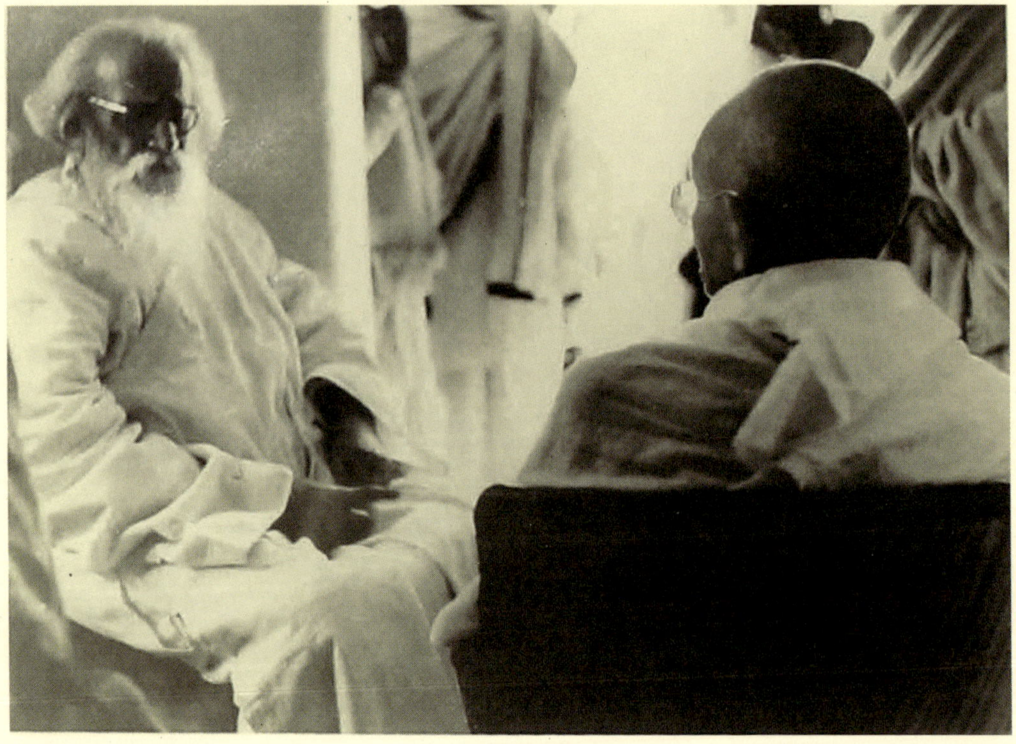

Rabindranath Tagore and Mahatma Gandhi at Shyamali
Shambhu Shaha // Santiniketan // Cultural Archives, IGNCA

DRD Wadia

A part of India's independence movement, photographer DRD Wadia shared a personal connect with Mahatma Gandhi. His lens has captured some iconic, individual perspectives on the public life of one of the most inspiring world figures. He came from a family that contributed extensively to the cultural, business and judicial life of Bombay and took a deep and sincere interest in the socio-cultural evolution of the country. One of the founders of the Photographic Society of India that formed in 1937, his work is noted for its unique portrayal of many thinkers and artists of the 40's in India, Europe and America.

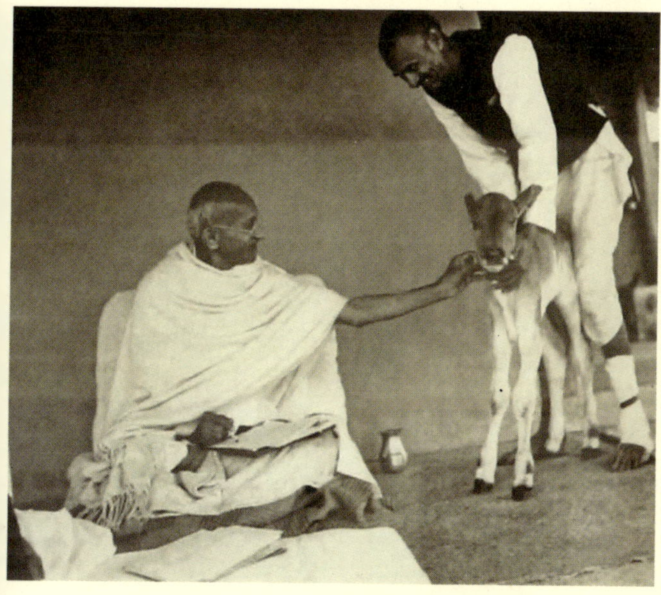

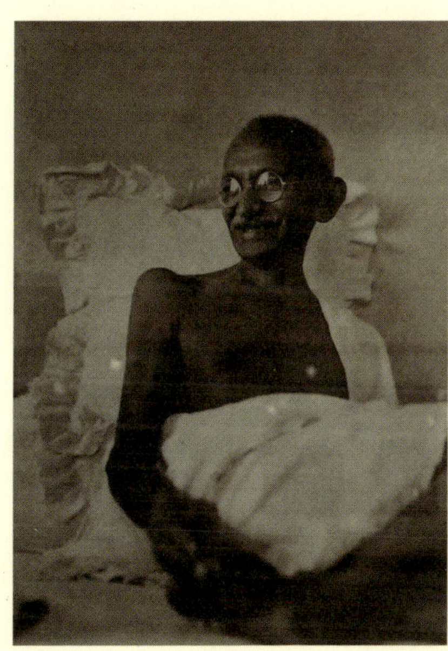

DRD Wadia // Cultural Archives, IGNCA

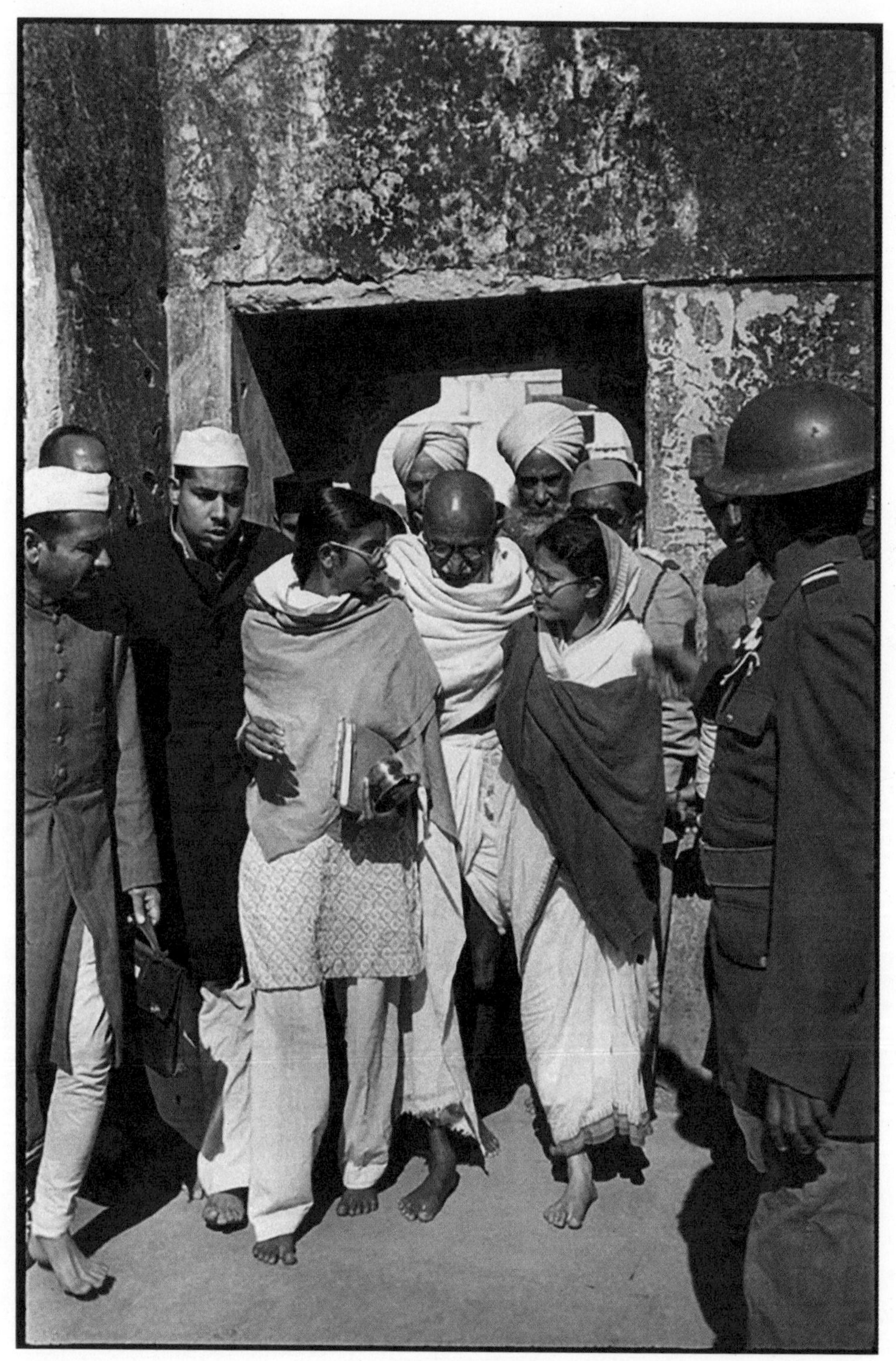

Henri Cartier-Bresson

Mahatma Gandhi's is perhaps one of the most publicly documented and photographed life amongst world leaders throughout history. Photographer Henri Cartier-Bresson, widely known for his imagery that was at once documentative and surreal, is the eye and mind behind capturing some of the most magnetic moments during Gandhi's life and death. Like Gandhi, Bresson was a man occupied with inquiry into truth, purpose, enriching the self and working tirelessly towards it. Like Gandhi, he believed in simplicity, in precision, in carrying minimal equipment so as to become invisible and offer the entire stage to the moment being caught, to the work being done.

He seemed to connect with Gandhi with a wavelength on which his pictures entwine like pages of poetry.

Opposite:

Mahatma Gandhi leaving the Muslim Shrine, Mehrauli. This was one of his last appearances during the time between the end of his fast and his death.

Henri Cartier-Bresson // Delhi, 1948 // Cultural Archives, IGNCA

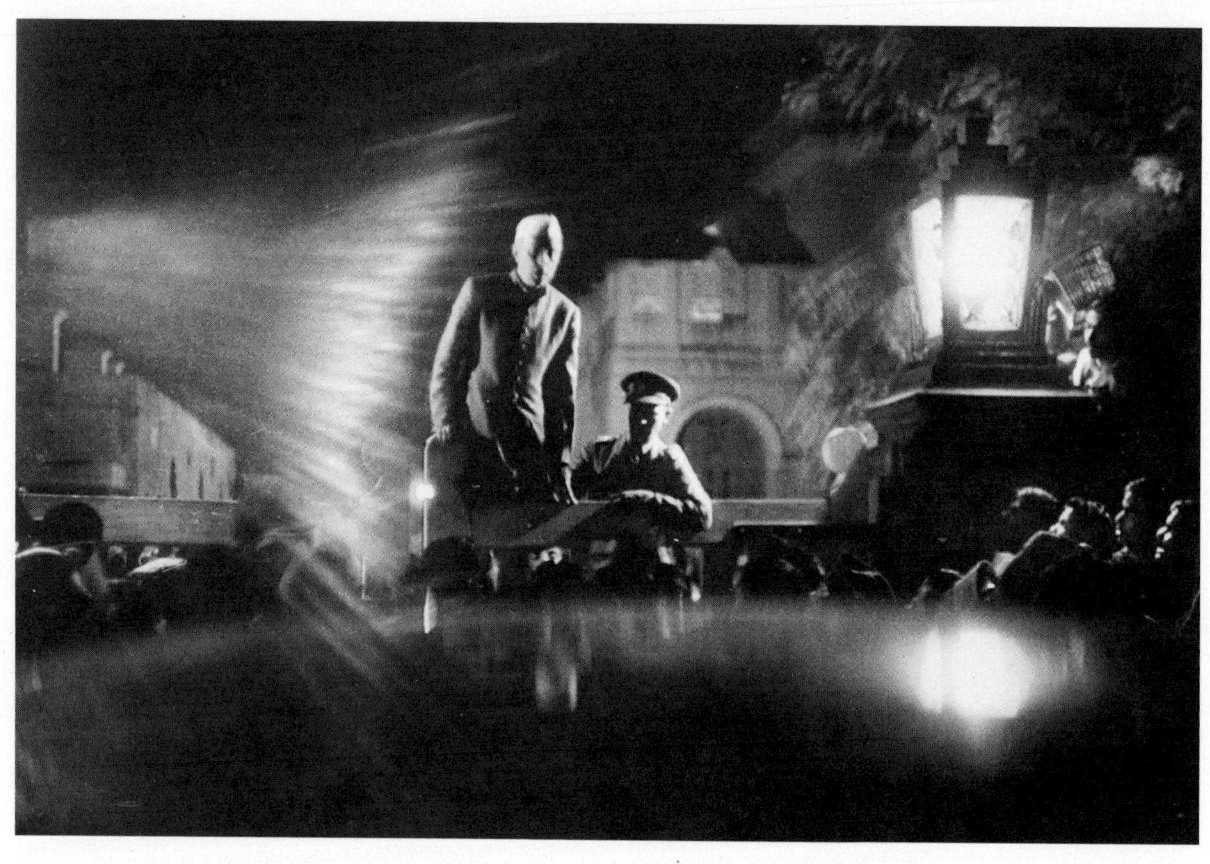

Pandit Jawaharlal Nehru announces the news of Gandhiji's death at the gates of Birla House. Pandit Nehru came out to address the huge gathering of nearly two lakhs which had surrounded Birla House, but broke down with grief more than once when he spoke.

Henri Cartier-Bresson // Delhi, 1948 // Cultural Archives, IGNCA

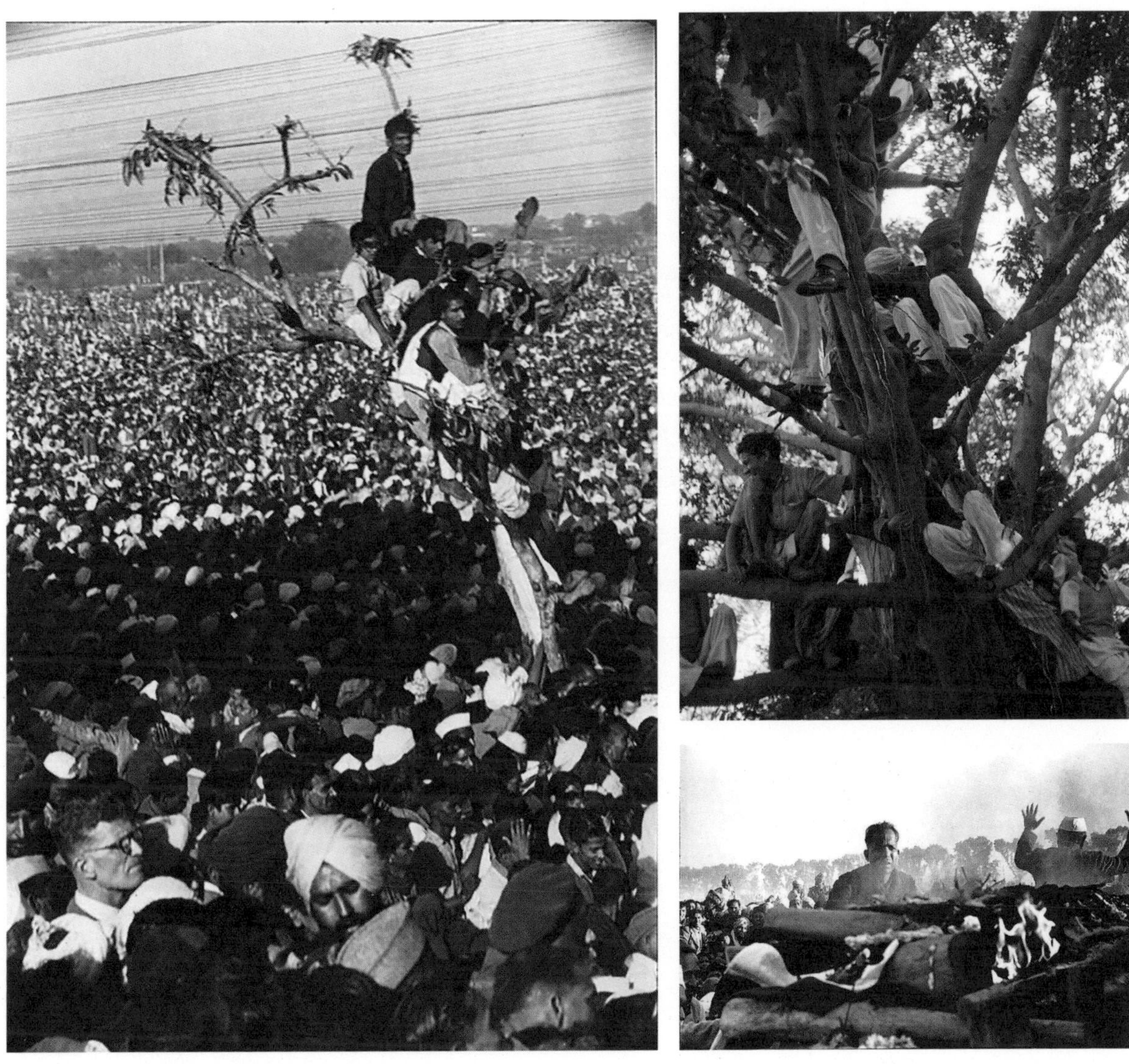

Moments from Mahatma Gandhi's final journey.
Henri Cartier-Bresson // Delhi, 1948 // Cultural Archives, IGNCA

Sunil Janah

For his sensitivity and profound human connect through his photographs, Sunil Janah was awarded the Padma Shri in 2012. His work is a venturing into the realities of British Imperialism as he observed through his eye, his heart. It documents India's journey from its struggle for freedom, its ordinary people and their turmoil, catastrophes like famines and riots to the swift industrialization that followed the country's independence.

Opposite:
Mahatma Gandhi at a prayer meeting
Sunil Janah // Mumbai, 1945 // Cultural Archives, IGNCA

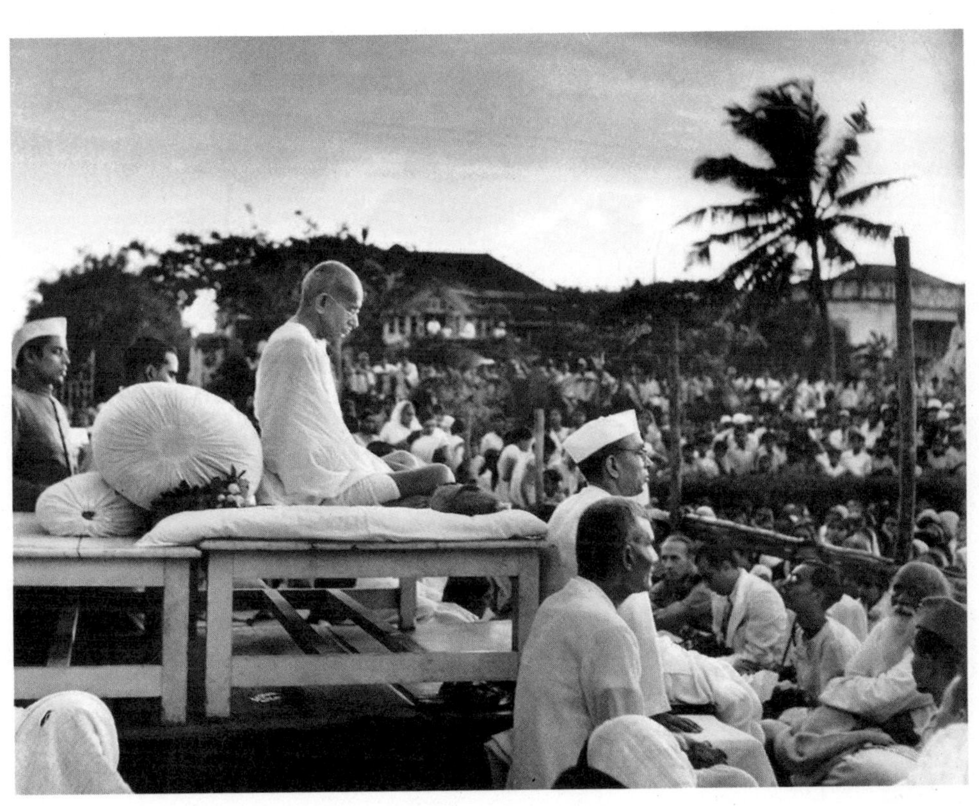

Elizabeth Brunner

Like a muse, India has wandered the imagination of many across the world, across time, especially of those seeking a spiritual axis. In that manner, she came to Elizabeth Brunner in a dream, in the form of a man with a white beard holding a candle. Her mother Elizabeth Sass Brunner, an artist herself, instinctively identified the man as Rabindranath Tagore and thus began their journey to India in1930. Here, Elizabeth painted voraciously the figures, the philosophies and the essence of this land. Her work reveals a meditative collage of visions, impressions and a travelling of the spirit impacted by the people she met, by her seeking of truth and by the India she felt she saw. Deeply influenced by her meetings with Mahatma Gandhi, their journey seems to run hand in hand in its searching, its resolve and the perseverance of a mind open to receiving.

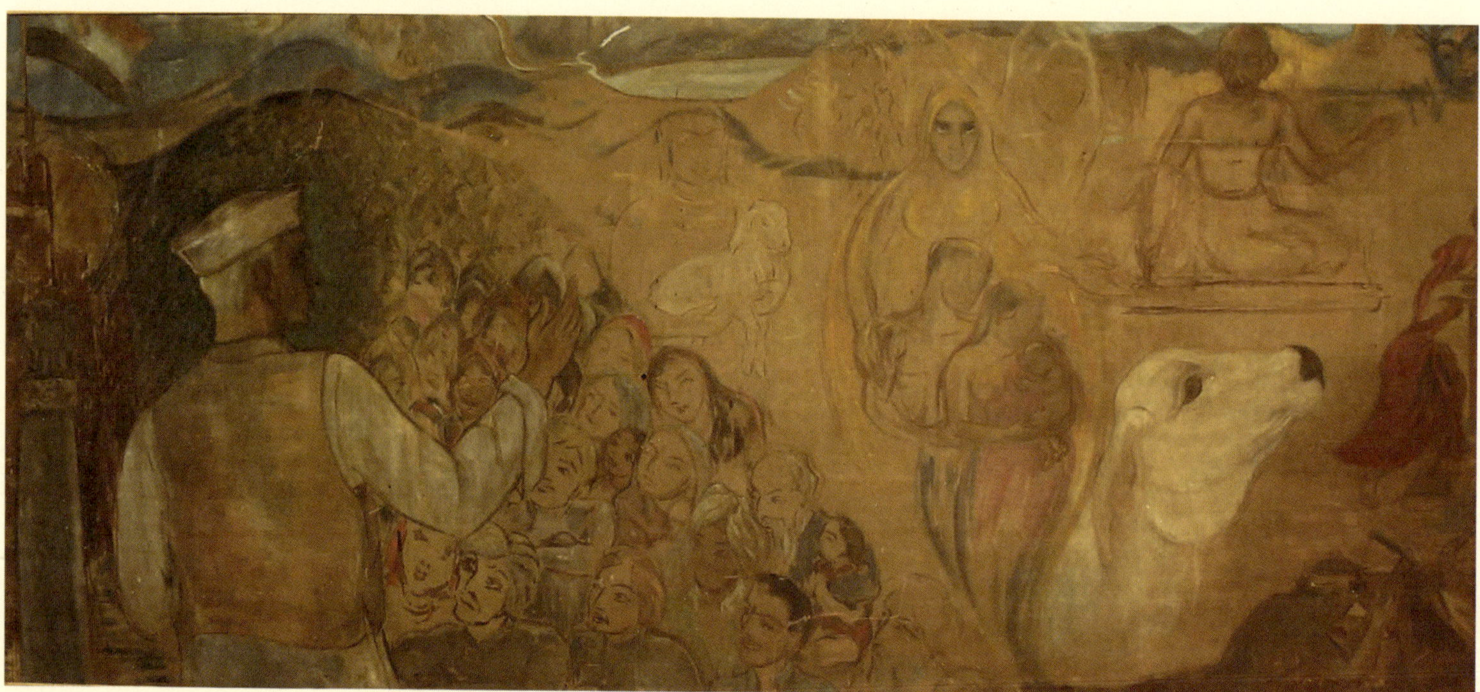

Elizabeth Brunner // Cultural Archives, IGNCA

In every palm
There is a leaf
As you read it
The tree grows
In you

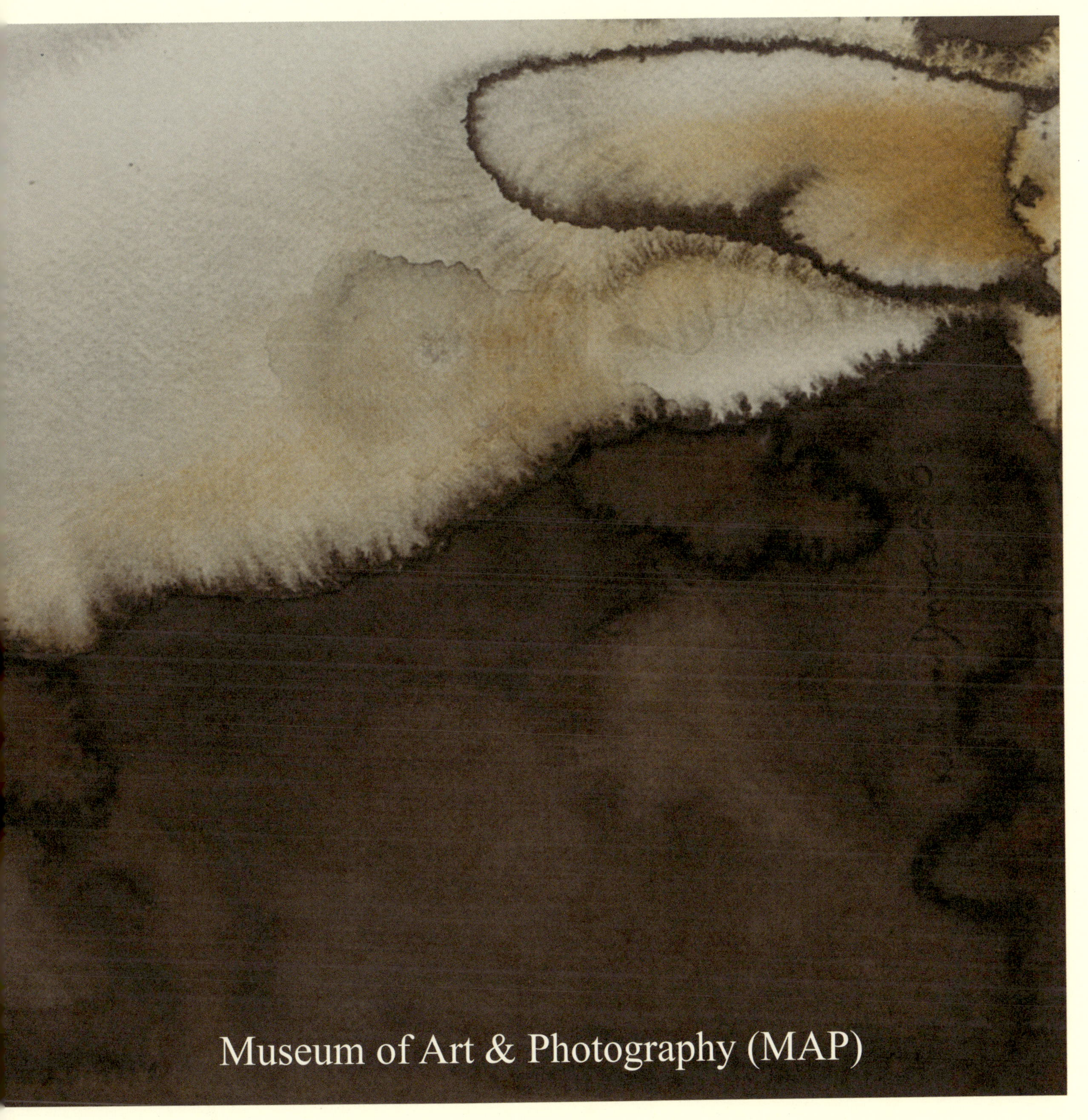
Museum of Art & Photography (MAP)

THE MUSEUM OF ART & PHOTOGRAPHY (MAP) IS SET TO OPEN ITS DOORS in December 2020. Located in Bengaluru, it is slated as south India's first extensive private art museum. Its mission is to make art and culture inclusive, educational and accessible to a wide and diverse audience.

Through its galleries, auditorium, research facilities and outreach programmes with schools, MAP intends to weave a community where the next generation has ample scope to engage with its growing collection of over 18,000 works of art. Predominantly, these works are from the Indian subcontinent and date from the twelfth century until present day. With historical and contemporary photography as well as popular culture being its core strength areas, the Museum's collections are catalogued and archived under six key areas: Modern and Contemporary, Photography, Folk and Tribal, Popular Culture and Textiles, Craft and Design and Pre-Modern Art.

MAP lends to Santati, pieces from its rare collection of paintings and chromolithographs.

"And he is no spinner who has no control over his wheel."

Mahatma Gandhi

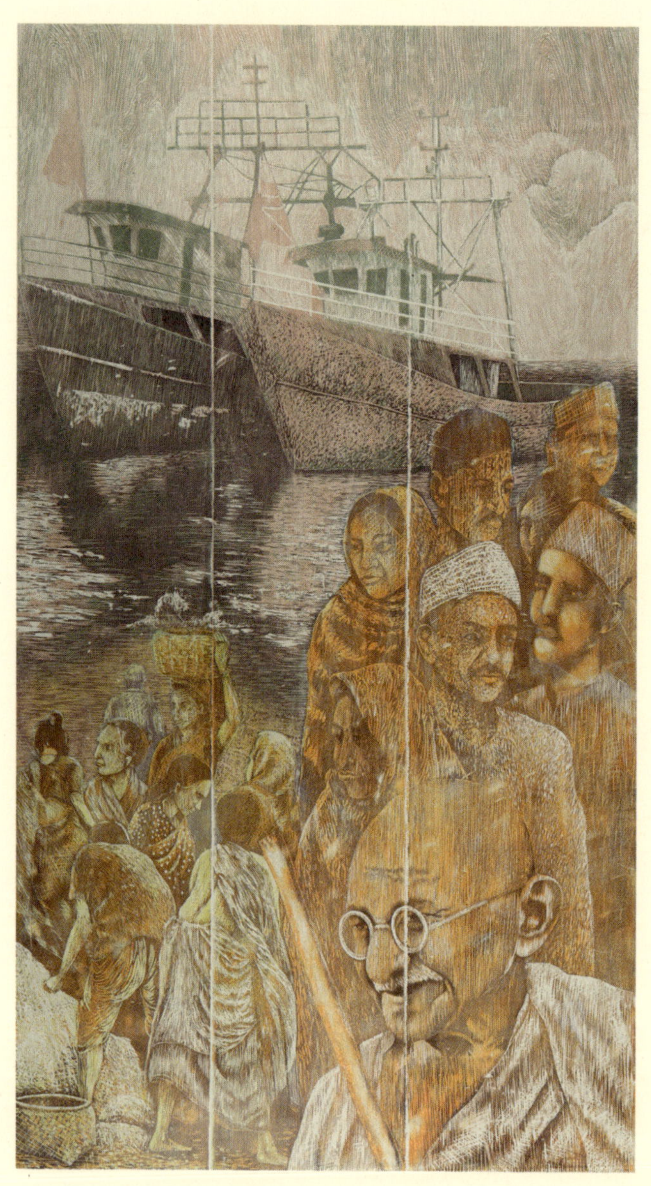

Satyagraha, 2007
Jagadeesh Thammineni, (b. 1988)
Woodcut prints // 190 × 105 cm

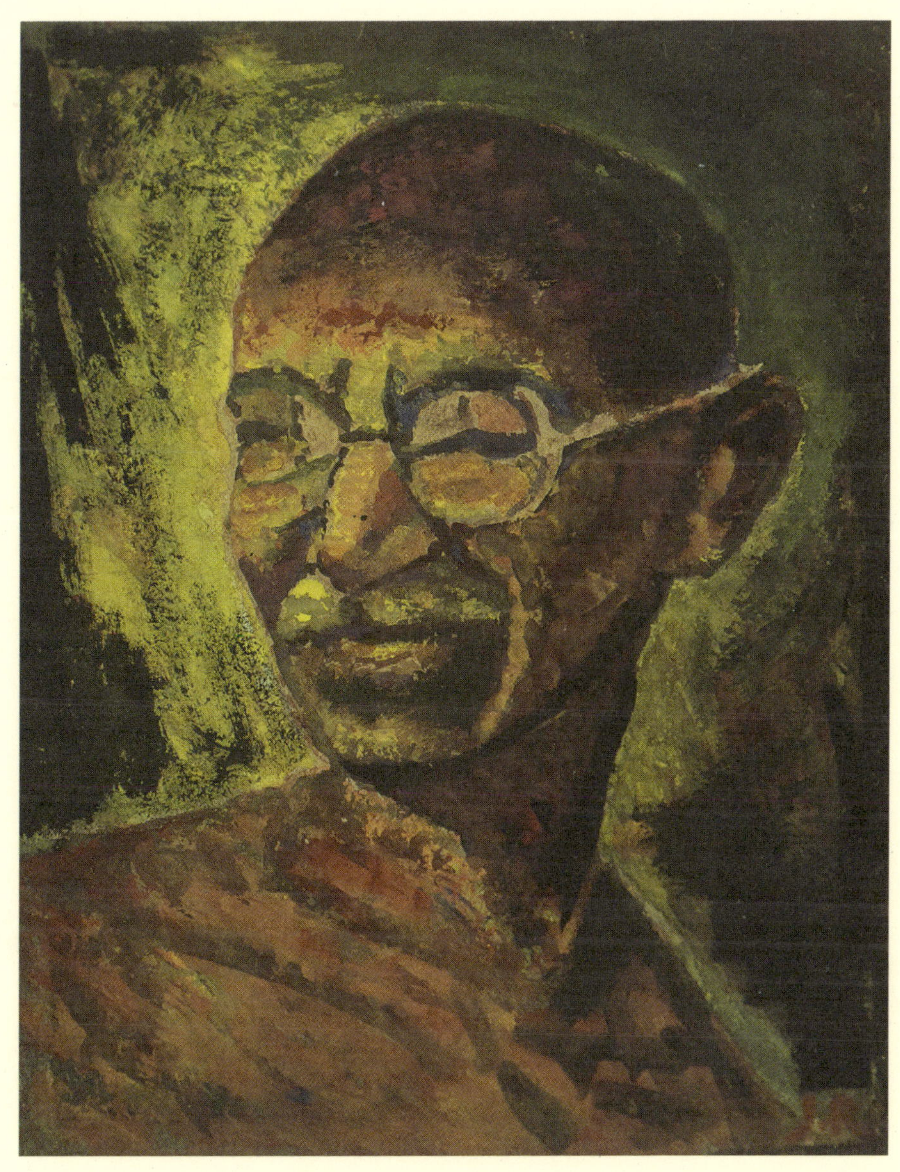

Old Gandhi, c. 1940
Jamini Roy, (1887–1972)
Tempera on board // 35 × 27 cm

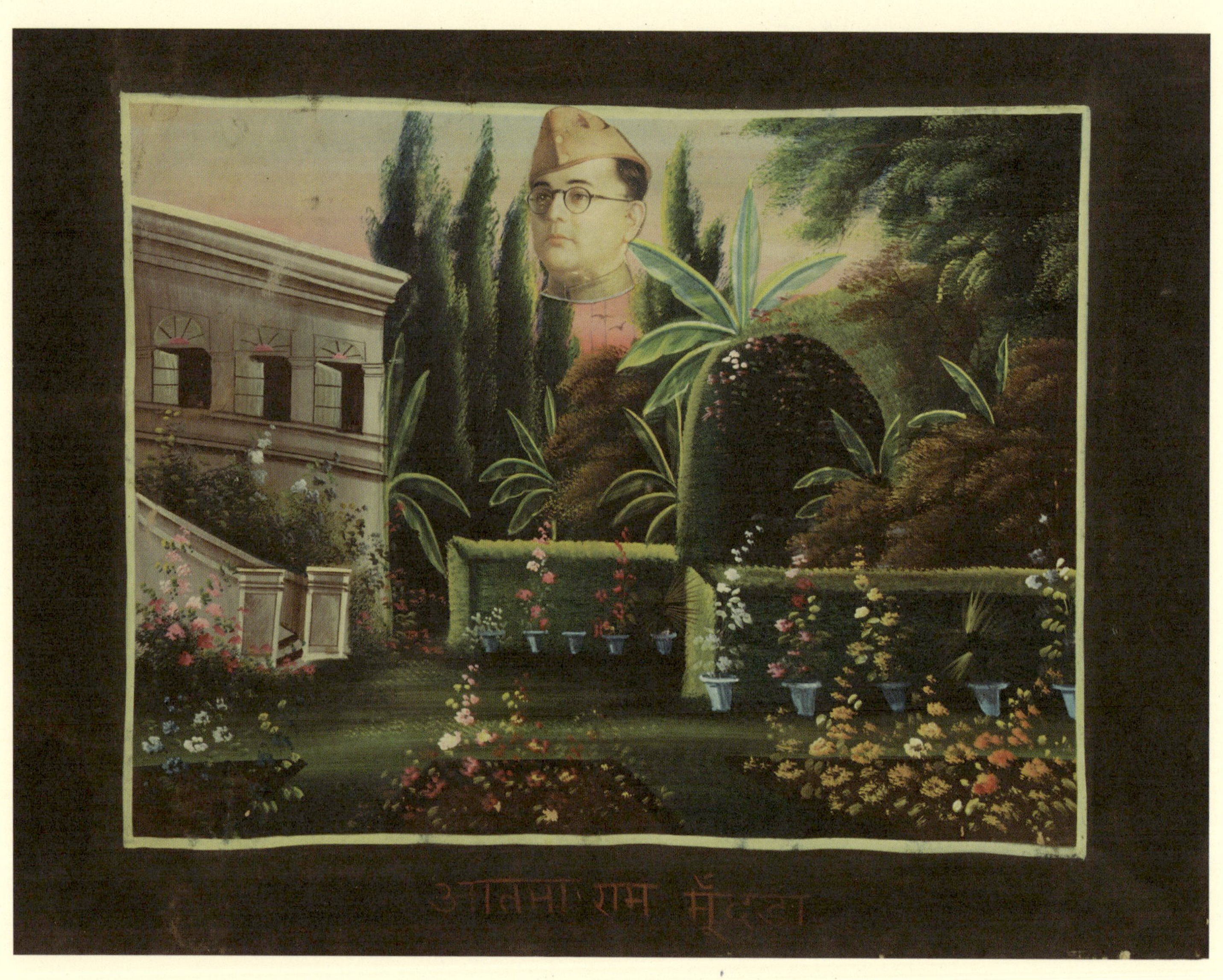

Collage depicting Subhash Chandra Bose, c. 1930s
Chromolithograph cut-out on a painted backdrop // 28.9 cm x 37.6 cm

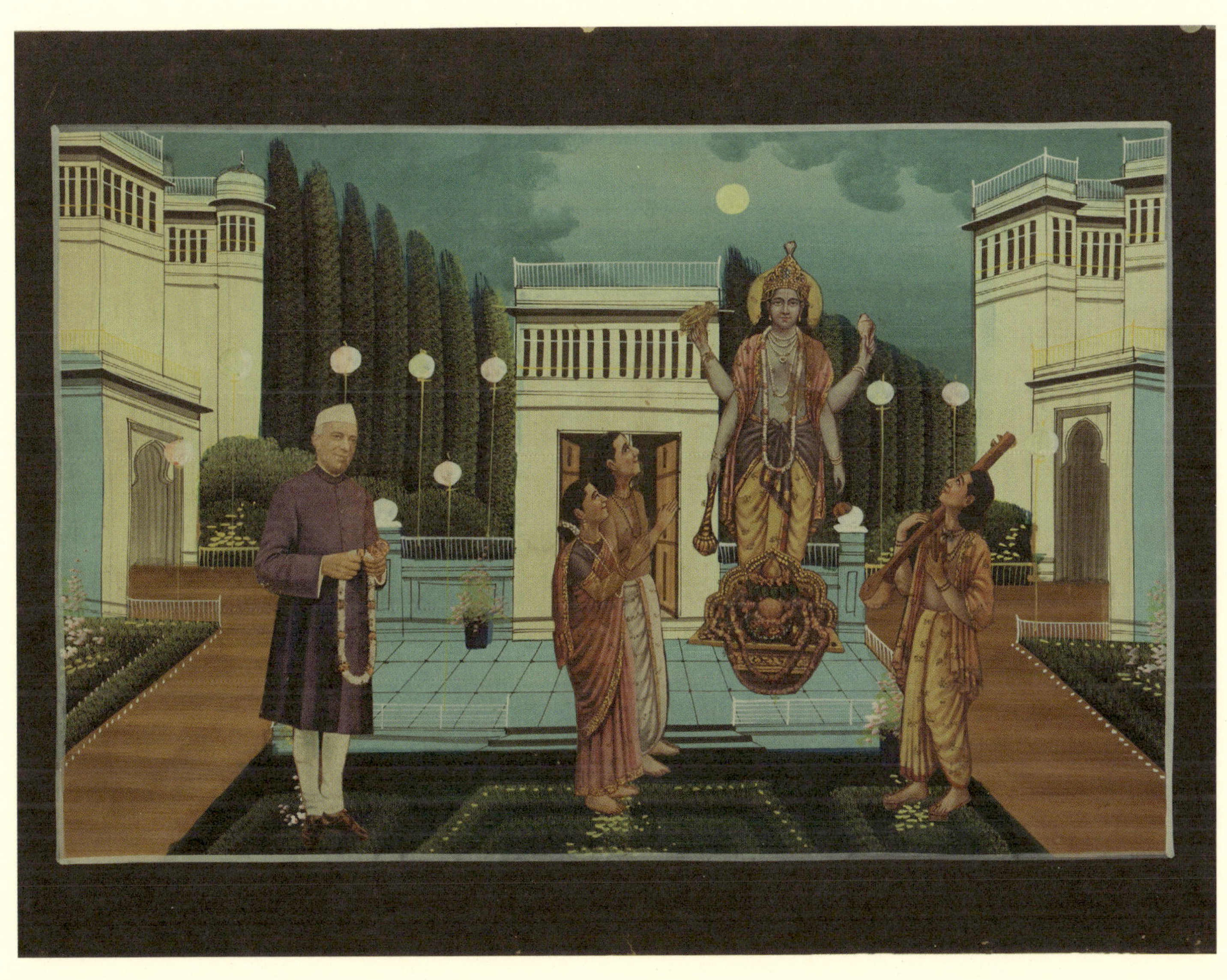

Collage depicting Satyanarayan and Jawaharlal Nehru, c. 1930
Chromolithograph cut-outs on a printed backdrop // 28 x 43.5 cm

Beyond words
And lines and circles
Lies the embrace
Without seasons

"God is not a power residing in the clouds. God is an unseen power residing within us and nearer to us than fingernails to the flesh."

Mahatma Gandhi

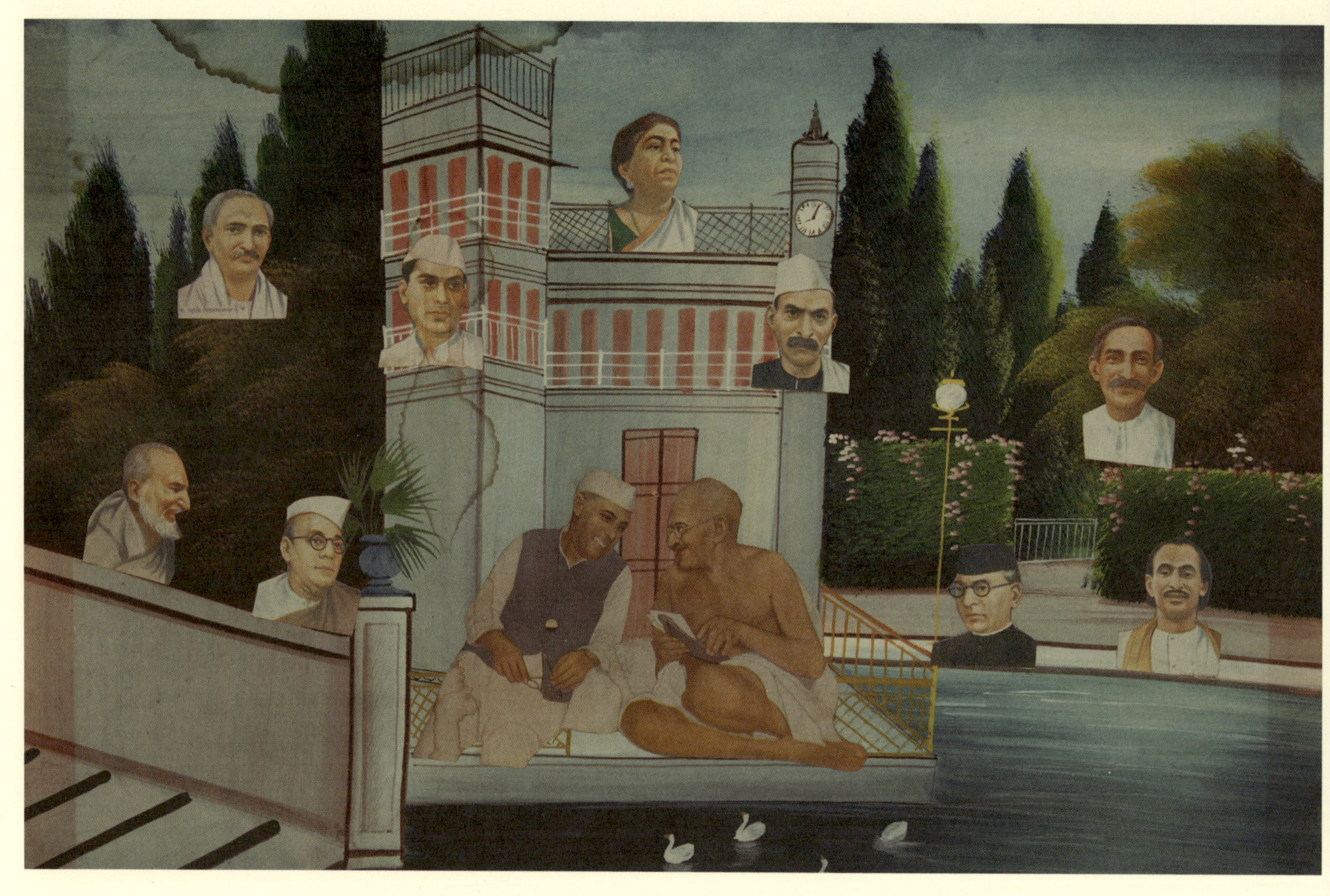

Collage depicting freedom fighters of India, c. 1930s
Chromolithograph cut-outs on a painted backdrop // 44.1 cm x 59.9 cm

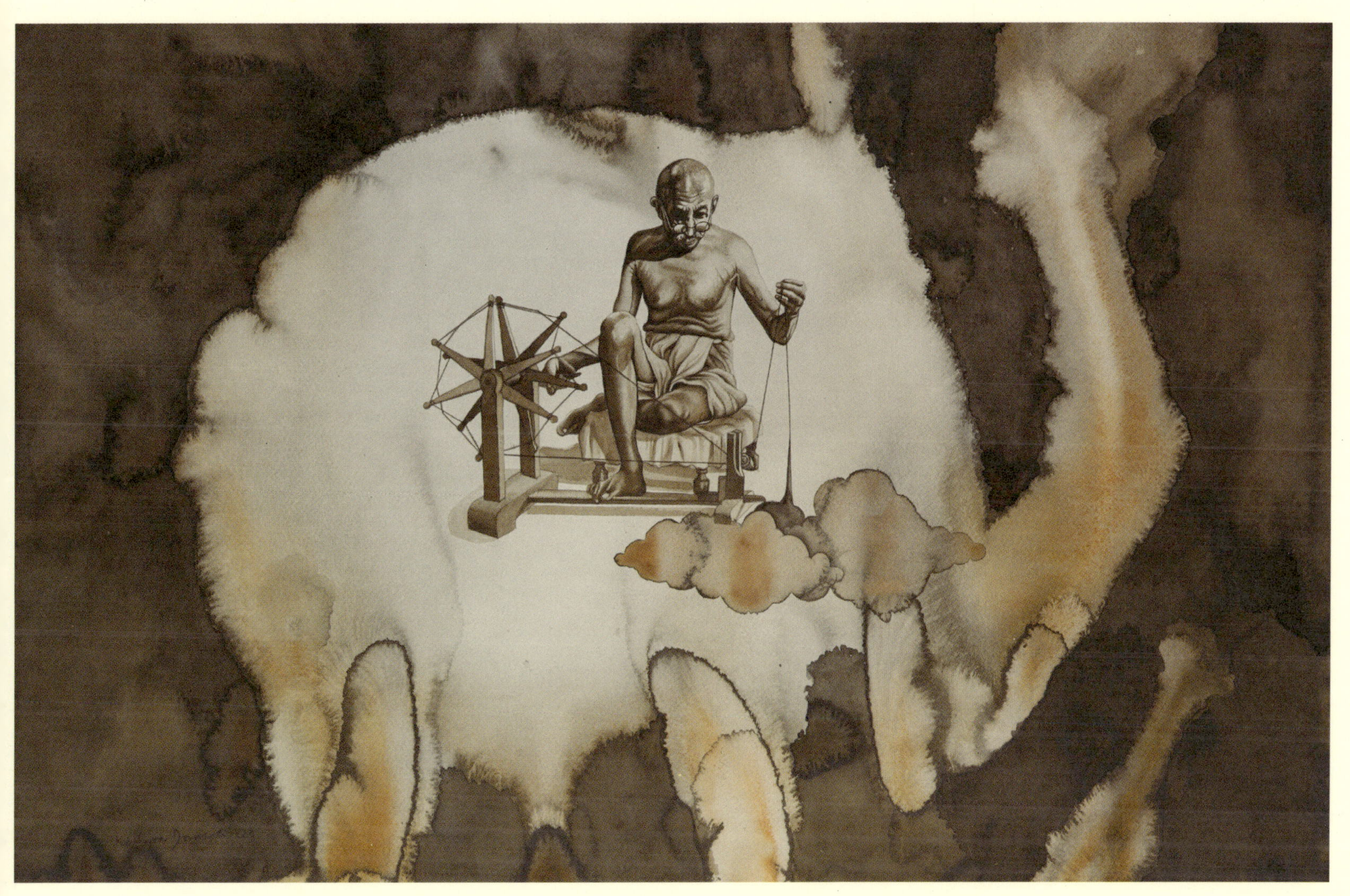

Swadeshi clouds, 2008
Kishan Duriseti, (b. 1970)
Watercolour on paper // 50 cm × 73 cm

"I see Beauty in Truth and through Truth. Whenever men begin to see Beauty in Truth, the true Art will arise."

Mahatma Gandhi

NOW

Can you hear me Bapu
I stand 150 years away from you
Can you bear it Bapu
What this land has come to
The wheel now churns
Lies after lies
Ideals reduced
To the shape of my clothes
I hoard
I lie
I steal
Oblivious to those
Whose bodies dry
Parched more each day
With the passing of my waning soul
My memory begins to fail me Bapu
Your message begins to gather dust
I wander alone
A madman guideless
In a cemented jungle
Clothed in lust
Your fluid figure
So easy to sketch
Is becoming harder to draw from
The form I'm taking
Ferocious flamboyant fickle
Is it legible to you
Can you still hear me Bapu
For I could never hear you

WE LIVE IN A WORLD OF "extinction rebellion", dire climate change and a universal nervousness around the threat to living species, human and otherwise. Yet as portrayed, it is a world where we are made to believe we have the power to be heard, to influence, to mobilize. On one hand this all might seem like a cosmic joke but on the other it evokes a sharp, gnawing sensation arising from the messages and lessons that were laid out for us, crystal, sharp, uncomfortable.
Prophetic and precise, Mahatma Gandhi's messages were a design in mindful living, deeply aware that the path of truth one often has to tread alone.

The artists featured in this chapter of *Santati*, embarked on creating unique works embodying their interpretation of Gandhi. With his philosophy as their primary canvas, these artists from the textile, fashion and design industries intend to show how precise, ultra-modern and firm yet liberal Gandhi's message was and remains. A message gaining more relevance today than ever, as the consciousness of the world makes a leaping shift from the obvious to the real.

“I and others may be revolutionaries but we are disciples of Mahatma Gandhi, directly or indirectly. Nothing more nothing less. ”

Ho-Chi-Minh, Former President of North Vietnam

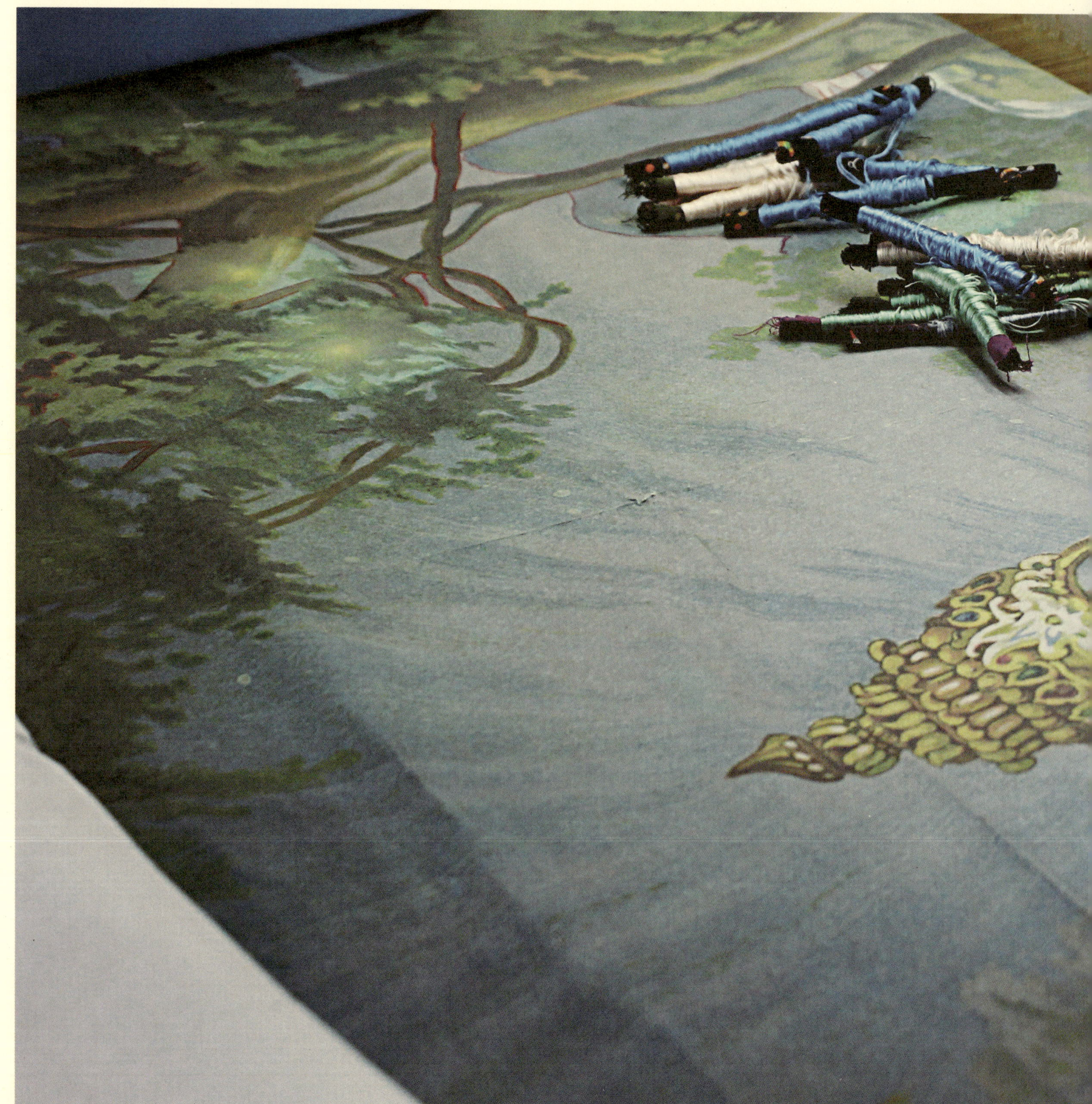

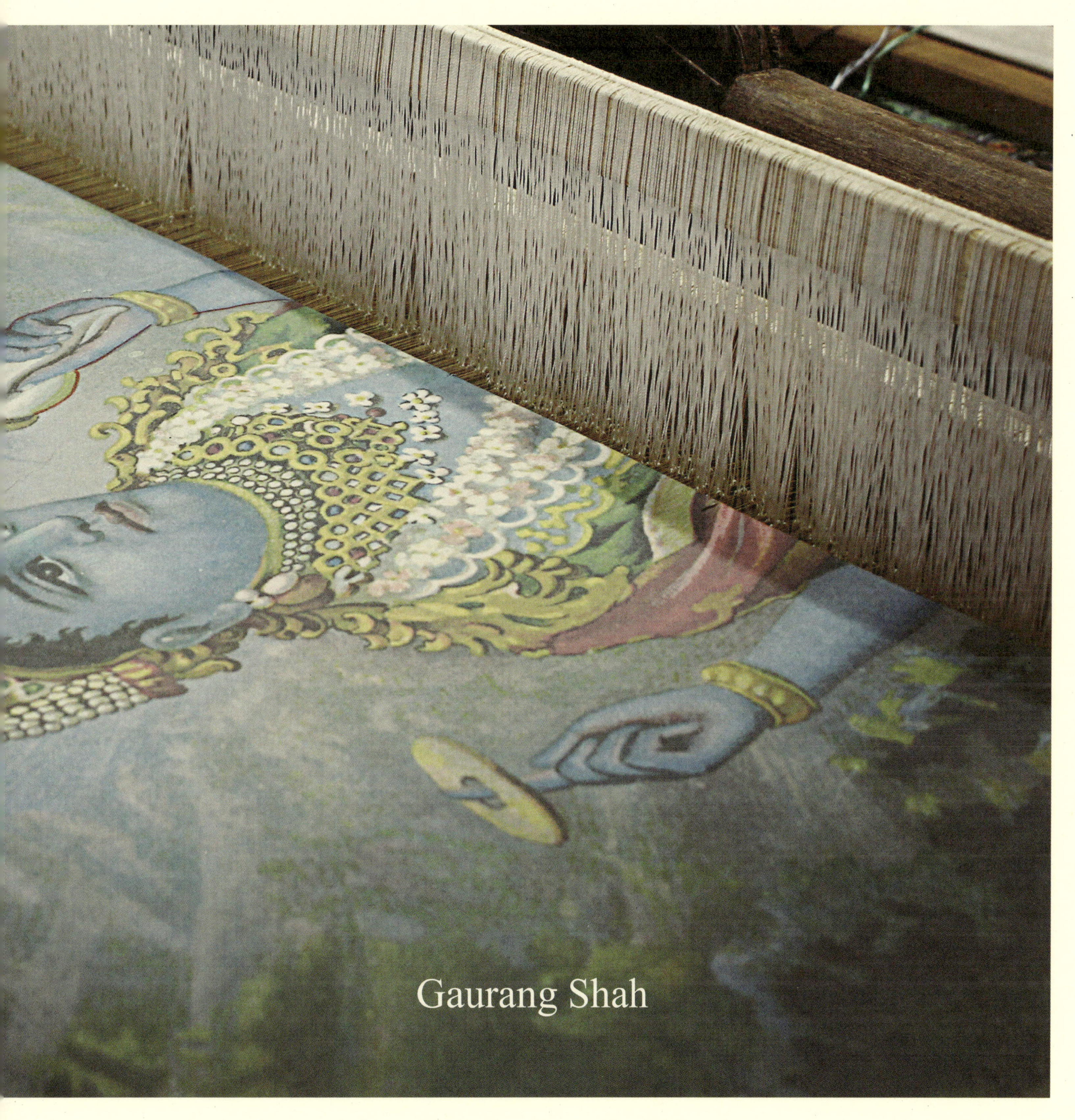

Gaurang Shah

Gaurang Shah

Textile Designer

One of the prominent driving forces behind Santati, Gaurang Shah along with curator Lavina Baldota first dreamt up this mammoth, never-done-before project around seven years ago. The task was to interpret landmark paintings from artist Raja Ravi Varma's work on to pallus of saris woven in hand-spun khadi, translating the art into wearable canvases. Paying tribute to the swadeshi philosophy of Mahatma Gandhi, these mythological scenes were transferred, warp by warp, on to saris with each sari taking between six months and two years to complete. The silk yarns used for the jamdani weaving were all naturally dyed. Delving further than the basic colours possible in natural dyeing, 600 shades and hues were developed to recreate the paintings, paying heed, throughout, to the time and light they were created in. Gaurang repeatedly attributes Junaid Khatri from Kutch in Gaujarat as the instrumental master craftsman who, through unconventional methods and his knowledge of natural dyeing, created never-before-seen colours.

The weaving was done in the villages of Chapara, Badam, Kodara and Karapalle of the Srikakulam District in Andhra Pradesh. With over forty artisans involved, each sari was woven at a 150 count weft and 150 count warp. Simply put, it means that just around two centimetres of the sari width would be woven in a day. While weaving is now perceived as a dwindling craft, these unprecedented works bring it into stark spotlight and showcase its sheer possibilities.

Through these saris, Gaurang highlights the potency of khadi and *jamdani* from their loom-to-luxury journey, making it crucially relevant in an age where turning inwards and towards indigenous industries seems to hold the future of progress.

A master, a pioneer and a visionary, Gaurang Shah has, for nearly two decades, worked tirelessly towards the revival of handwoven textiles in India. The backbone of his work draws strength from a profound and beautifully challenging idea of positive social reform.

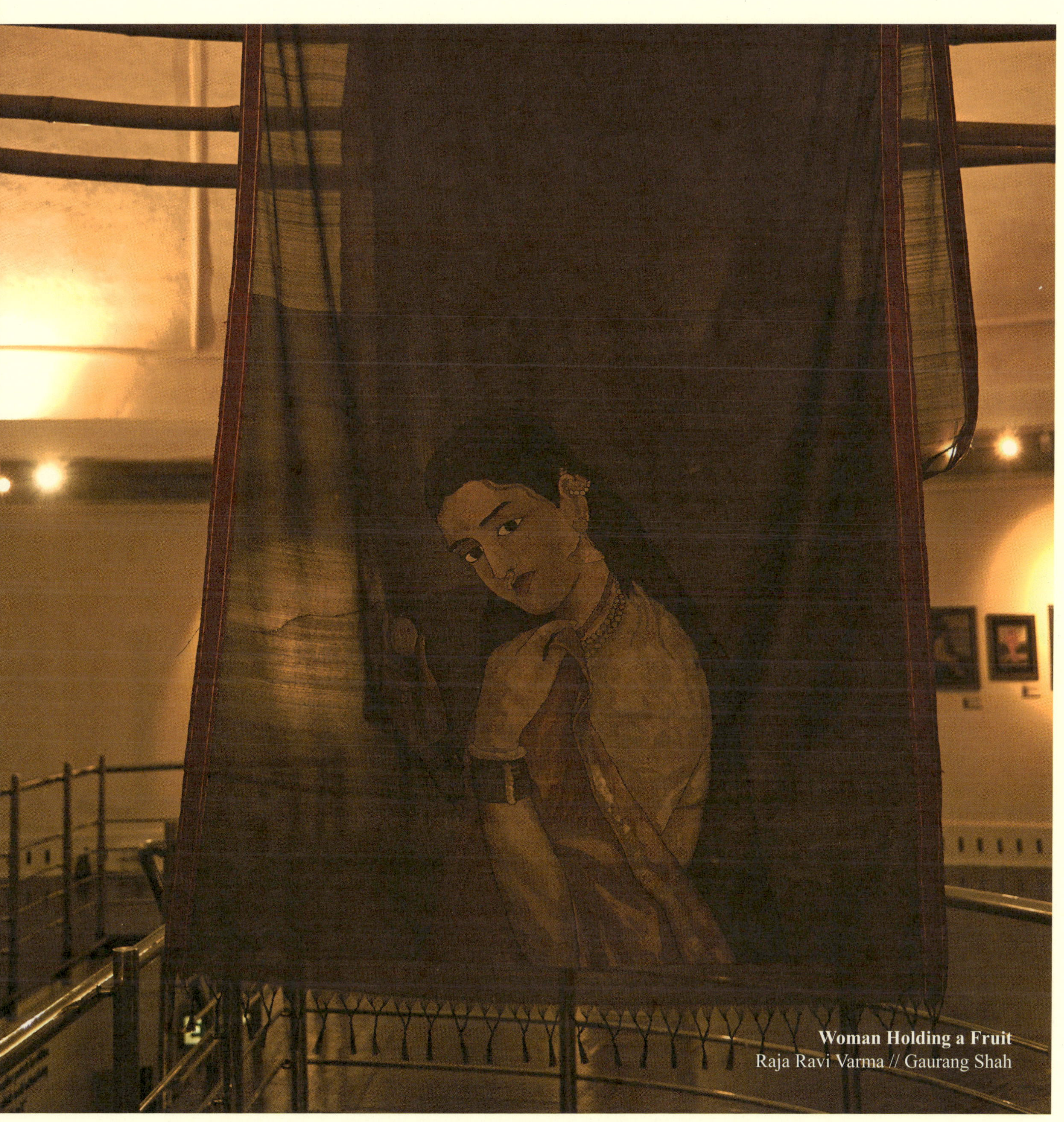

Woman Holding a Fruit
Raja Ravi Varma // Gaurang Shah

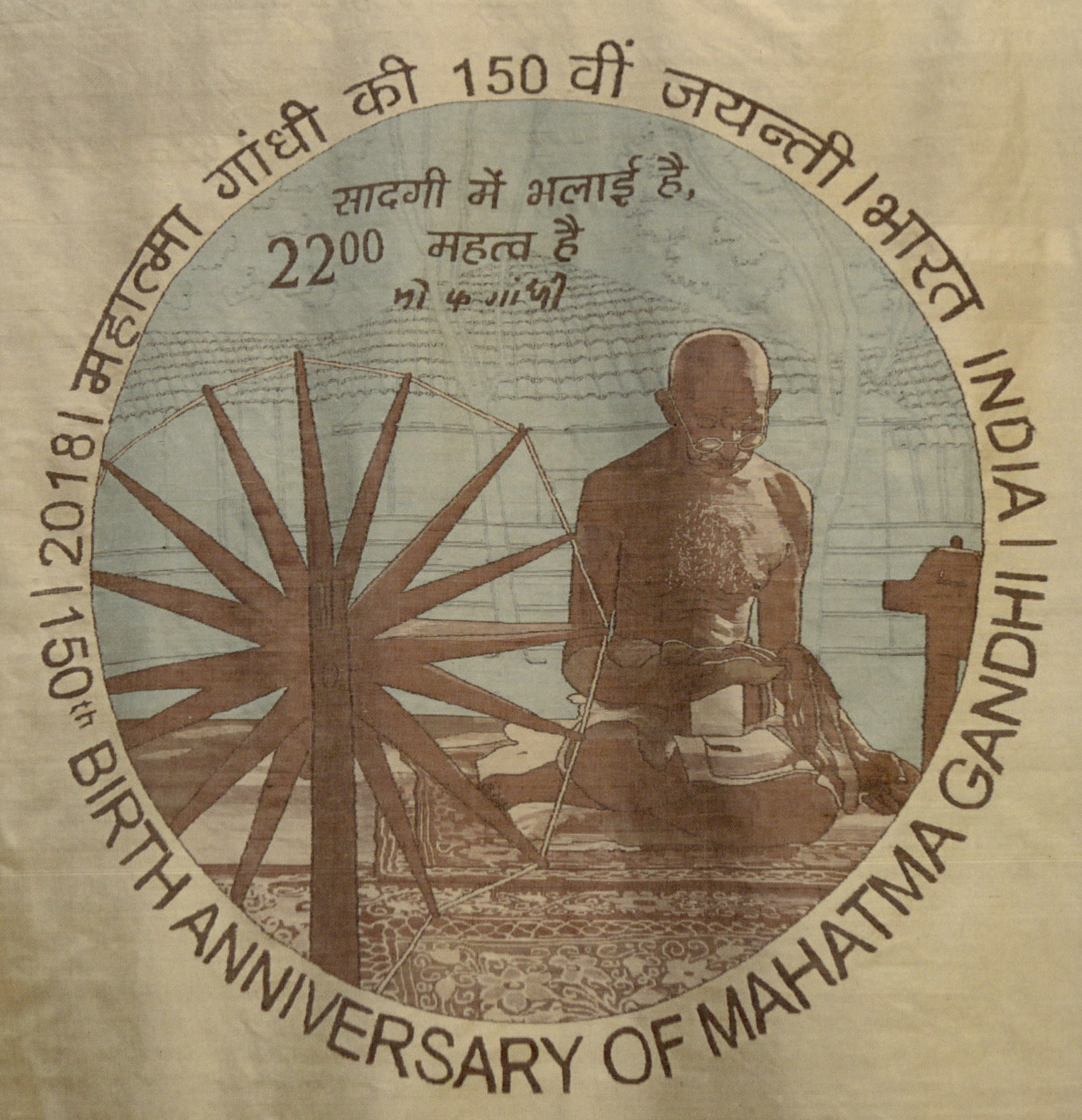

महात्मा गांधी की 150 वीं जयन्ती । भारत
INDIA
150th BIRTH ANNIVERSARY OF MAHATMA GANDHI
2018
सादगी में भलाई है,
महत्व है
मो क गांधी
22.00

A world will stand still
A world will take heed
A world can begin
To turn around
In the quiet spinning
Of a wheel

रुक सा गया है समय
पलटने लगा है काल
धीमी सी चरखे की चाप
एक गूंज एक भूचाल

Opposite: Stamp commemorating the Mahatma's 150th birth anniversary, woven on khadi // Gaurang Shah

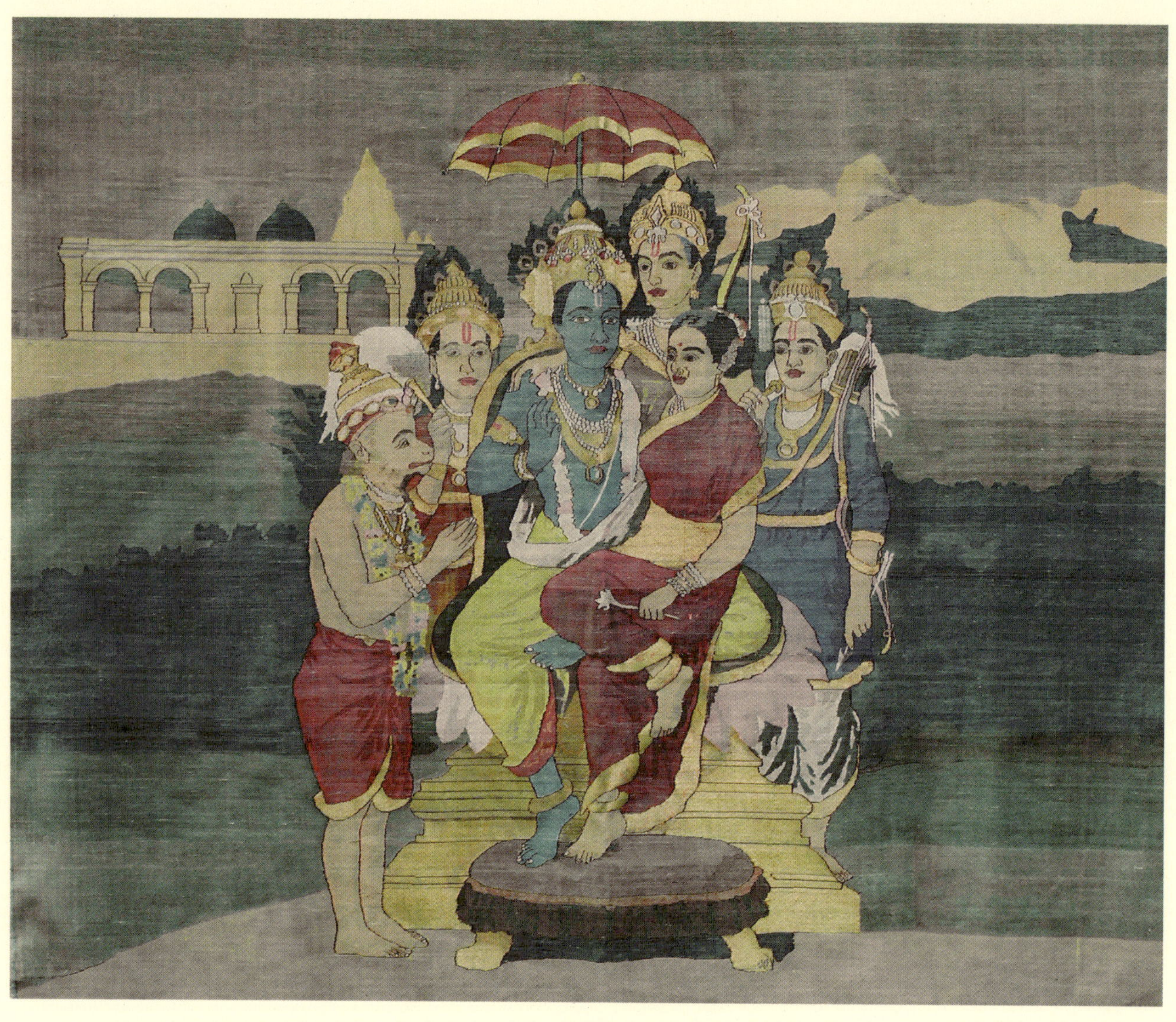

My heart begs
To the giver of day
For it to stay
As long as this moment divine

Pause just here my beloved
Hold that gaze the smile
Let me hold the moment that
Each moment passes by

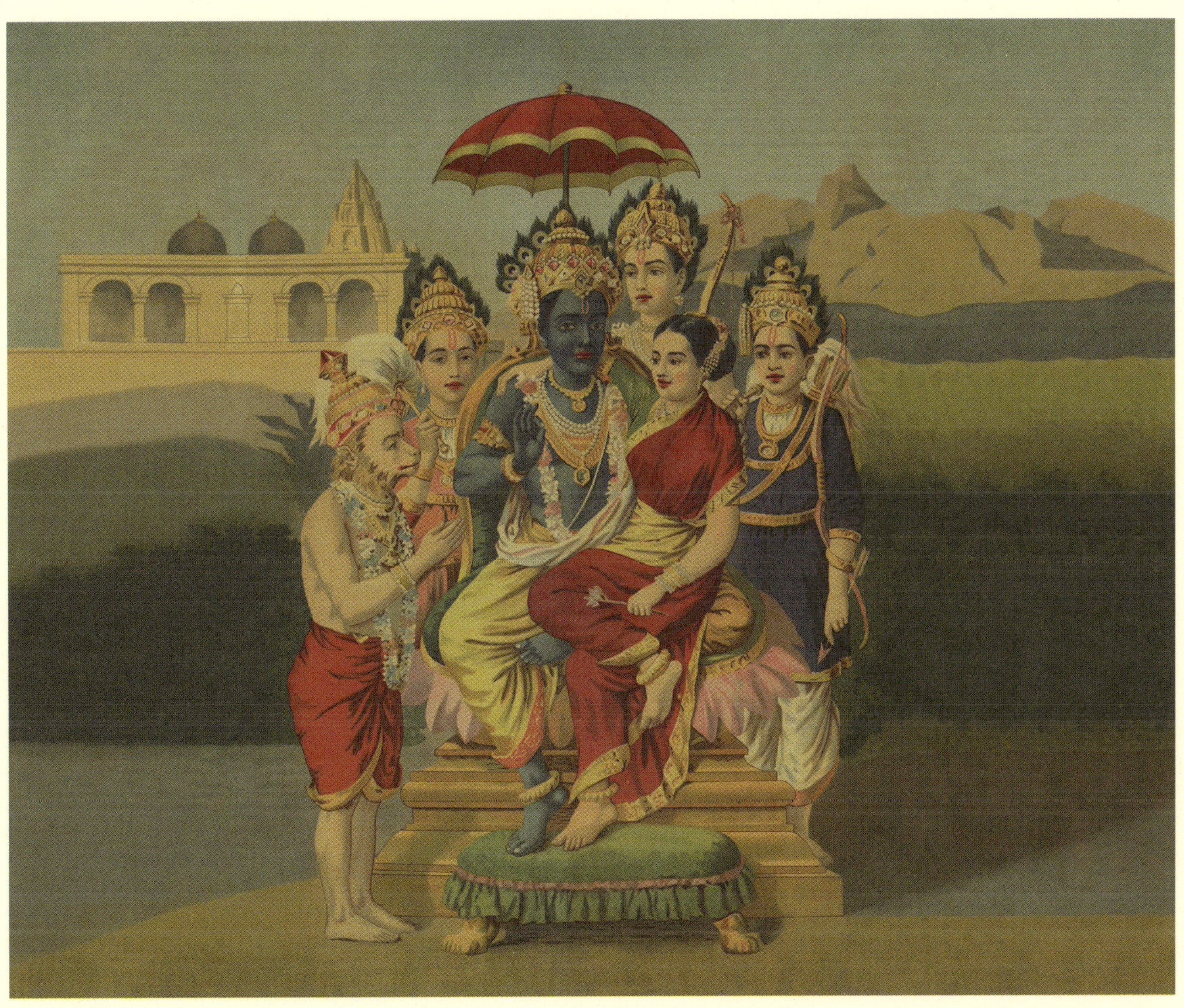

Ram Panchayatan

A moment of true reunion holds in it, a quiet intensity and unspoken reverence. It is a meeting of souls severed and hearts aching for the balm of the sight of those we have loved, lived, longed for. Panchayatan translates as containing the five. This painting is a quiet scene of Lord Ram's return to his erstwhile home and palace in Ayodhya after fourteen years of *vanvaas*, a time of solitary life in the jungles. With him are Sita, Lakshman, Bharat and Hanuman, all kindred spirits greeting each other in silent worship, before life in the palatial realm resumes.

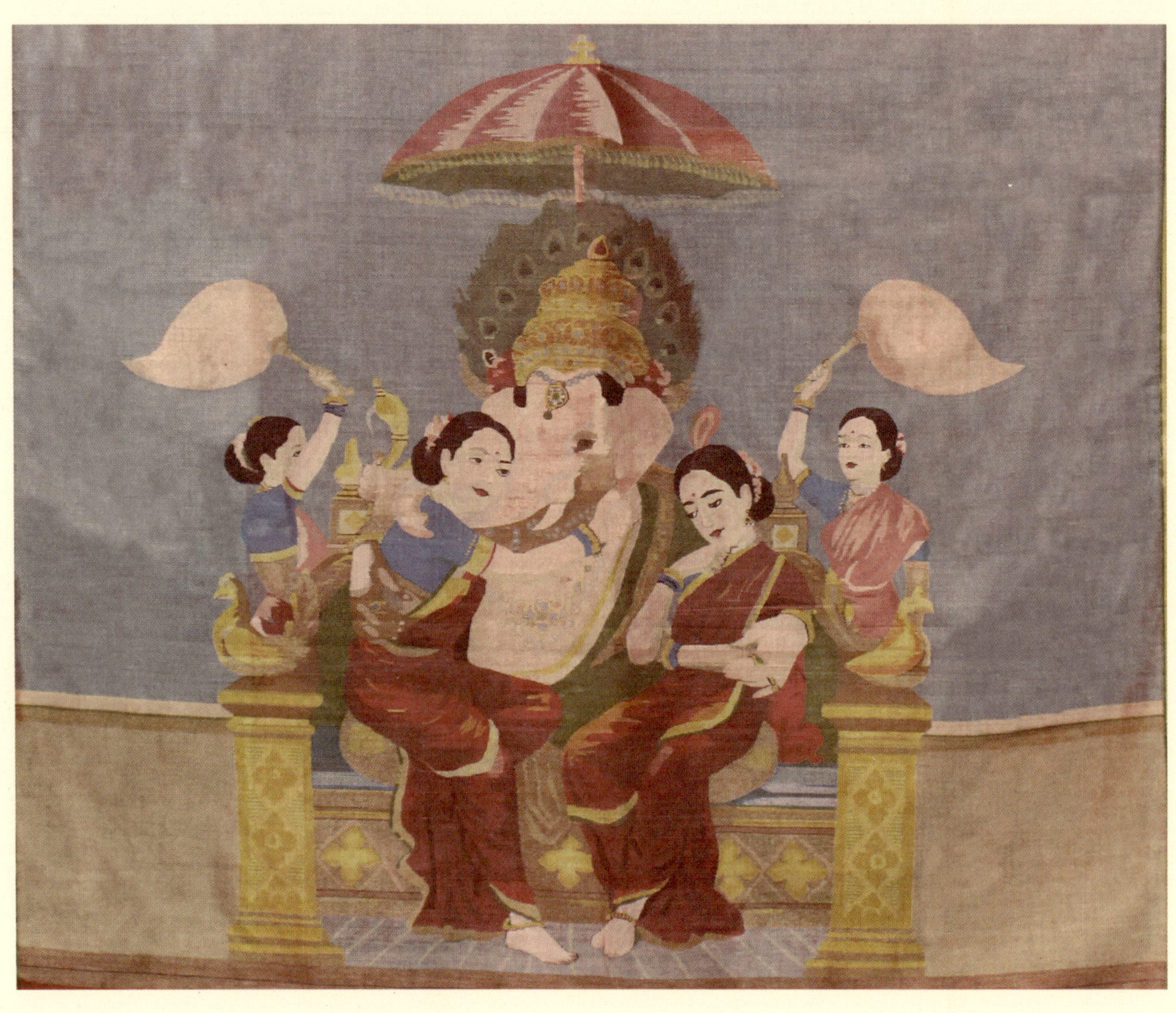

May our lives
Be prayers
To the truth
Of love

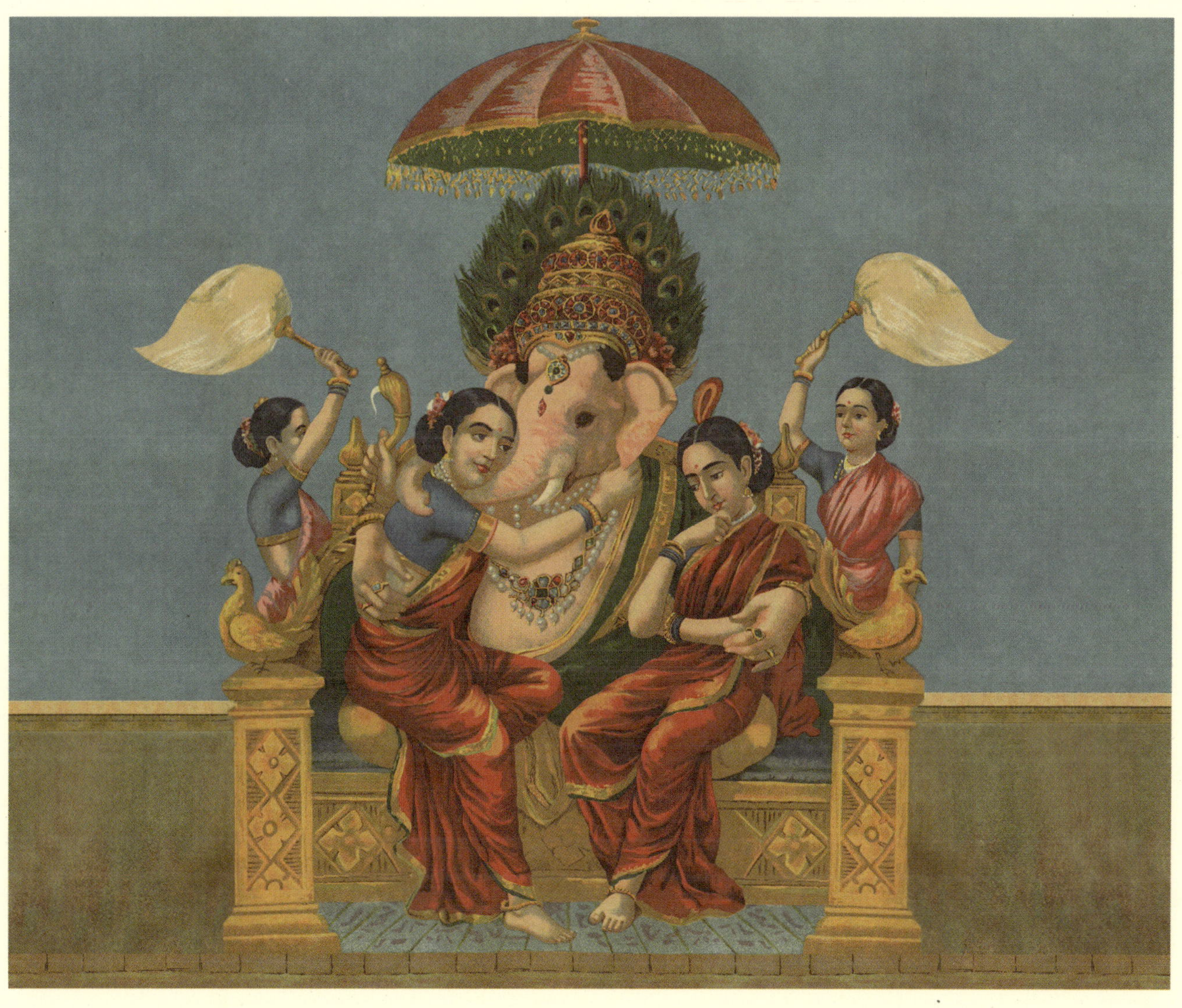

Ganapathi with Riddhi Siddhi

Together with his consorts Riddhi and Siddhi, Lord Ganapathi takes the throne to paint a picture of colourful prosperity and a joy shaded from all hurdles. As Lord Brahma manifested Riddhi and Siddhi (prosperity and power) for Ganapathi, so they are believed to together bring abundance and great luck to those who seek their blessings.

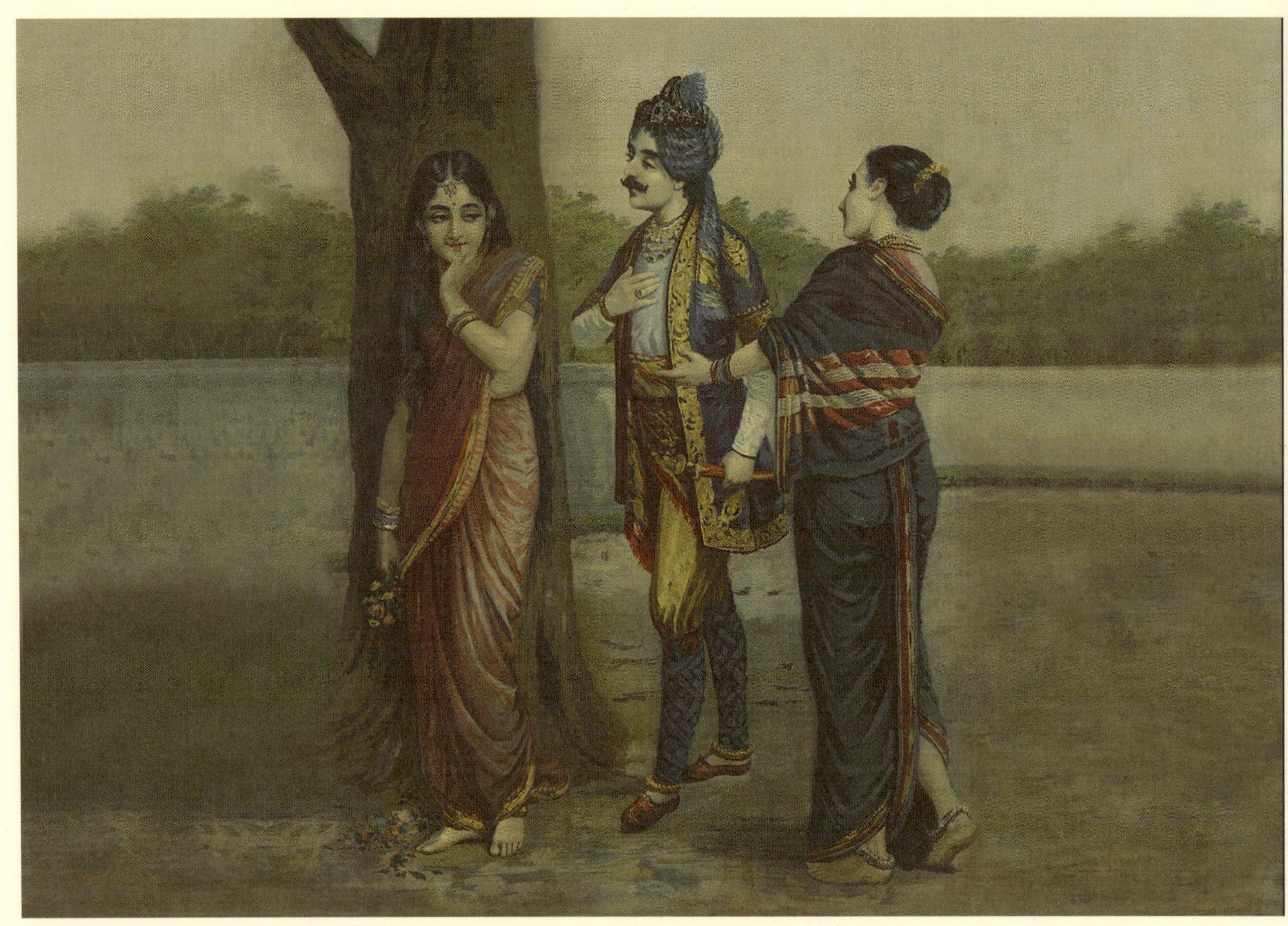

You look into my eyes
And I disappear and
With me, this world

Madalasa and Rutudwaja

Legend has it that King Rutudwaja killed the demon Pataalketu, rescued the beautiful Madalasa from his clutches and sought her hand in marriage. While versions of the nature of their marriage vary, this scene holds no ambiguity in its soft, radiating romance and the hope of promises made with love.

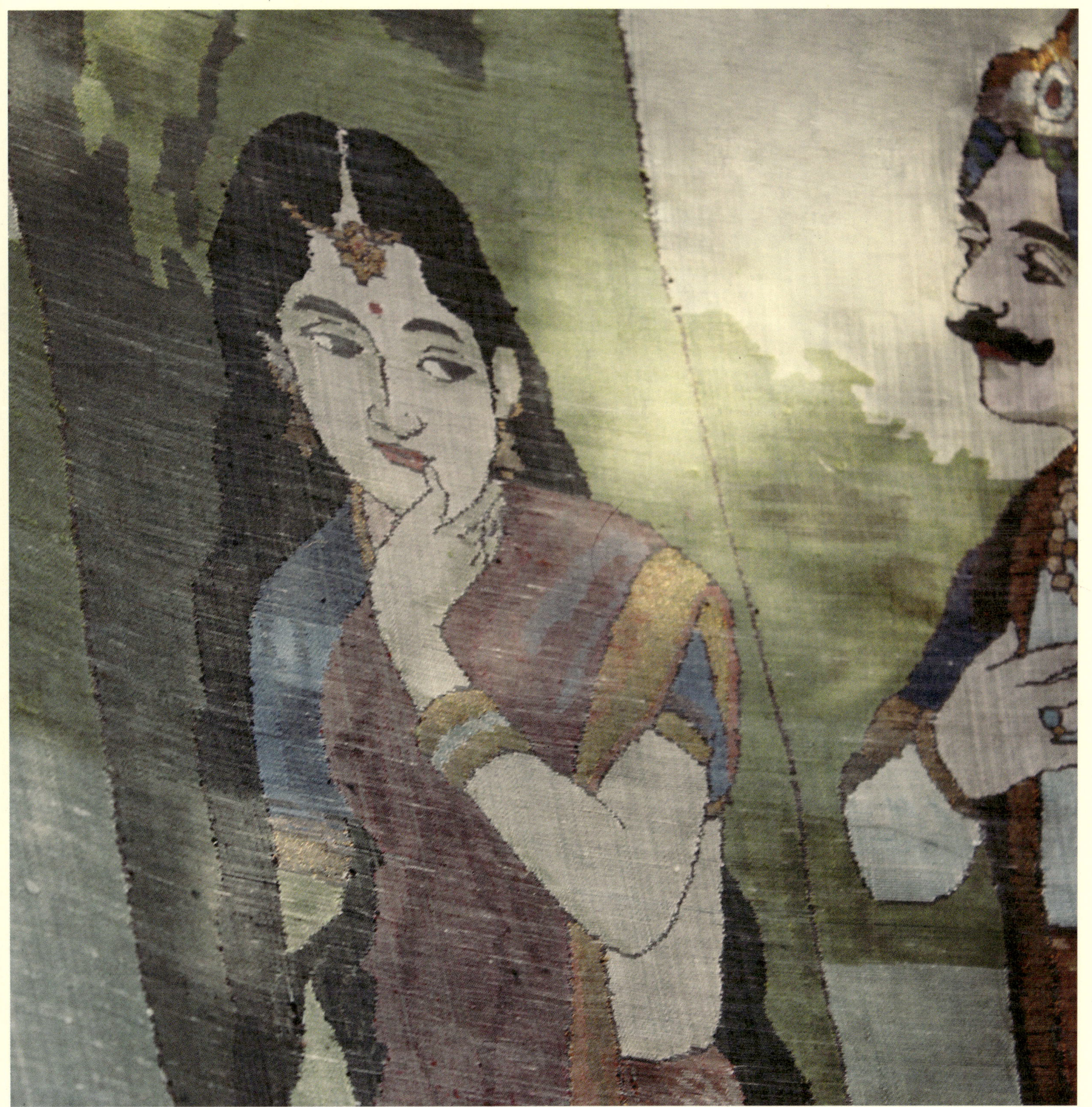

PADMINII

Where do you
Keep your words
When I look at you

With the lightness of her spirit she seems to rise above all that is around her, akin to the lotuses and sheer like the fabric swirling about her form.

Padminii is second in a series of three portraits of nymphs, fluid in their gesture, ethereal in their strokes.

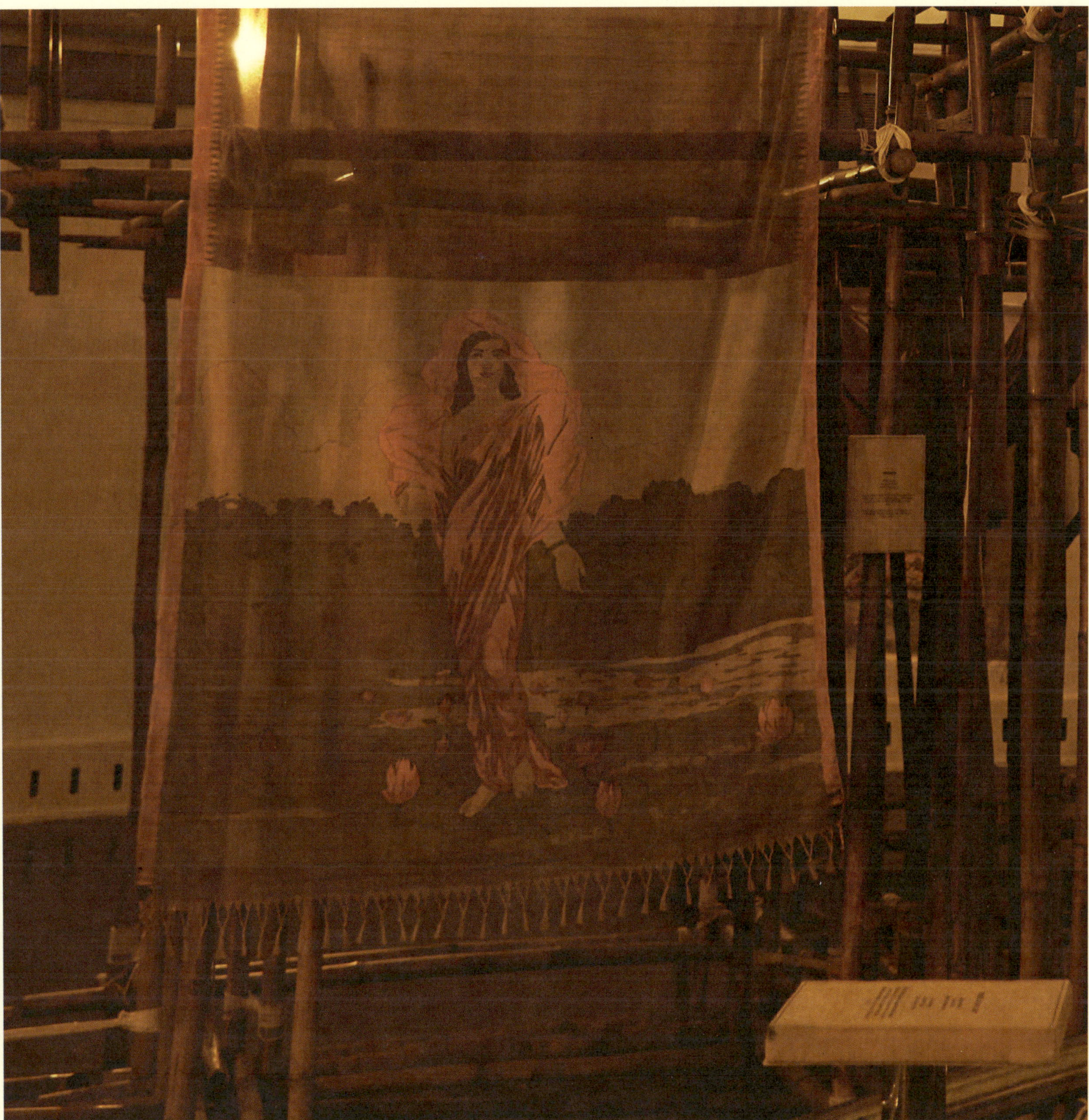

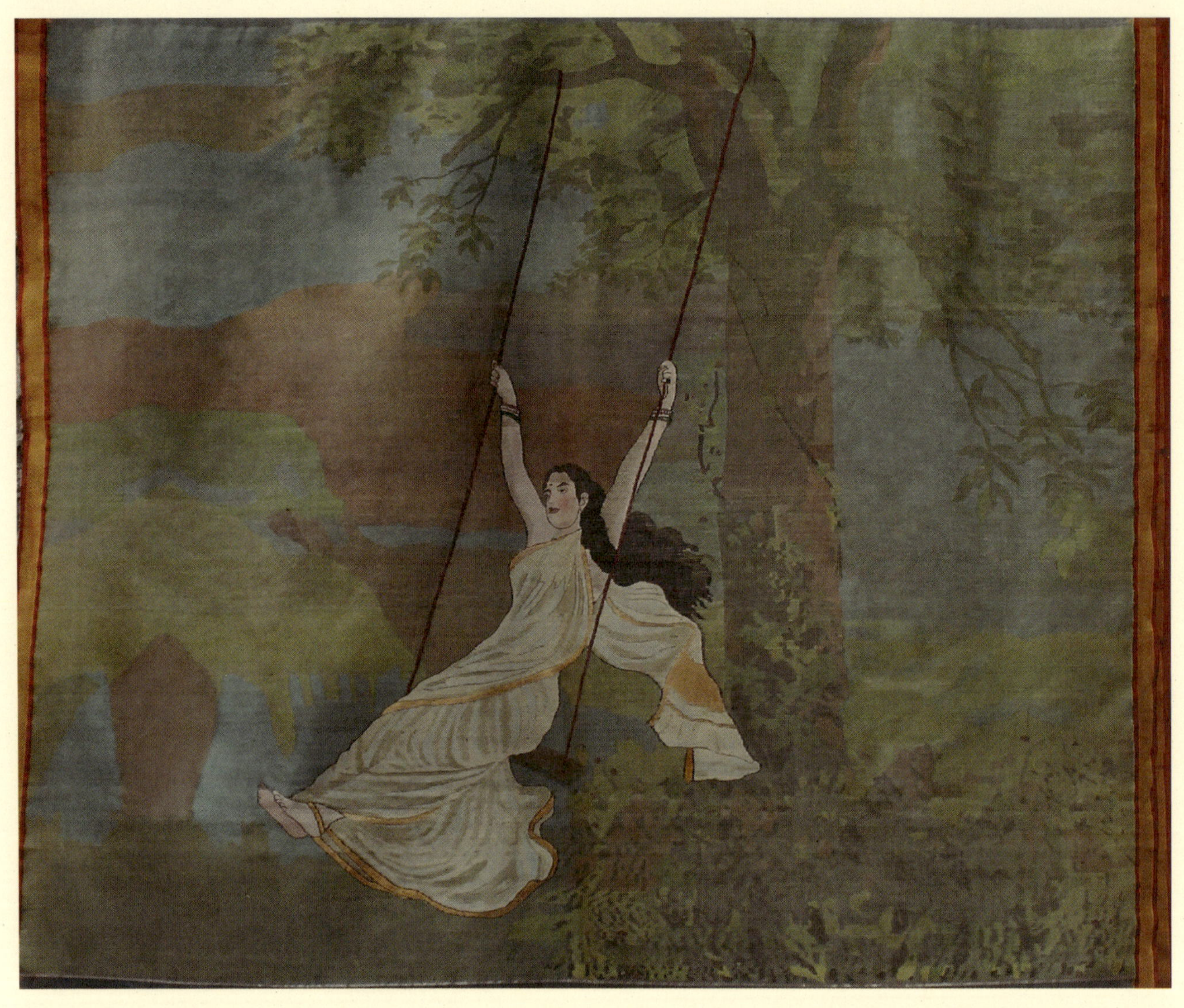

With a finesse
Not known to man
Her feet slowly move
The slightest sway
Of her thought
Overturns
The universe

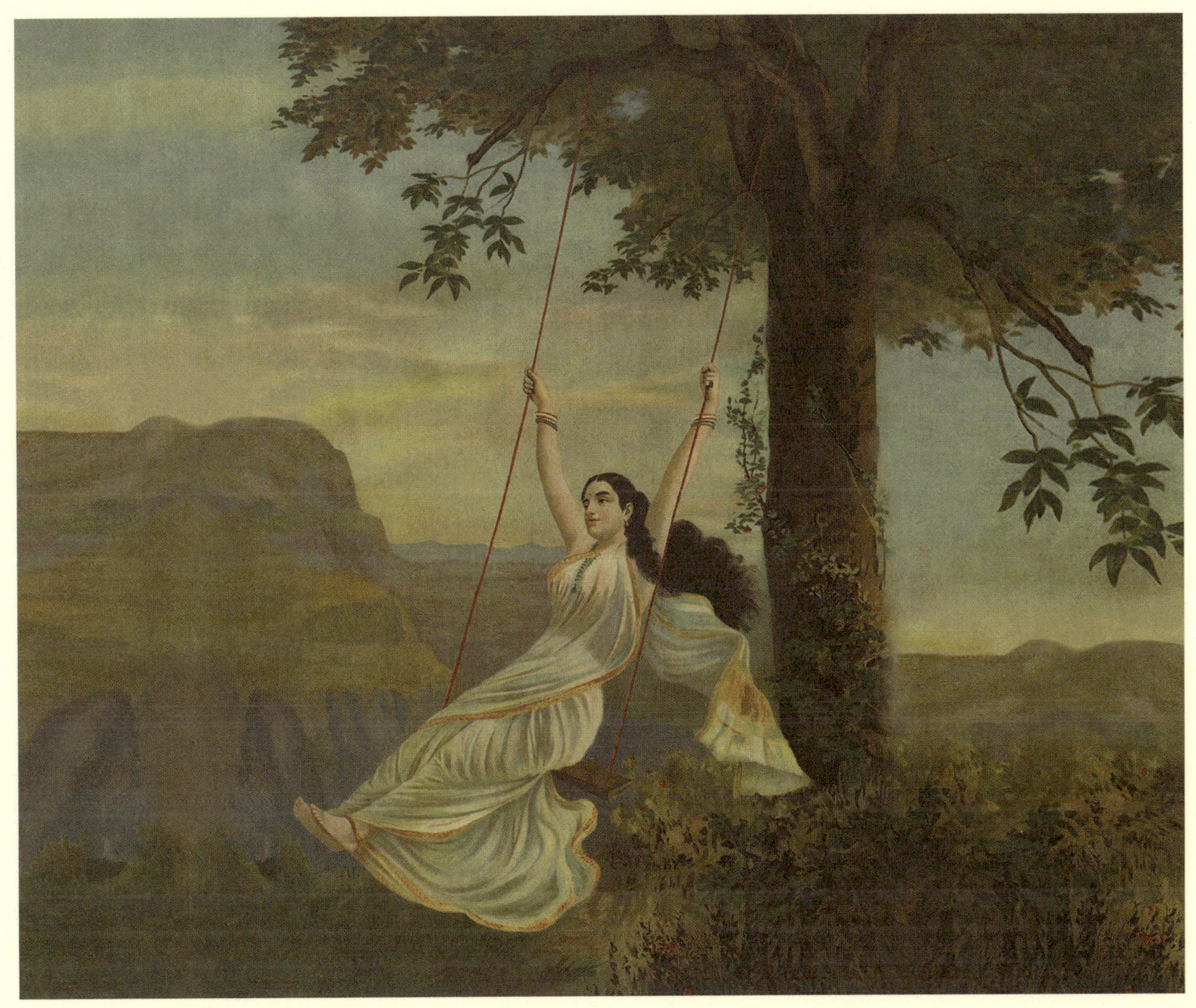

Mohini

As if swinging between parallel realities, Mohini, an avatar of Lord Vishnu descends in her pristinely alluring form to deceive the *asuras*, the demons so she can pass on the divine nectar to the *devas*, the gods. This *amrit*, the nectar of immortality could be perceived as a metaphor to her name which means she who entrances.

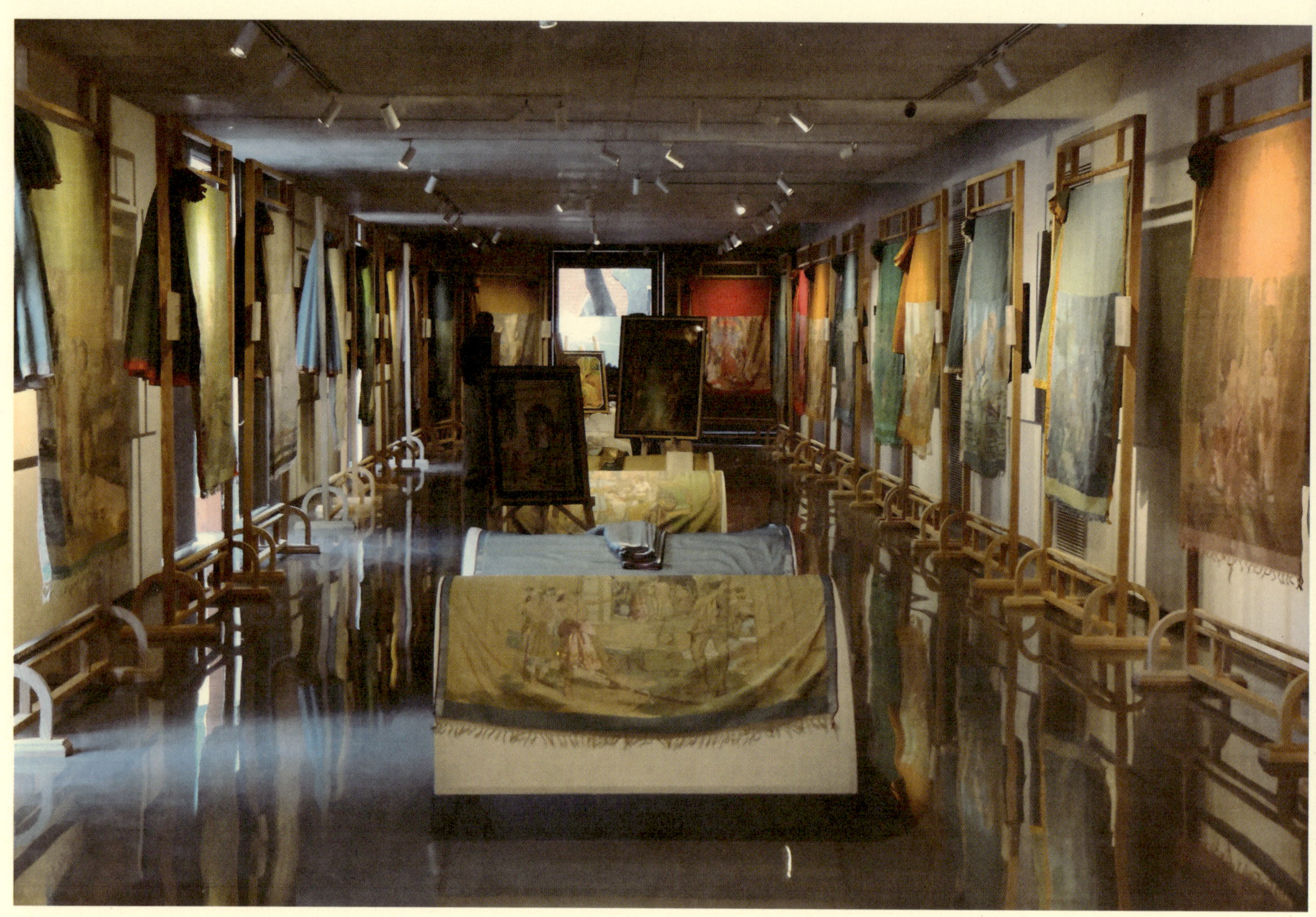

"The textile history of India and the expertise in the field were major reasons for India's prosperity in the ancient era. But under colonial rule, the British destroyed India's textile industry. Under Gandhi's swadeshi movement khadi production was encouraged, enabling Indians to regain their confidence of self-reliance and to be free from foreign clothes. As a textile artist these handwoven khadi saris are my tribute to Gandhi's philosophy and showcasing the potency of khadi from its loom to luxury journey. Gandhi's motto of swadeshi has influenced me to work with the weaving clusters of all states. Every citizen of India should use 'Made In India'."

Gaurang Shah

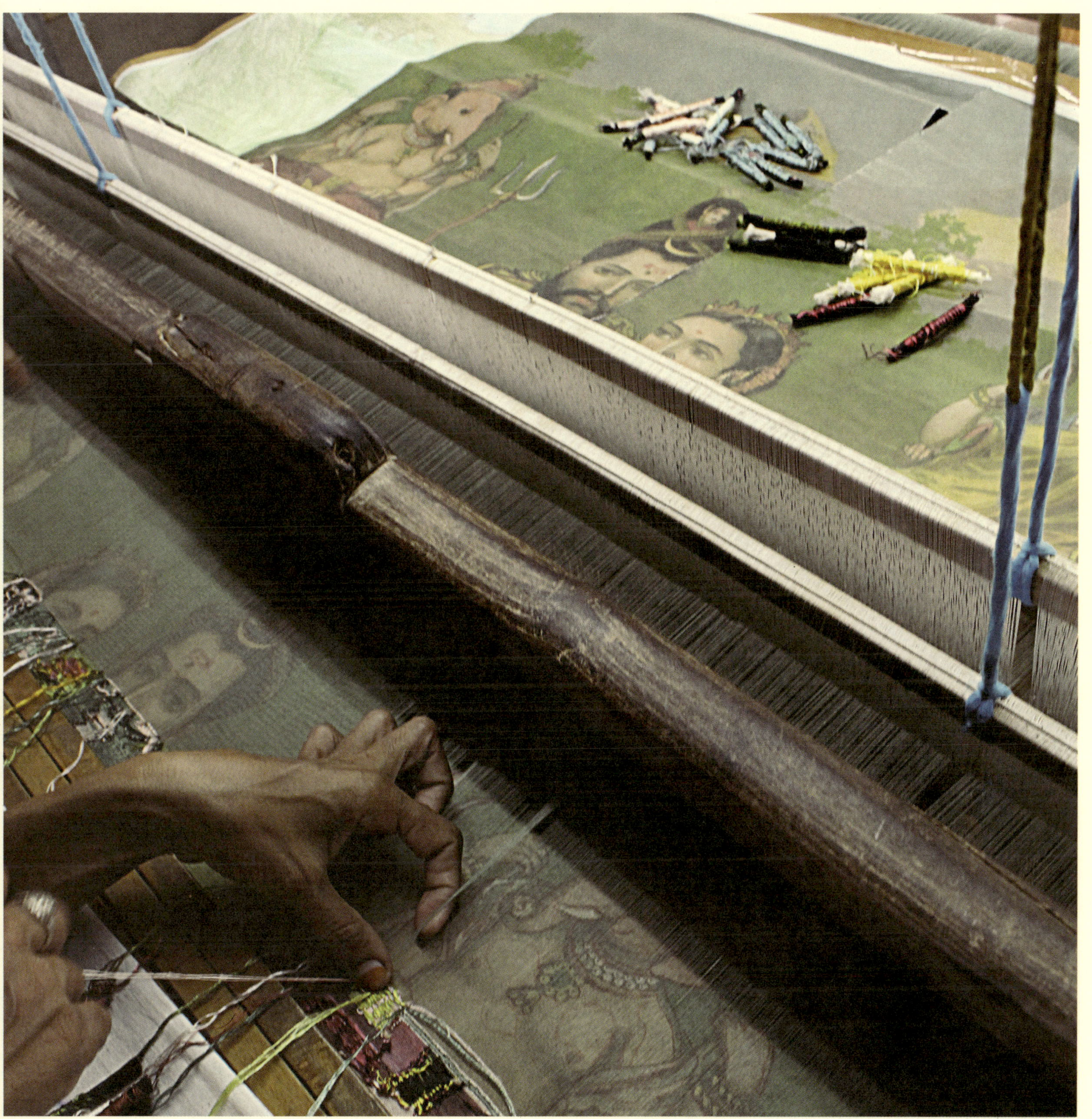

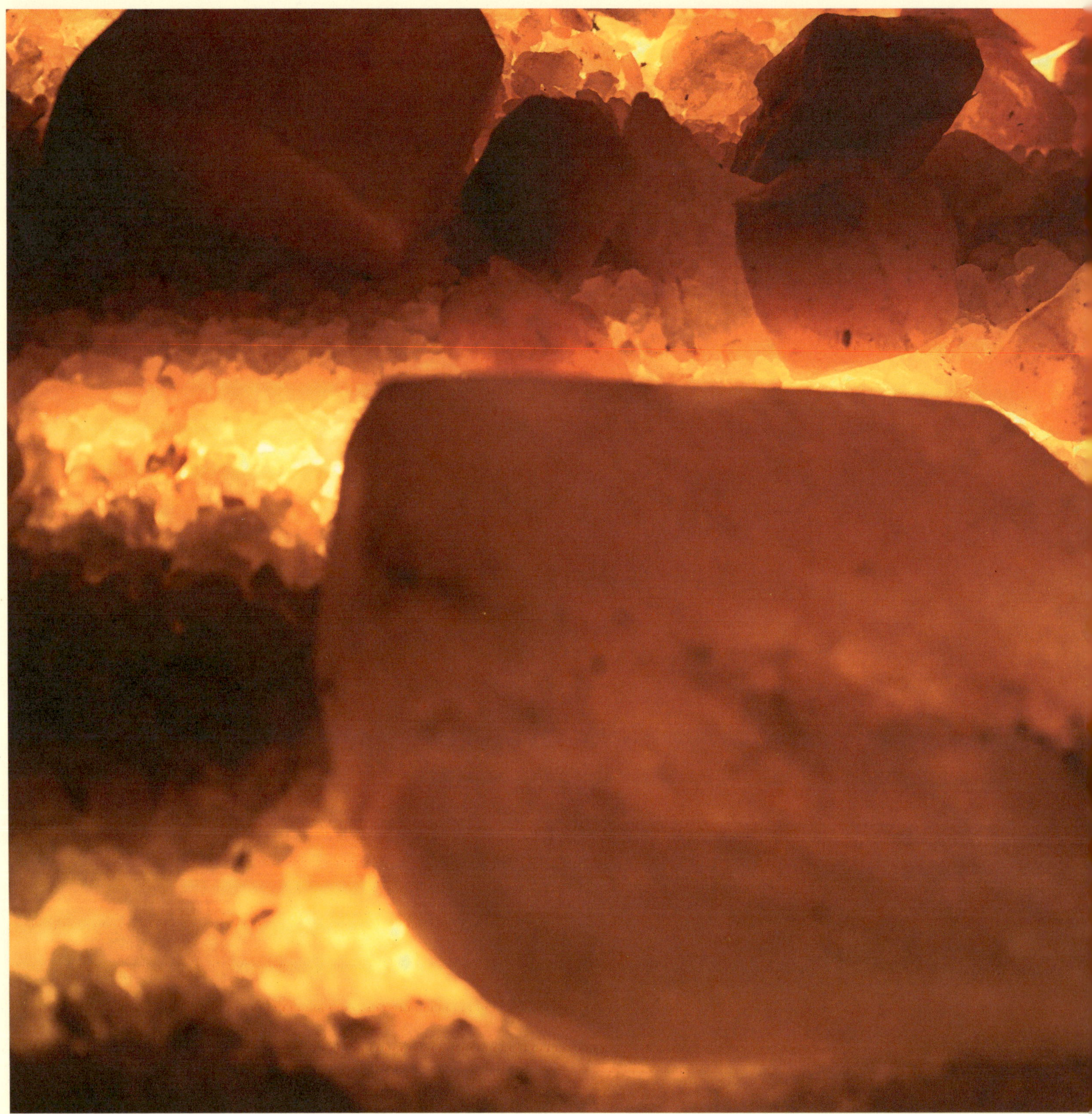

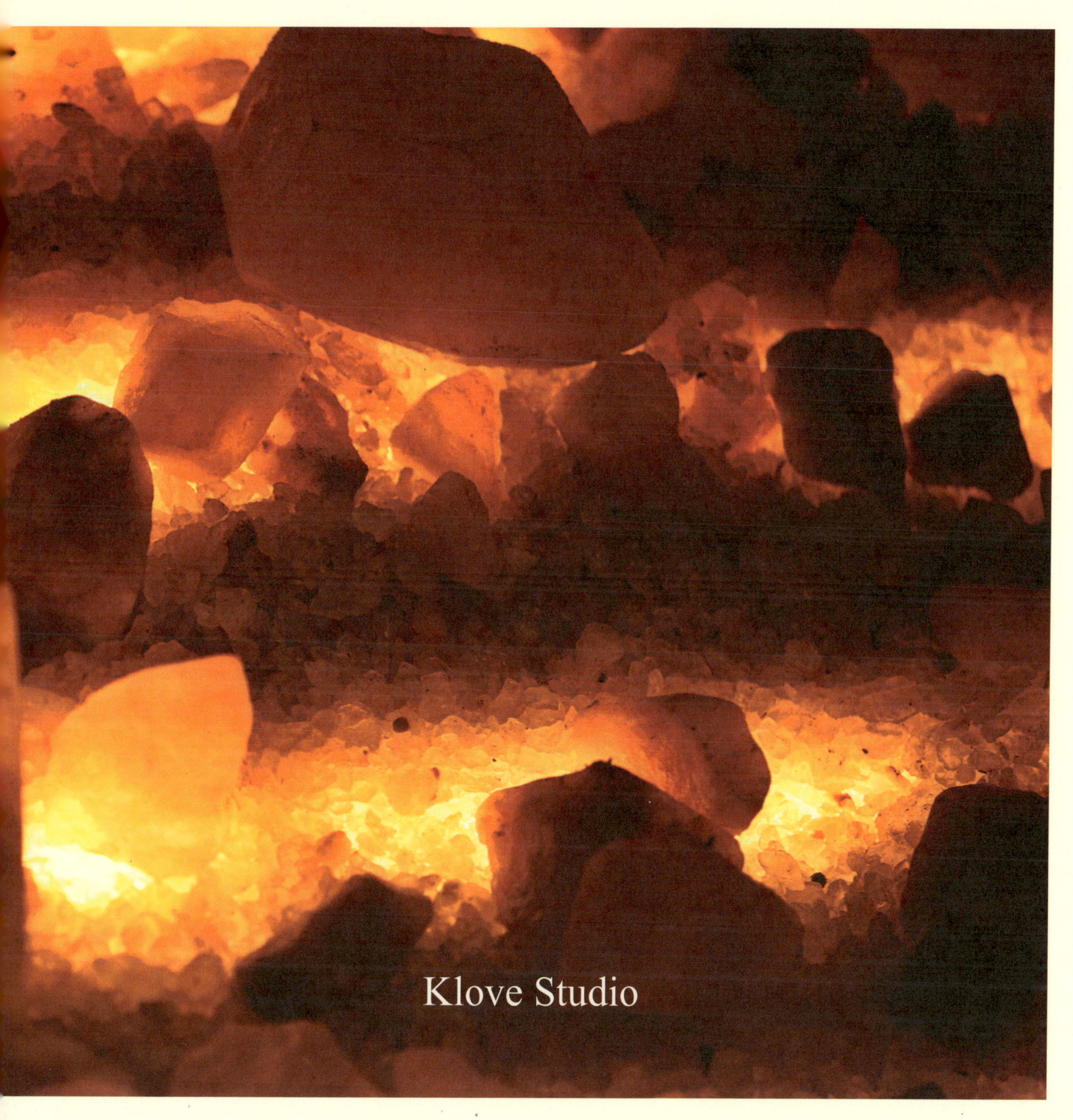
Klove Studio

Klove Studio

Light Designers

The metal frame of Mahatma Gandhi's iconic spectacles, the Dandi march to initiate the salt *satyagraha* and his firmness in humanity form the basis of Klove Studio's vision and installation titled *Ahimsa*. Their work is an allegorical, almost mysterious display where metal, mirrors and lighting merge to form the word *ahimsa* or non-violence – an historic movement initiated by Gandhi during India's struggle towards freedom. It is highlighted through optical and spatial play, rock salt and delicate illumination. Reflective of the simplicity of Gandhi's message and of modern history, this three-dimensional mid-century installation chronicles Gandhi's powerful belief, "In a gentle way, you can shake the world".

Pioneers in the art of blown glass and light design, Klove Studio has been and remains a progressive brand in luminosity and space aesthetics. Founded by designers Prateek Jain and Gautam Seth, Klove Studio continues to forge newer paths through the path of light.

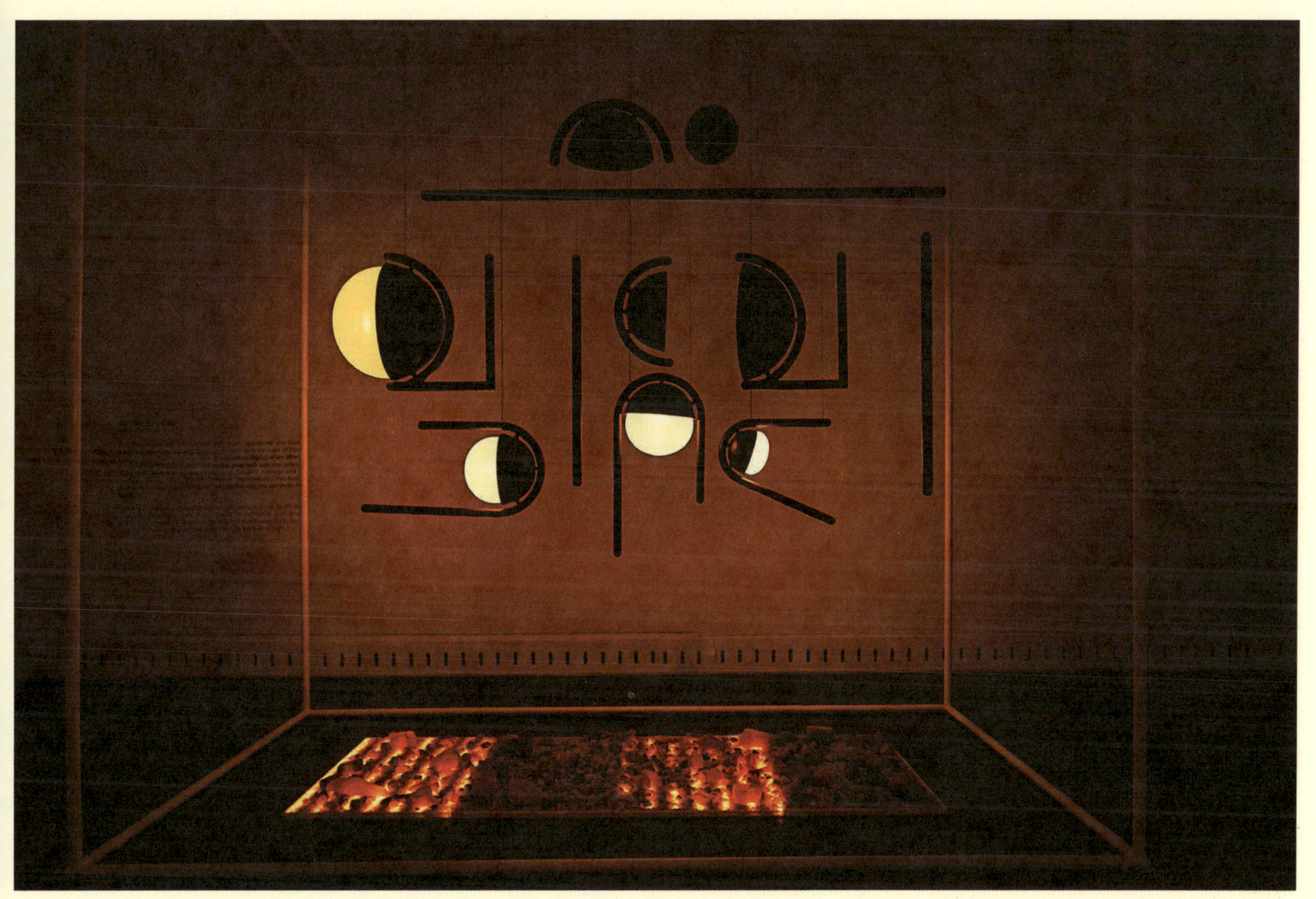

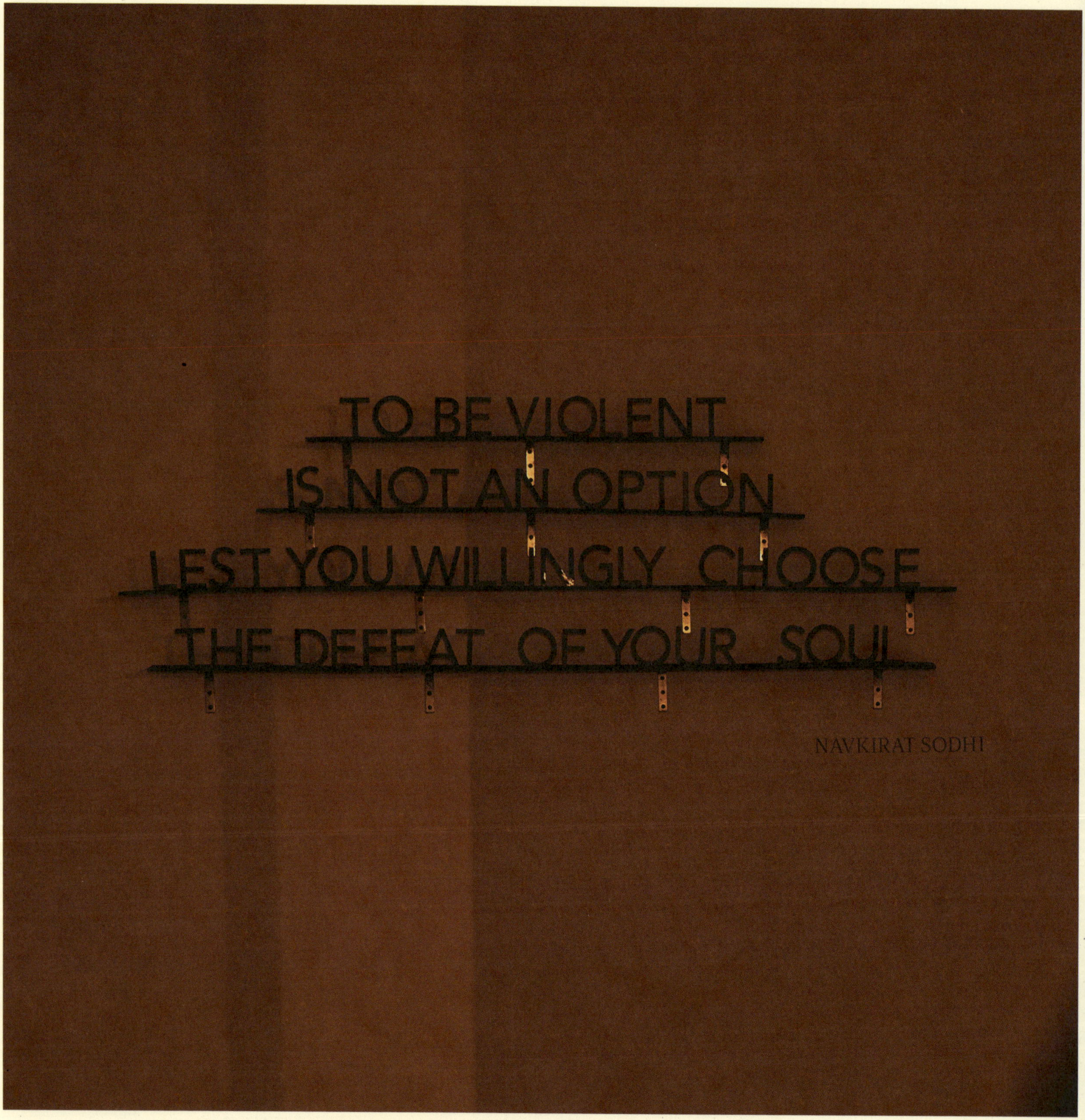

TO BE VIOLENT
IS NOT AN OPTION
LEST YOU WILLINGLY CHOOSE
THE DEFEAT OF YOUR SOUL

NAVKIRAT SODHI

हिंसा कोई विकल्प नहीं
है मानवता के सार से परे
या स्वेच्छा से हम स्वीकृत करें
आत्म पतन

"Non-violence is the first article of my faith. It is also the last article of my creed."

Mahatma Gandhi

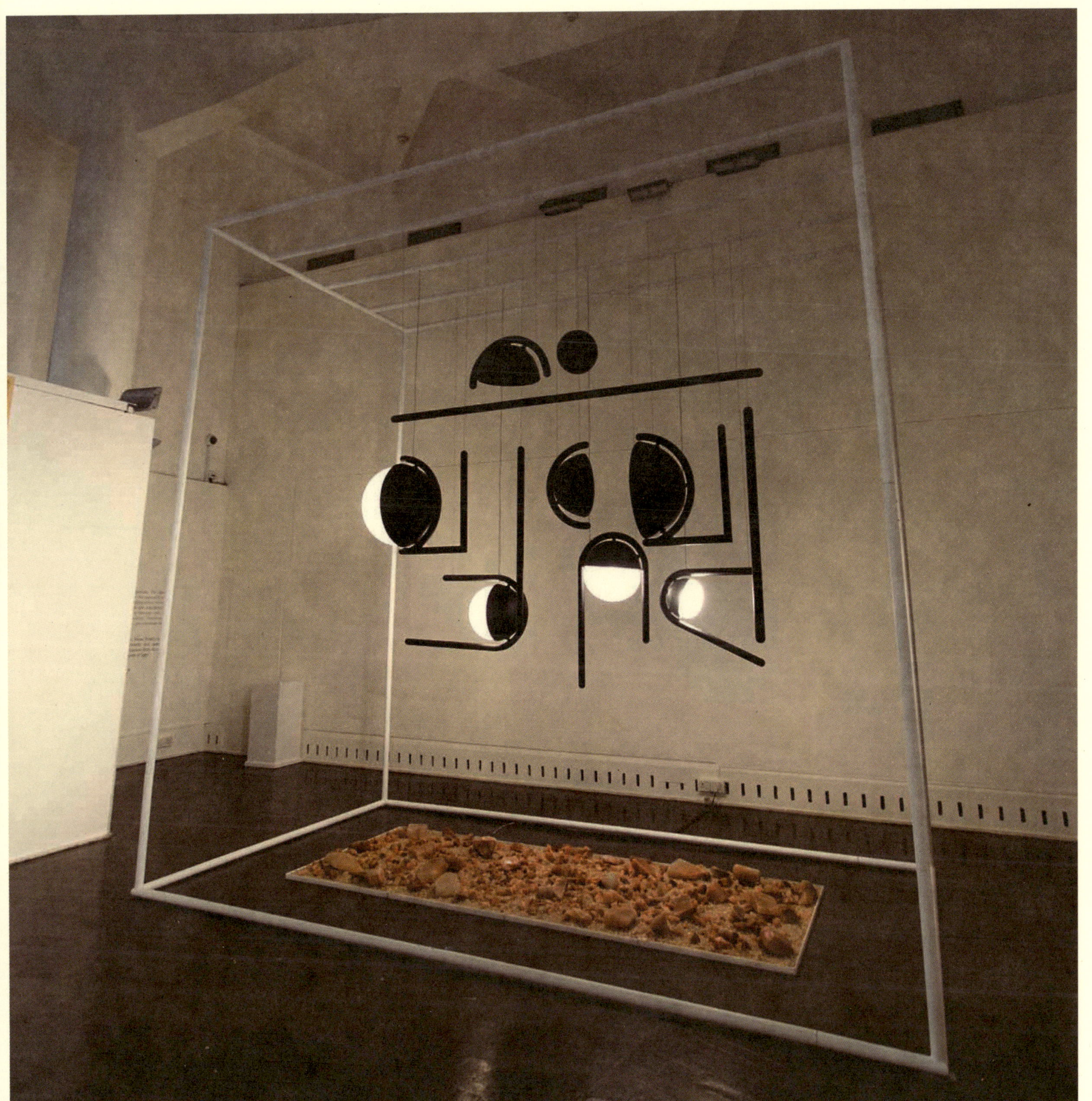

"The modern and simplistic design is a representation of Gandhi's character, a man who lived his life with honesty and humility. As a champion for human rights through non-violence he is a man respected and cherished by the world for being one of the most inspirational figures of all time."

Klove Studio (Gautam Seth, Prateek Jain)

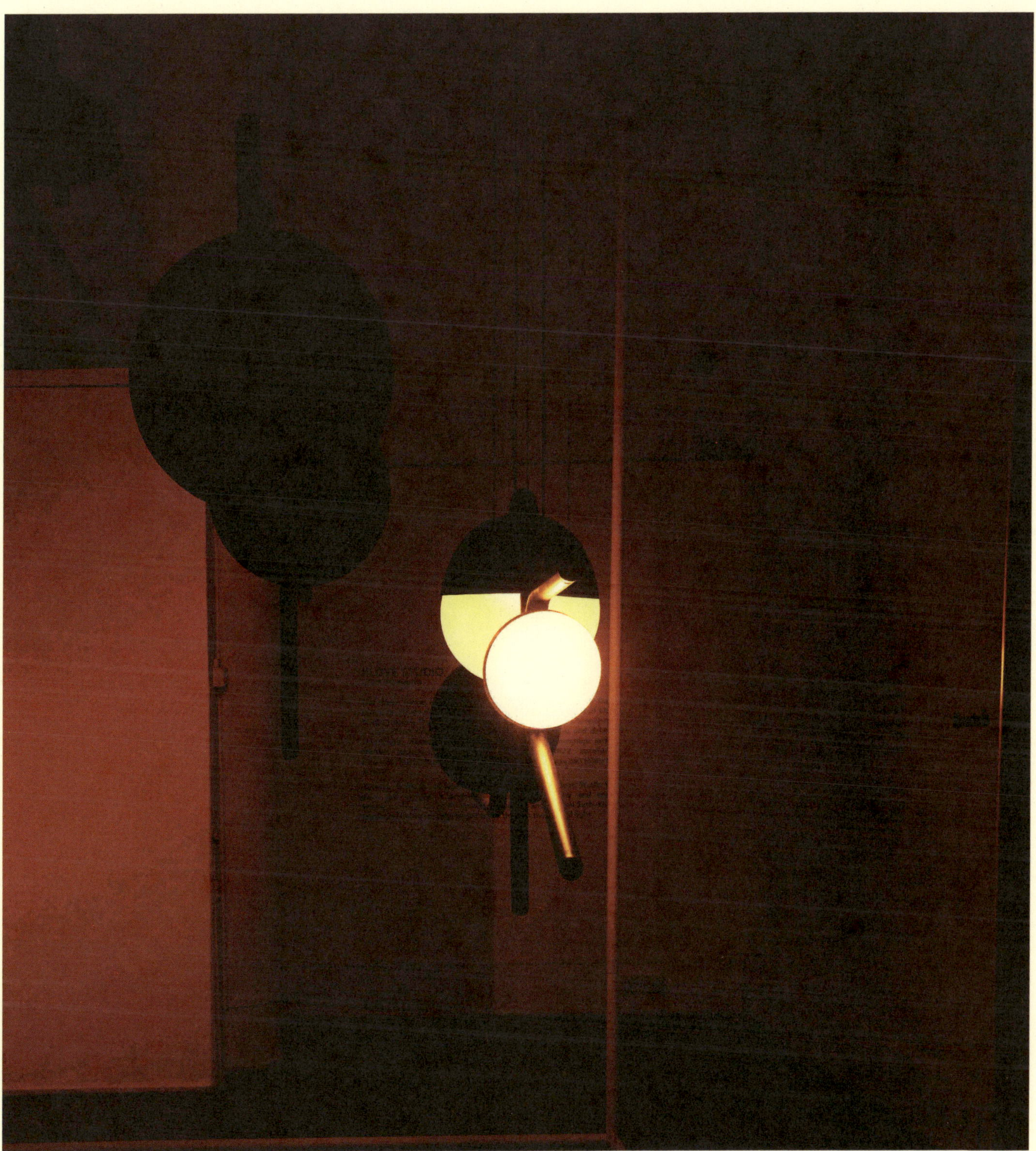

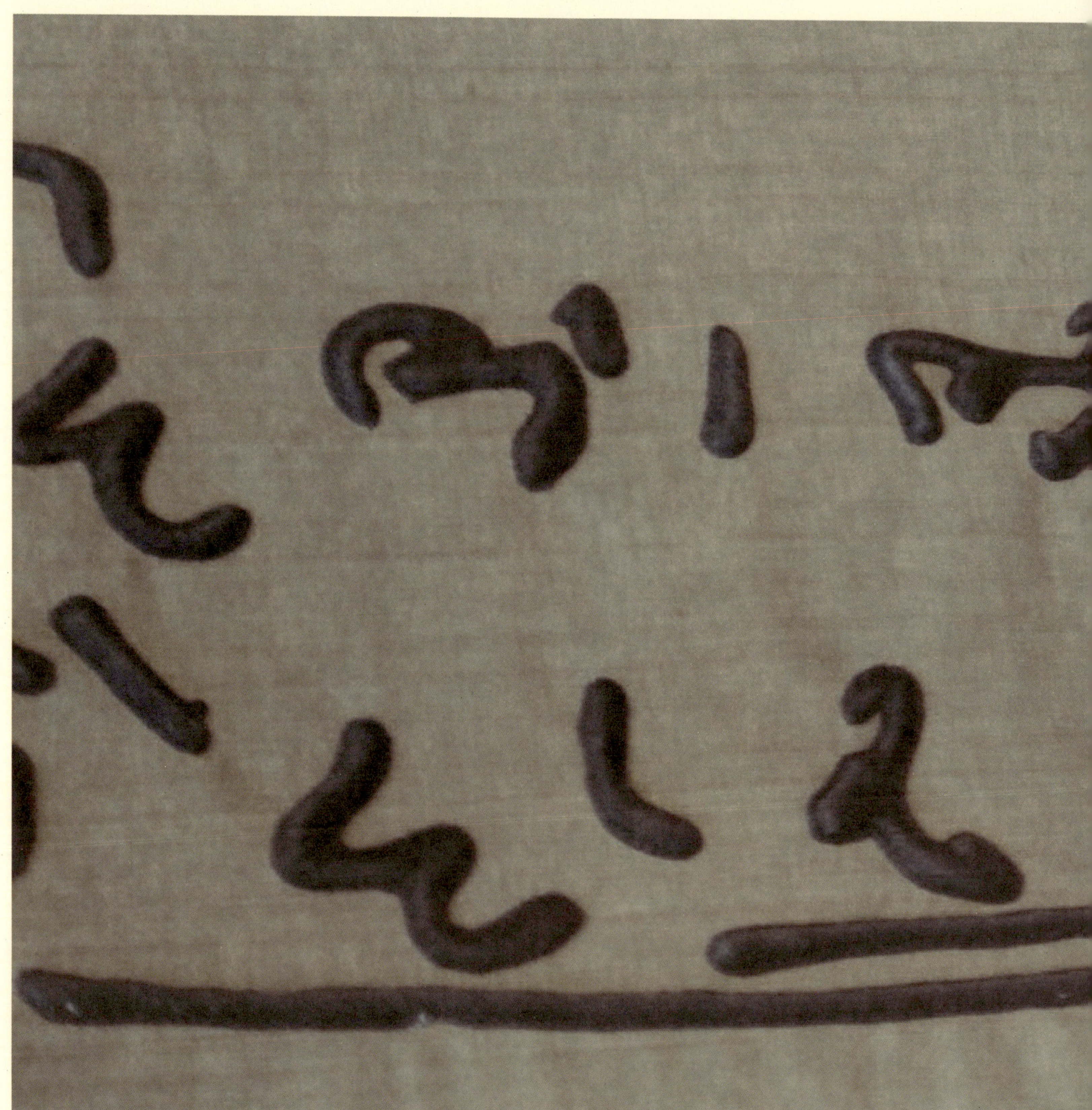

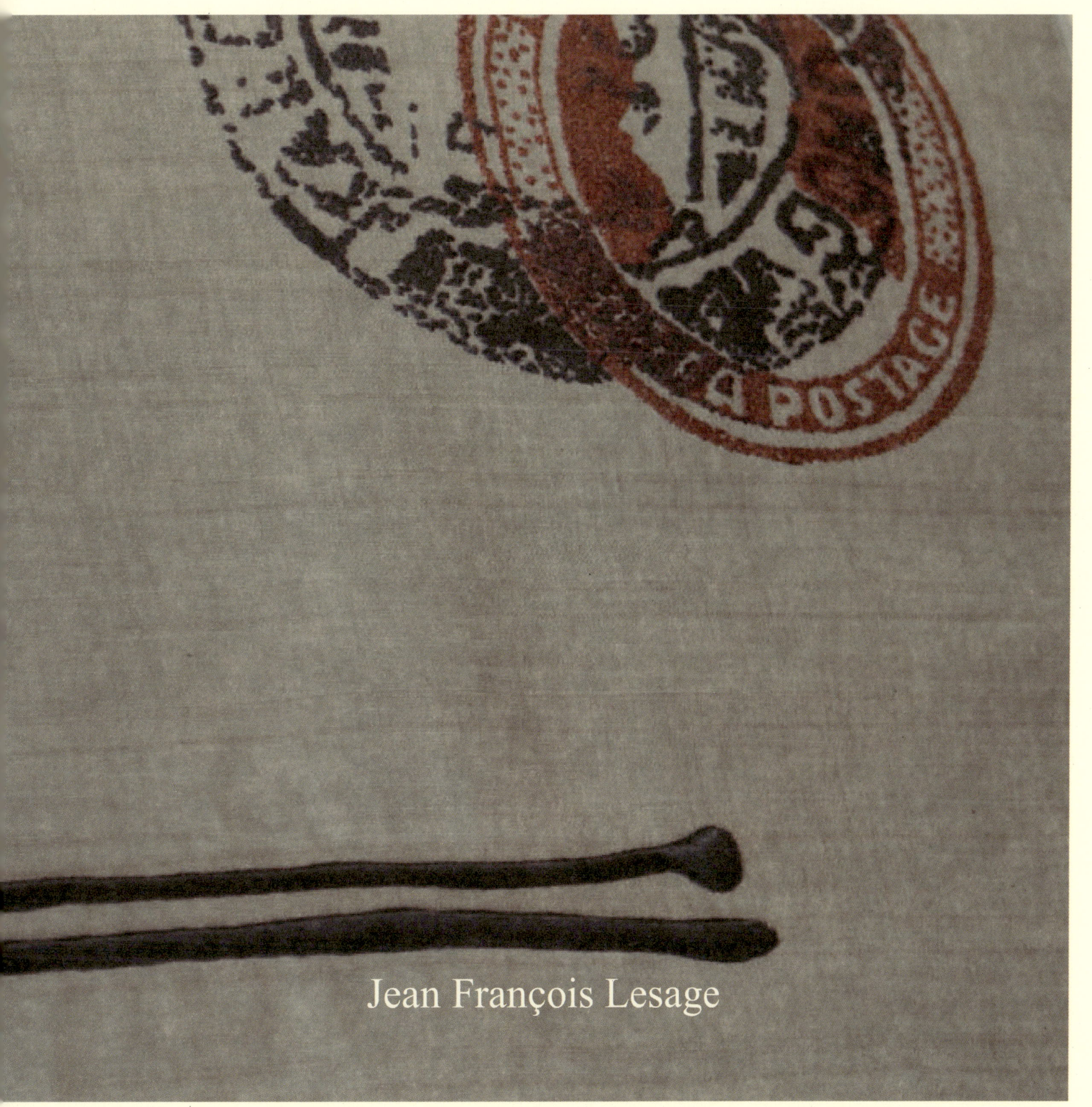
A POSTAGE
Jean François Lesage

Jean François Lesage

Couture Embroiderer

Jean François Lesage renders Mahatma Gandhi's salt *satyagraha* march to Dandi and his handwritten letters through hand embroidery on hand-spun khadi. As the eye roves over the route of the march and Gandhi's handwriting stretched on tall canvases, each thread seems to recount the man's resilience and crystallized faith in fighting for freedom. The layering of sheer fabric with printed letters creates a semblance of depth. A depth akin to Gandhi's messages – always succinct, always carrying multiple layers. And always marching.

Associated with couture since the 1920s, the Lesage family has rendered design through embroidery for foremost international couture houses. Jean François Lesage leads the formidable atelier and takes the legacy forward through a close and long-standing relationship with Indian artisans.

All letters imprinted for embroidery are a part of the private collection of Shri Kishore Jhunjhunwala

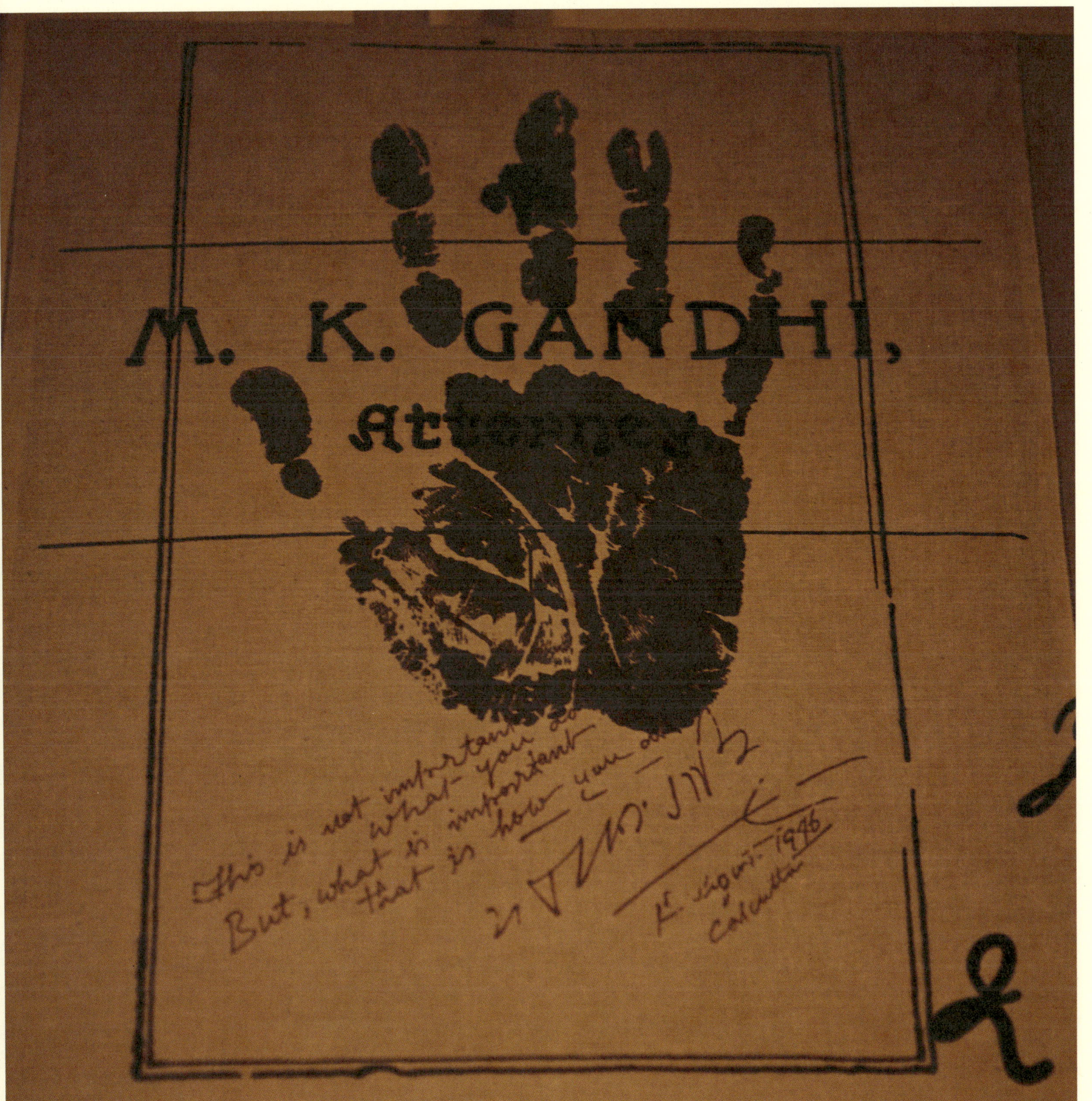
M. K. GANDHI,
This is not important
But, what what you do
that is important
is how you do
1st August 1946
Calcutta

DANDI MARCH

My dear Jawarlal
you must not be
stunned. Rather re-
joice that God gives
strength to drive him
to do my Duty. I could

Yours sincerely
M K Gandhi

M. K. GANDHI.

21-24 Court Chambers,

Johannesburg

"True morality consists not in following the beaten track, but in finding out the true path for ourselves and in fearlessly following it."

Mahatma Gandhi

I want world sympathy in this battle of Right against Might.
Dandi M.K.Gandhi
5.4.'30

My dear Jawaharlal
You must not be
stunned. Rather we
should rejoice. God gives
strength and direction
to do my duty. I could
not ... otherwise. As
the author of the newspaper...
tion, a heavy respon-
sibility lies on my shoul-
ders. Be quiet in
writing your im-
pressions of Lucknow
& Cawnpore. Let
drink the cup
... ...

I want world sympathy
in this battle of
Right against Might.

Dandi
M.K.Gandhi
5.4.'30

Till the stale waters
Of slavery
Evaporate from the salt
Of our essence
We will march

यह यात्रा न होगी खत्म
जब तक गुलामी का जीर्ण तत्व
हो हर सूक्ष्म, हर सुप्त
लहू के लवण से लुप्त

Ahmadabad
Sanand
Mahi
Kaira
Nadiad
Anand
Borsad
Cambay
BARODA
Kangapour
Dabhoi
Nandod
Broach
Golfe de Cambaye
Surat
Salines de Dandi
Navsari
Jalalpour

उरान दीवान,
काम करनी कर
ने ताके करता न
रा भाग का हूँ कि
नि देश्या का नी
मेरी कहानी और
मैं आपको देता र
धरम स्थ और उन

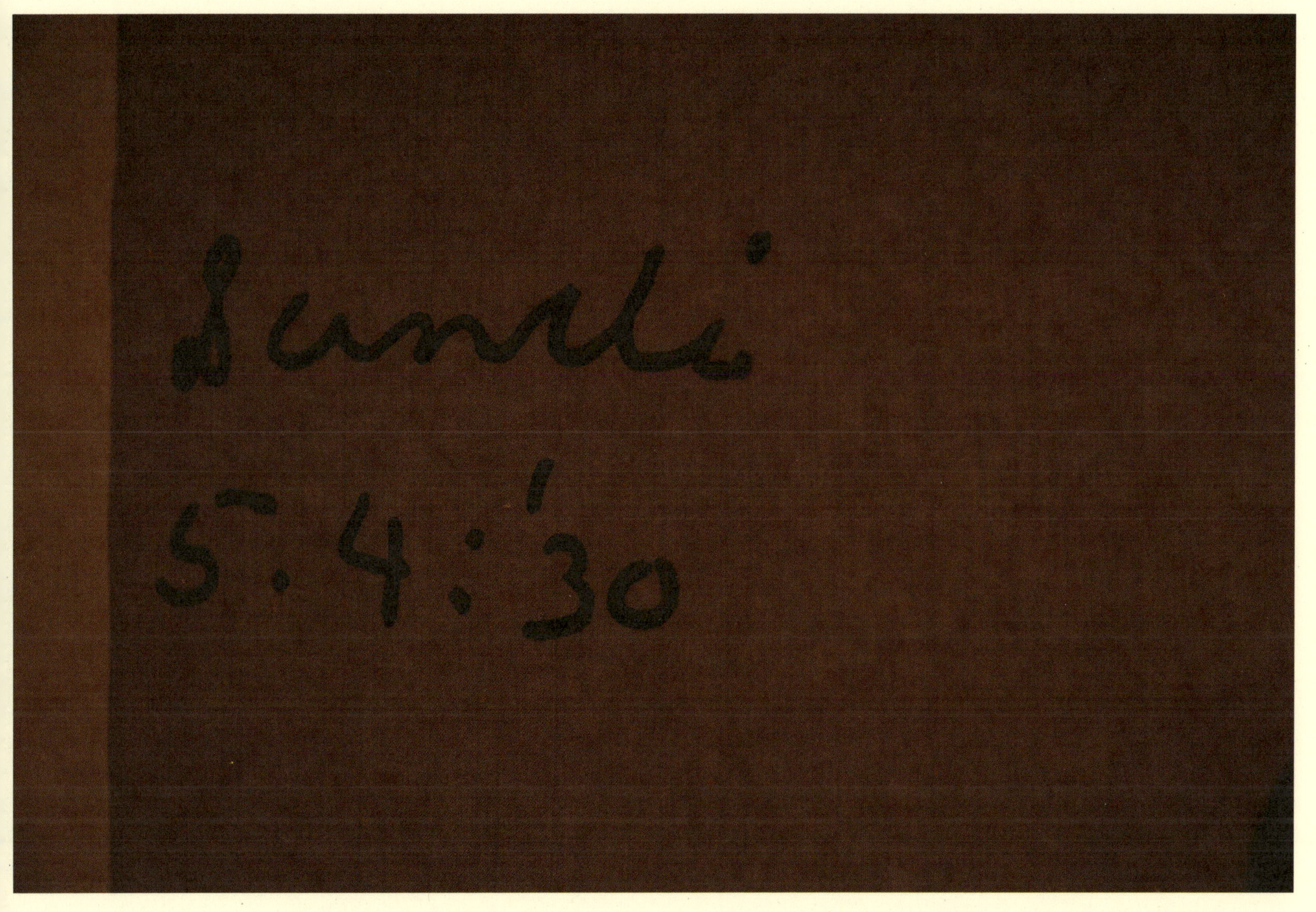

"Ours is a human project which revolves around people, craft and the beauty of handwork."

Jean François Lesage

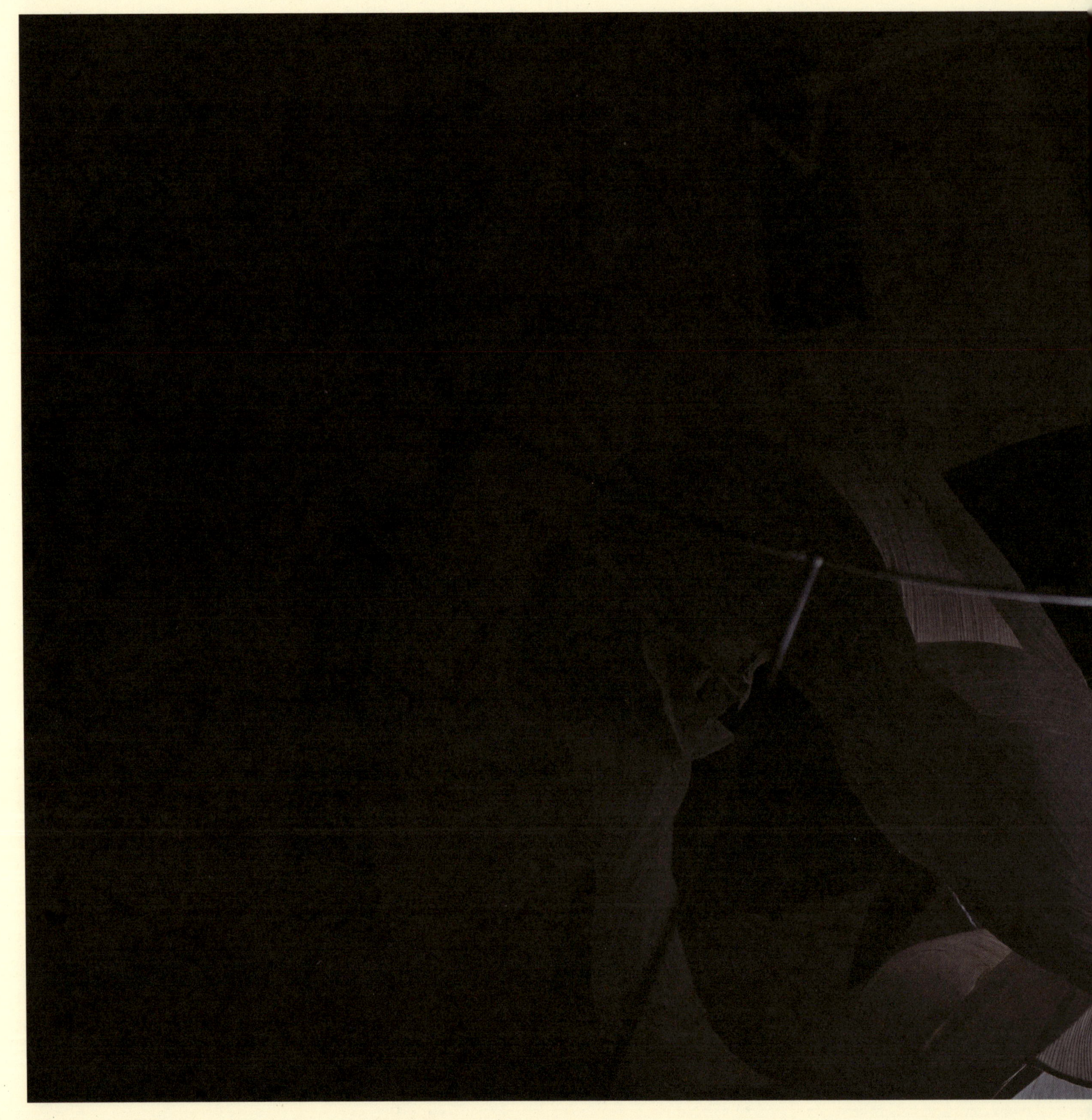

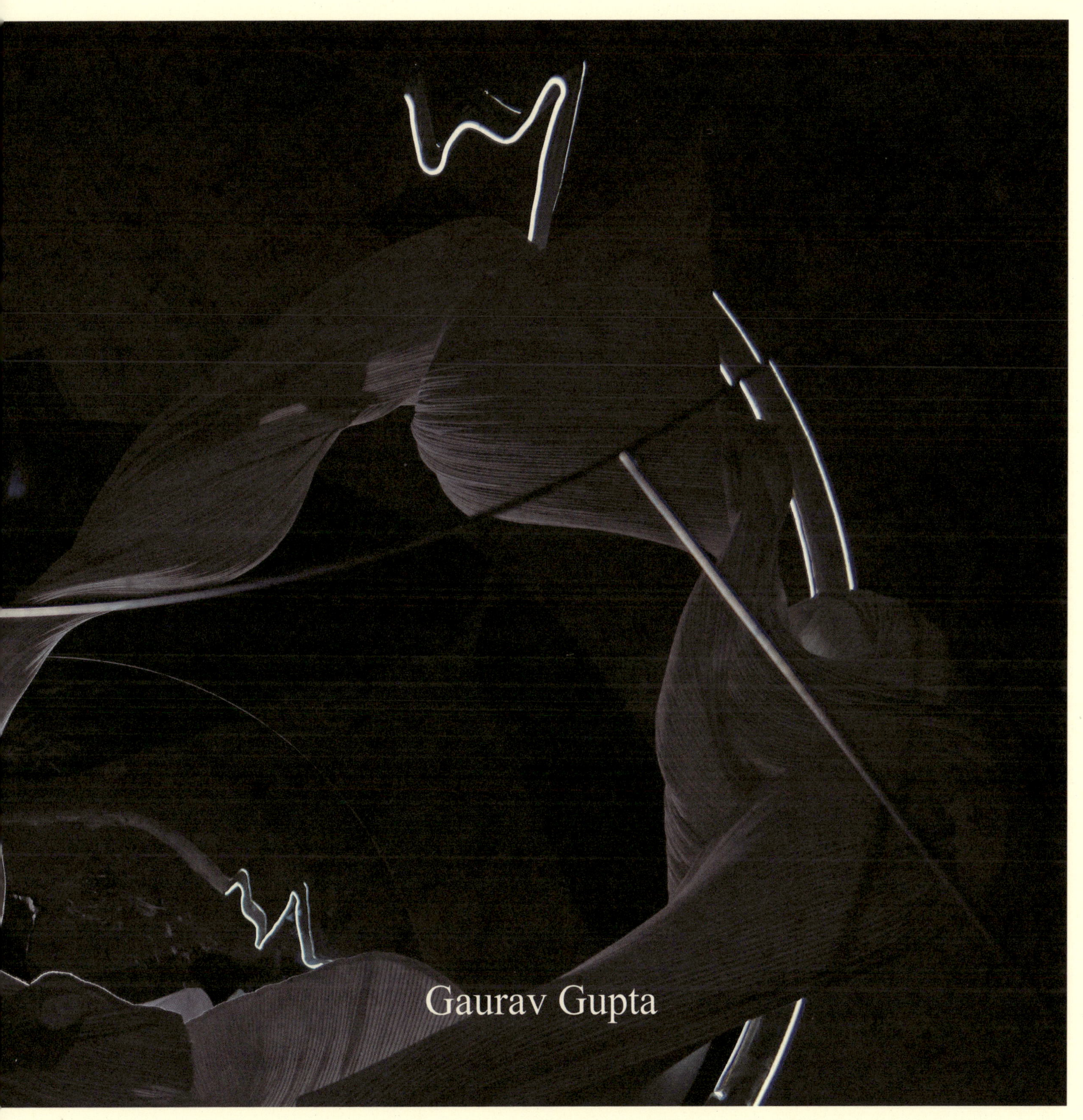
Gaurav Gupta

Gaurav Gupta

Couturier

Precisely planning a life that would have naturally gone on for 125 years, Mahatma Gandhi's each action and idea fiercely echoed his claim, "my life is my message". For Gaurav Gupta the inspiration behind the "Tunnel of Infinity" lay in the clarity, rhythm and sound of Gandhi's perfect heartbeat, symbolic of the cyclical nature of absolute truth. This sound forms the accompanying backdrop for the work. Taking his love for sculptural draping forward, Gaurav imagines the philosophy of Mahatma Gandhi as a reflective, infinite tunnel that holds up a mirror to mankind. The fluid, floating sculpture in khadi, a revolutionary fabric, represents the endless possibilities that can emerge from sustainable practice, from reflecting, from peeping deep into ourselves.

Recognized for his successful experiments with couture and ushering radical ideas in clothing and space design, Gaurav Gupta's work emerges from a dialogue between anatomy, art and architecture. A continual undercurrent of ideas like infinity, fluid form and the abstract continues to inform his design landscape.

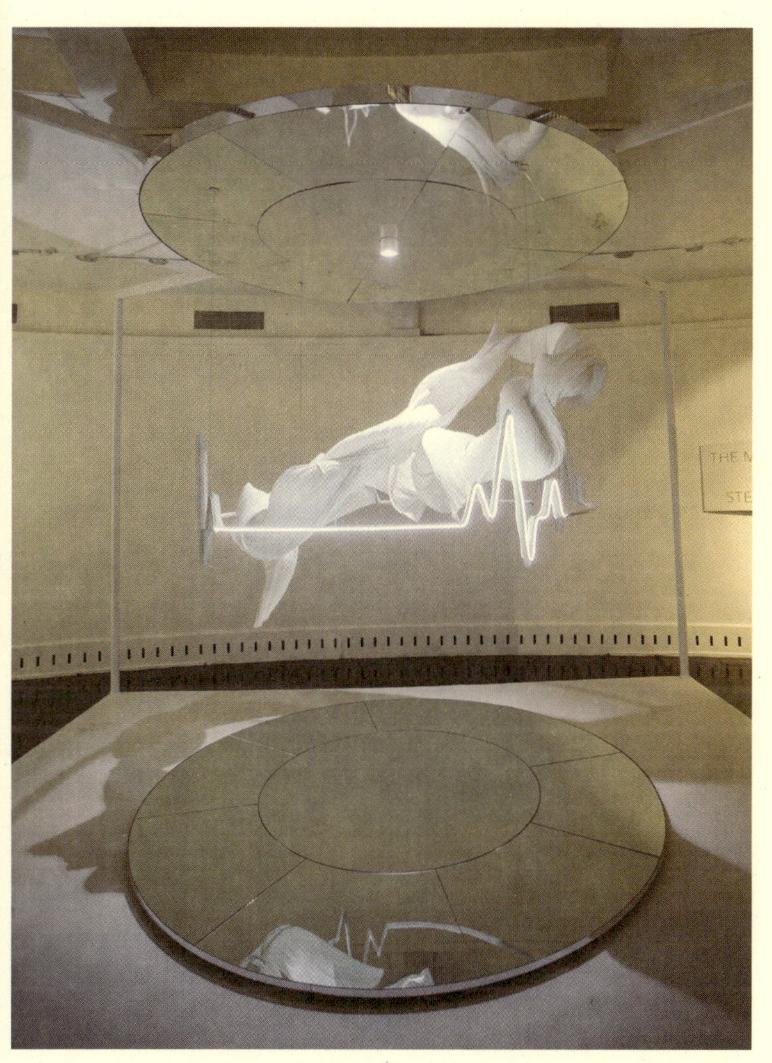

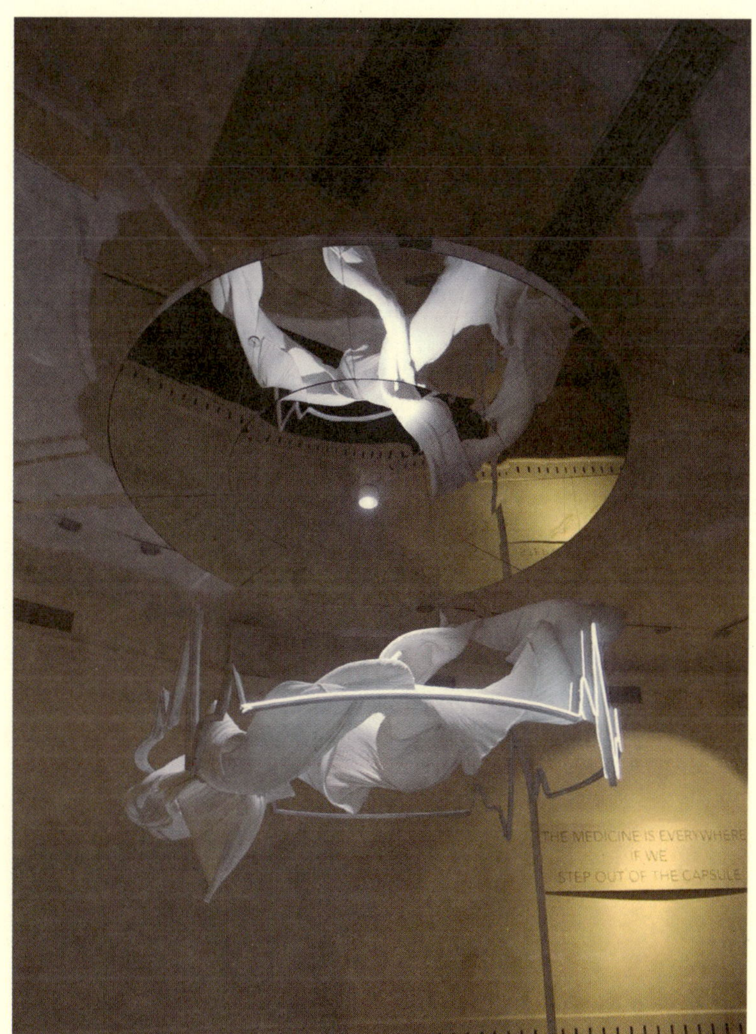
THE MEDICINE IS EVERYWHERE
IF WE
STEP OUT OF THE CAPSULE

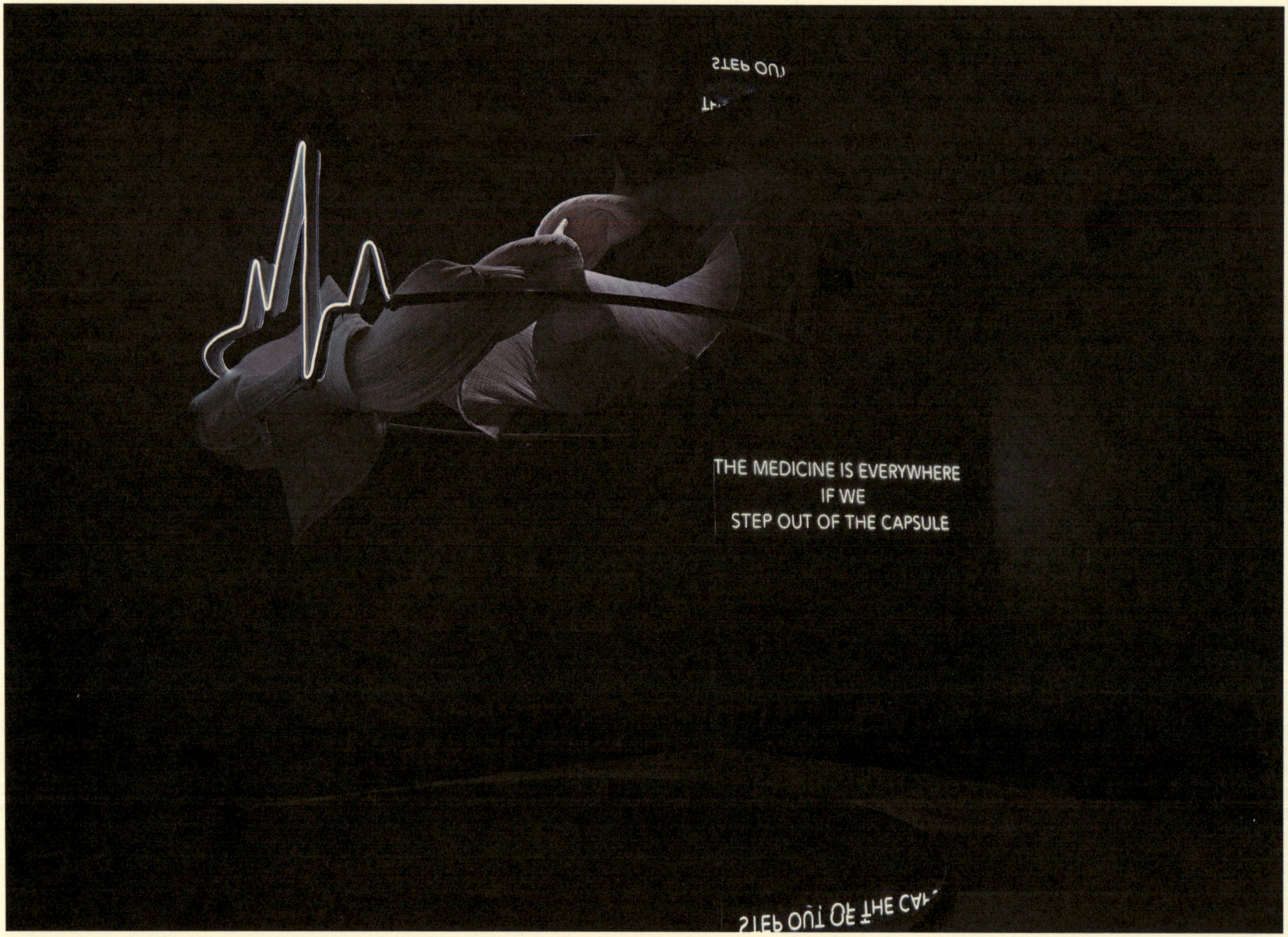

THE MEDICINE IS EVERYWHERE
IF WE
STEP OUT OF THE CAPSULE

सर्वत्र है उपचार
फिर औषधि में सीमित
क्यों हम लाचार

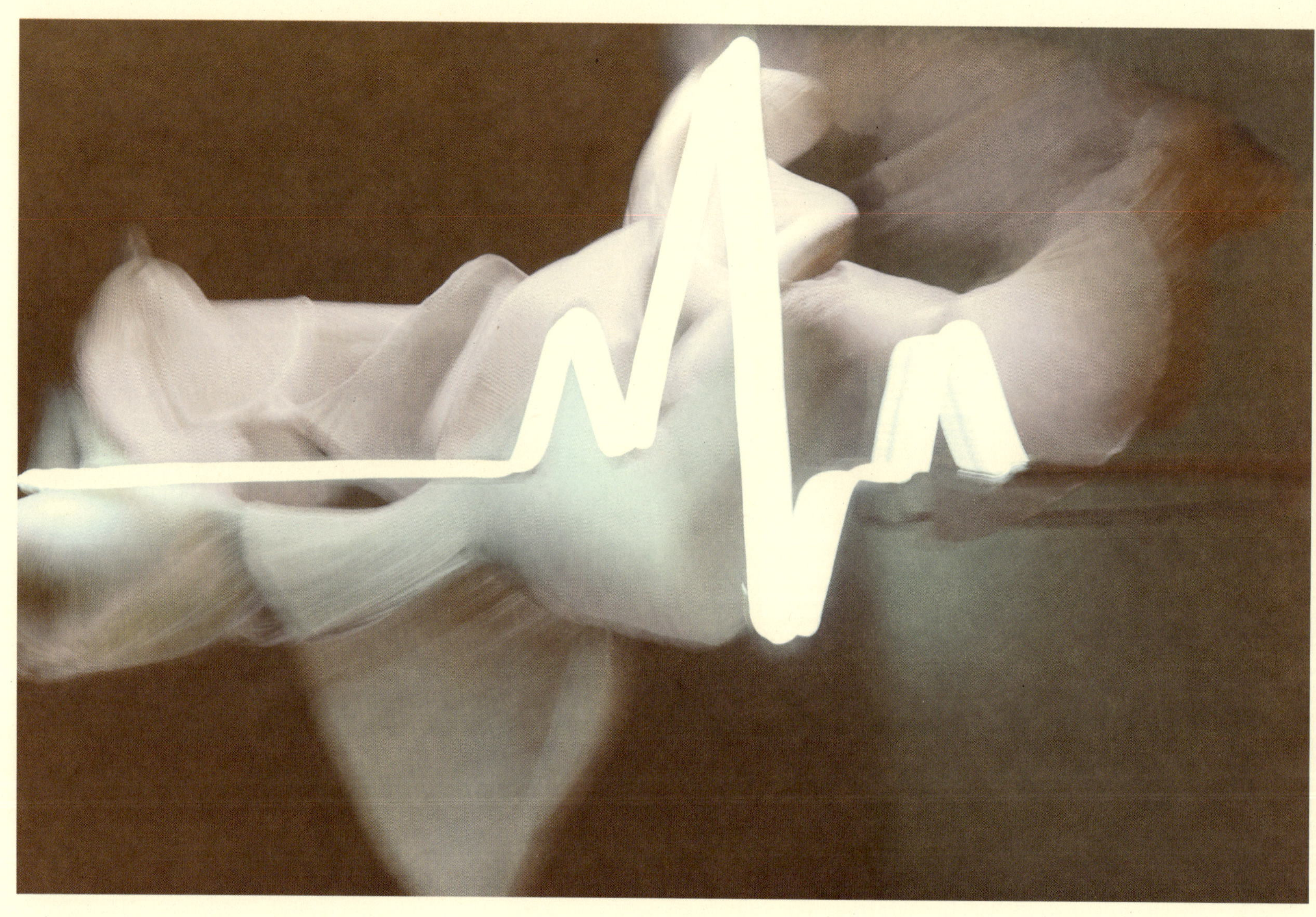

"Therefore the means of deliverance from all those evils from which men suffer lies only in one thing, the inner work of each man upon himself."

Mahatma Gandhi

"Gandhi is an amorphous soul just like the power of truth, the power of belief, the power of light—it follows a continuum and forms a loop of infinity. It is intense, immense, spiral. Through this work, I want people to talk to the Gandhi inside of them by reflecting on the Gandhi in front of them."

Gaurav Gupta

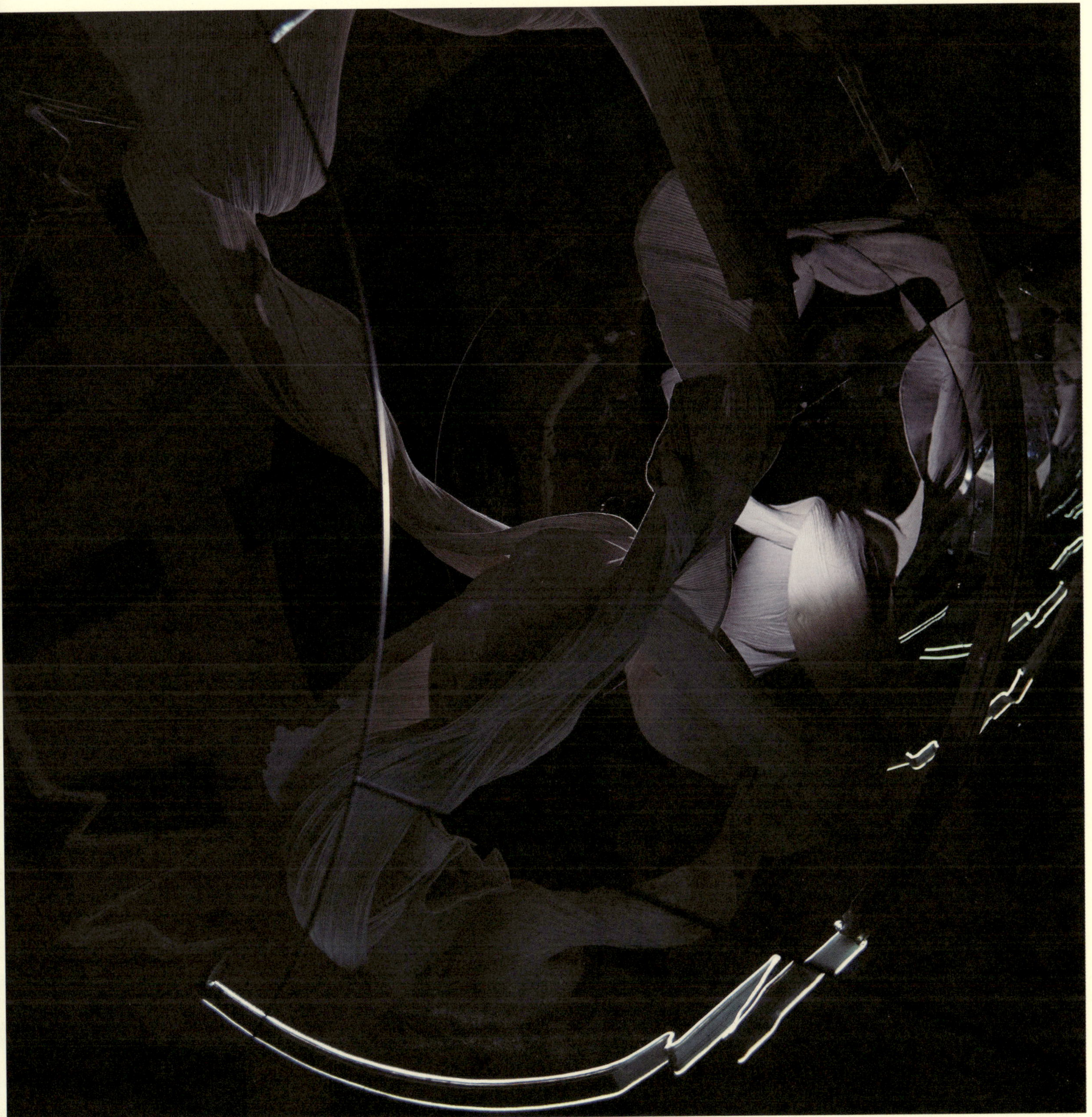

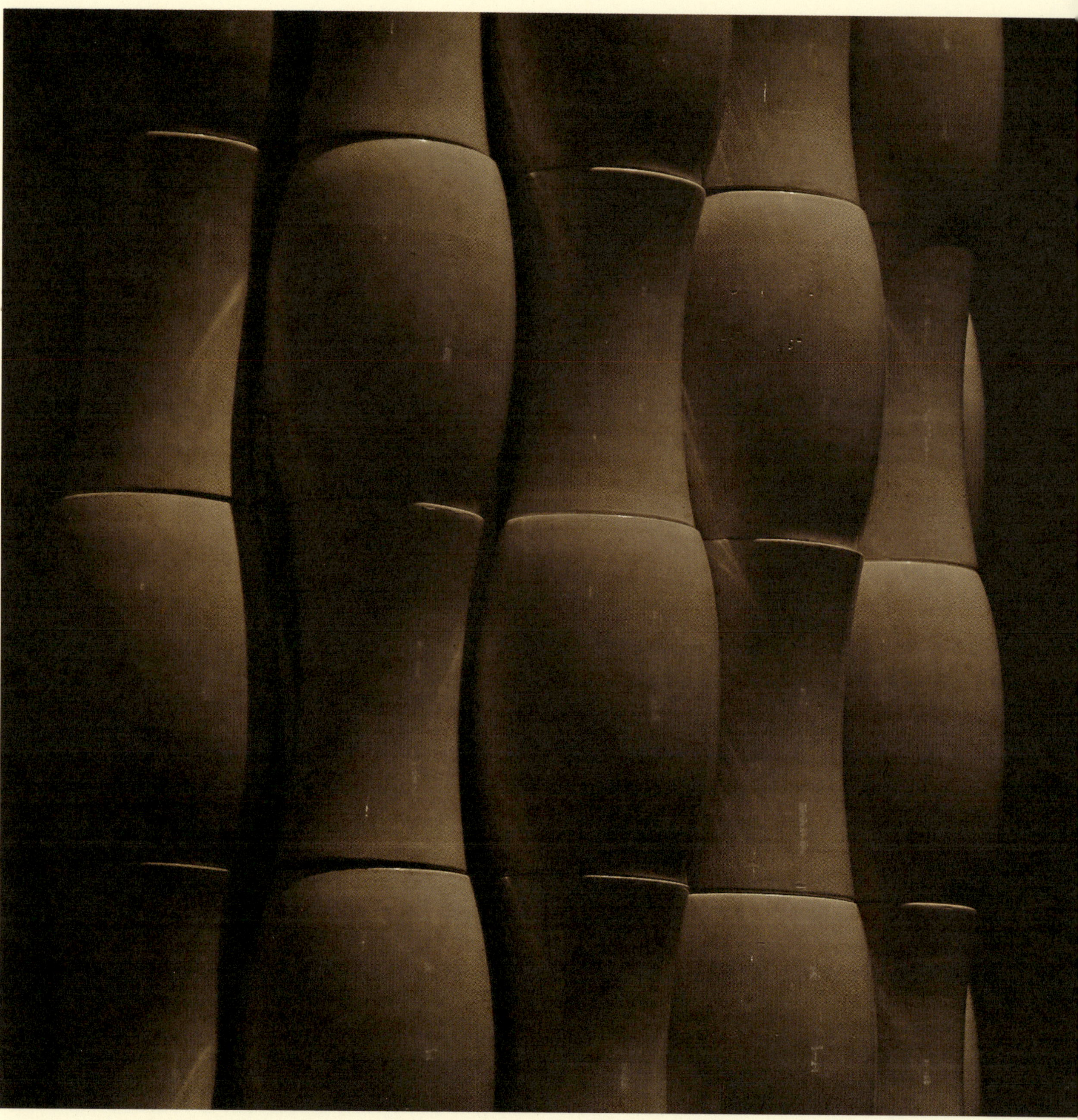

Ashiesh Shah

Ashiesh Shah

Architect

Ashiesh Shah reflects upon Mahatma Gandhi's idea of *swadeshi*, of less is more and the lightness of spiritual minimalism. His work is fuelled by persistent and devoted concentration on collaborating with Indian craftsmanship, believing, as Gandhi did, that "the soul of India lives in its villages." Craft forms like Longpi from Manipur, Channapatna from Karnataka and Kantilo from Odisha are a few that merge into his design language, interpreted by modern aesthetic to challenge prevailing perceptions.

Amongst India's coveted minds in space design, Ashiesh Shah is widely known as an interiors' architect. His practice is rooted in wabi sabi, the Japanese aesthetic philosophy of the transience of beauty, of accepting its incompleteness, its imperfection.

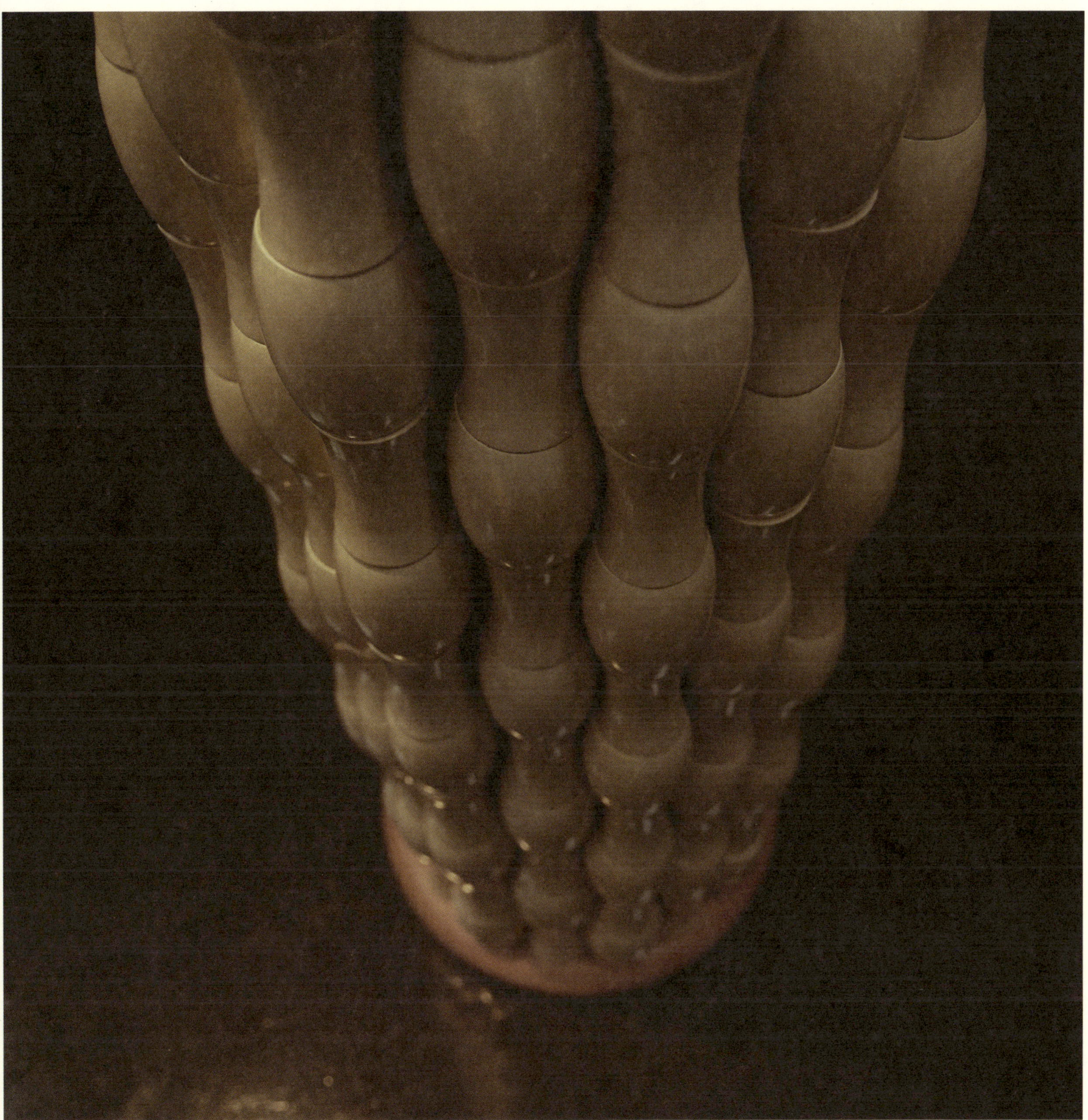

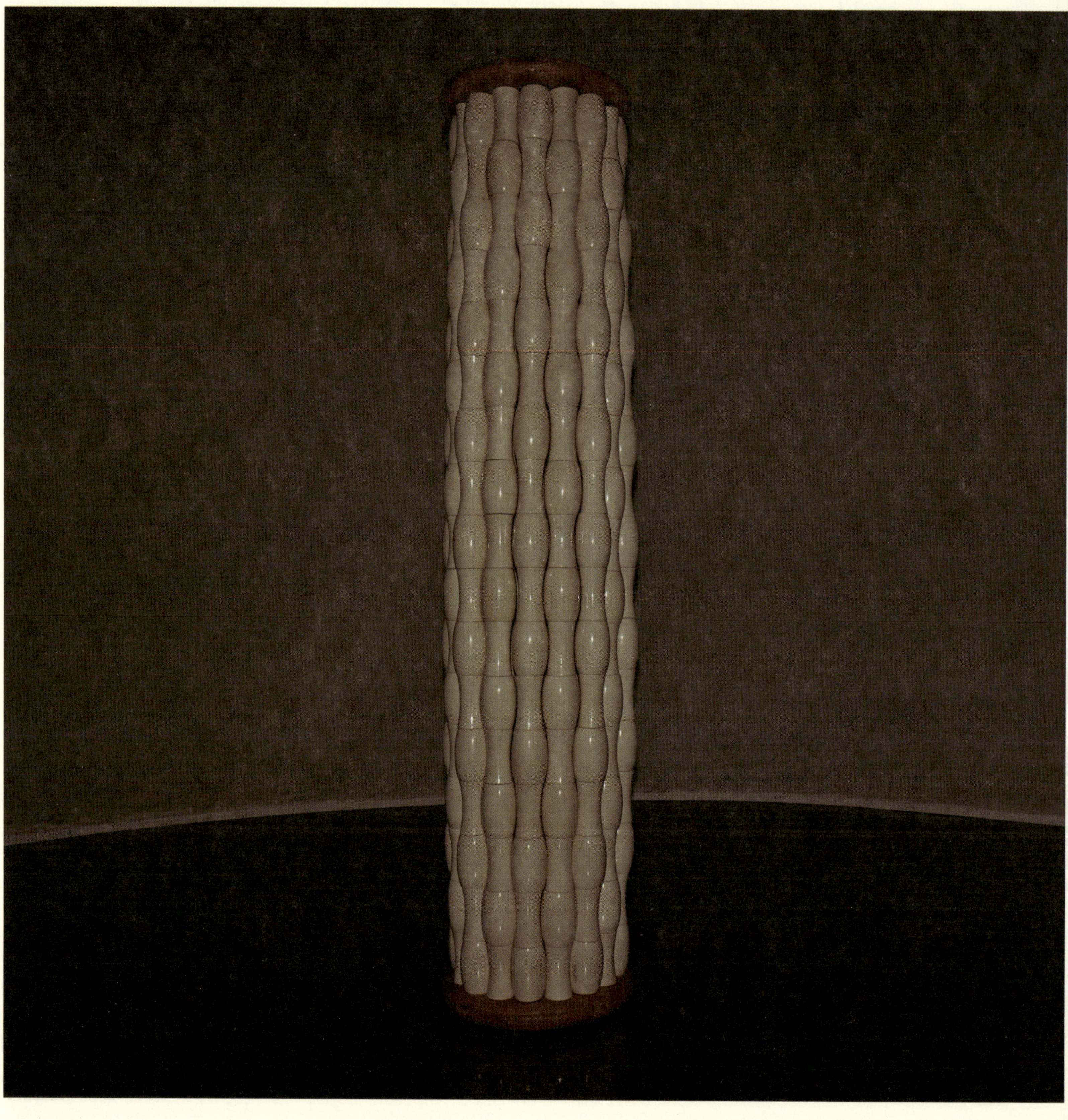

The Shanti Totem

The “Father of the Nation”, reflected through “The Shanti Totem”, characterizes itself with skin-coloured terracotta disks, enveloped in off-white *channapatna* beads, softened at the edges, replicating Gandhi’s handwoven khadi attire. Shanti or “peace force”, is driven through the tranquility of the coloured beads, perfectly imperfect in stature. Each piece, moulded by hand, pays homage to the handicrafts of India, the epitome of wabi sabi.

The lanky yet well-composed height, runs up to 1.64 metres, a handcrafted embodiment of the visionary himself.

“Gandhi always said ‘India lives in its villages,’ the way things are moving, villages now live in the cities. While we find ourselves gazing towards the West for inspiration, our own country is debouching with handicrafts and inspiration that’s self-made.”

Ashiesh Shah

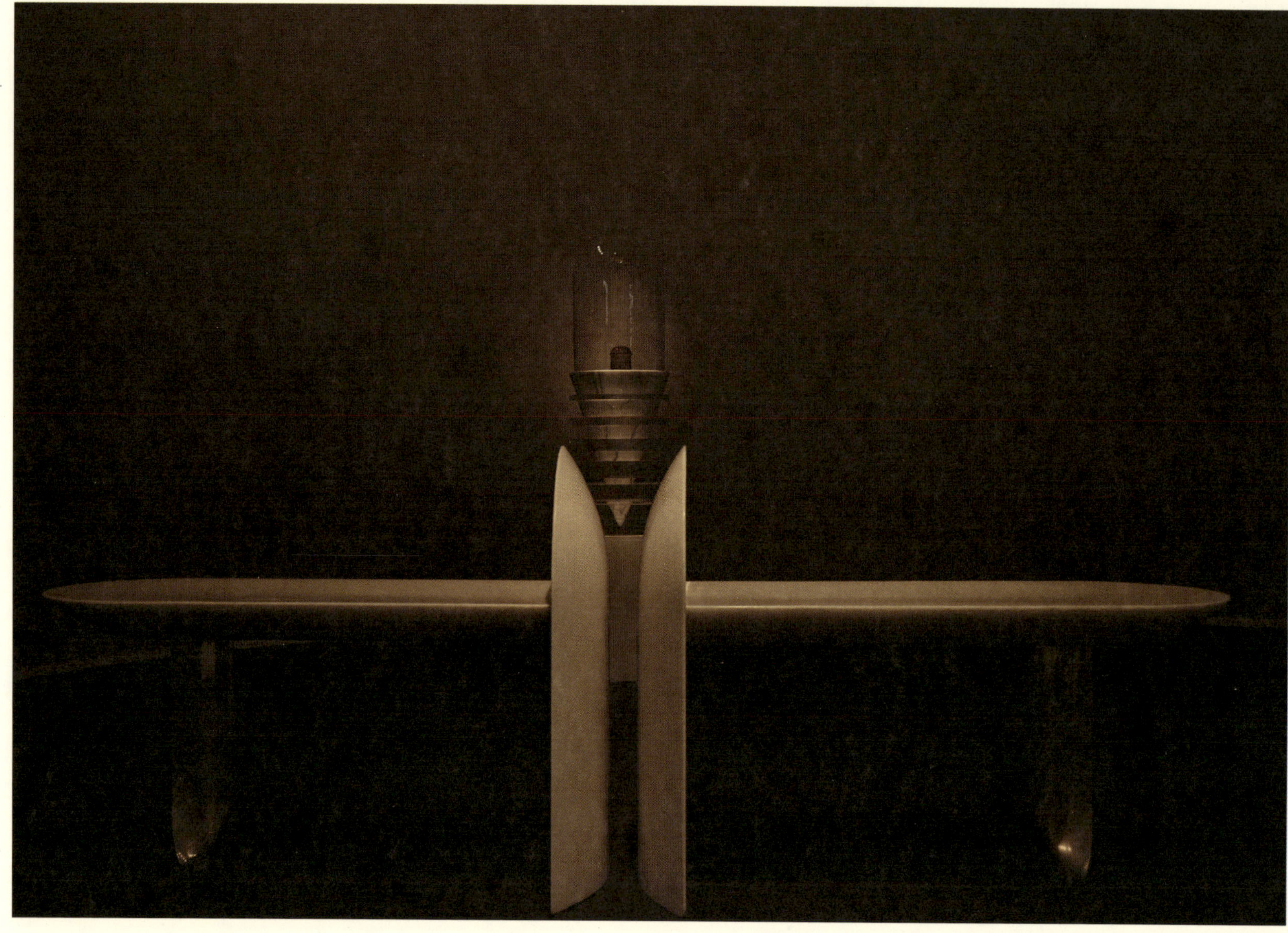

Asthi

Mahatma Gandhi's ashes (lent from the collection of Shri Kishore Jhunjhunwala) finds solace, amongst weightless white marble and resin. An octagonal pedestal laden with "The Intersect Stool", is covered with a glass vitrine by Klove. The entire assembly is a play of perspectives, characterized by presence and absence drawing from the divine being himself. A space of contentment and tranquility completes itself with the sculptural "Lingam Benches". A ray of light cuts through the installation casting a perfectly centred halo.

"I have no fear of death. I would regard it with relief and satisfaction. But it is impossible for me to think that that is the end. I have no proof."

Mahatma Gandhi

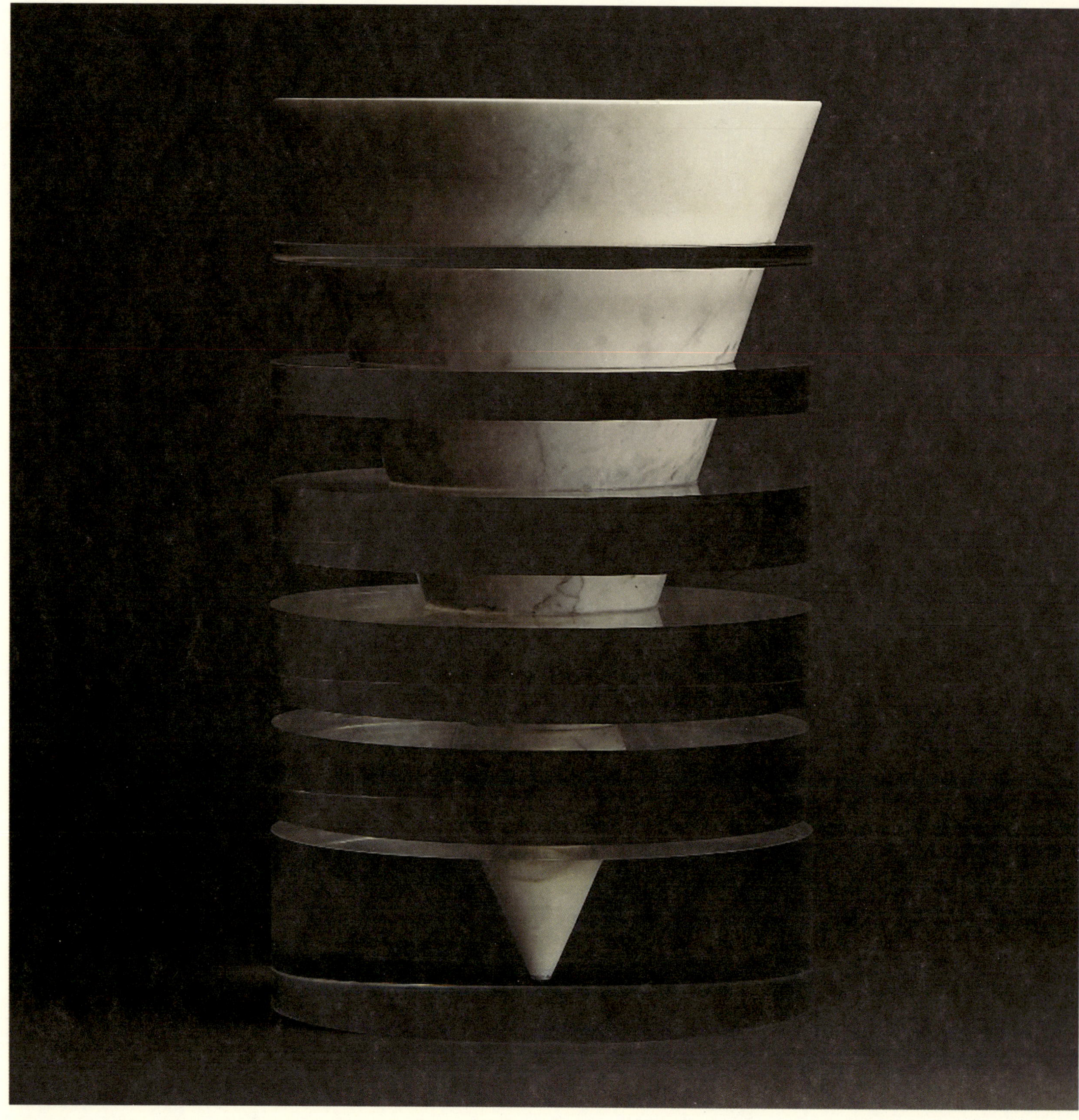

But we must return
Time and again
To fathom how
To gather this
Eternity of knowledge
In a fistful of life

तिनके सी ज़िन्दगी
सागर सी ज्ञप्ति
पुनः आगमन
पुनः विमोचन
पुनः मनन
यही है संतति

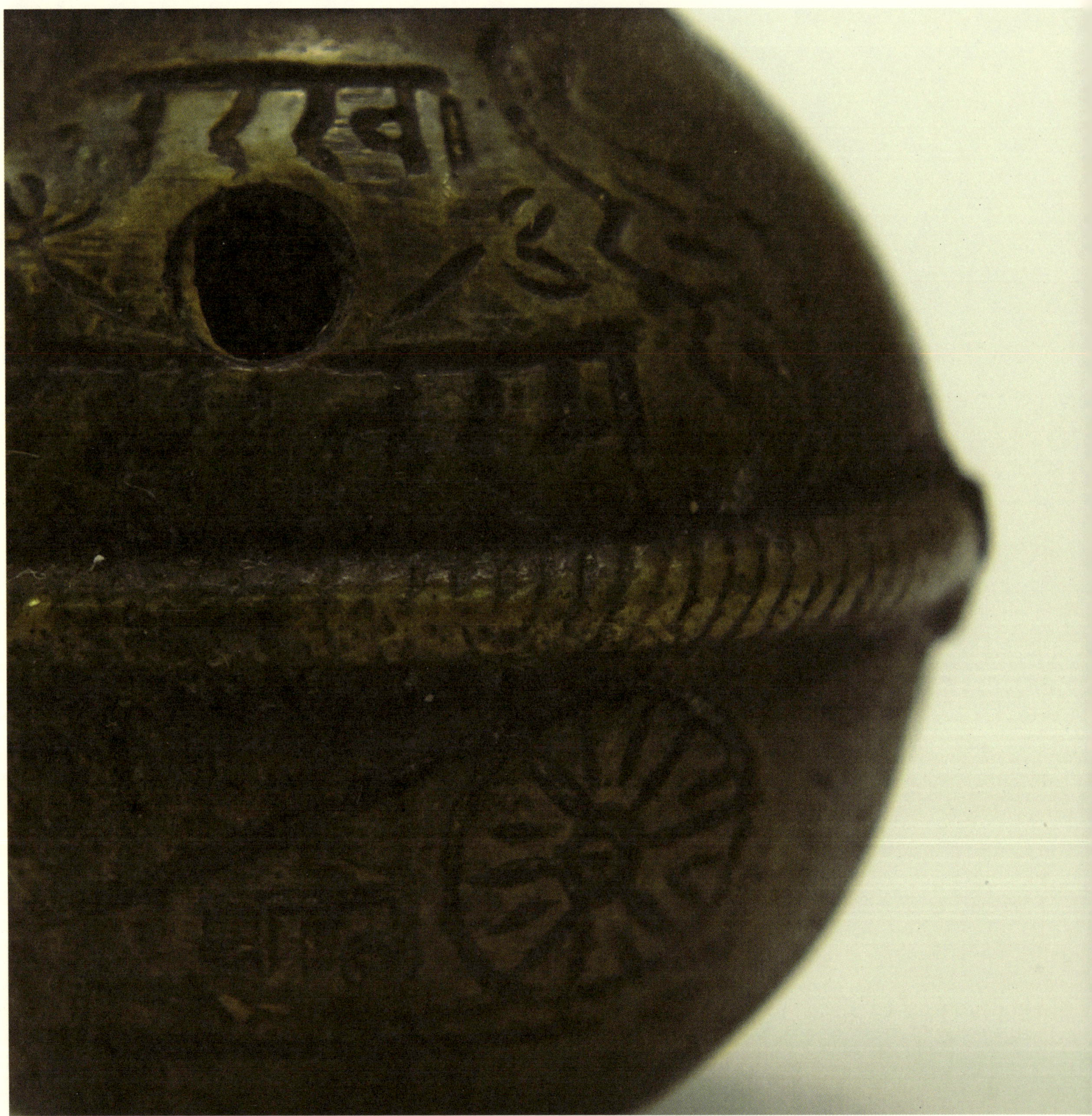

Kishore Jhunjhunwala

Kishore Jhunjhunwala

Collector, Philatelist, Numismatist

Collecting objects, imprints and ideas related to Mahatma Gandhi, living in the footsteps of his ideologies, following the trail of his journeys and making this his life's singular passion is what has consumed collector Kishore Jhunjhunwala for more than half a century. With over 10,000 collectibles and memorabilia of Gandhi, Jhunjhunwala's greatest regret remains not having met the Mahatma himself.

In a large alcove-like space in his Mumbai home, Kishore Jhunjhunwala has created, over years, a library, a museum, a cave almost. A cave that keeps safe the tireless collection of his journeys in the hope to imbibe his Gandhi.

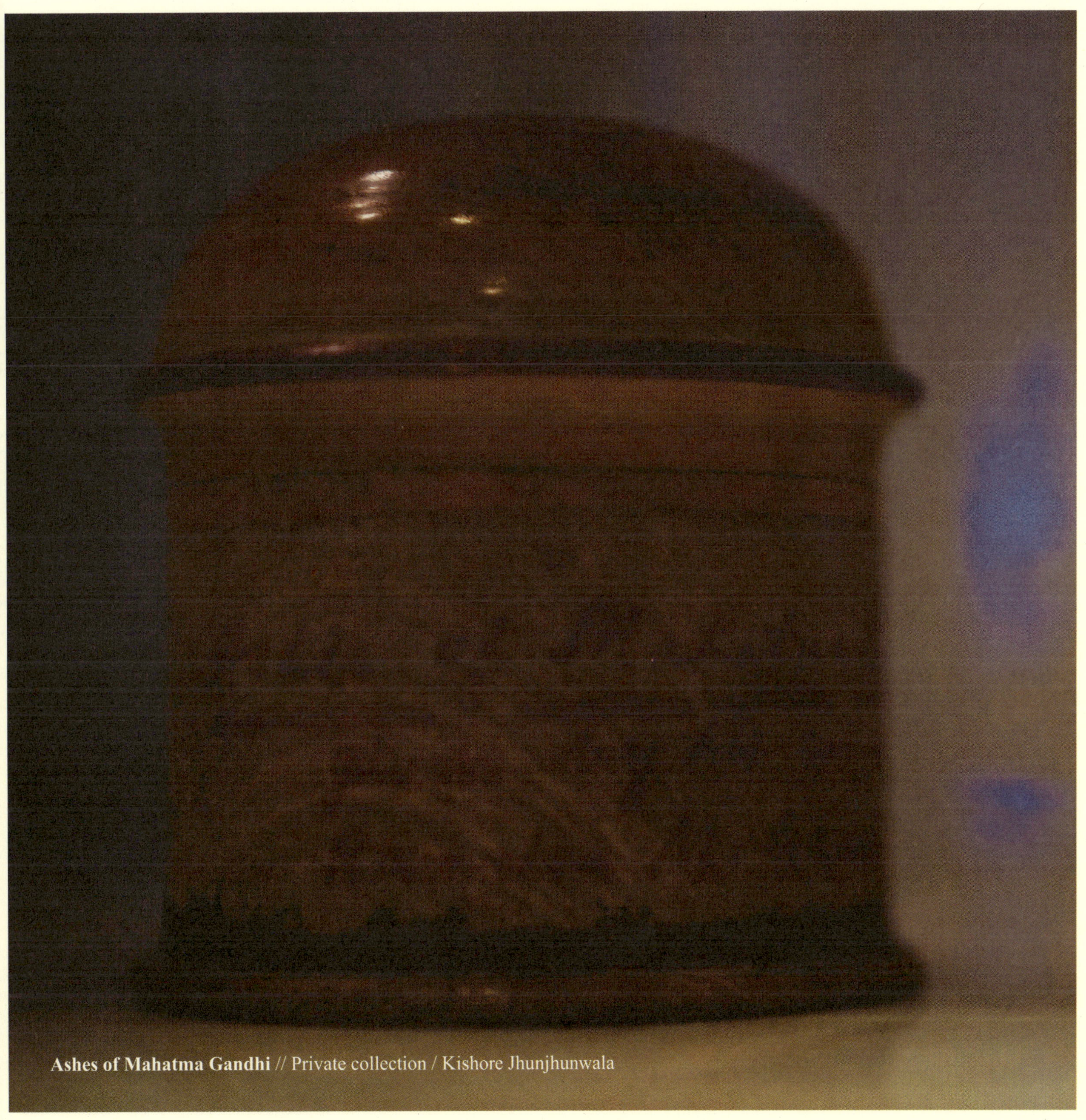

Ashes of Mahatma Gandhi // Private collection / Kishore Jhunjhunwala

THE "DAILY PRATAP" LAHORE. 17th August 1930.

MAHATMA GANDHI IN PRISON

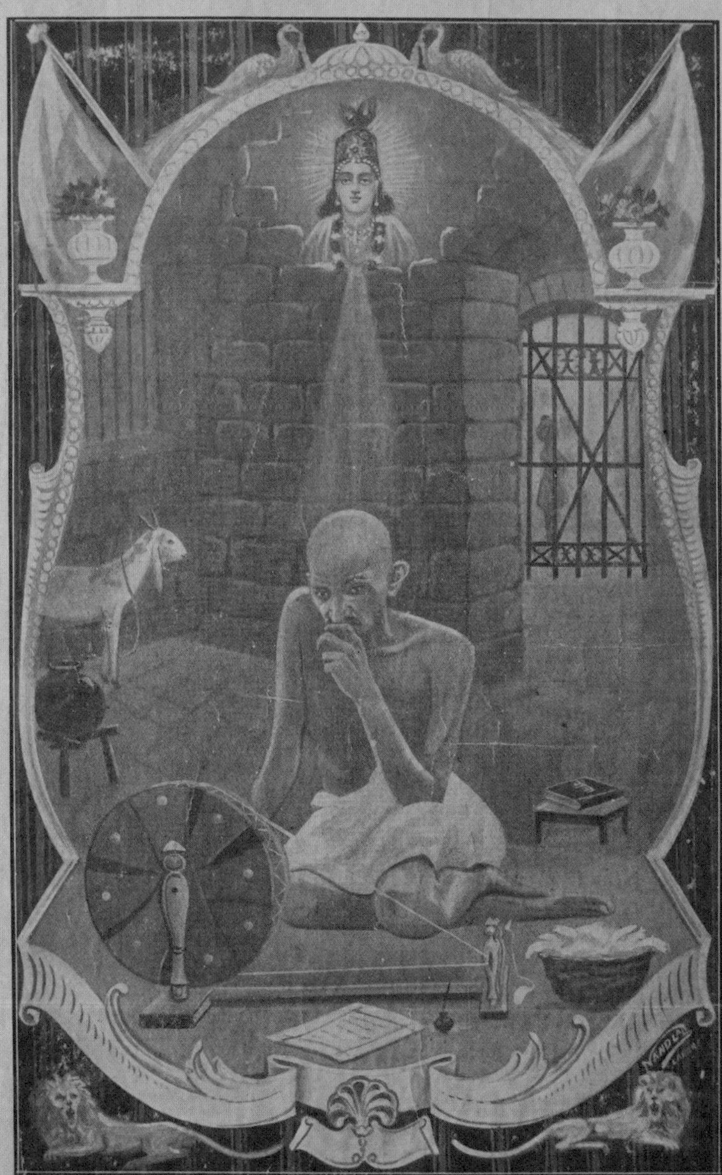

LORD KRISHNA SHOWERING HIS BLESSINGS ON HIM.

Printed at Arorbans Press Anarkali Lahore and published from the Pratap Office, Hospital Road, Lahore by L. Nanak Chand Naz, Printer and Publisher.

"Love is mute, it does not complain. Love is blind, it sees no fault. Love is deaf, it hears no tales. Love ever gives, never demands. Love is constant, never varying whether in adversity or prosperity. Love is never hurt. Love never tires. How has yours fared of late!"

Mahatma Gandhi

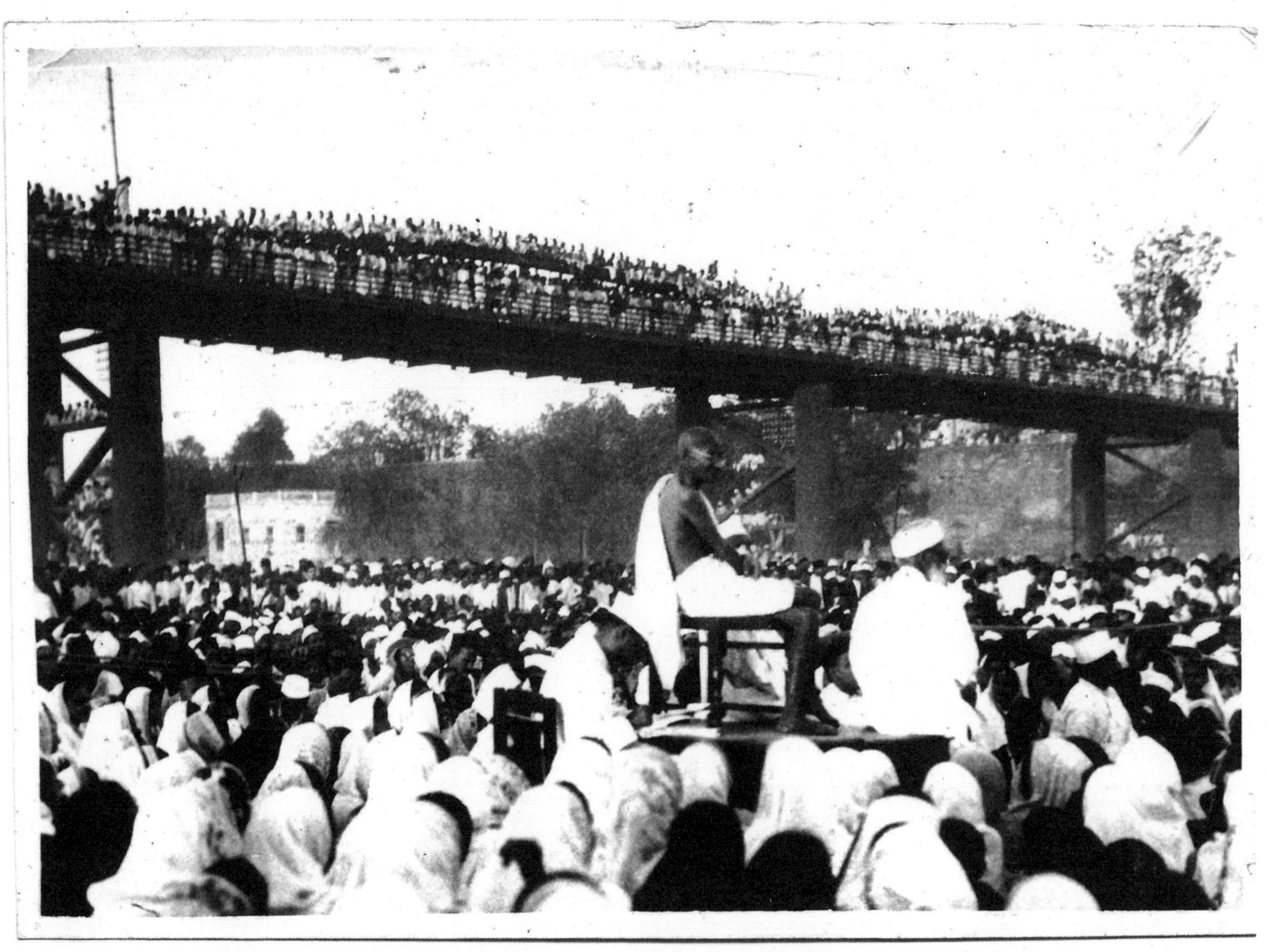

Above and opposite: A scene from and a hand-embroidered route for the Dandi march respectively.

Kishore Jhunjhunwala walked from Transval to Pretoria, the trail Mahatma Gandhi followed to initiate the Civil Disobedience Movement in South Africa. The journey took 21 days by foot.

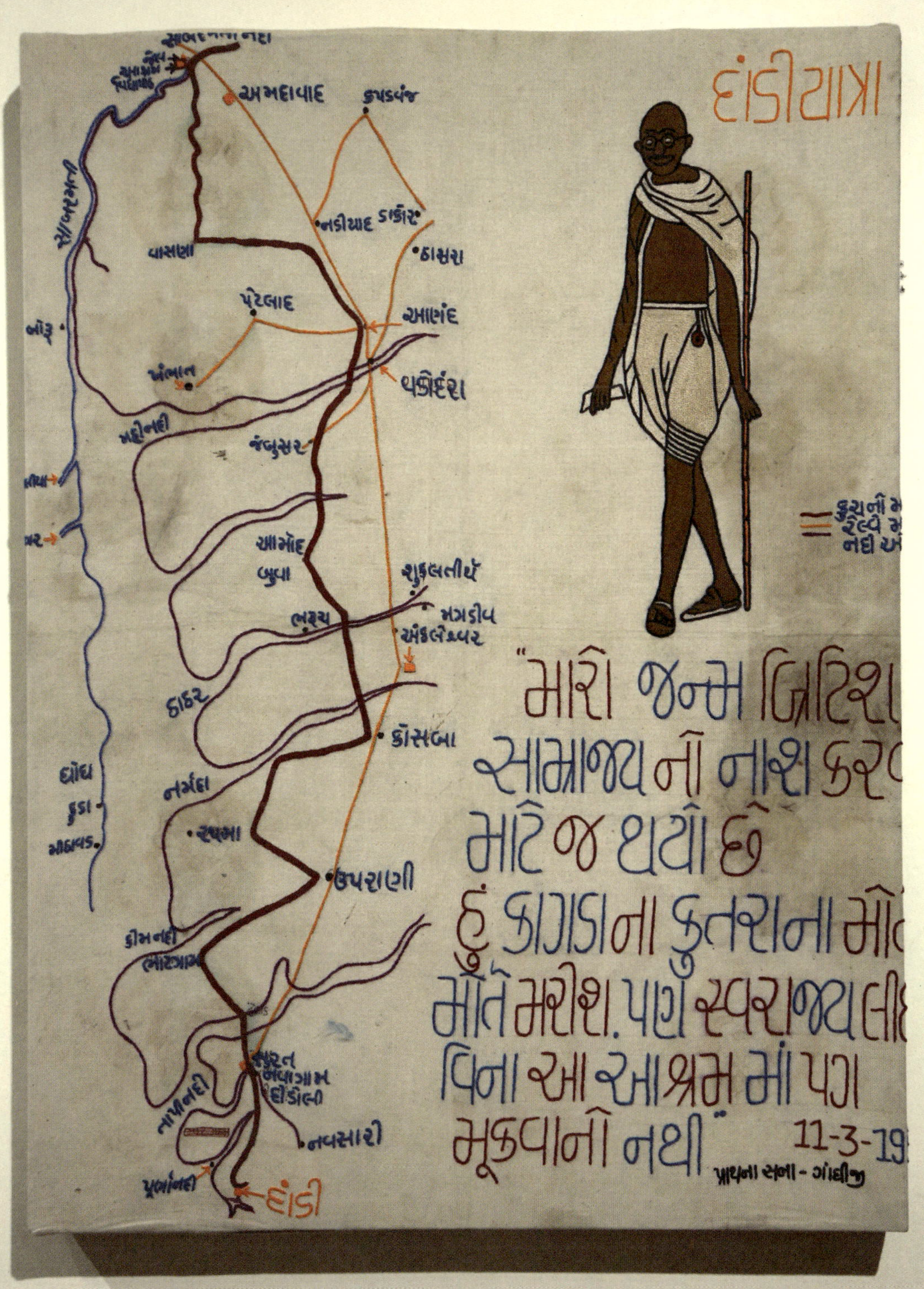

દાંડીયાત્રા
અમદાવાદ
કપડવંજ
નડીઆદ
વાસણા
આણંદ
ખંભાત
મહીનદી
જંબુસર
આમોદ
શુકલતીર્થ
ભરૂચ
અંકલેશ્વર
નર્મદા
કીમનદી
સુરત
નવસારી
દાંડી
"મારો જન્મ બ્રિટિશ
સામ્રાજ્ય નો નાશ કર
માટે જ થયો છે
હું કાગડાના કુતરાના મો
મોતે મરીશ. પણ સ્વરાજ્ય લી
વિના આ આશ્રમ માં પગ
મૂકવાનો નથી"
11-3-19
પ્રાથના સભા - ગાંધીજી

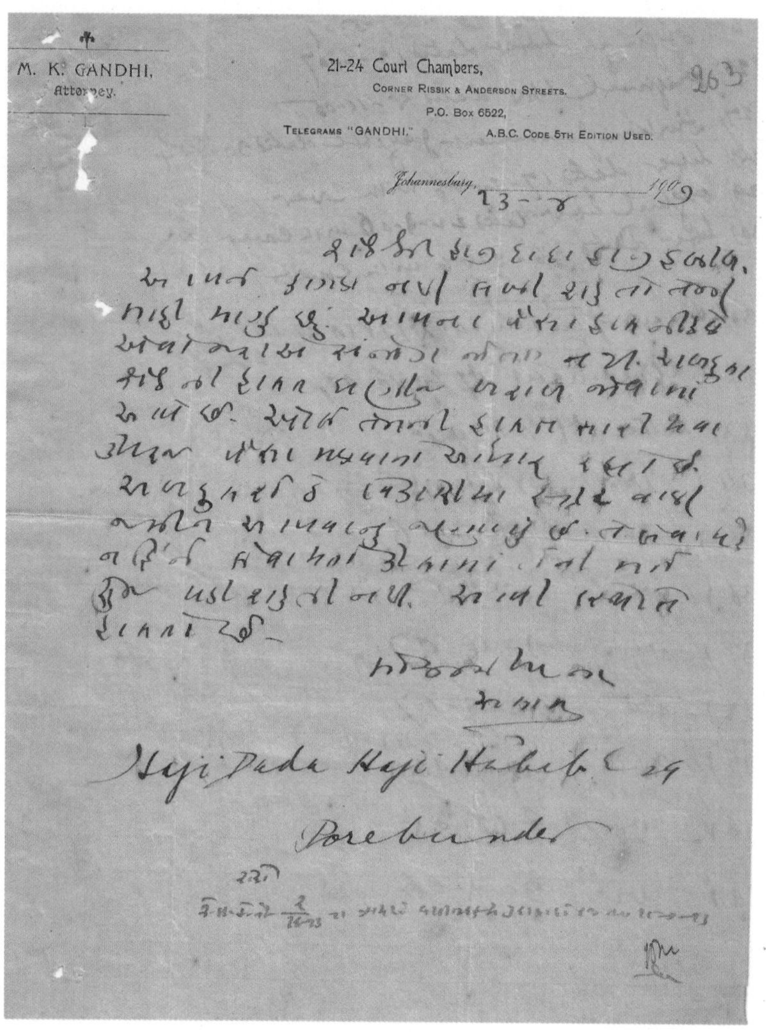

M. K. GANDHI,
Attorney.

21-24 Court Chambers,
Corner Rissik & Anderson Streets.
P.O. Box 6522,
Telegrams "GANDHI." A.B.C. Code 5th Edition Used.

Johannesburg, 13-8 1909

Haji Dada Haji Habib & Co
Porebunder

Mahatma Gandhi's handwritten letter, 1909, Johannesburg

GANDHI

Culver Pictures, Inc.
150 West 22nd Street
Suite 300
New York, New York 10011
(212) 645-1672

Culver Pictures
New York 16, N. Y.

This Picture is loaned for one reproduction only. Must not be used for advertising without written permission.

INDIAN LEADER OF NATIONALIST MOVEMENT.

MAHATMA GANDHI, leader of the Indian National Movement, who asks "Are English men and English women prepared to rely for the safety of their lives and property on the good will of the people, rather than on their gun mounted forts. "If they are not ready there is no dominion status that will satisfy me or my people..." states.

1860874

PE0063 CP007 019 People: FRO - GAR
Origin:Culver Pictures Inc Old# Print BW
Gandhi, Mohandas K. "Mahatma" (1869-1948) Indian nationalis
+ spiritual leader who practiced nonviolent disobedience.

JayParmo.com
QP178

141309

"The most valuable items in my collection are his ashes, his handwritten letters and copies of notes of his after-prayer sermons written by his personal assistants, which he later corrected in his own handwriting."

Kishore Jhunjhunwala

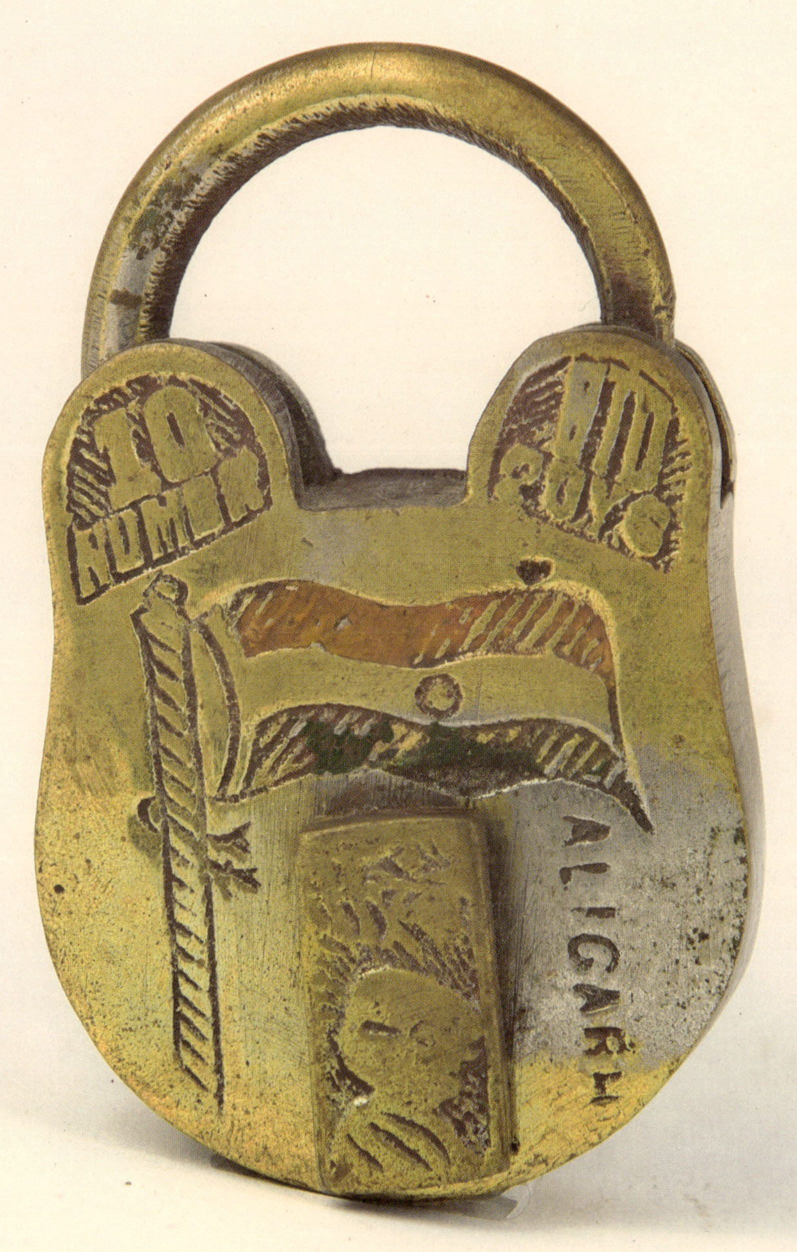
ALIGARH

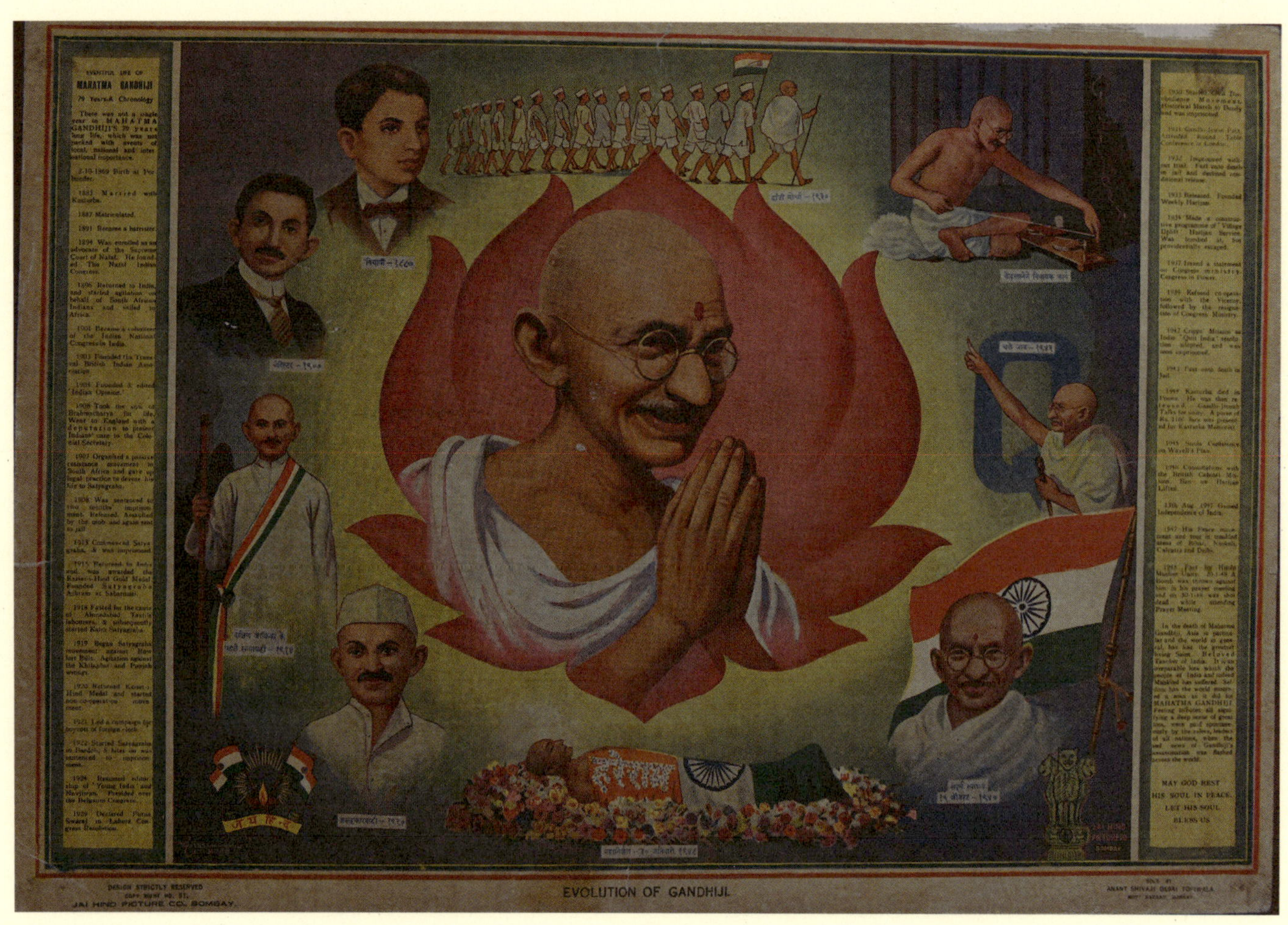

"Not since Buddha has India so revered any man….Not since St. Francis of Assisi has any life known to history been so marked by gentleness, disinterestedness, simplicity of soul and forgiveness of enemies…We have the astonishing phenomenon of a revolution led by a saint."

Will Durant

Writer

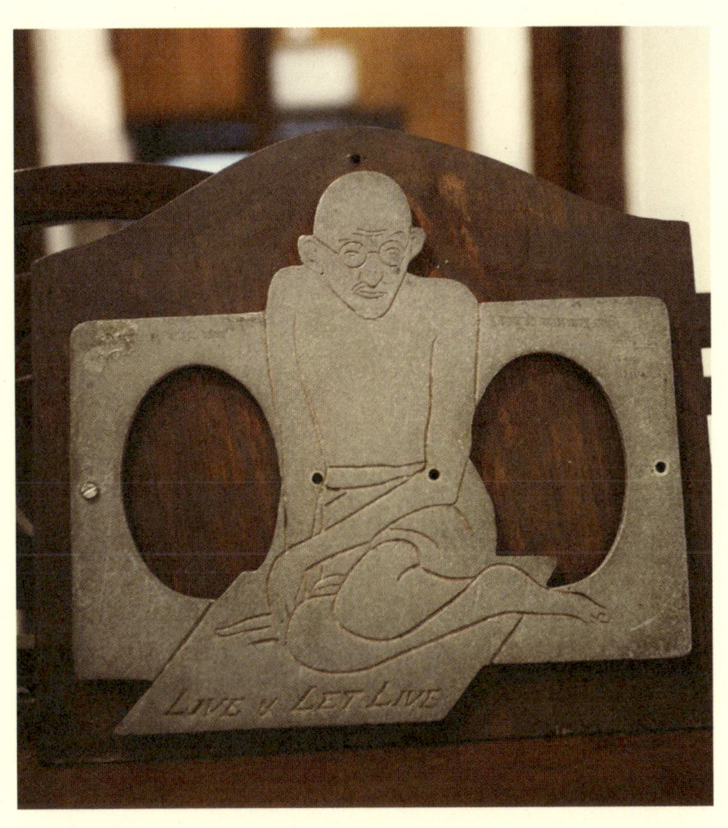
LIVE & LET LIVE

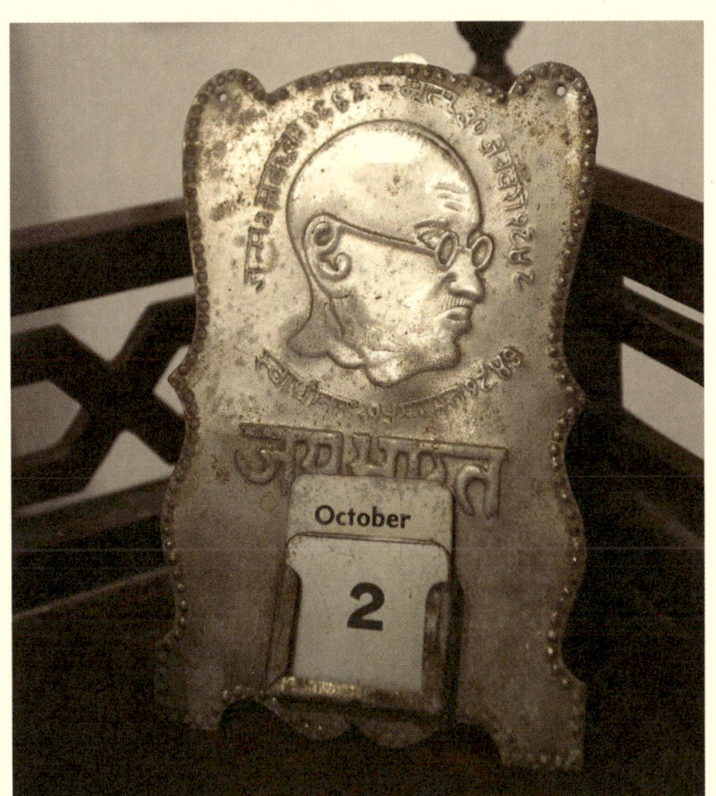
October
2

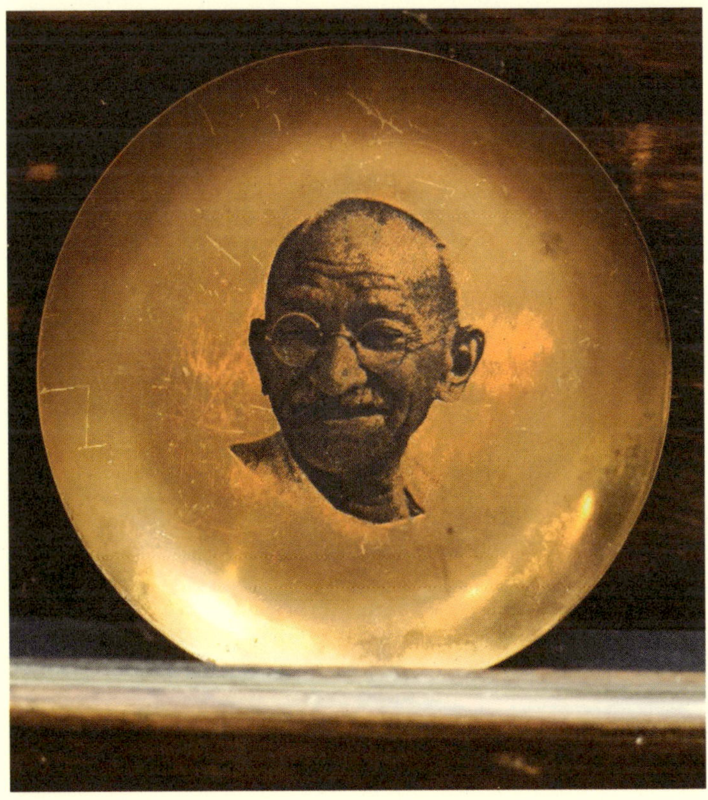

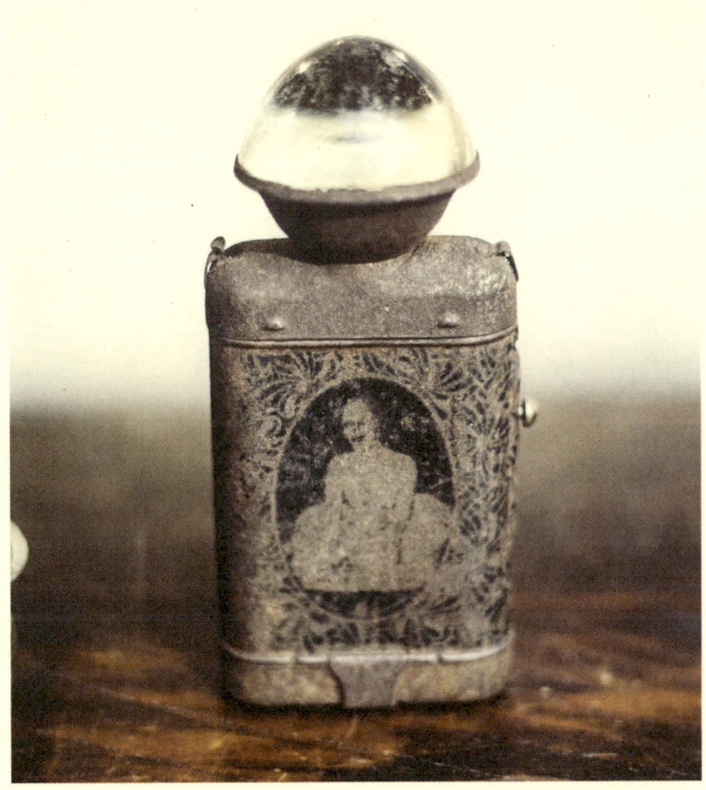

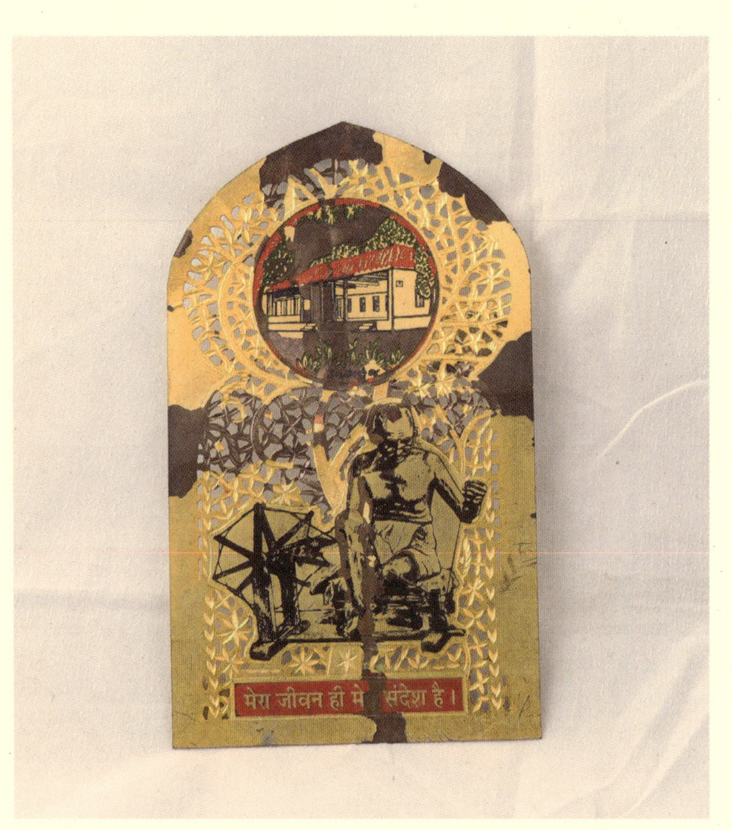
मेरा जीवन ही मे संदेश है।

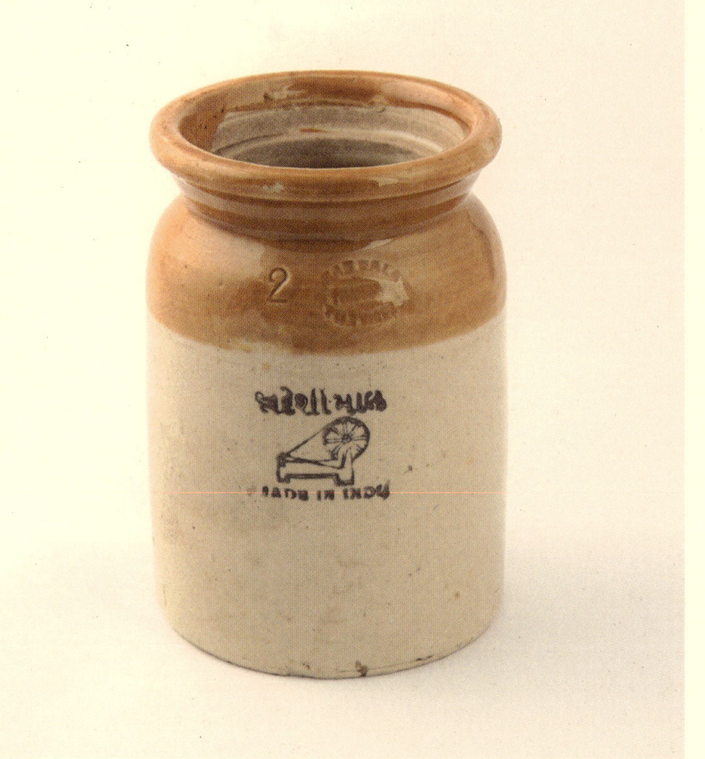

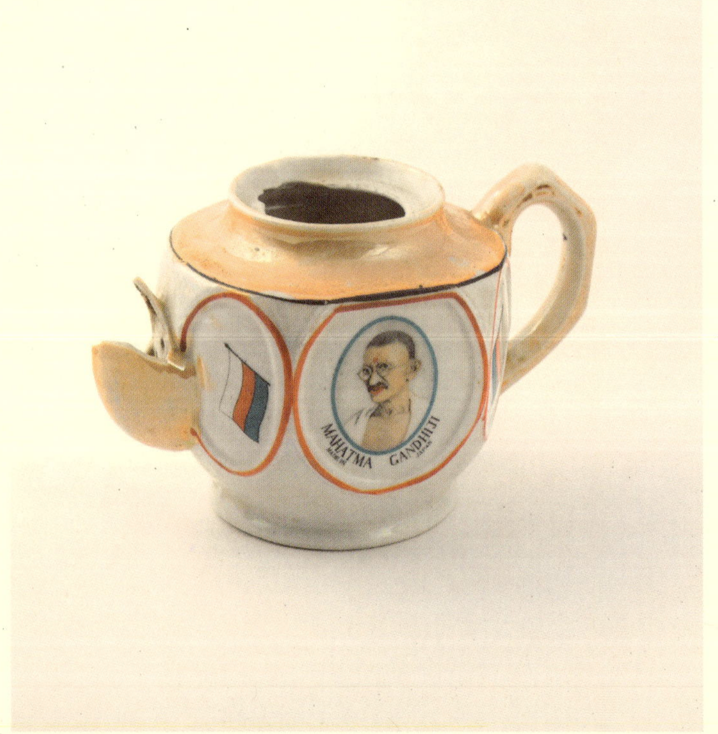
MAHATMA GANDHIJI

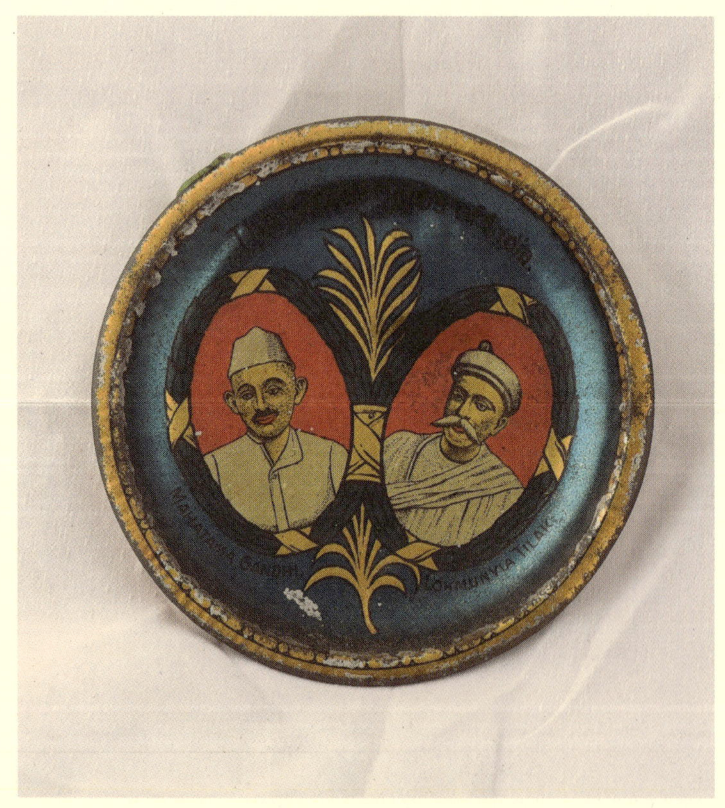
GANDHI
TILAK

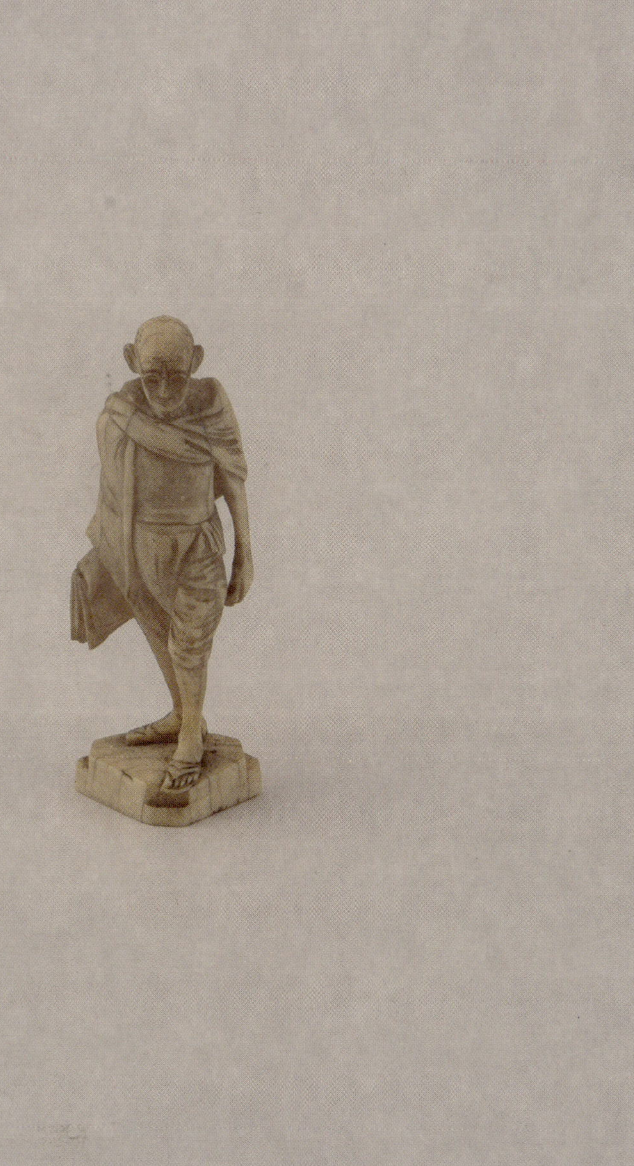

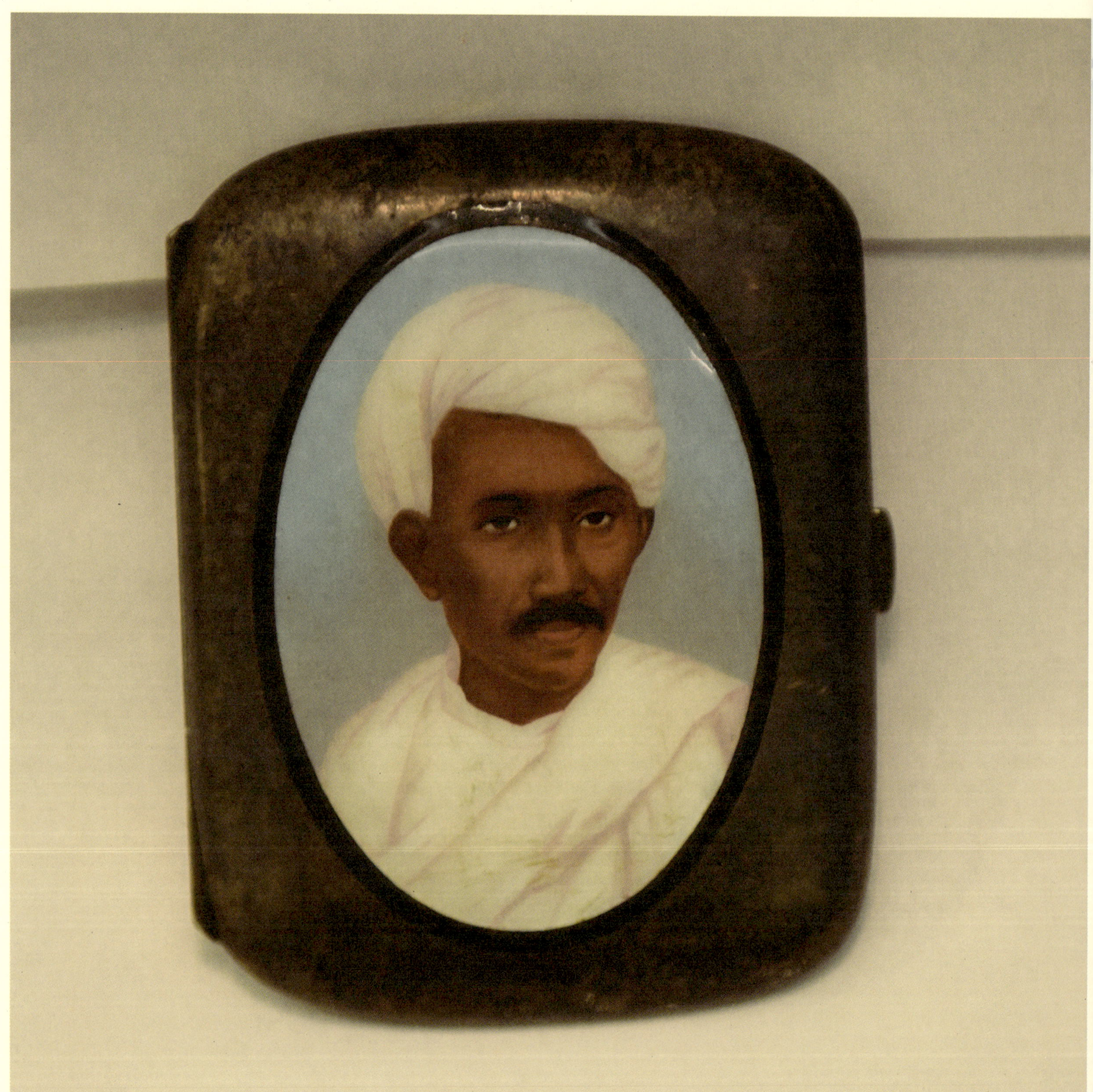

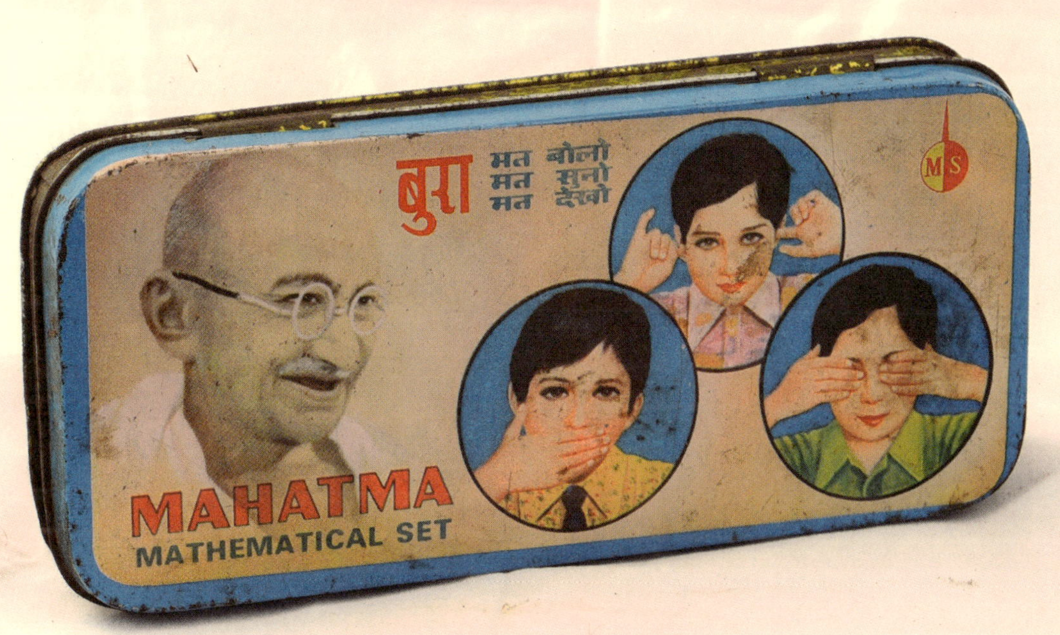
बुरा
मत बोलो
मत सुनो
मत देखो
MS
MAHATMA
MATHEMATICAL SET

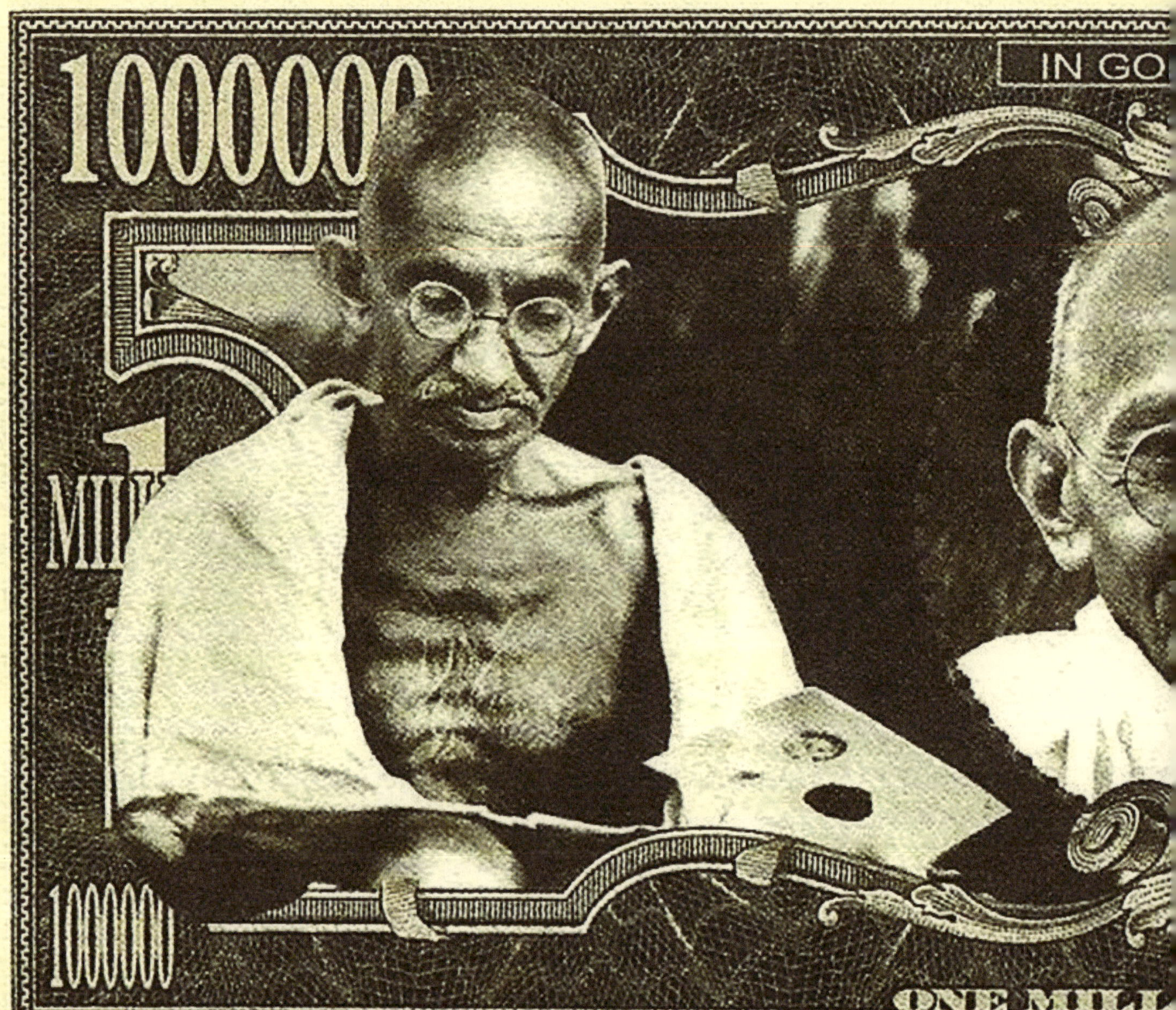

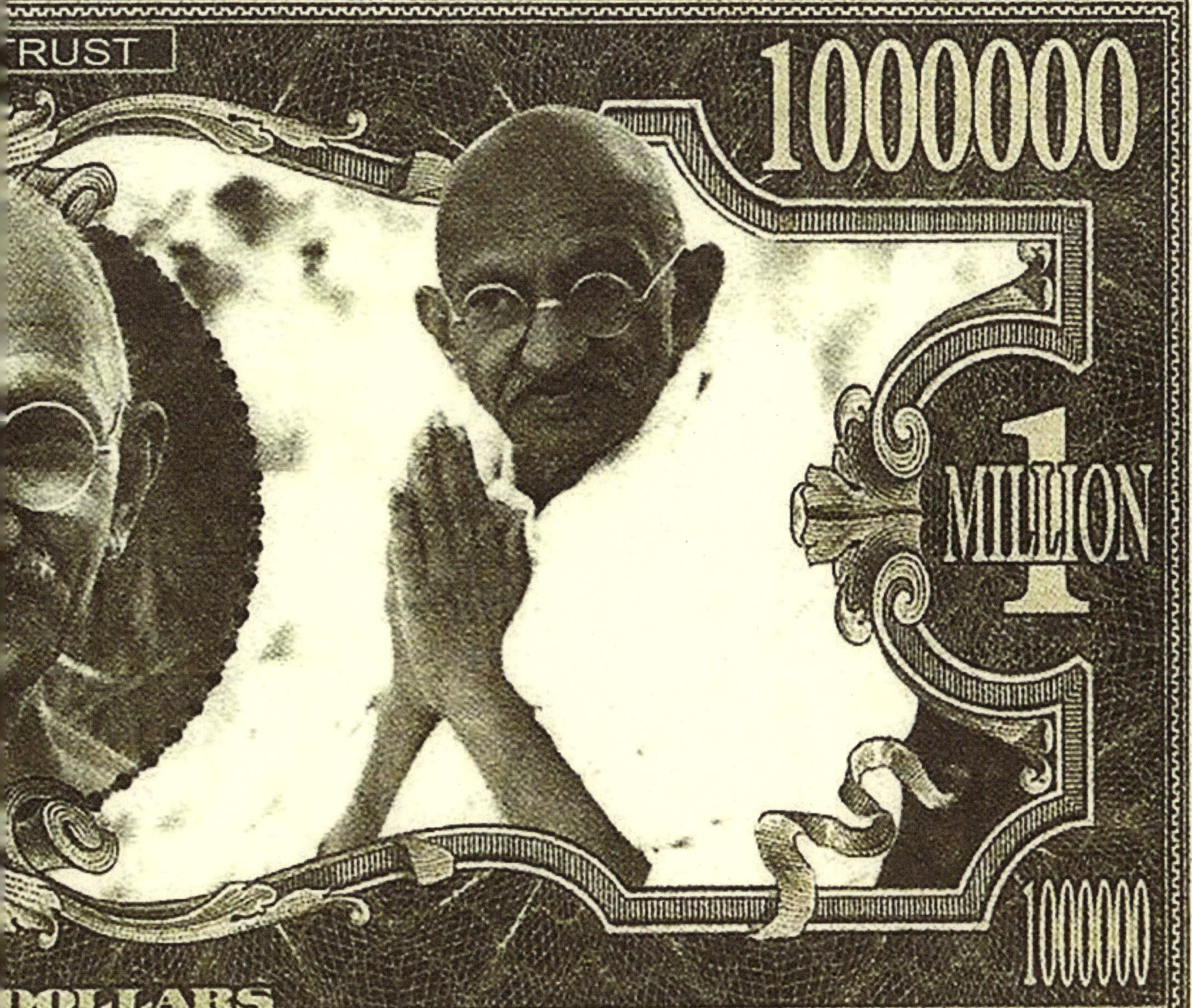
TRUST
1000000
1
MILLION
1
100000
DOLLARS

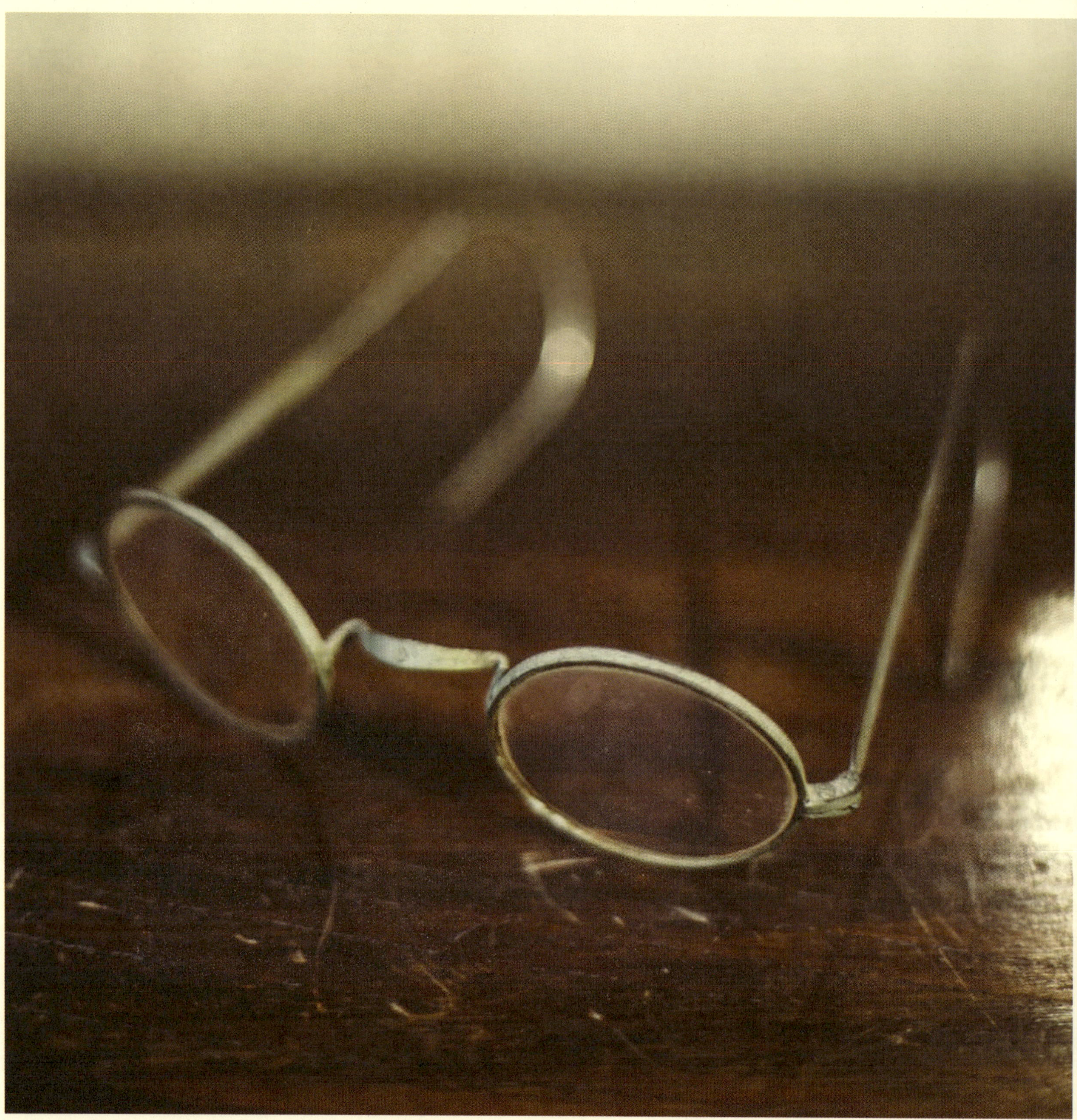

The sum of me
Is nothing but an attempt
To be
A mirror

कुल मिलाकर मेरा अक्स
सिर्फ शून्य का आभास
केवल एक प्रतिबिंब
केवल एक प्रयास

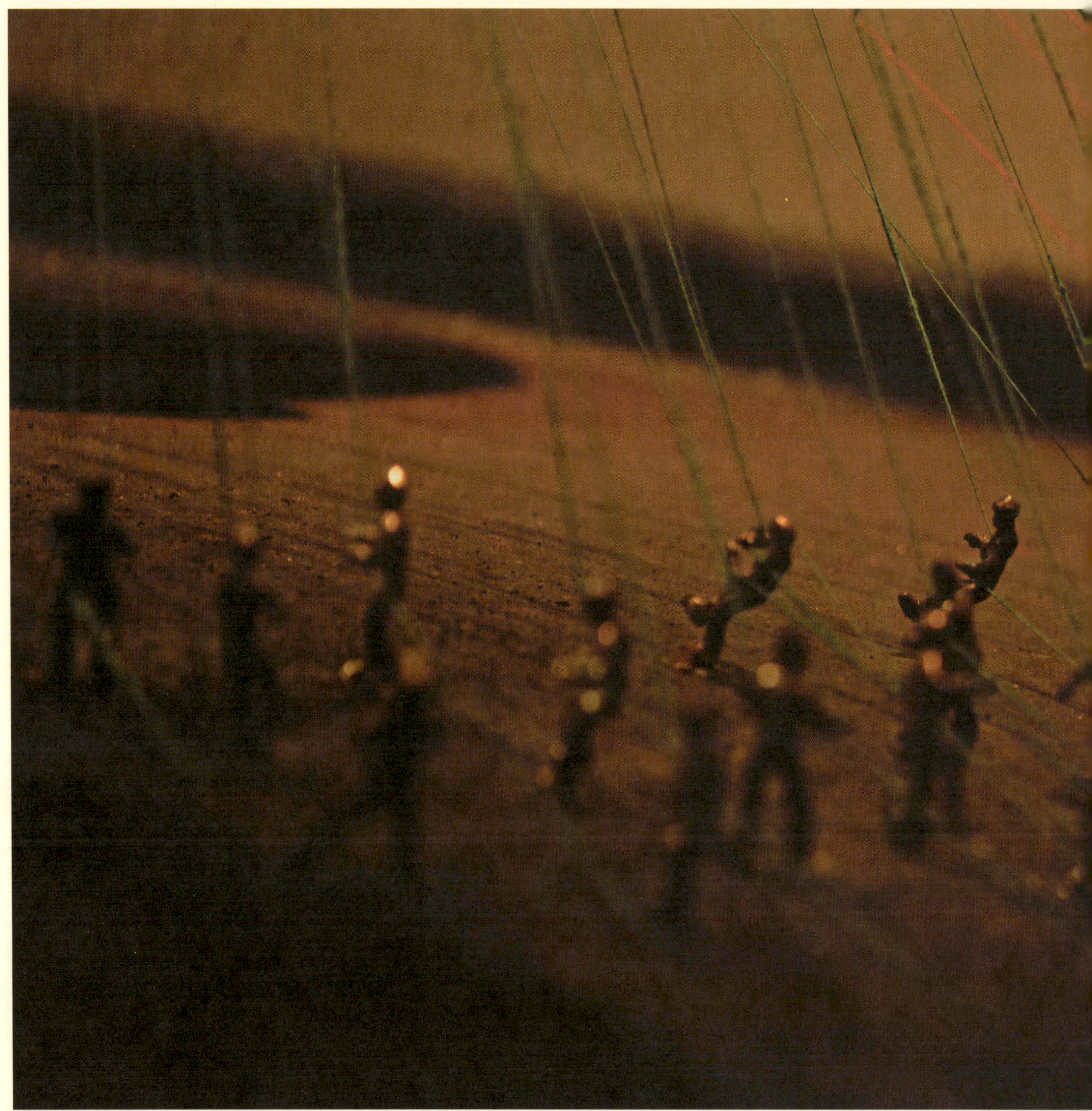

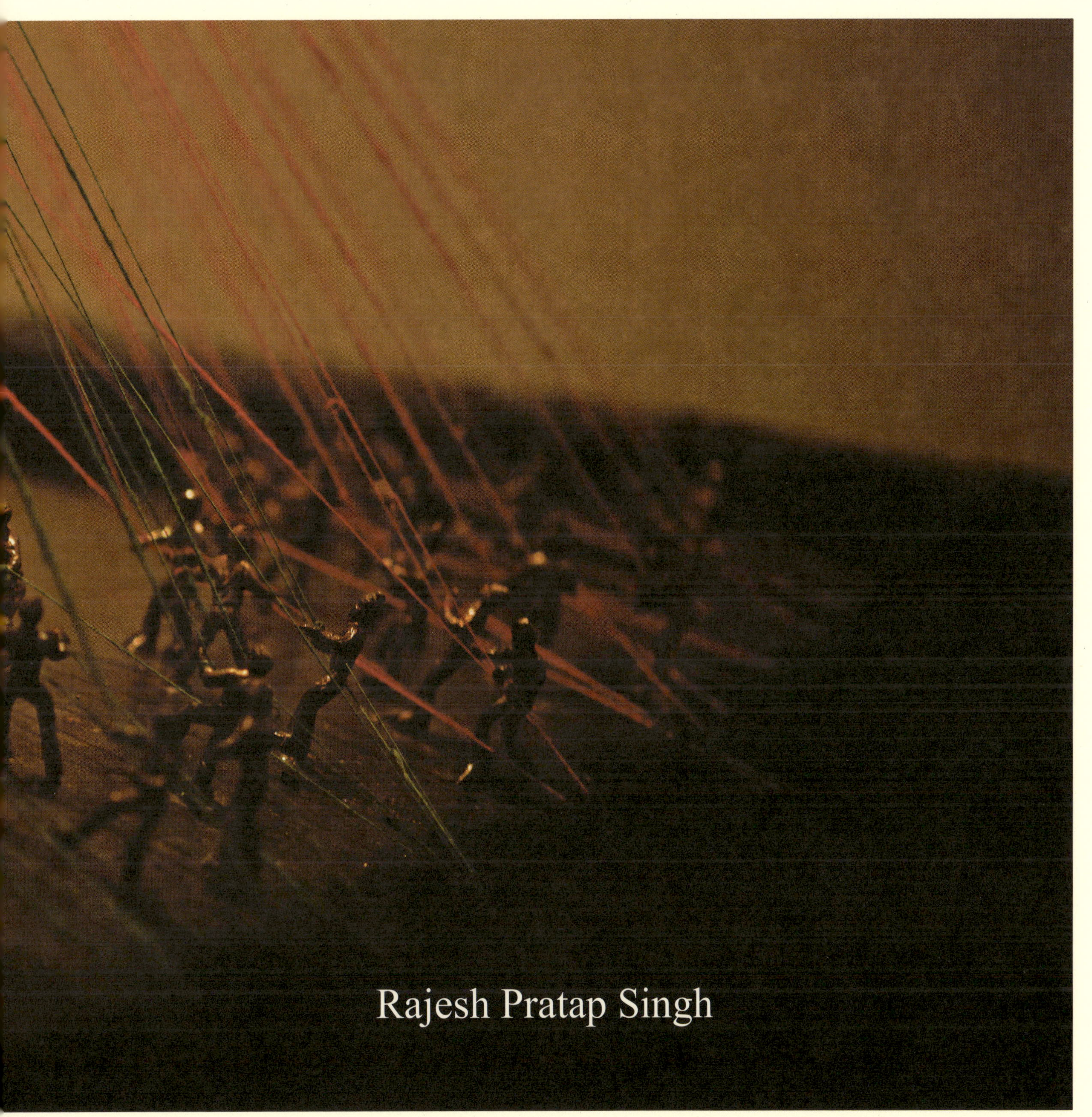
Rajesh Pratap Singh

Rajesh Pratap Singh

Designer

Rajesh Pratap Singh's work *Neel* is a study in how Mahatma Gandhi has been observed by the world. The liberal nature of Gandhi's ideas lent him a canvas-like quality, a canvas people felt free to draw on with the strokes of their own beliefs and perceptions. They kept trying to nail their Gandhi in the hope of justifying their various wishes for and from India. They tilted him to suit their inclinations.

He remained however, a giant force with a vision always vaster than the pettiness of personal motives. His struggle and victory for the indigo farmers of Champaran was one of many in his battle of "Right against Might". The pool of indigo is belief, is heat, is churning, and also a reminder of the dark, regurgitated hurdles that will inevitably line the way of those who walk the path of Truth.

Rajesh Pratap Singh is respected for his distinctive design language that subtly draws from Indian roots to craft artisanal garments. A delicate and detailed balance of clean lines and complex concepts has lent his work noted appeal. Closely associated with Indian fabric mills, Rajesh Pratap's work in textile experimentation spans both, the very high-tech as well as the deeply traditional.

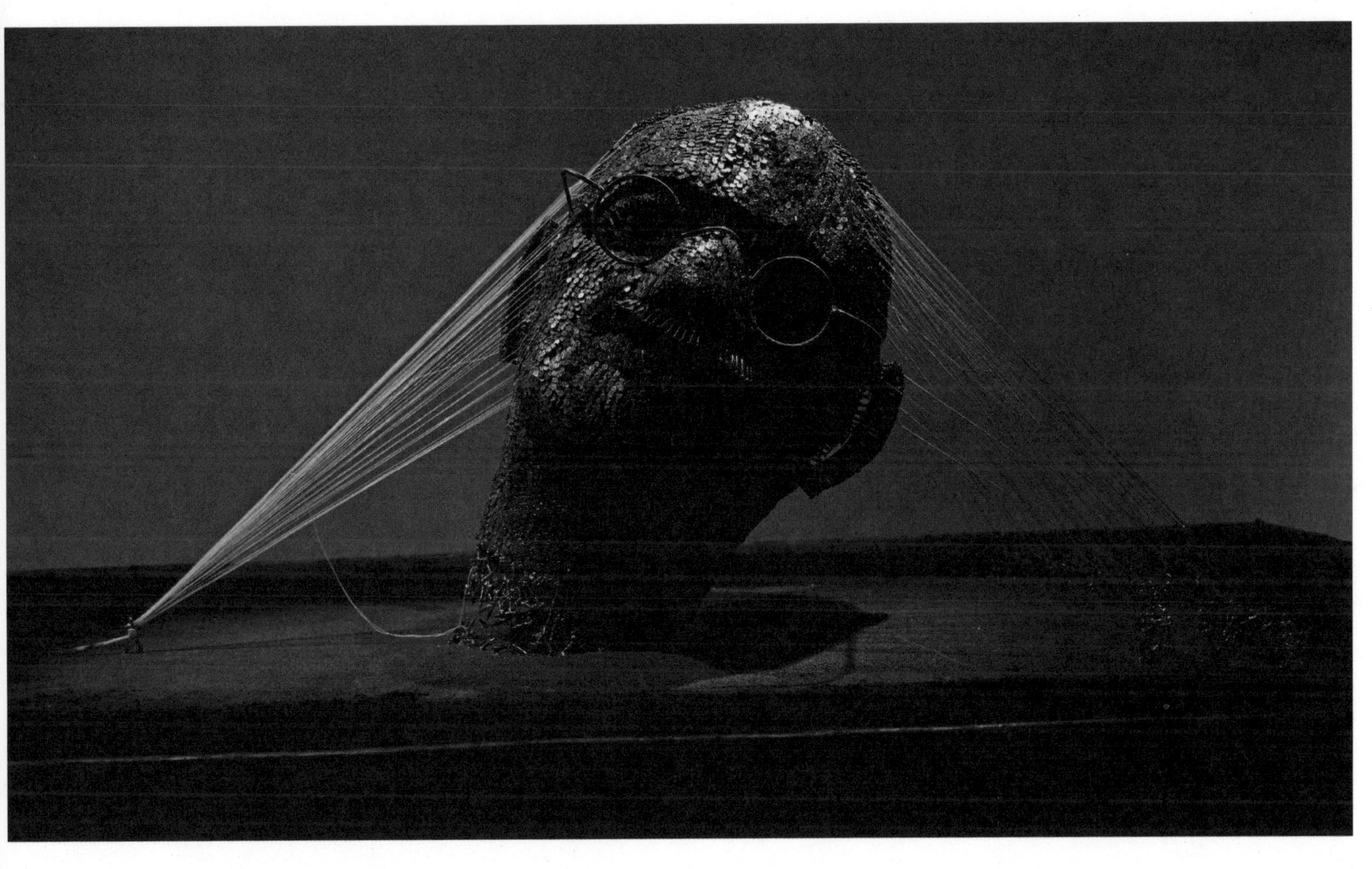

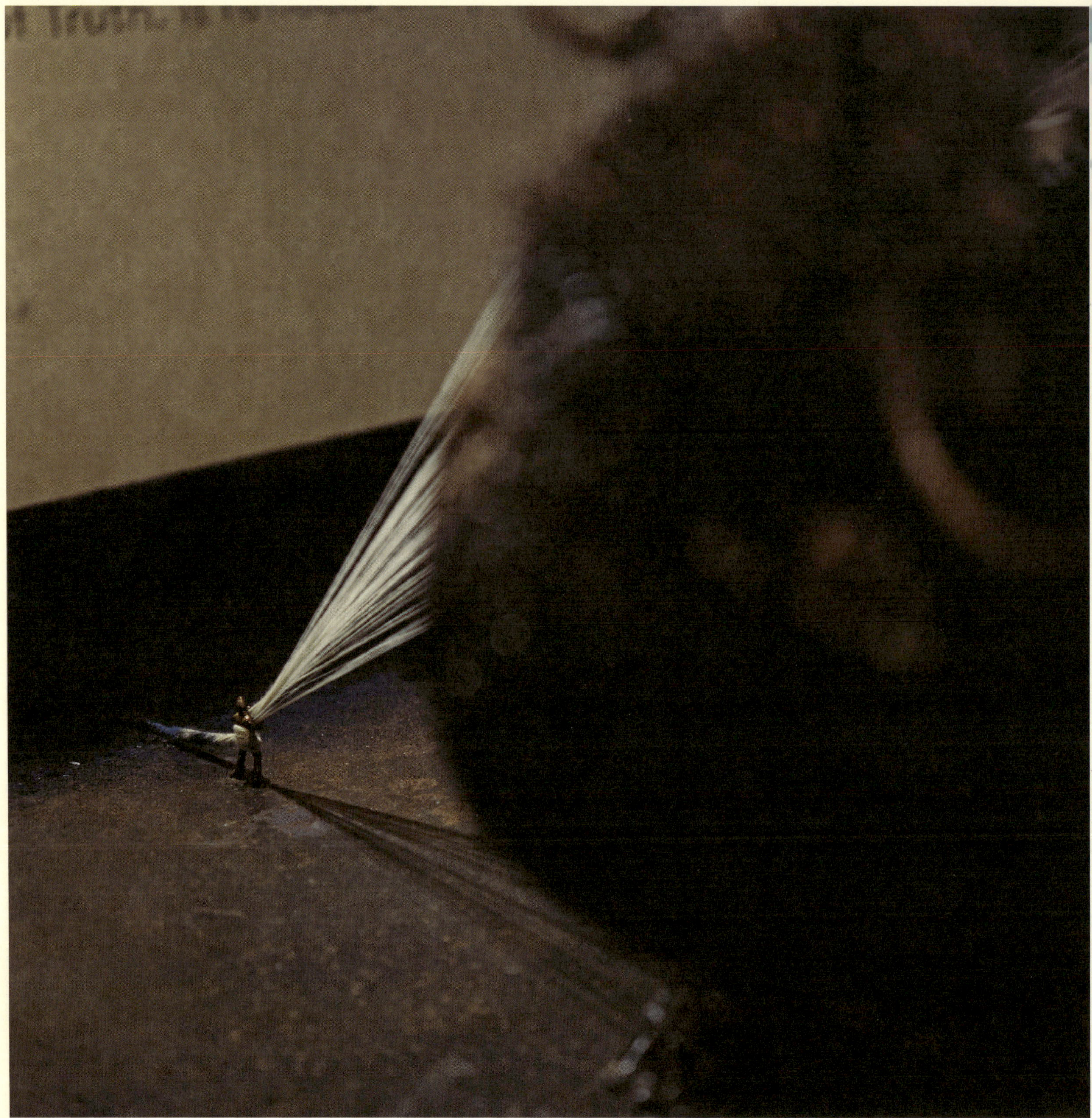

"Impressions of Gandhi? You might as well ask for someone's impression of the Himalayas."

George Bernard Shaw

Playwright

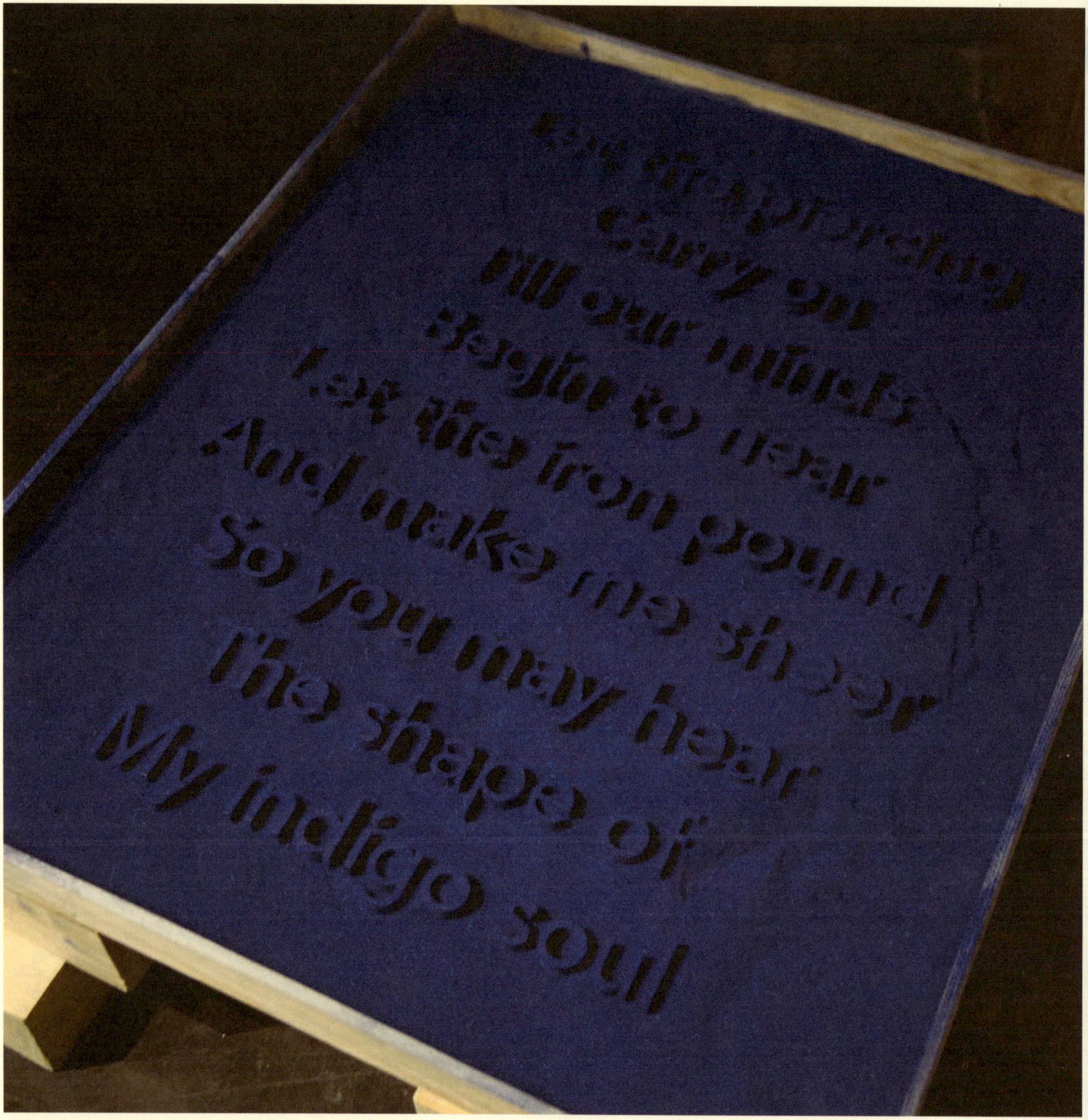

So you may hear
The shape of
My indigo soul

Let the piercing
Carry on
Till our minds
Begin to near
Let the iron pound
And make me sheer
So you may hear
The shape of
My indigo soul

सोच मिले जब तक
जारी रहे चुभन
अहम पिघले तब तक
तेज रहे तपन
फिर शायद खोज पाऊं
अंतरंग में बसा, नीला
आत्मन

"Truth means existing at all times."

Mahatma Gandhi

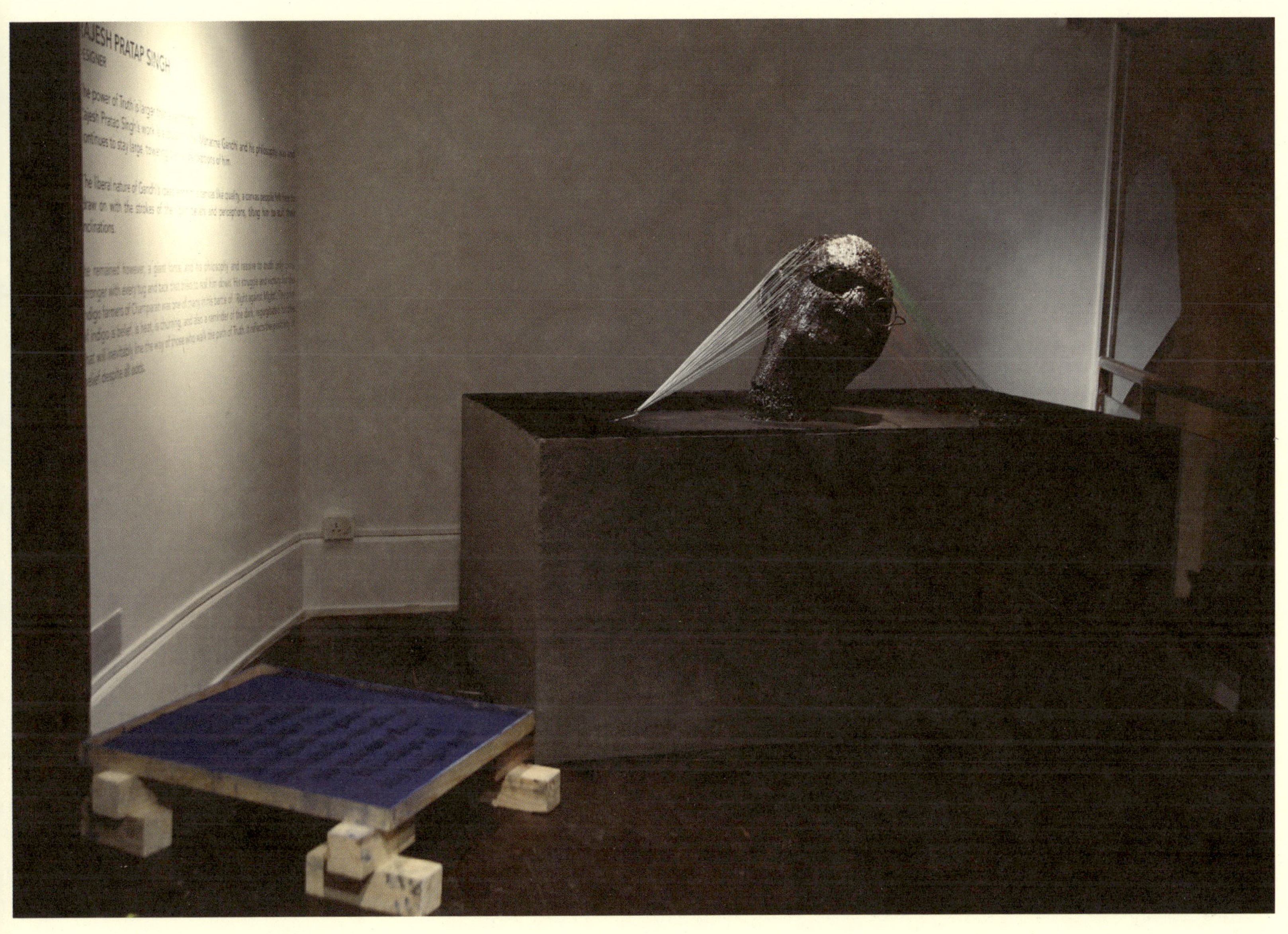

"Mahatma Gandhi's message is like an anchored axis one can keep returning to when pulled by the world in myriad ways."

Rajesh Pratap Singh

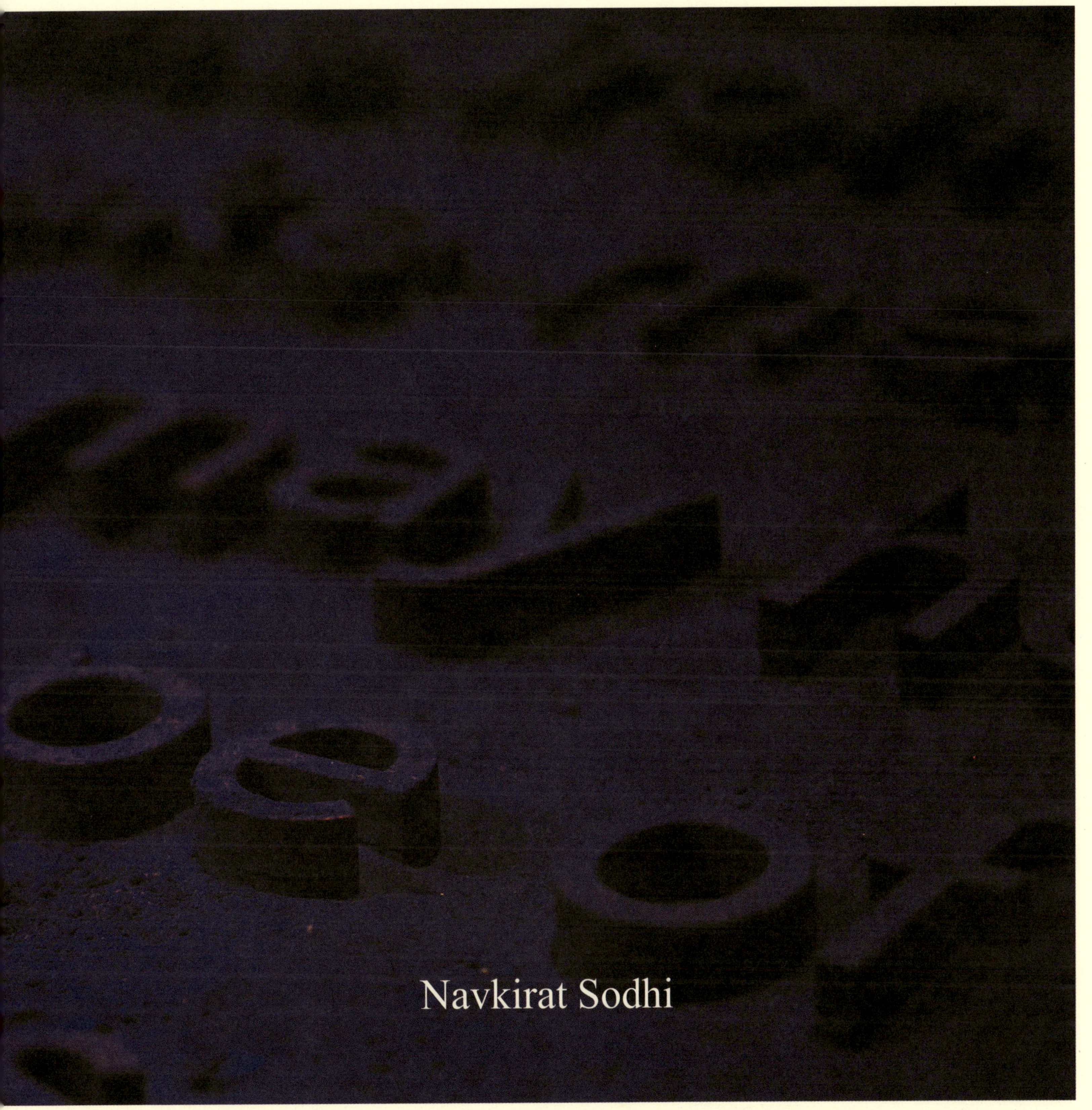
Navkirat Sodhi

Navkirat Sodhi

Poet

Navkirat Sodhi contributes to Santati by writing words and verses for the exposition. She pays her tribute with experiential poetry written around the spiritual and philosophical significance of Mahatma Gandhi's messages.

Navkirat Sodhi writes on the lust for knowing, on existential love, on travel and art. She believes poetry lives outside of pages. Visual stories told through verse and live performances have helped extend the boundaries of her expression.

There are holes
Carved in me
By the history
Today will become
It is riddled by the hunger
Of those who are full

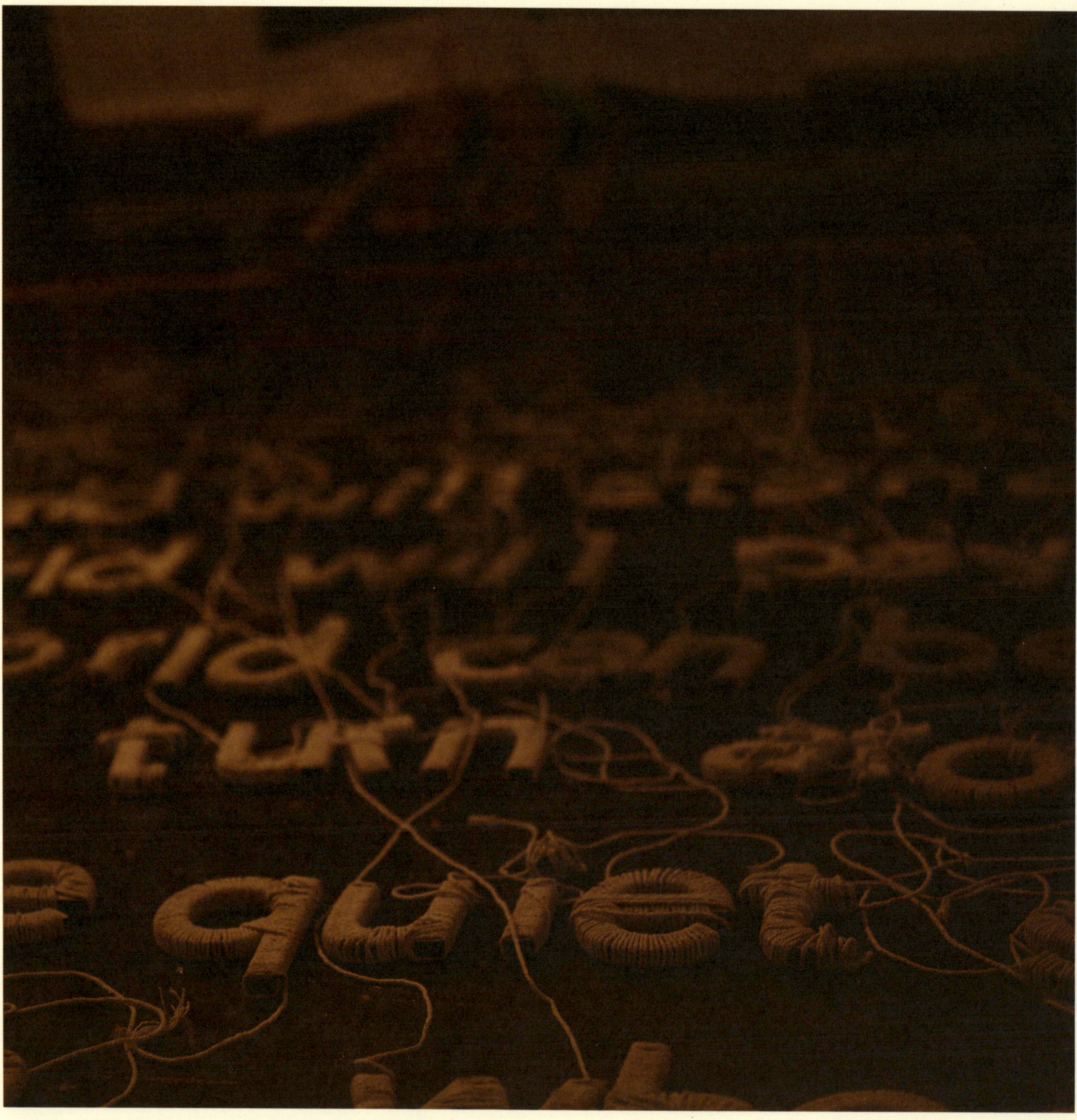
turn
quiet

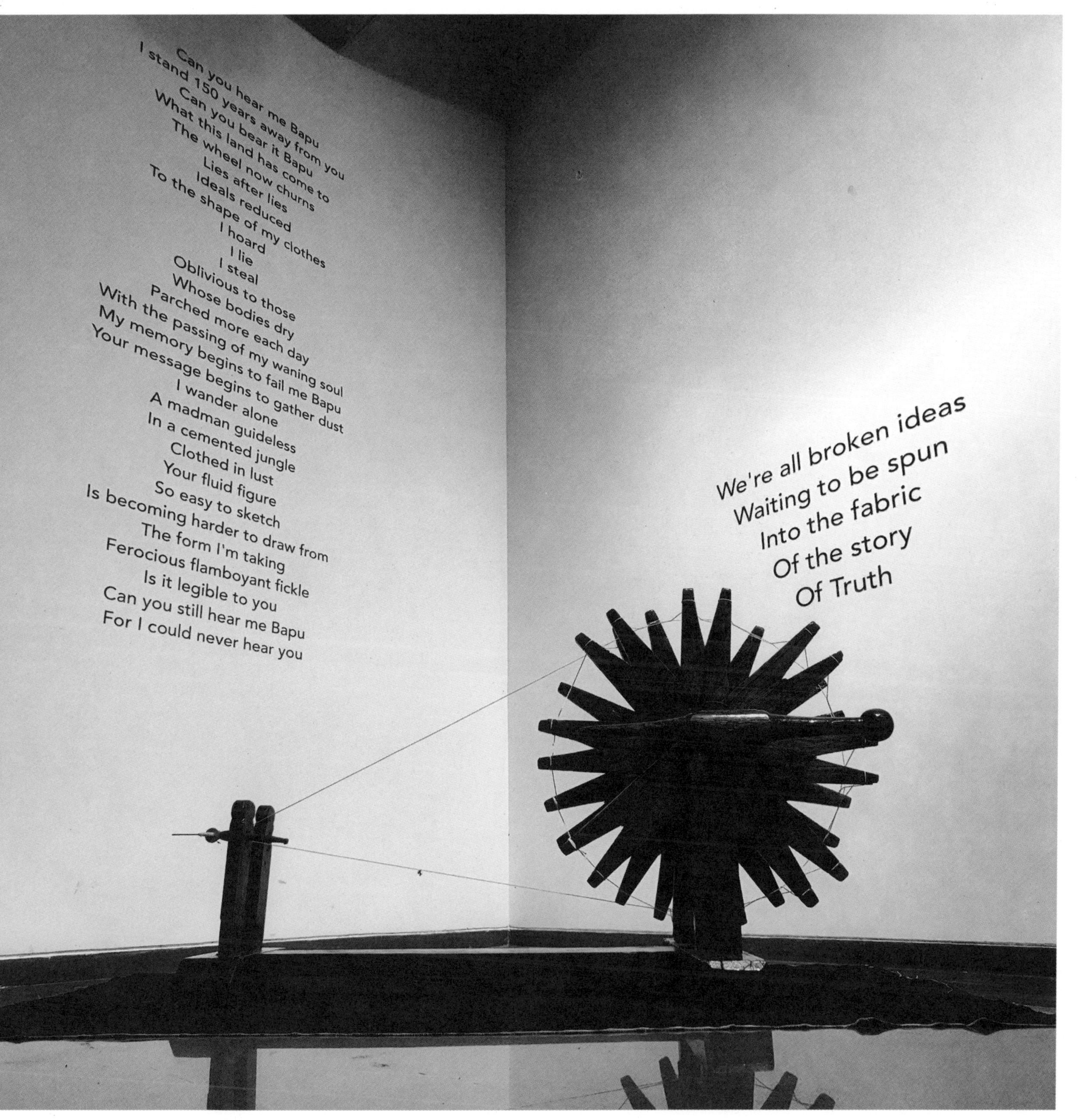
Can you hear me Bapu
I stand 150 years away from you
Can you bear it Bapu
What this land has come to
The wheel now churns
Lies after lies
Ideals reduced
To the shape of my clothes
I hoard
I lie
I steal
Oblivious to those
Whose bodies dry
Parched more each day
With the passing of my waning soul
My memory begins to fail me Bapu
Your message begins to gather dust
I wander alone
A madman guideless
In a cemented jungle
Clothed in lust
Your fluid figure
So easy to sketch
Is becoming harder to draw from
The form I'm taking
Ferocious flamboyant fickle
Is it legible to you
Can you still hear me Bapu
For I could never hear you
We're all broken ideas
Waiting to be spun
Into the fabric
Of the story
Of Truth

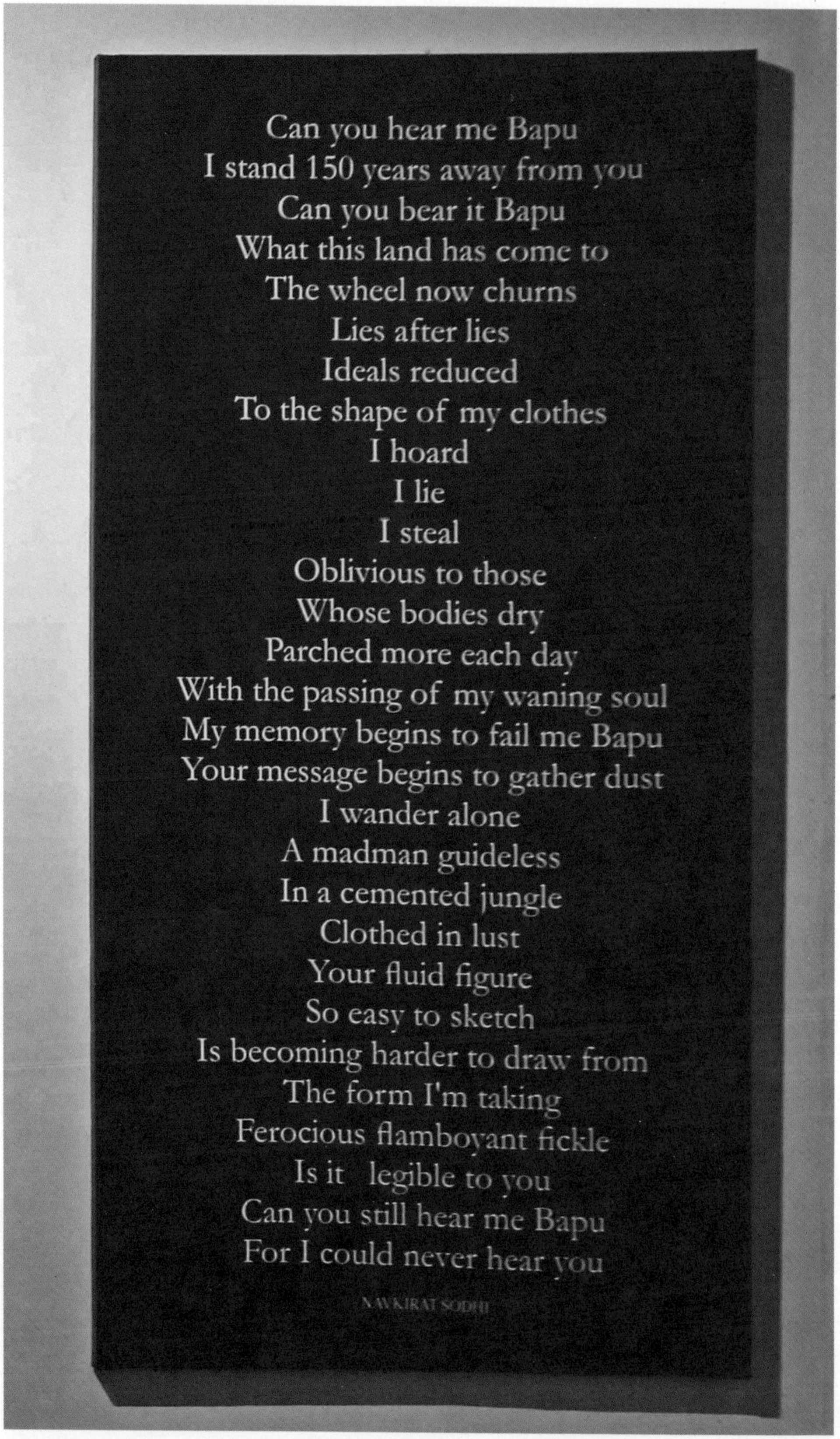

Can you hear me Bapu
I stand 150 years away from you
Can you bear it Bapu
What this land has come to
The wheel now churns
Lies after lies
Ideals reduced
To the shape of my clothes
I hoard
I lie
I steal
Oblivious to those
Whose bodies dry
Parched more each day
With the passing of my waning soul
My memory begins to fail me Bapu
Your message begins to gather dust
I wander alone
A madman guideless
In a cemented jungle
Clothed in lust
Your fluid figure
So easy to sketch
Is becoming harder to draw from
The form I'm taking
Ferocious flamboyant fickle
Is it legible to you
Can you still hear me Bapu
For I could never hear you

NAVKIRAT SODHI

“Insofar as we have made the modern materialistic craze our goal, we are going downhill on the path of progress.”

Mahatma Gandhi

"I cannot think of permanent enmity between man and man, and believing as I do in the theory of rebirth, I live in the hope that, if not in this birth, in some other birth, I shall be able to hug all humanity in friendly embrace."

Mahatma Gandhi

NEXT

If there is a will
To climb uphill
The mountain presents itself

A mountain that has studied
Your stamina
Your trajectory
It knows how shallow how steep
Lie the crests of your determination
And presents your path
With equal parts
Stinging and balm

It carries in its heart
The same map you hold within
Where future intersects with the past
To show you at every altitude
The very vast distance you travelled
Thirsty to become "me"

You might find some water at the peak
If you carry on

Drink it carefully
It is believed
To turn off your hallucinations
Show you that you still stand
So still at the base
That it's not
At its top
But deep in its heart
Where the mountain holds
Its peak

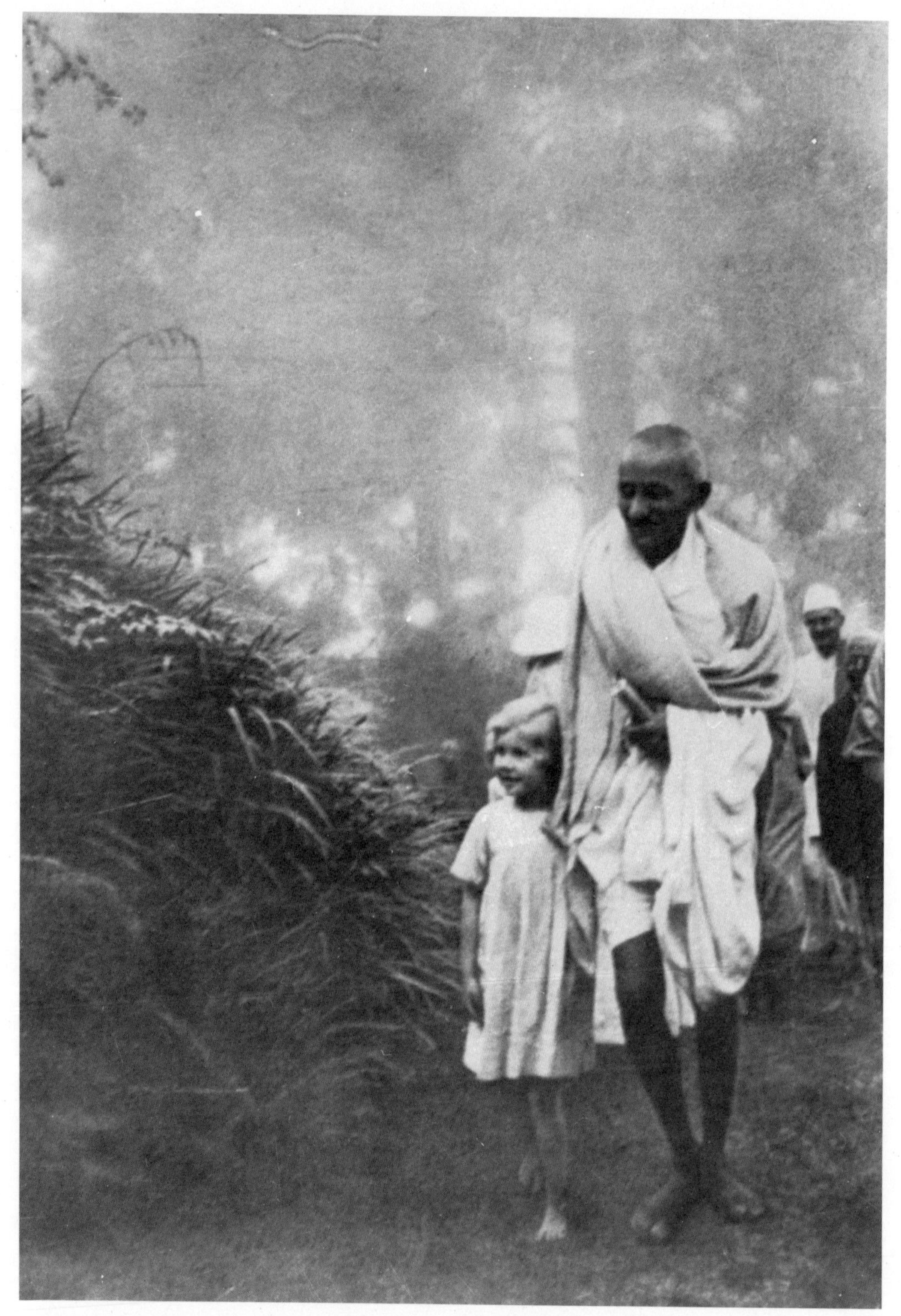

Keep walking
Till you know
This journey knows
No end

न थमें
न ठहरें
बस चलते रहें
जब तक ज्ञात न हो
इस पथ की इति
है क्षितिज से परे

Opposite:
Mahatma Gandhi in Simla before departing for the Round Table Conference in England
Simla, 1931 // National Gandhi Museum Archives

AS IF LAID OUT FOR US LIKE A BLUEPRINT, there are messages and indications in Mahatma Gandhi's words which seem to hold prophetic truths about our future, about the next. They exist not to comfort us but to rattle our perceptions, to ask tougher questions, to exit the personal and enter the cosmic "me". They warn us of the precarious spiral that stands before us, ready to devour, without exception.

The present world is proof.

Gandhi's legacy goes deeper than a socio-political movement. It serves as a trigger for a personal and imperative churning of which, the entire fight and struggle for freedom was just the beginning.

"No one is too old to grow, certainly not I."

Mahatma Gandhi

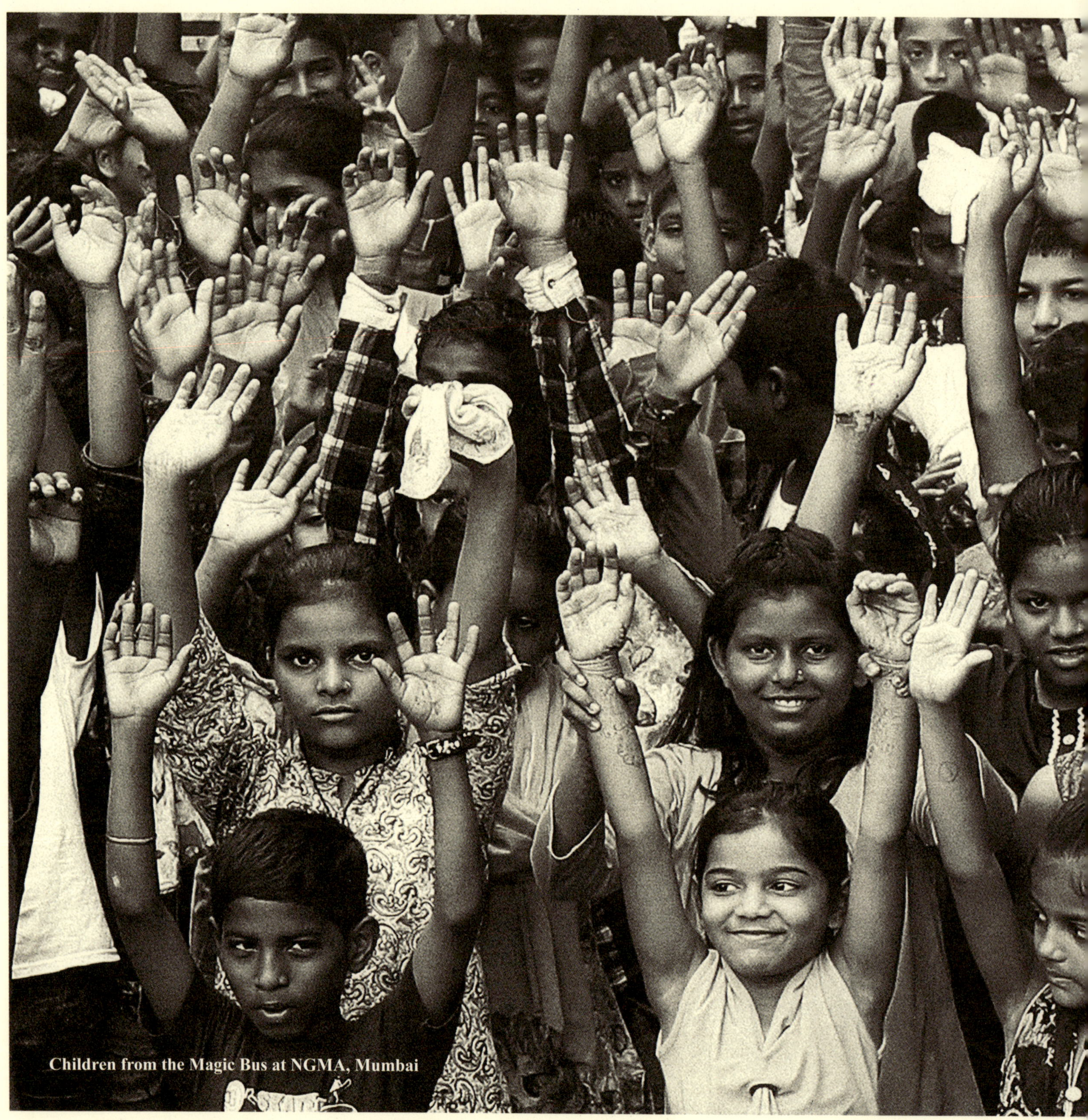

Children from the Magic Bus at NGMA, Mumbai

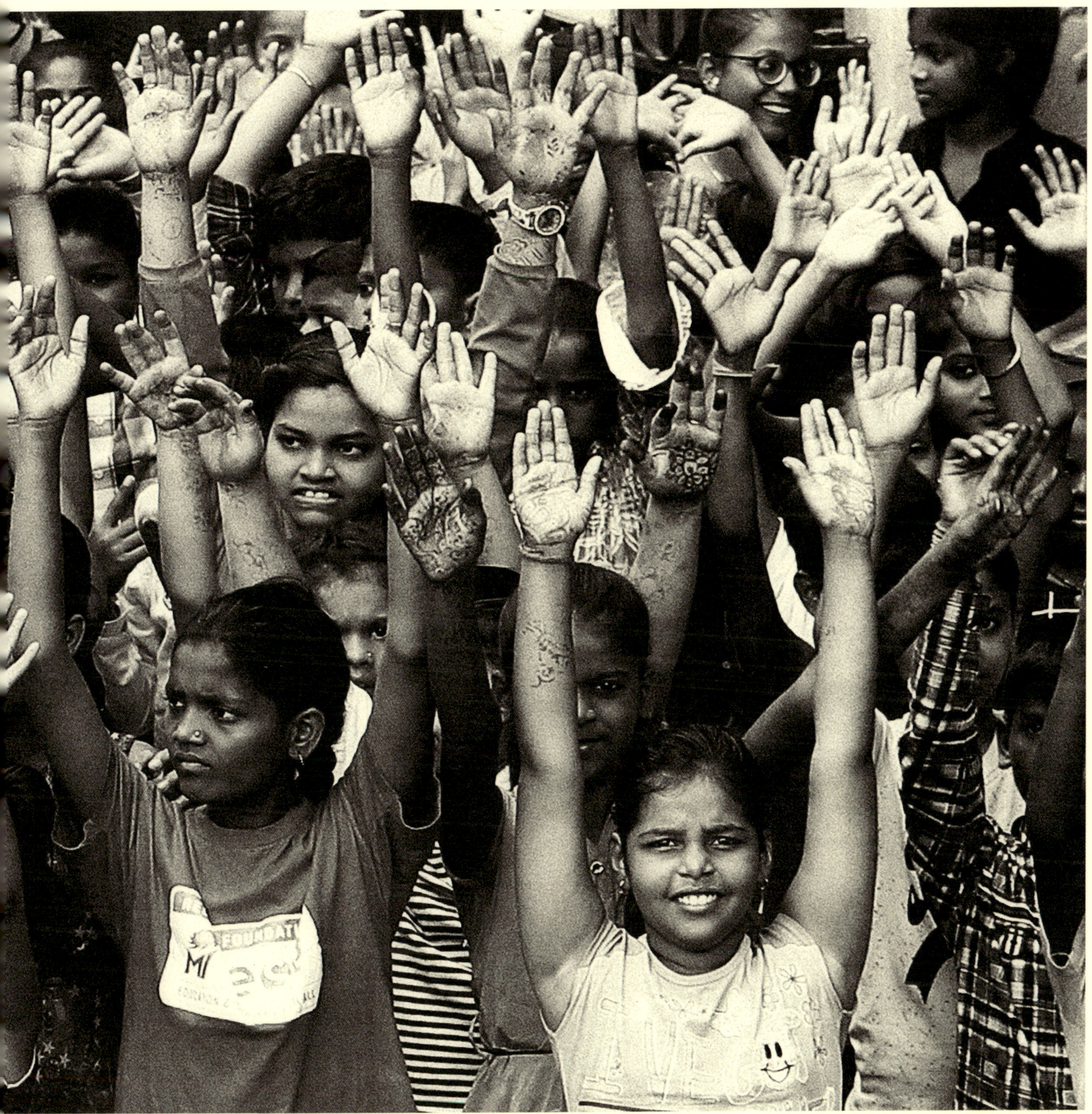

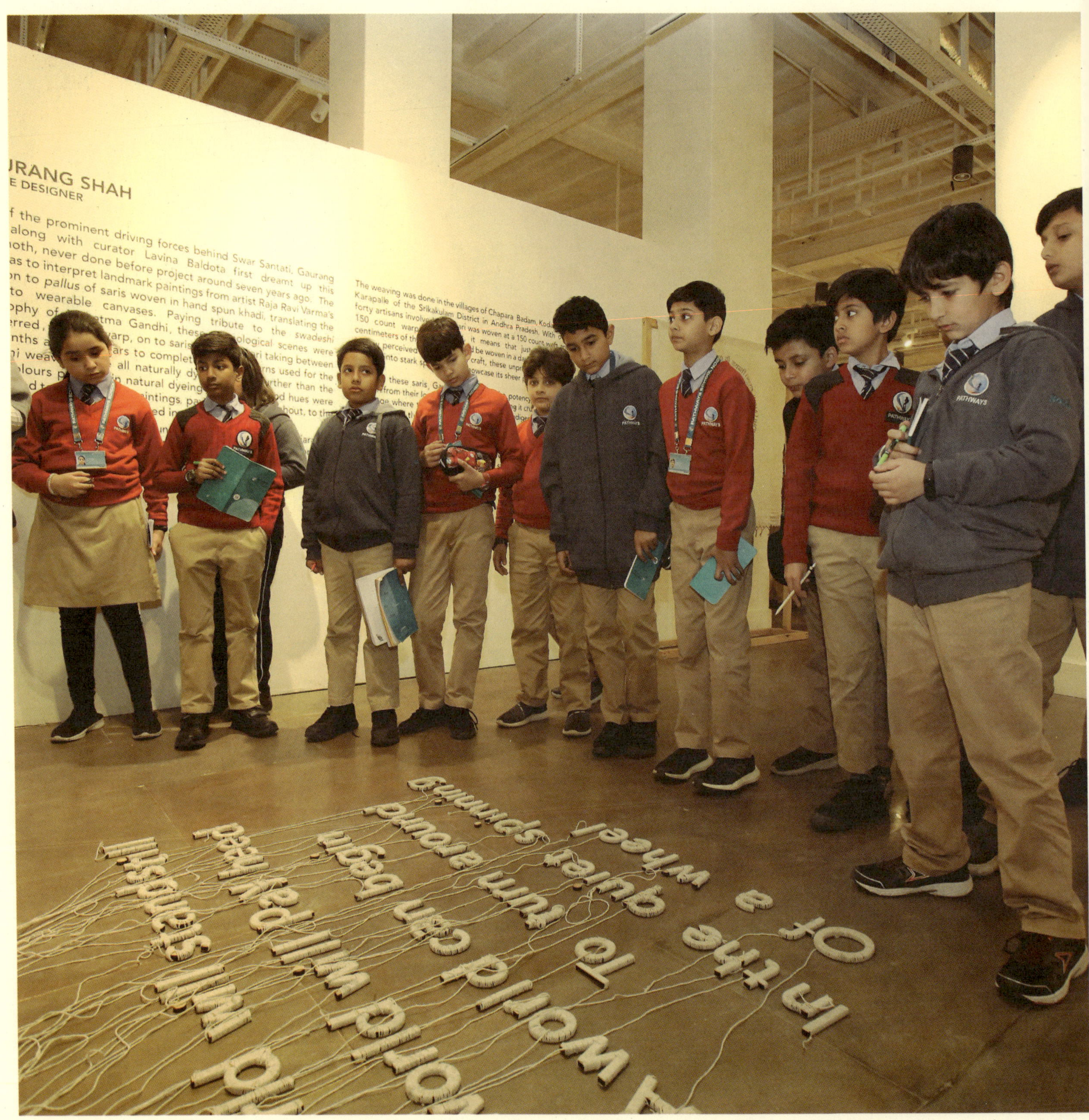
URANG SHAH
E DESIGNER
f the prominent driving forces behind Swar Santati, Gaurang
along with curator Lavina Baldota first dreamt up this
noth, never done before project around seven years ago. The
as to interpret landmark paintings from artist Raja Ravi Varma's
on to pallus of saris woven in hand spun khadi, translating the
to wearable canvases. Paying tribute to the swadeshi
The weaving was done in the villages of Chapara Badam, Koda
Karapalle of the Srikakulam District in Andhra Pradesh.

The verse accompanying Gaurang Shah's handwoven paintings on saris says

A world will stand still
A world will pay heed
A world can begin
To turn around
In the quiet spinning
Of a wheel

At the outset, Gaurang's work ethic founded on Mahatma Gandhi's ideal of swadeshi, might seem Utopian for a world that was hitherto moving with relentlessly rapid motion. However, as the spread of a global pandemic caused by the Corona Virus increases, economies are likely to be forced to plan and employ alternatives. Unless the world emerges from this lockdown unchanged, unaffected and heads towards a further downward trial, it can reap positively from the economic map laid down by Mahatma Gandhi. His progressive, futuristic and simplistic plans can help shape an economy which not only sustains itself prosperously but also holds the capacity to supply indigenous art, craft, agricultural produce and a more circular way of living to the world outside.

Opposite:
Young minds from the Pathways School tour and observe the Santati exhibition as part of their Art Inquiry. Their experience, apart from seeing the installations, involves imagining and delving into personalities of the artists whose works are on display.
Delhi, 2020// IGNCA

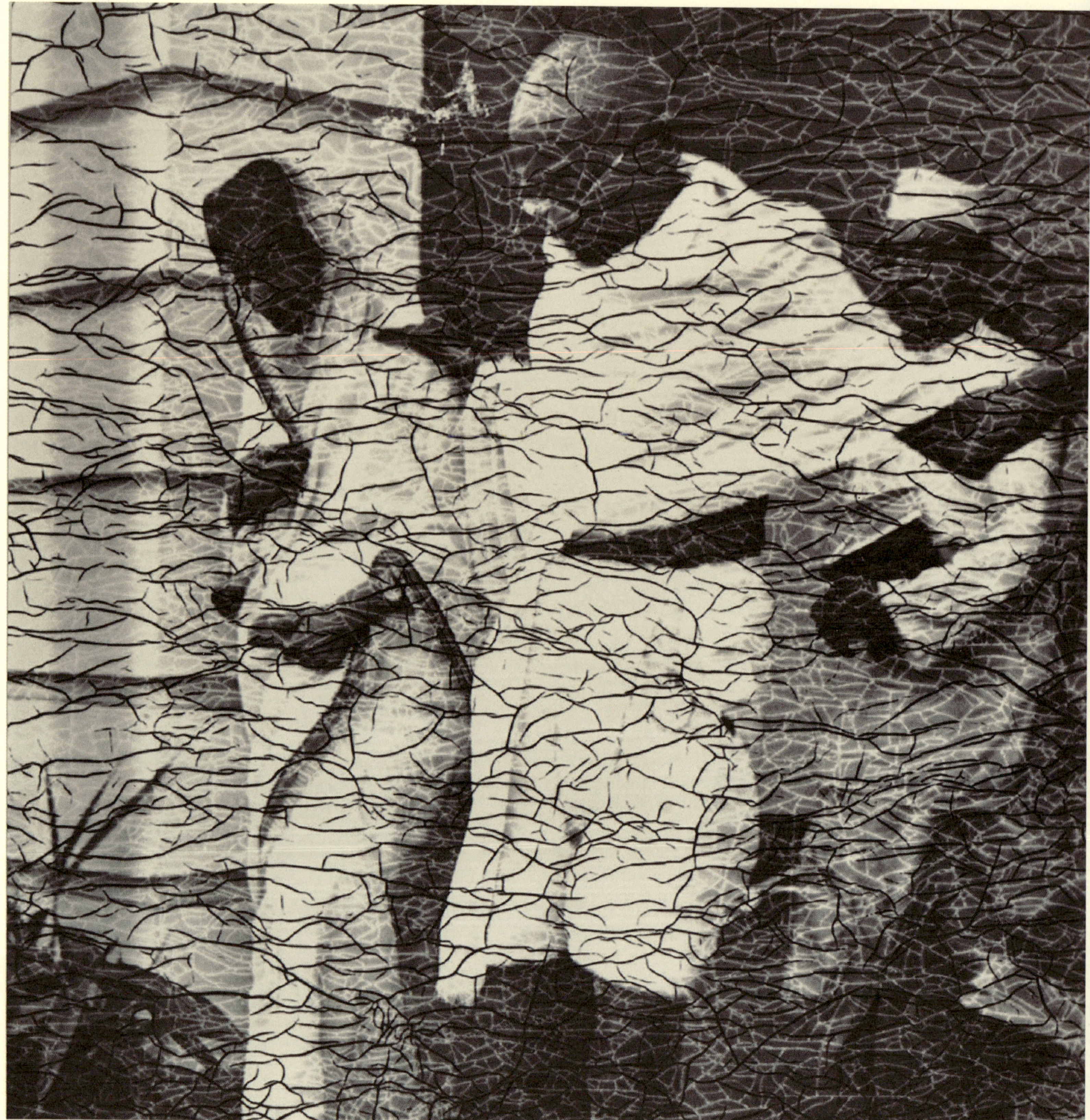

Let's leave no leaf
Unturned
Till the jungle reveals
Itself in a vein

Opposite:
Mahatma Gandhi with Rajkumari Amrit Kaur
Kulwant Roy
Broken negative // NGMA Archives

“True worth of a man seems to me to consist in his capacity to resist his surroundings. It is the measure of his self-realization. If we control ourselves we cannot be controlled by others, not even by our surroundings, not fashion, nor food, nor spectacles, nor games, nor company, nor hobbies. There is no true happiness without this real SELF RULE. You have a unique opportunity of acquiring it. May it be your lot to do so.”

Mahatma Gandhi

Opposite:
Artwork from Sir JJ School of Art Archives

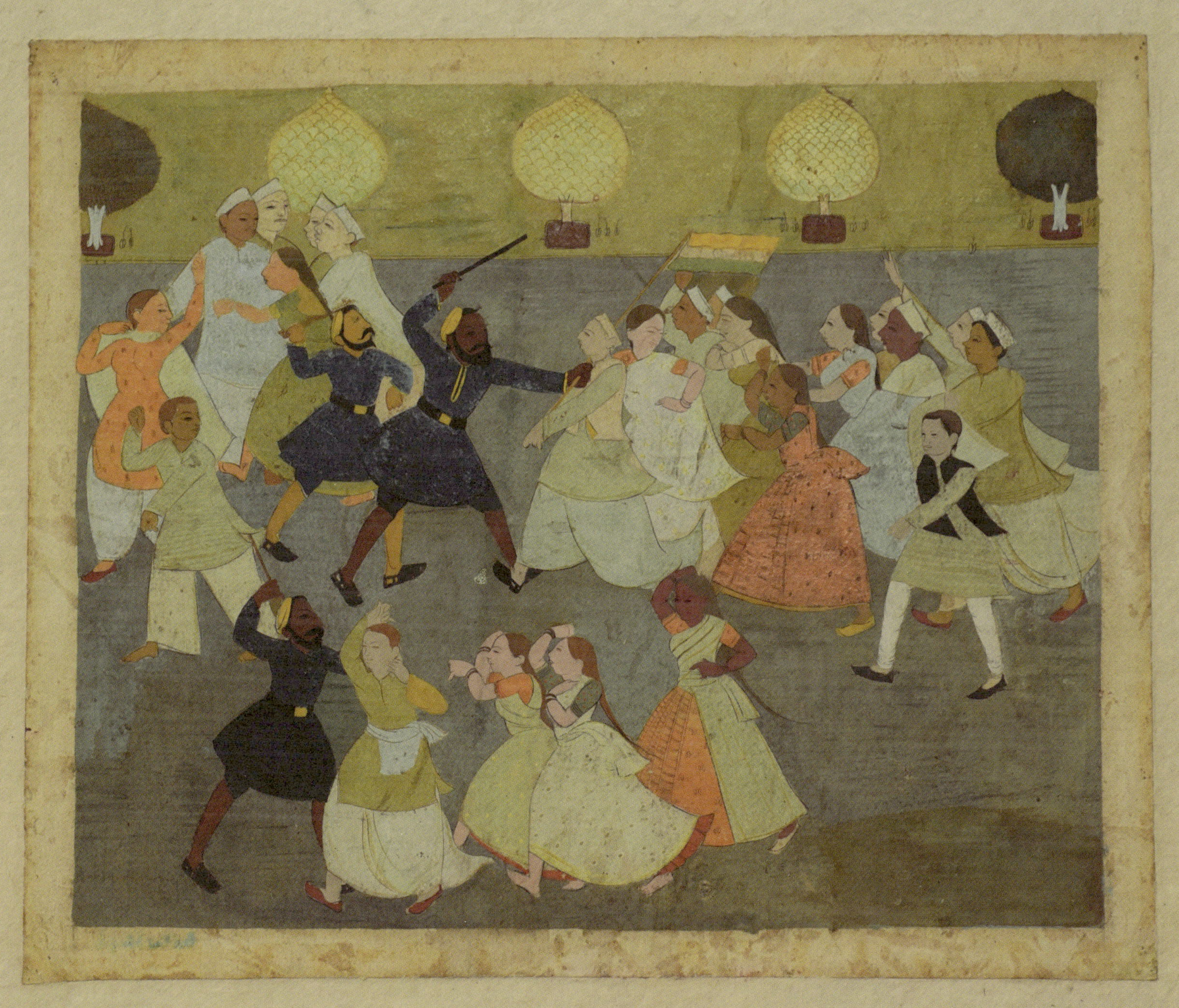

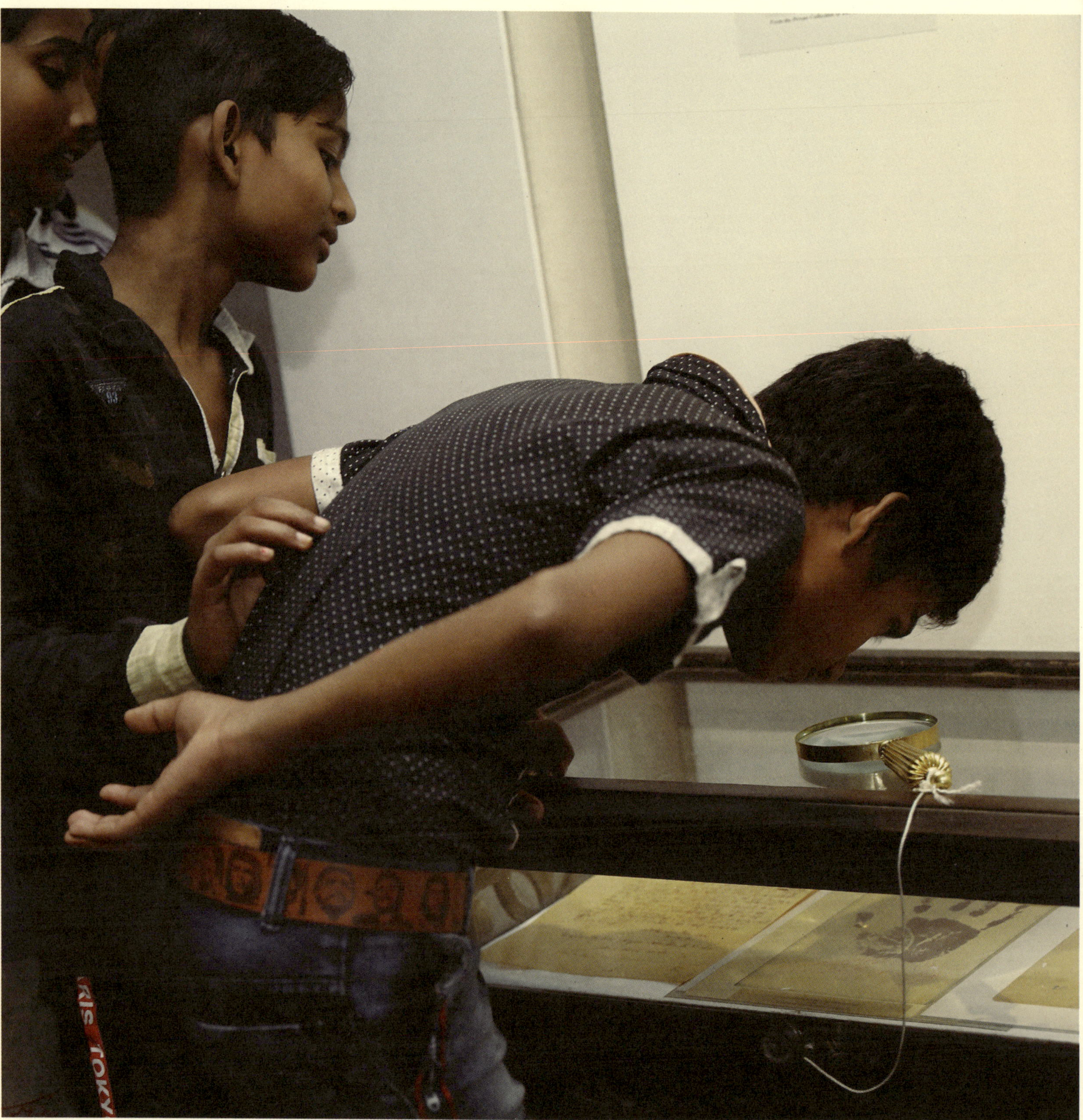

"Ultimately what we have to learn is that the whole world is one."

Mahatma Gandhi

Opposite:
Children from the Magic Bus peer into the private collection of Shri Kishore Jhunjhunwala, as they try to observe Mahatma Gandhi through their tour of Santati.
Location: National Gallery of Modern Art, Mumbai

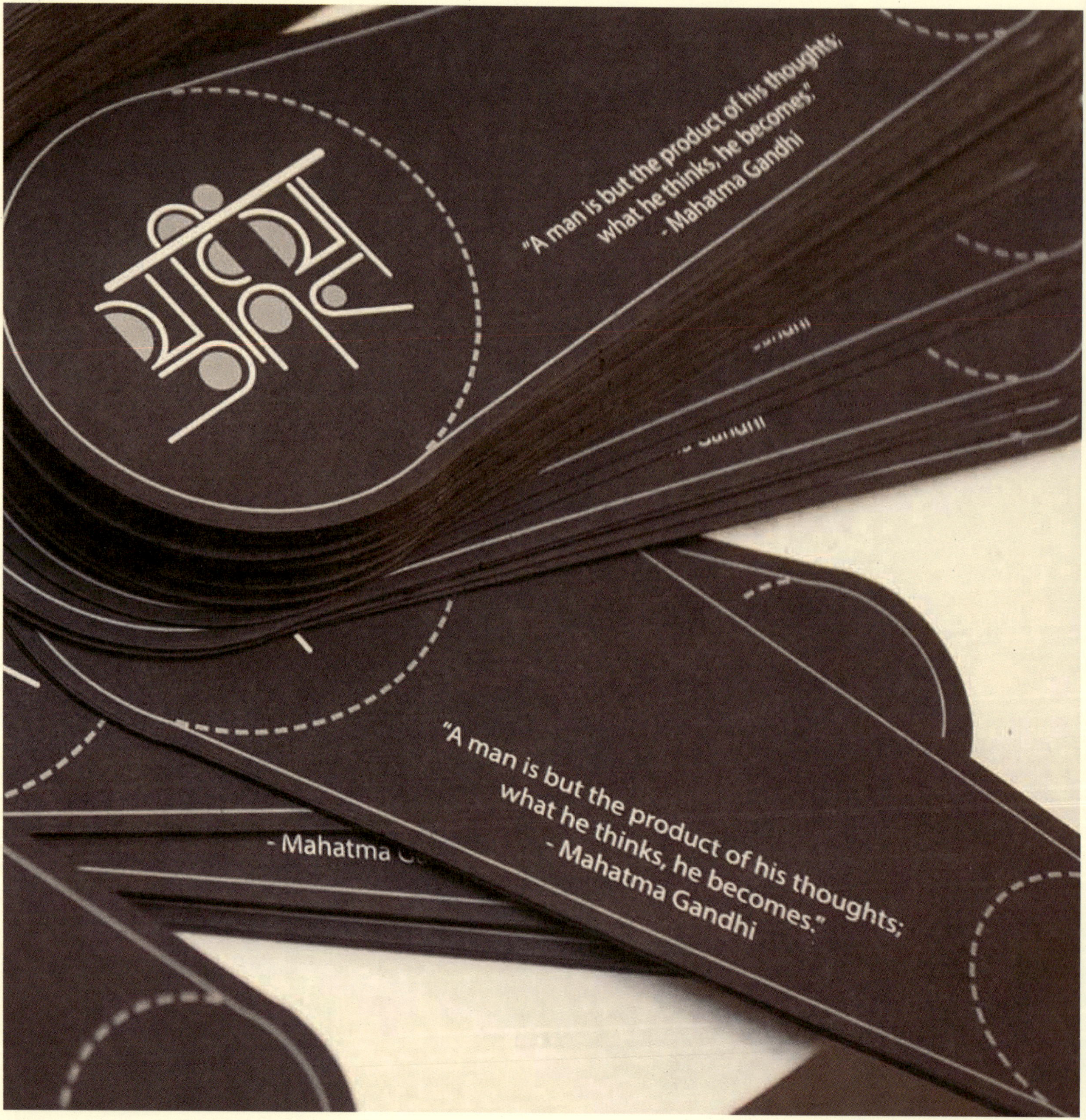

"A man is but the product of his thoughts; what he thinks, he becomes."
- Mahatma Gandhi

"A man is but the product of his thoughts; what he thinks, he becomes."
- Mahatma Gandhi

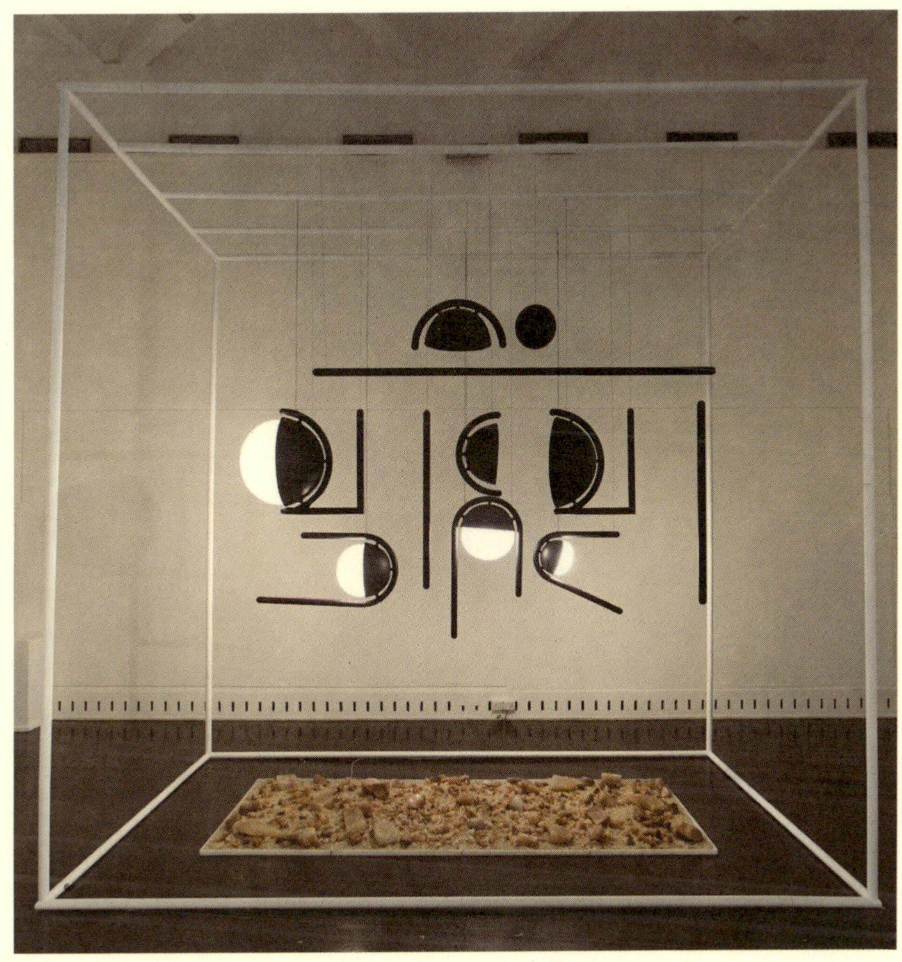

Mahatma Gandhi was fanatically against violence in any form, gross or subtle. Vehemently he advocated ahimsa or non-violence in deed, word and thought. He was deeply interested in the route of actions and sought to purify their journey from the seed of thought to the tree of action.

His method of study from effect to cause becomes more pertinent by the day for our world that is perched precariously between collective action and consequence. To re-imagine or re-calibrate the next world, a collective lens of *ahimsa* is the only one that can steer us towards genuine progress and a breathable future. And so Ahimsa, Gautam Seth and Prateek Jain's installation from Klove Studio stands as a stark chronicler of a truth that time cannot fray.

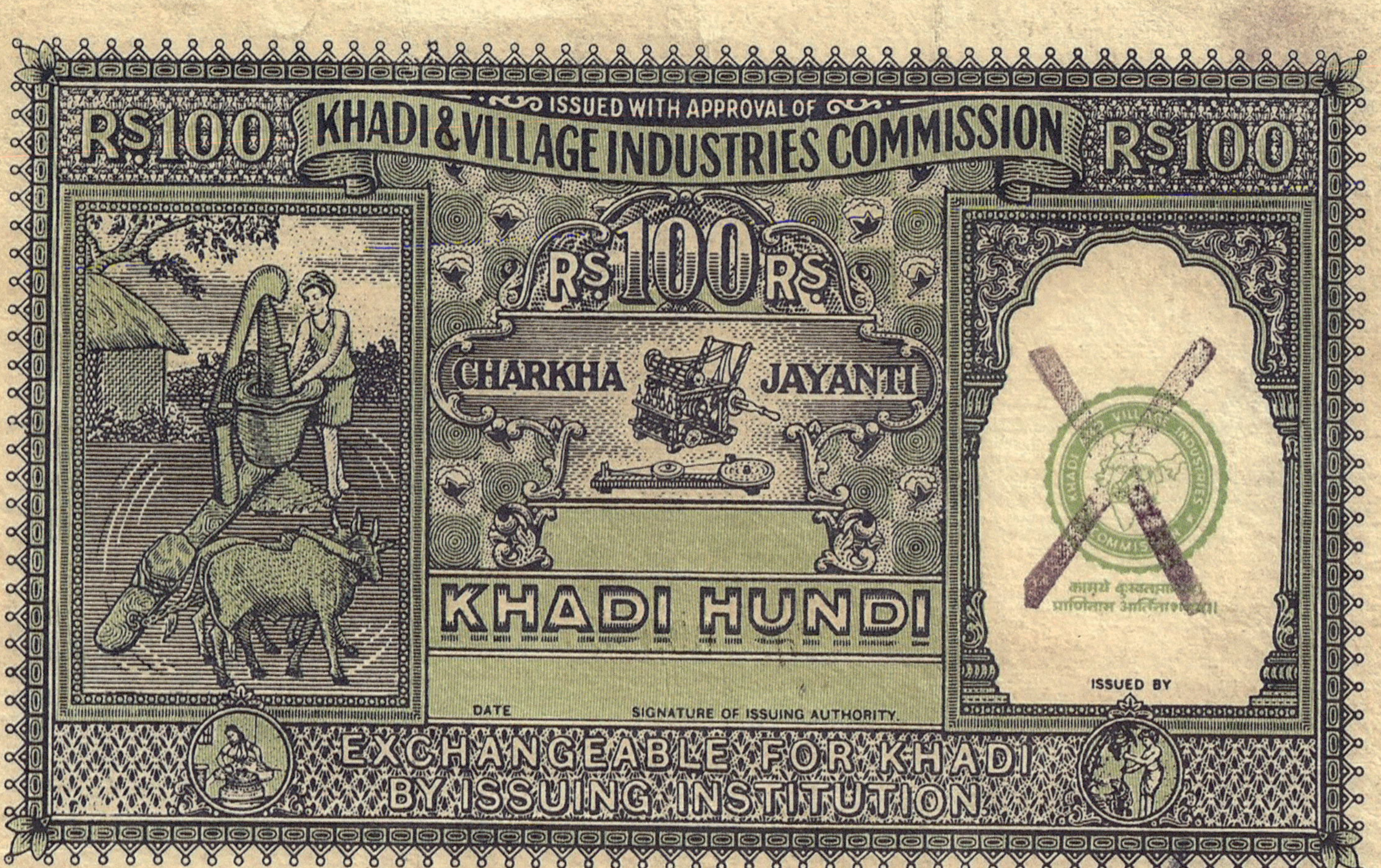

ISSUED WITH APPROVAL OF
KHADI & VILLAGE INDUSTRIES COMMISSION
RS.100
RS.100
RS 100 RS
CHARKHA JAYANTI
KHADI HUNDI
DATE
SIGNATURE OF ISSUING AUTHORITY.
ISSUED BY
EXCHANGEABLE FOR KHADI
BY ISSUING INSTITUTION
REDEEMABLE BY ISSUING INSTITUTION.
VALID, IF SIGNED, FOR ONE YEAR FROM THE DATE OF ISSUE.

"God forbid India should ever take to industrialism after the manner of the West. The economic imperialism of a single island kingdom is today keeping the world in chains. If an entire nation of 300 million took to similar economic exploitation, it would strip the world bare like locusts. Unless the capitalists of India help to avert that tragedy by becoming trustees of the welfare of the masses and by devoting their talents not to amassing wealth for themselves but to the service of the masses in altruistic spirit, they will end either by destroying the masses or being destroyed by them."

Mahatma Gandhi

Opposite:
Currency note from Kishore Jhunjhunwala's Private Collection

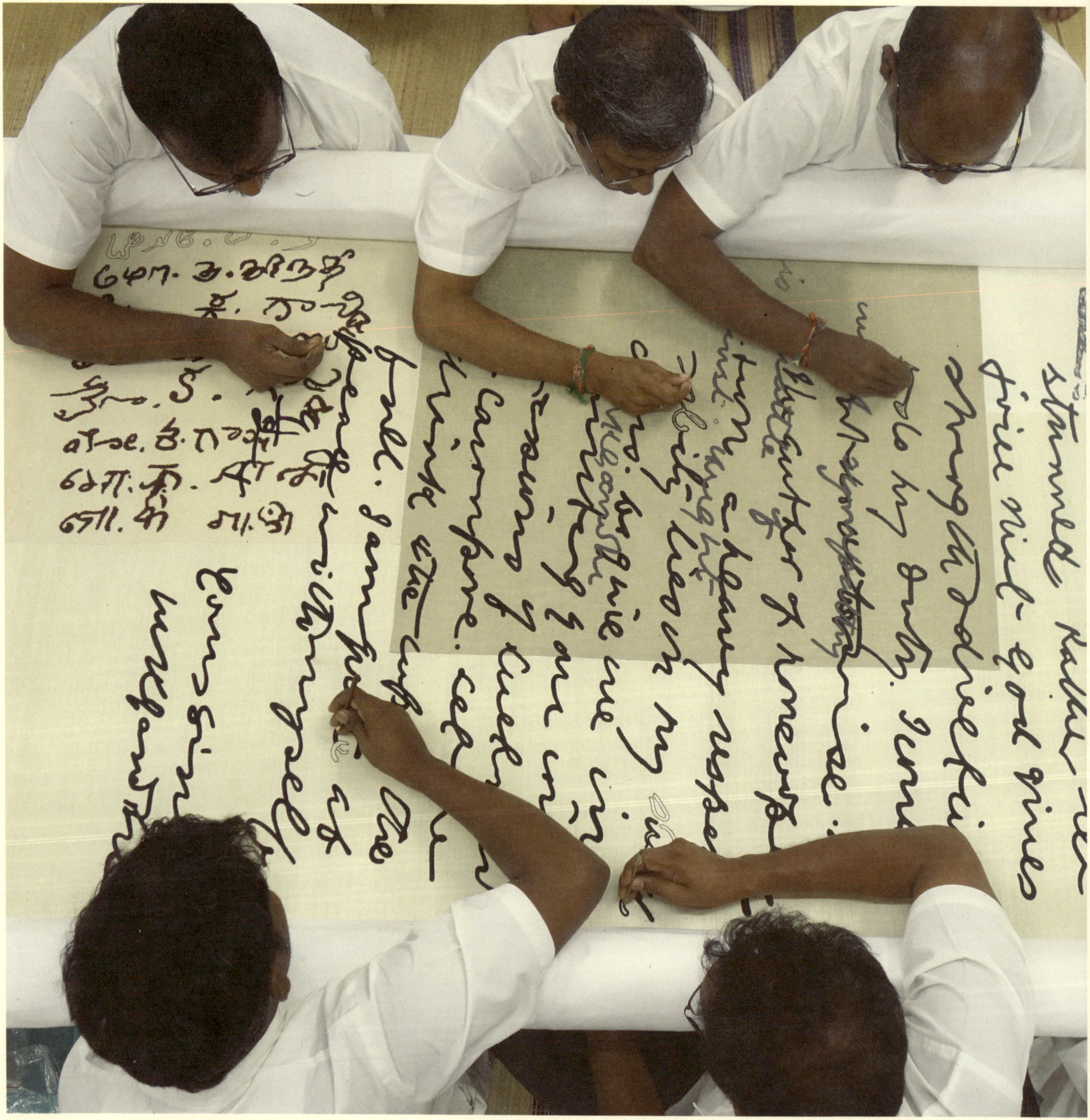

“India must protect her primary industries even as a mother protects her children against the whole world without being hostile to it.”

Mahatma Gandhi

Opposite:
Work in progress // Jean François Lesage

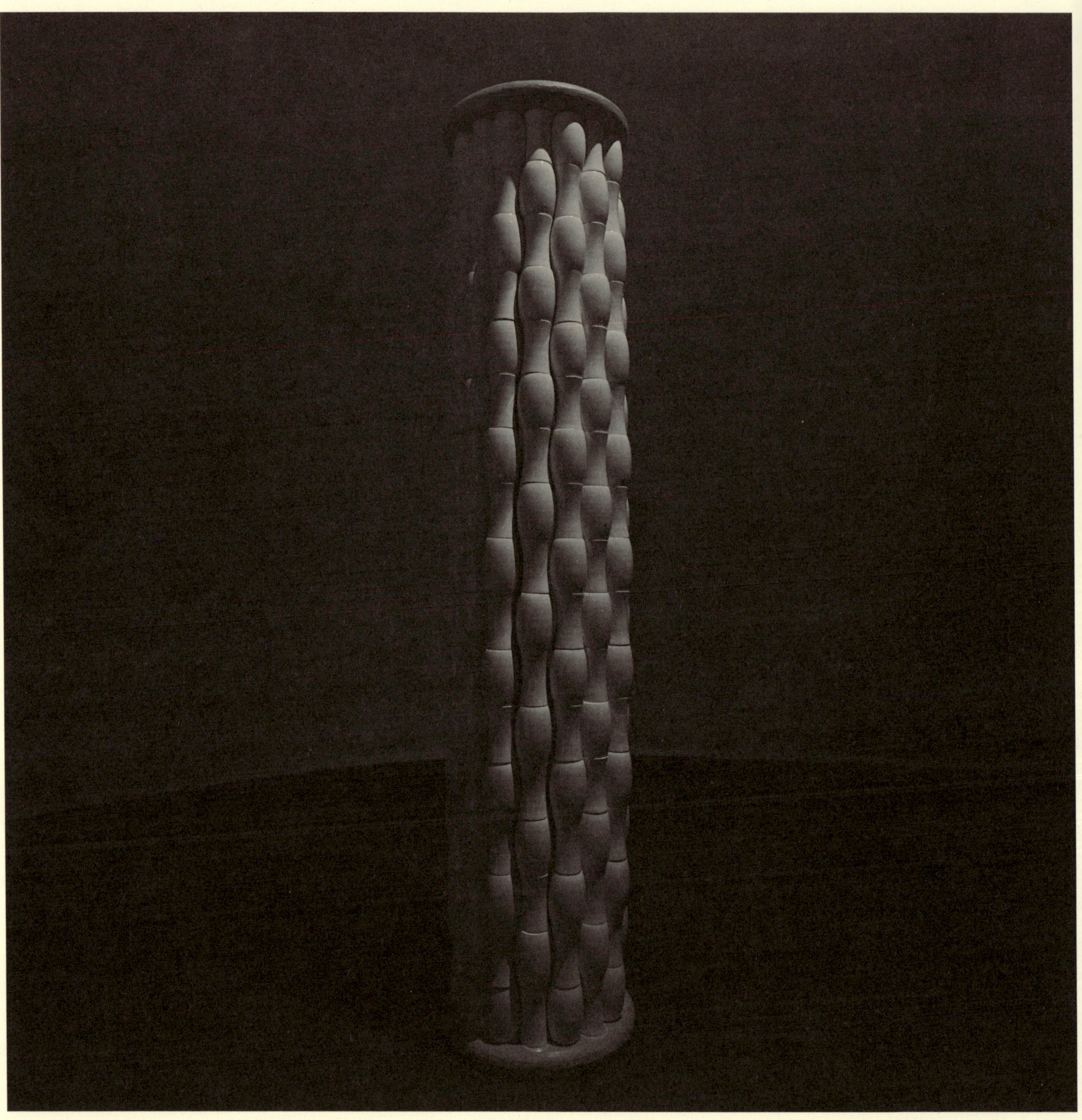

Mahatma Gandhi proposed a wholly circular system of production through consumption, a system which borrowed from nature and then gave back to it almost in its entirety. As a visionary he seemed to have a stark clarity when he saw the potential in India's native industries – be it textiles, agriculture, the arts or crafts. He envisioned an ecosystem with more than plenty for itself and surplus to supply to the outside world.

Ashiesh Shah employs Gandhi's ideology at all levels of his practice from working closely with artisans to creating works that lend back to the very sources they take from. The Channapatna beads on the totem can be upcycled again to create wooden toys and the circle goes on. Herein lies a philosophy to cure the world of its most pressing disease – climate change.

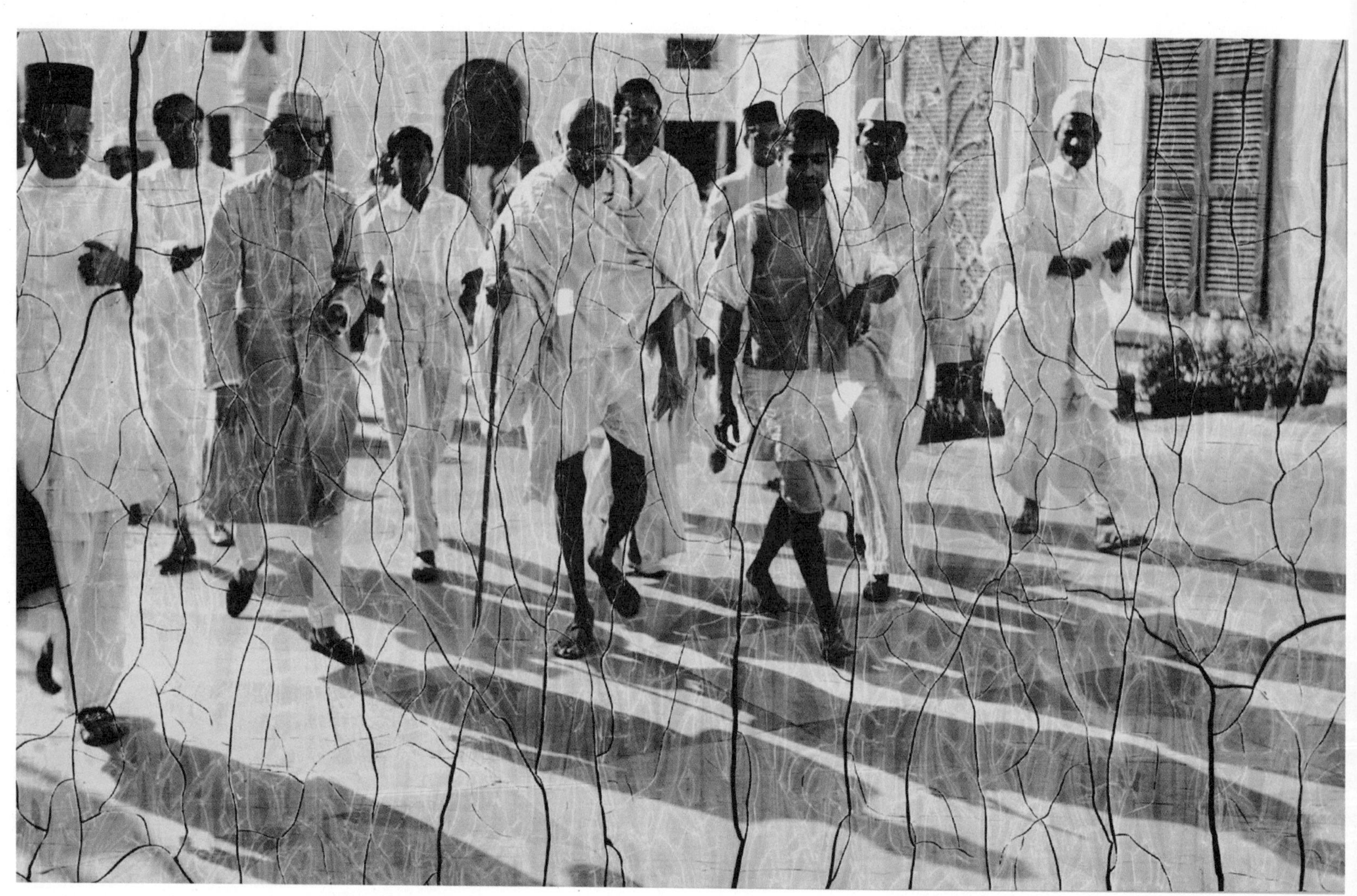

"Fearlessness is the first requisite of spirituality. Cowards can never be moral."

Mahatma Gandhi

Opposite:
Mahatma Gandhi and Dr Rajendra Prasad
Kulwant Roy
Broken negative // NGMA Archives

Somewhere while peeping into Gaurav Gupta's "Tunnel of Infinity", it dawns that Mahatma Gandhi's message does not belong to a fixed, chronological time. As one's reflection multiplies into infinity, the core of Gandhi's philosophy emerges from the tunnel as a singular, unwavering centre around which the winds of time blow.

What he proposed, foresaw and envisioned for India, for a way of life, begins to spiral around one's space, evoked more deeply by the rhythm of his still beating heart. His message becomes a fortress against the blows of time, the time gone by, the time that is yet to come.

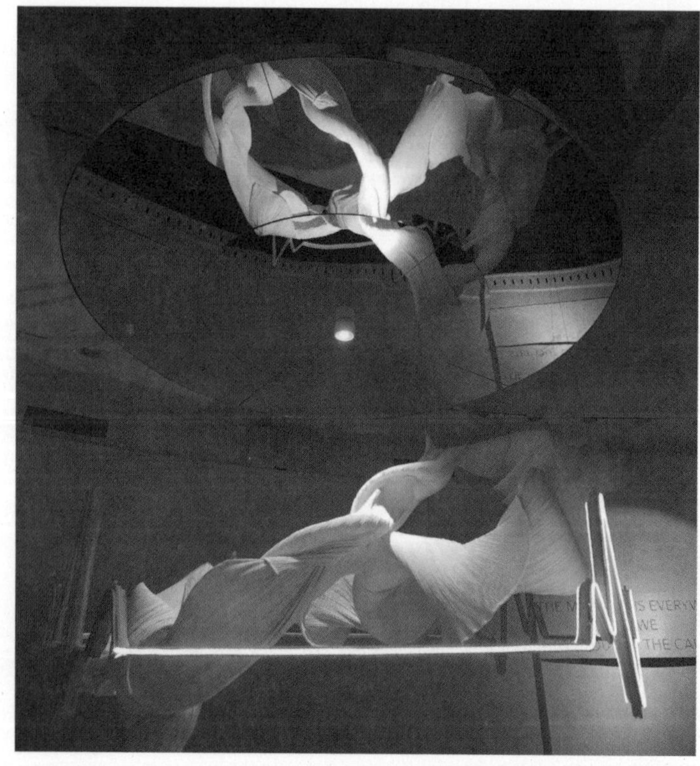

Opposite:
Tunnel of Infinity
Gaurav Gupta

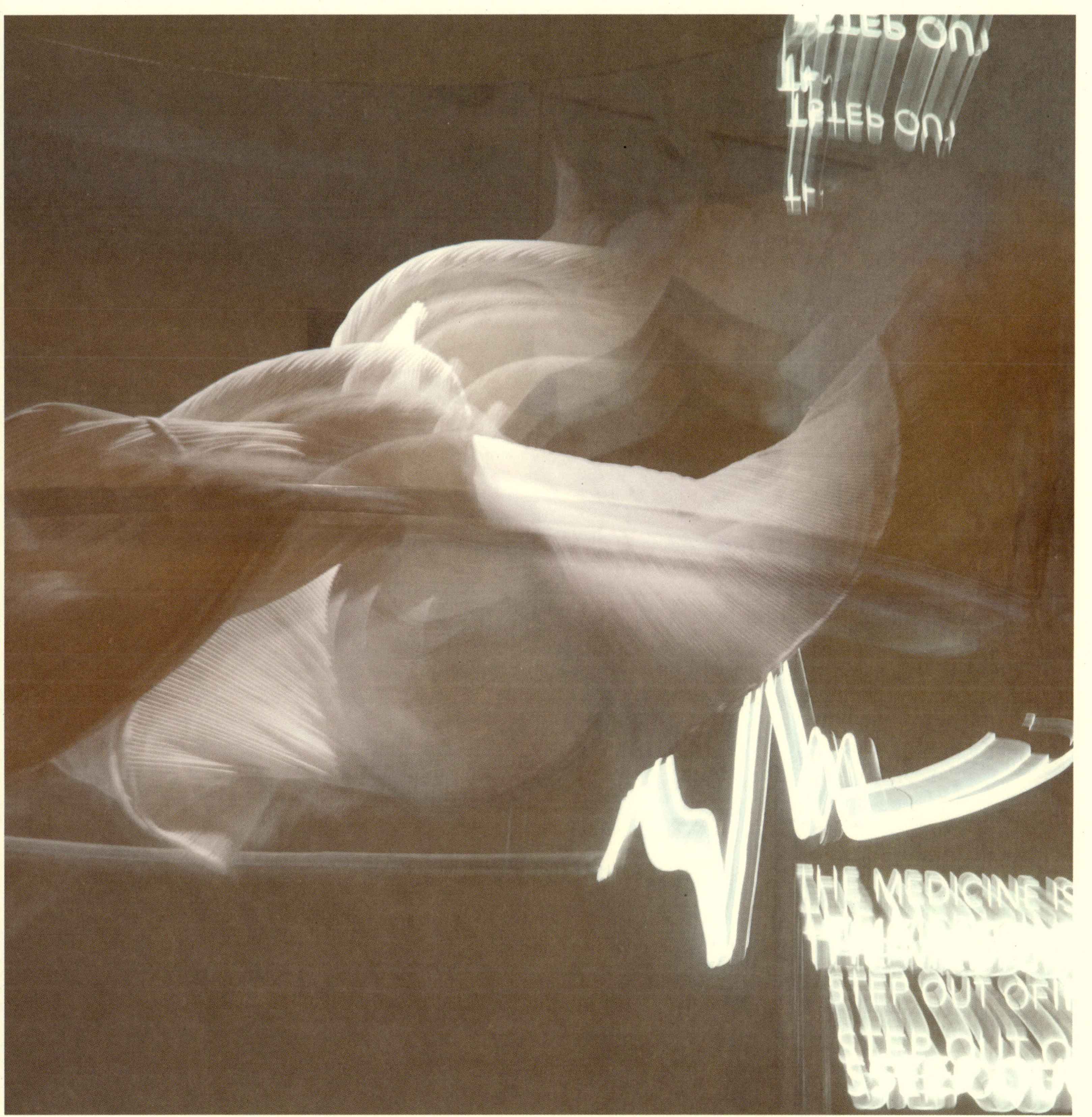
THE MEDICINE IS
STEP OUT OF

May we learn
Its power
Freedom
Is a risky wand

Opposite:
Private collection // Kishore Jhunjhunwala

CAN HITLER FIGHT US?

DECEMBER 1939
•
TWENTY-FIVE CENTS

The Men, The Events: History in the Making by

HUGH S. JOHNSON — DUFF COOPER — ABBÉ DIMNET — HENRY WOLFE and others

CURRENT HISTORY

MAHATMA GANDHI

FRANCE MAKES UP HER MIND

by Abbé Ernest Dimnet

THE TANKS ARE COMING

INDIA BALKS AGAIN

MARTIN DIES OF TEXAS

GERMANY'S VON RIBBENTROP

George V. Denny, Jr.—What's YOUR Opinion?

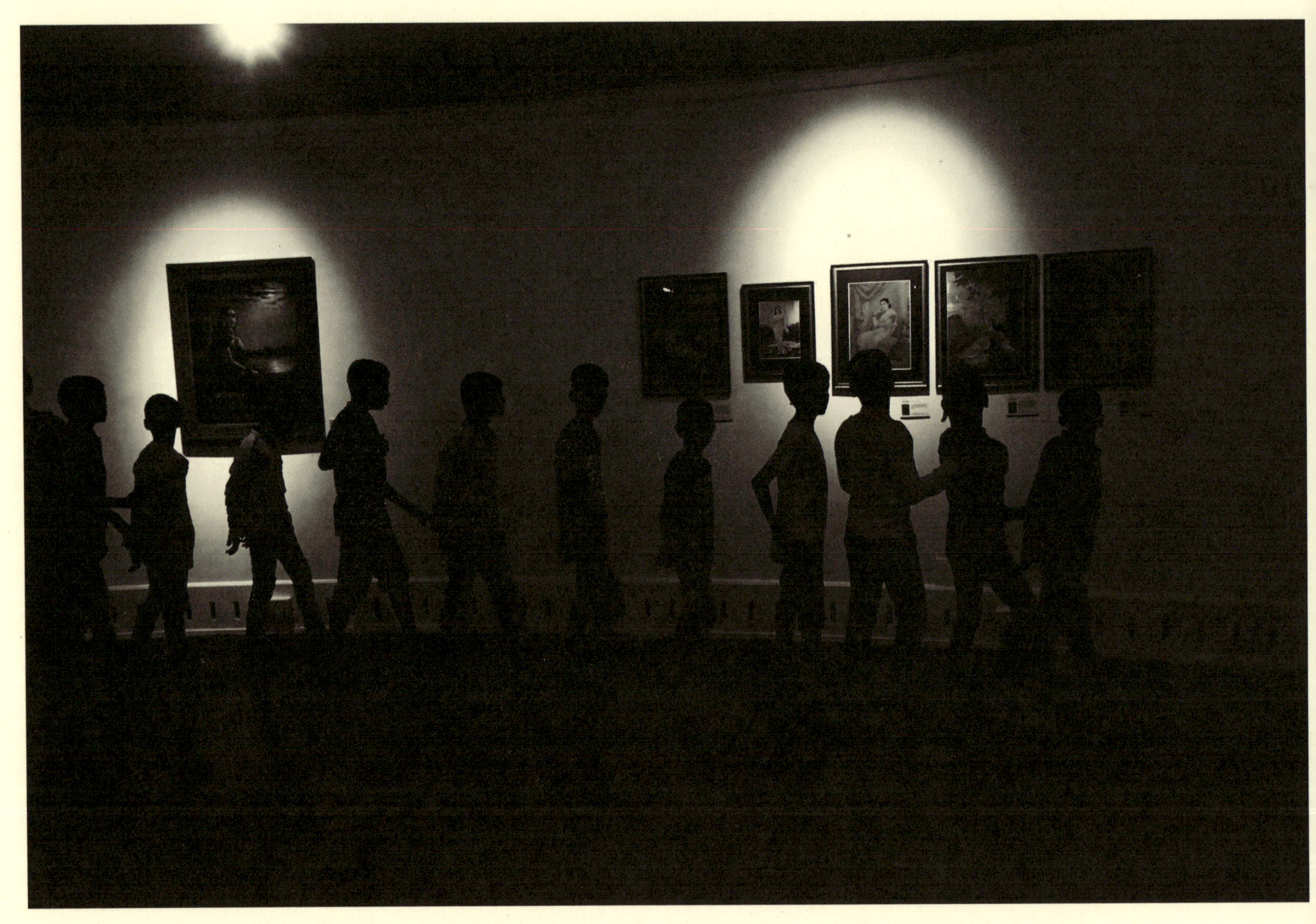

We start taking strides
When we know
The ground
Is transient

अवश्य उठेंगे कदम
उत्थान होगा ज़रूर
जब आभास हो जाए
ज़मीन है अस्थाई
जग क्षणभंगुर

"It is the privilege of friendship to lay the gentle finger on the weak spots. Friendship becomes a divine institution only when it educates friends. Let us try to elevate each other."

Mahatma Gandhi

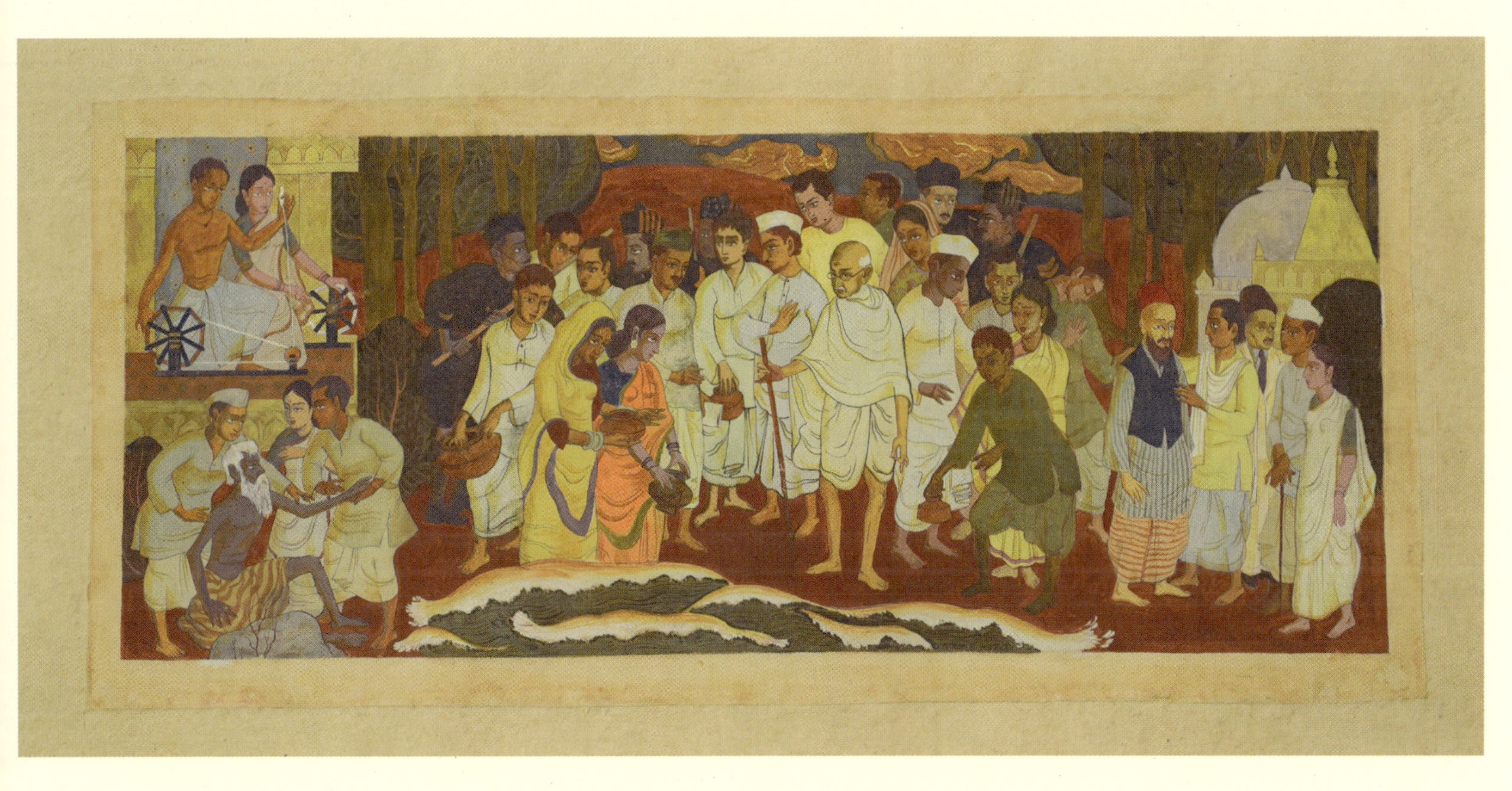

Artwork from Sir JJ School of Art Archives

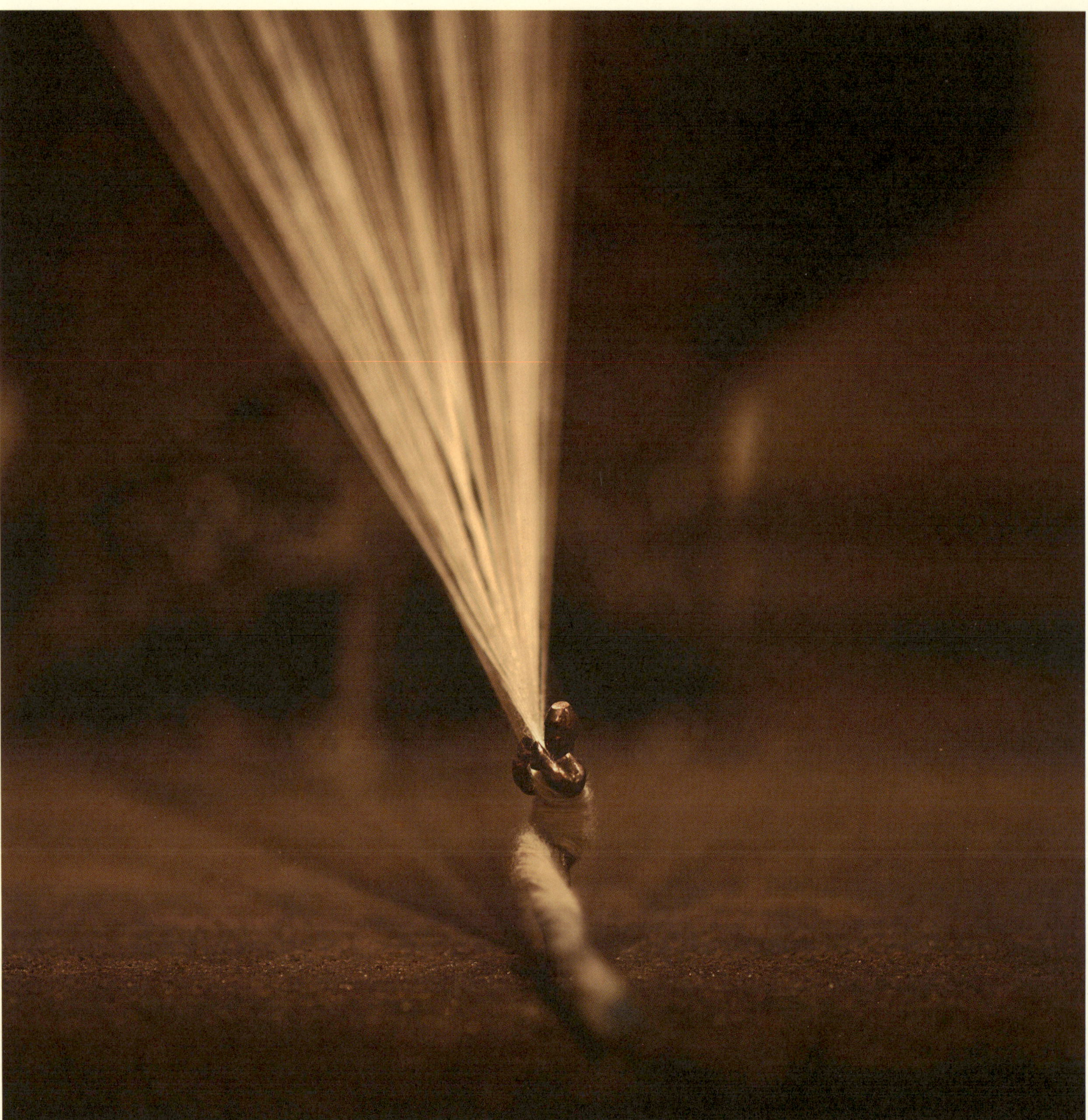

I want you to see
What I see
What lives beneath
Our soil
A seed that can
sprout into
The waking of this
world

Opposite: **Neel** // Rajesh Pratap Singh

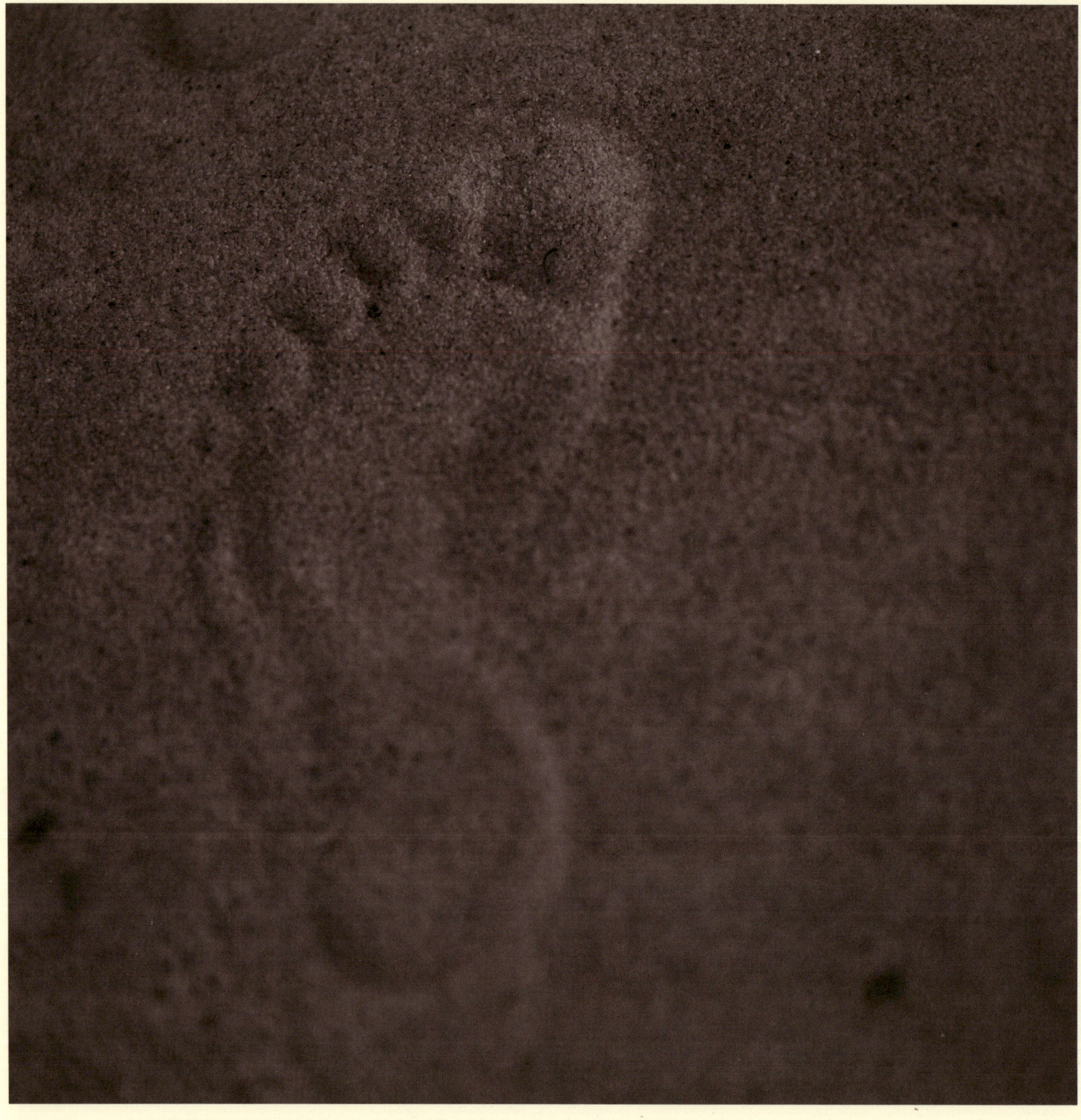

असत्य की नैया एकजुट
परस्पर तिर जाए
सत्य के मझधार का एकांत
स्वयं से परिचित कराए

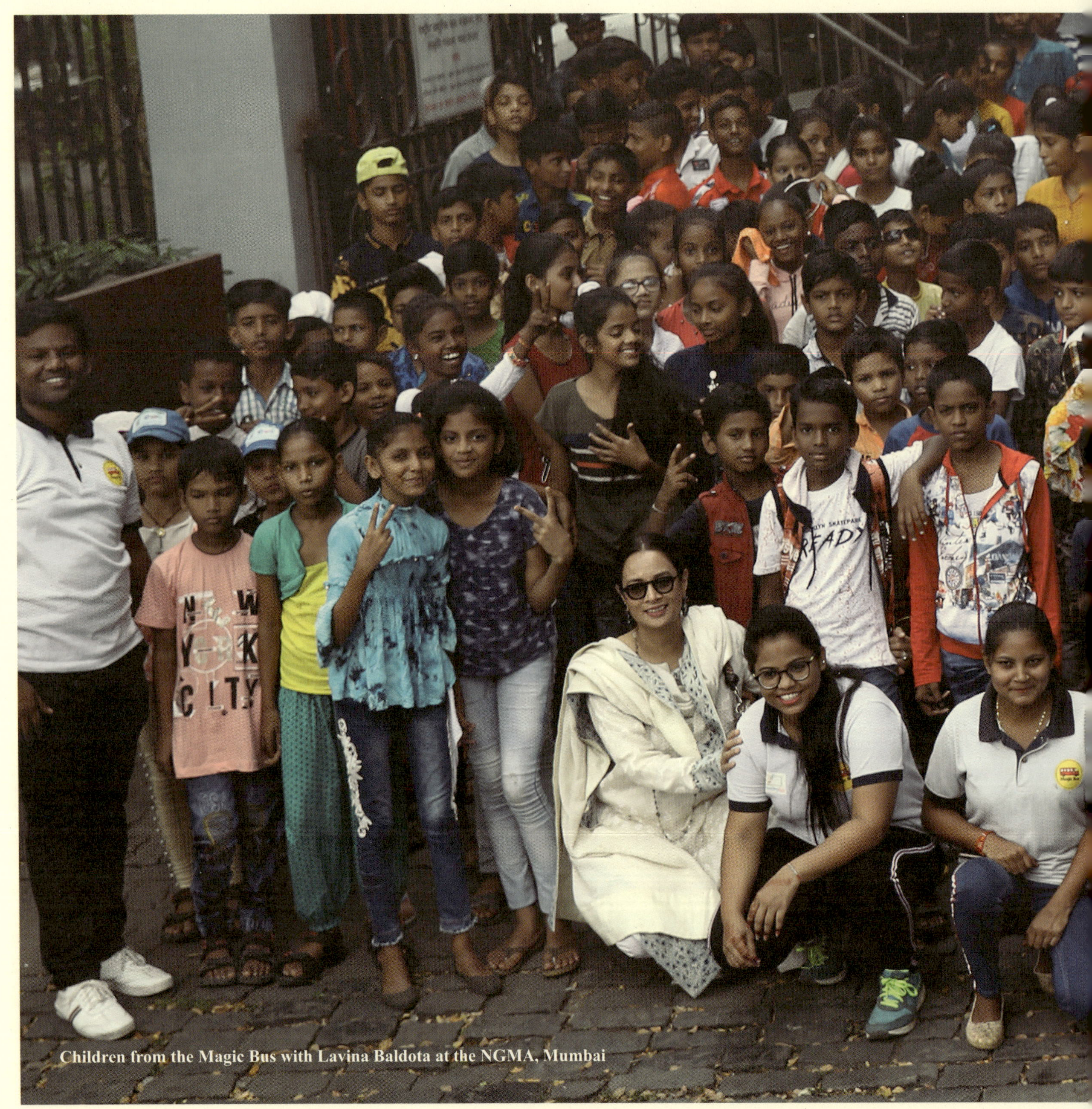
Children from the Magic Bus with Lavina Baldota at the NGMA, Mumbai

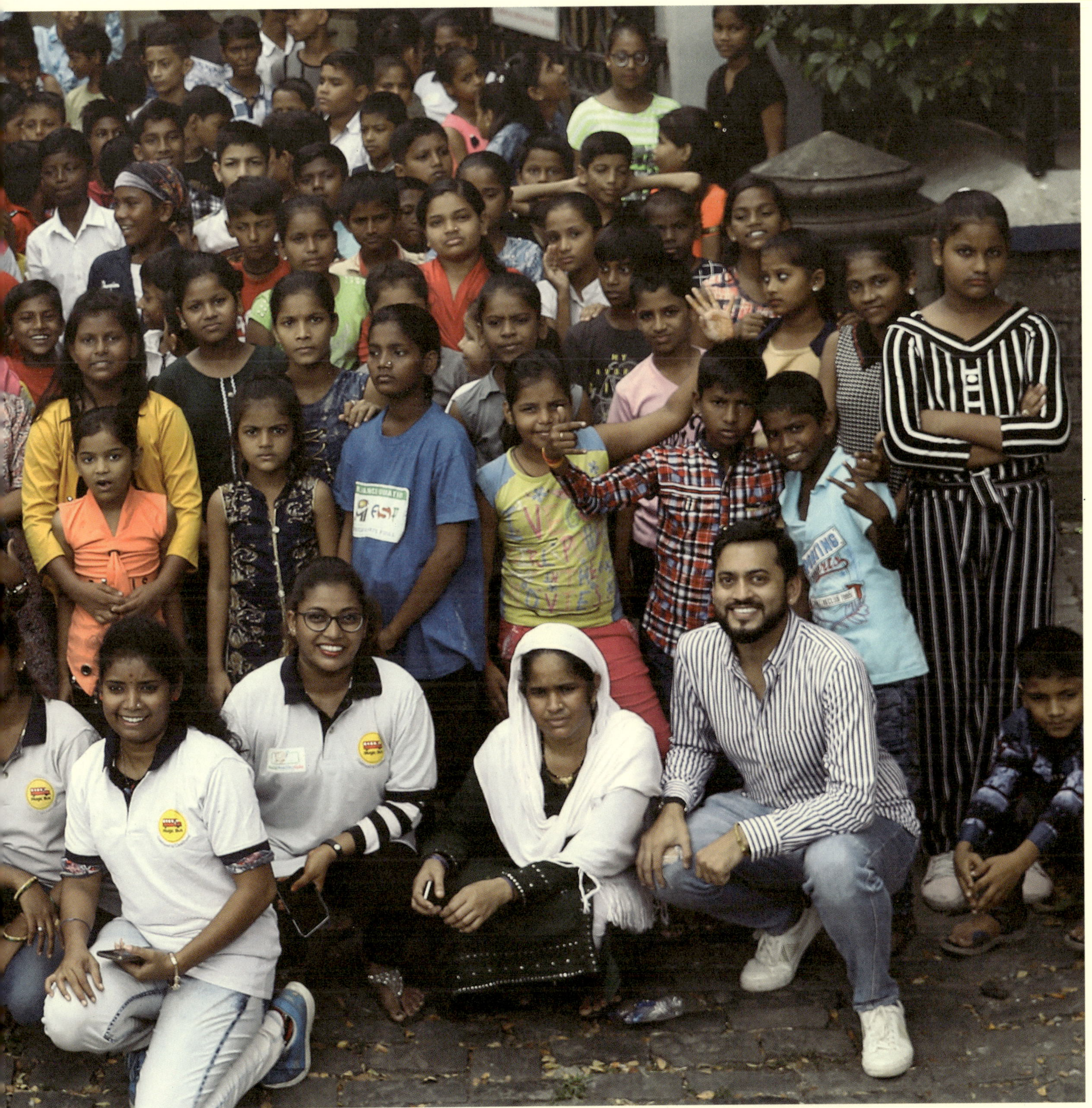
ASF

उत्कर्श की चाह हो अगर
प्रत्यक्ष हो जाए वह शिखर
वह जिसे है विदित
तुम्हारा सामर्थ
तुम्हारा मनोबल
वह जिसे है अवगत
कितना तरल,
कितना अचल
तुम्हारा संकल्प
ऐसा पथ, फिर हो विद्यमान
जहाँ चुभन और मरहम
है समान
जिसमें प्रतिबिंबित वही अक्स
मन में संजोया, तुम्हारा नक़्श
जहाँ भूत और भविष्य
हर पड़ाव पर दें अनुमान
तय हुए लम्बे सफ़र का प्रमाण
फिर और बढ़े,
तुम और चढ़े
मुझमें समाने की तृष्णा में लुप्त
और, शिर पर कुछ जल मिल जाए
मगर, ध्यान से होना तृप्त
कहते हैं, वह माया भंगुर है
खुद को पाओगे स्तब्ध,
शिखर के तले, स्थिर
जहाँ तुम्हें हो आभास
शिखर के ऊपर नहीं
अंतर है बसा
उसका शीर्ष

This was an amazing expeirience. - Siya

It was a spectacular display of MK Gandhi's life. - Saisha

Its like we came in 1990's - Aadya

I was amazed and could not belive my eyes of what I was seeing!! - Sarah

This was a amazing journey thanks a lot (Tejal)

I was amazed to see and it was a nice

I am sure children feel as inspired as I do as an educator. How every human being can be a meticulous & thought+ful artist to make a difference is a heart-warming thought. The whole wonderful efforts by the team - Kudos!!

- Sugandha

It felt like Gandhiji was with us right now.

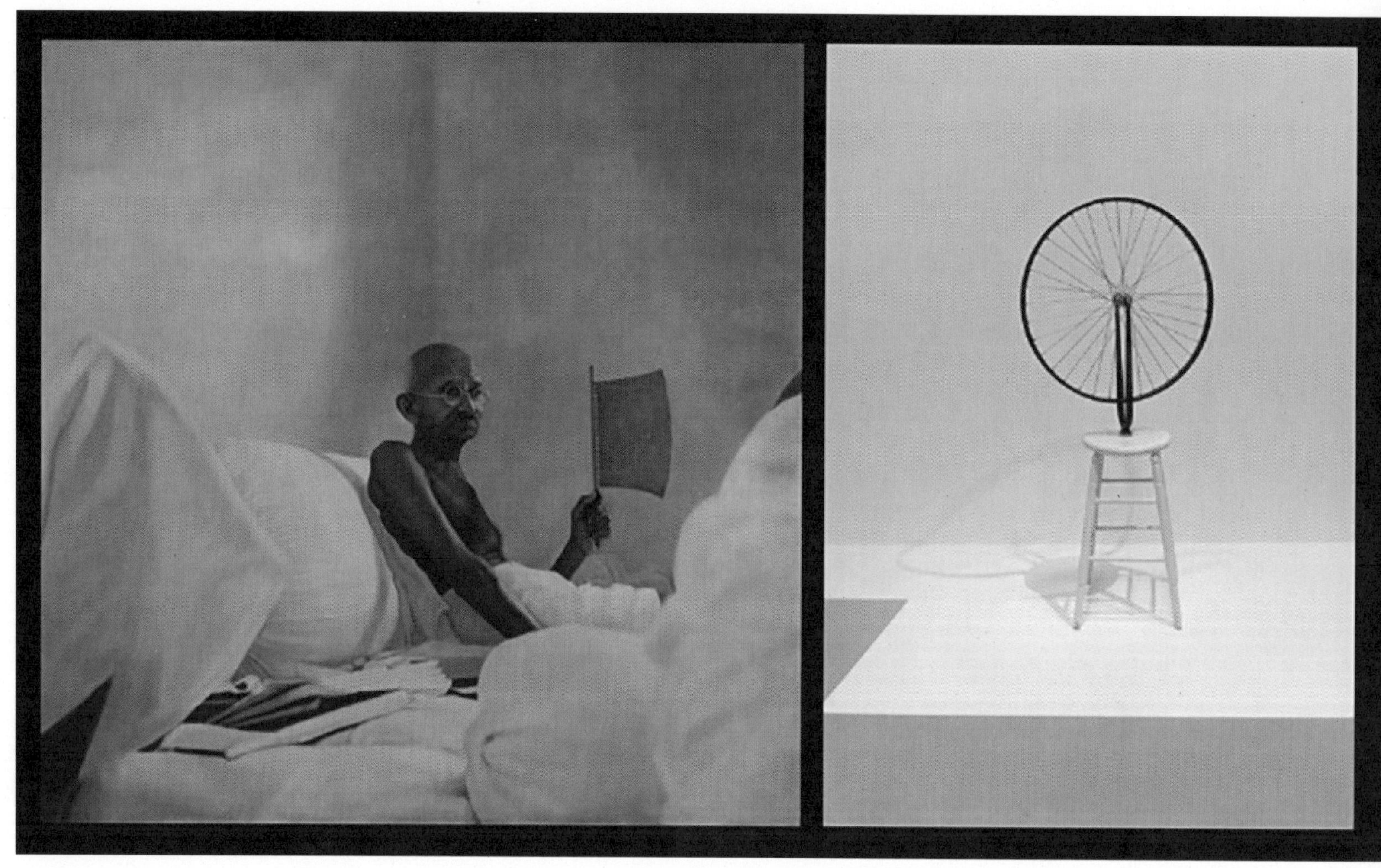

At Birla House, Bombay 1940
Atul Dodiya
2019
Left panel: Oil on canvas, 36 x 36 inches
Right panel: Archival digital print on hahnemuehle rag paper, 36 x 25 inches.
Collection: Sunil Advani, Mumbai

EPILOGUE

In this tribute of an epilogue, artist Atul Dodiya invites us into his impressions of Mahatma Gandhi and his life's impact on the artist and his work.

Atul Dodiya

Artist

Mahatma Gandhi once said, “I am not a seer, rishi or philosopher of non-violence; I am only an artist of non-violence and desire to develop the art of non-violence in the realm of resistance.” This statement has been a powerful trigger for much of the work I have done around Gandhi. His picking of salt, the Dandi march, the non-cooperation movement – all are rich conceptual acts. Reflecting on this, I have been painting Mahatma Gandhi for more than twenty years and this work forms a major part of my oeuvre. His ideals of compassion for all creatures and these active gestures of non-violence are important in our troubled times when we see so much violence, intolerance and hatred amongst human beings, not just in India but all over the world.

In 1997, when India was celebrating its 50 years of Independence, I started thinking about Gandhi’s absence. In 1999 I did a series of large-scale watercolour paintings depicting Mahatma Gandhi. After that, in diverse media, Gandhi remains a central subject in my oeuvre.

In the diptychs which have the painted Mahatma alongside the photographs of Modern European artists’ work, I have juxtaposed two histories – India’s freedom movement under Gandhi’s guidance, and the modern art movement which started in France in the early 20th century. I found it fascinating how in a certain time span, in different spaces, people struggled for freedom and creativity.

Trained in Mumbai and Paris, Atul Dodiya’s journey started garnering attention in the nineties for hyper-realist paintings depicting middle-class Indian life and for his watercolours and oil series on Mahatma Gandhi. In his paintings diverse traditions culminate – the written word, spiritual findings, national history, traumata and autobiographical narratives. Having shown across the world, Atul Dodiya’s work is at once progressively scriptural and vividly kinetic..

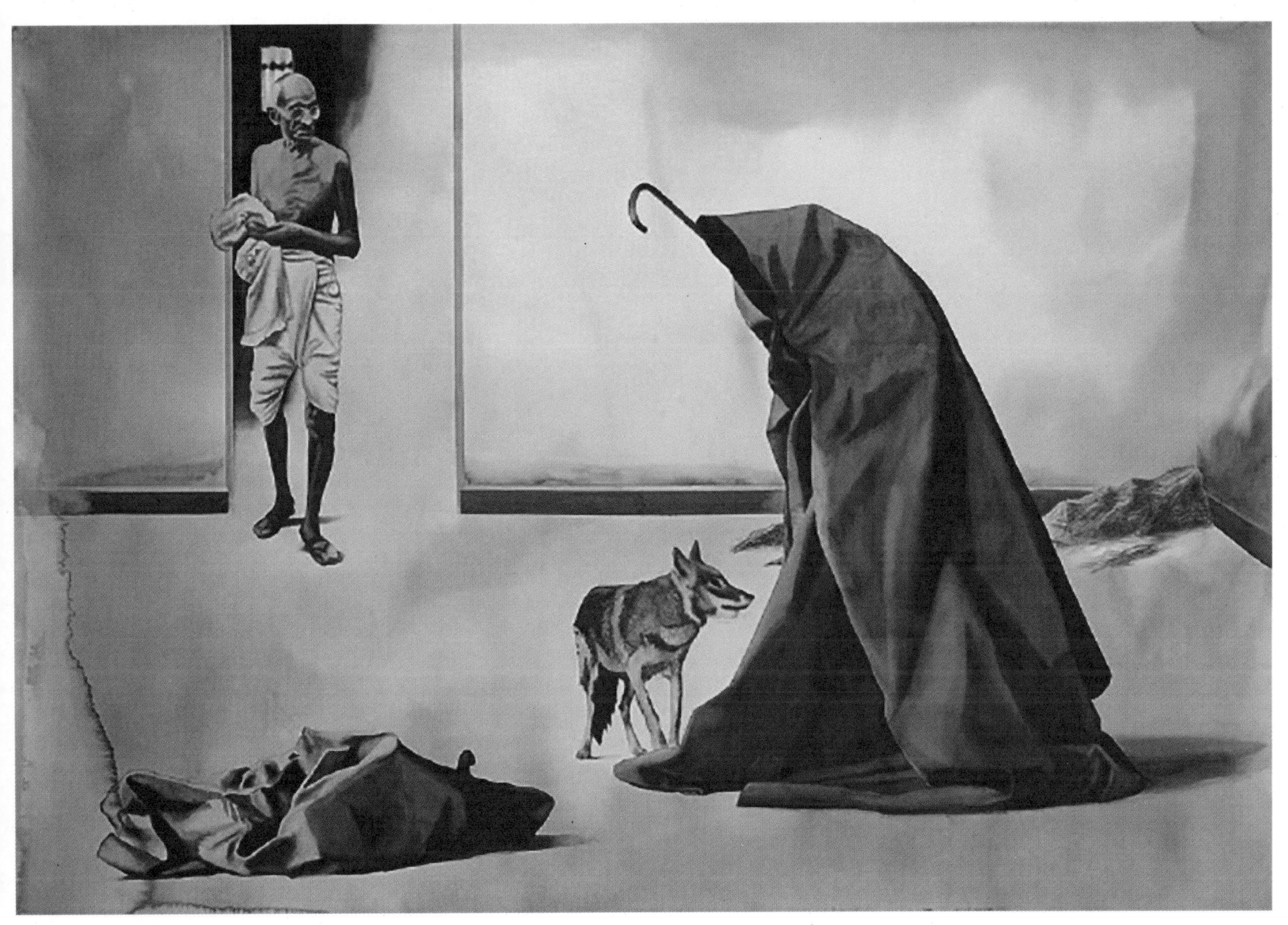

Bapu at Rene Block Gallery, New York, 1974
1998
Watercolour on paper
45 x 70 inches
Collection: Shireen Gandhy, Mumbai

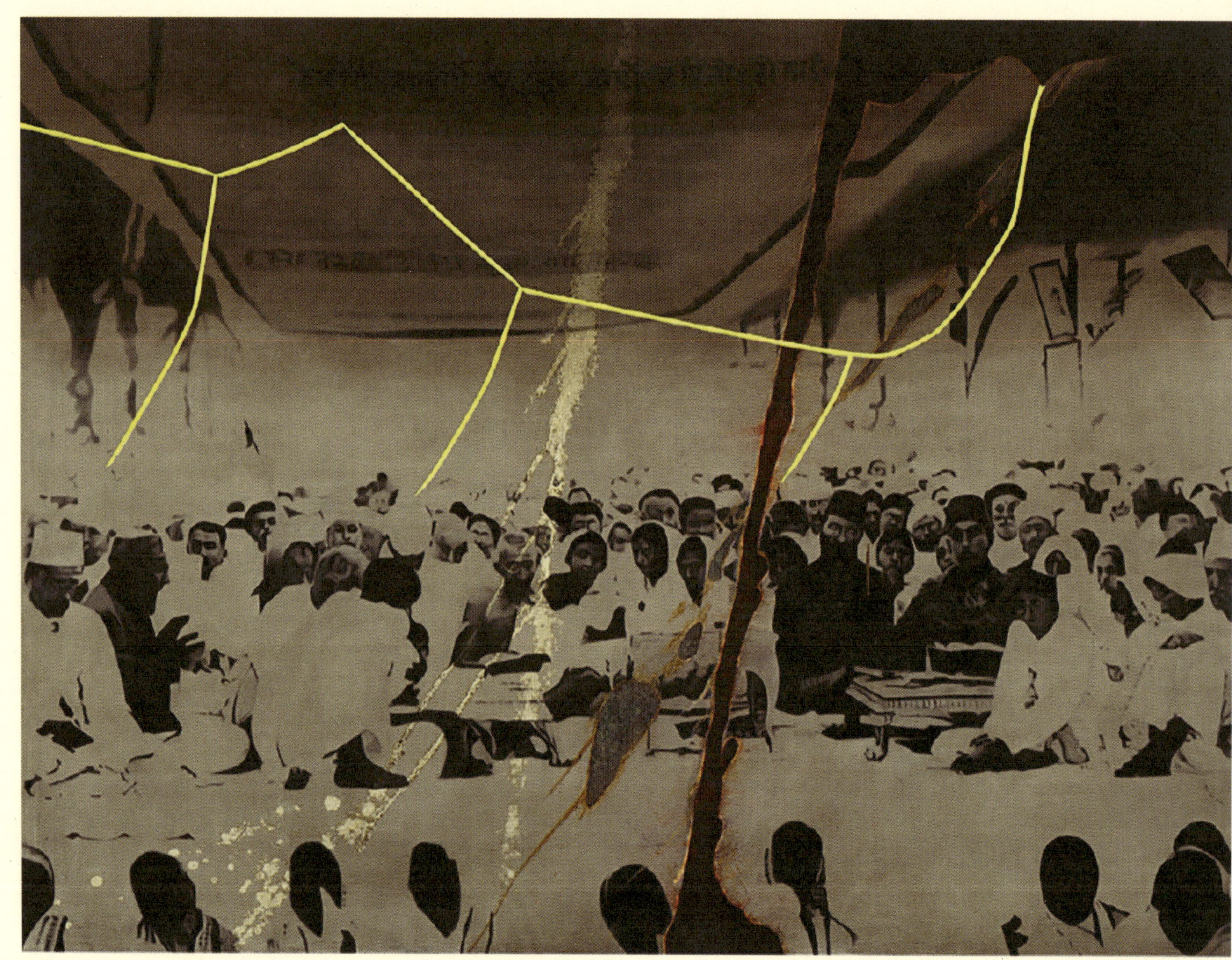

Congress session at Ahmedabad, Dec.1921
2015
54 x 76 inches
Oil on canvas
Collection: Atul Choksey, Mumbai

In the blink of an eye
It was made
It will go away
In a blink
Behold in me
What you hold within
Beyond the whole
Is the infinite

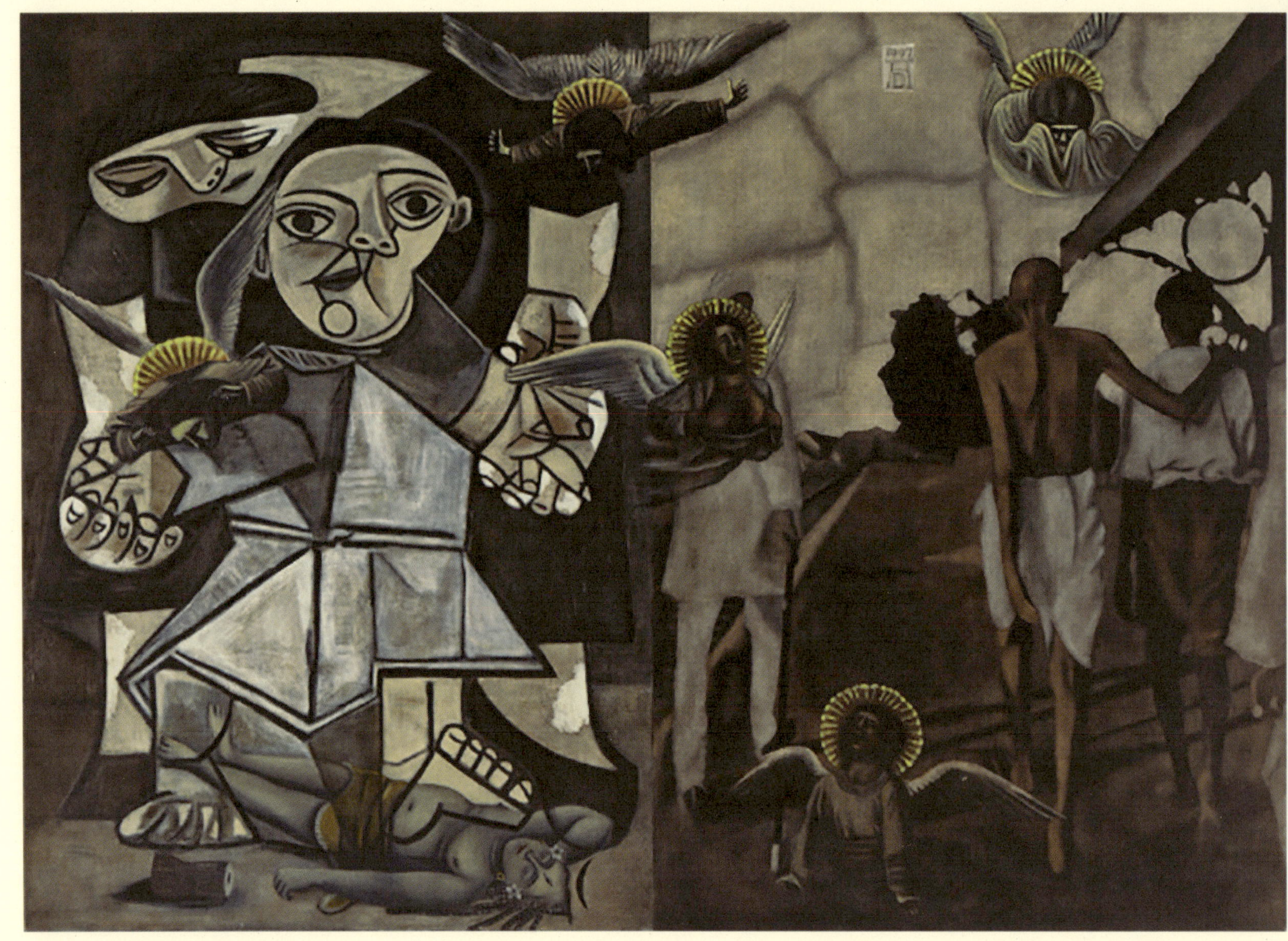

Lamentation
1997
69 x 96 inches
Oil, acrylic and marble dust on canvas
Collection: RPG, Harsh Goenka, Mumbai

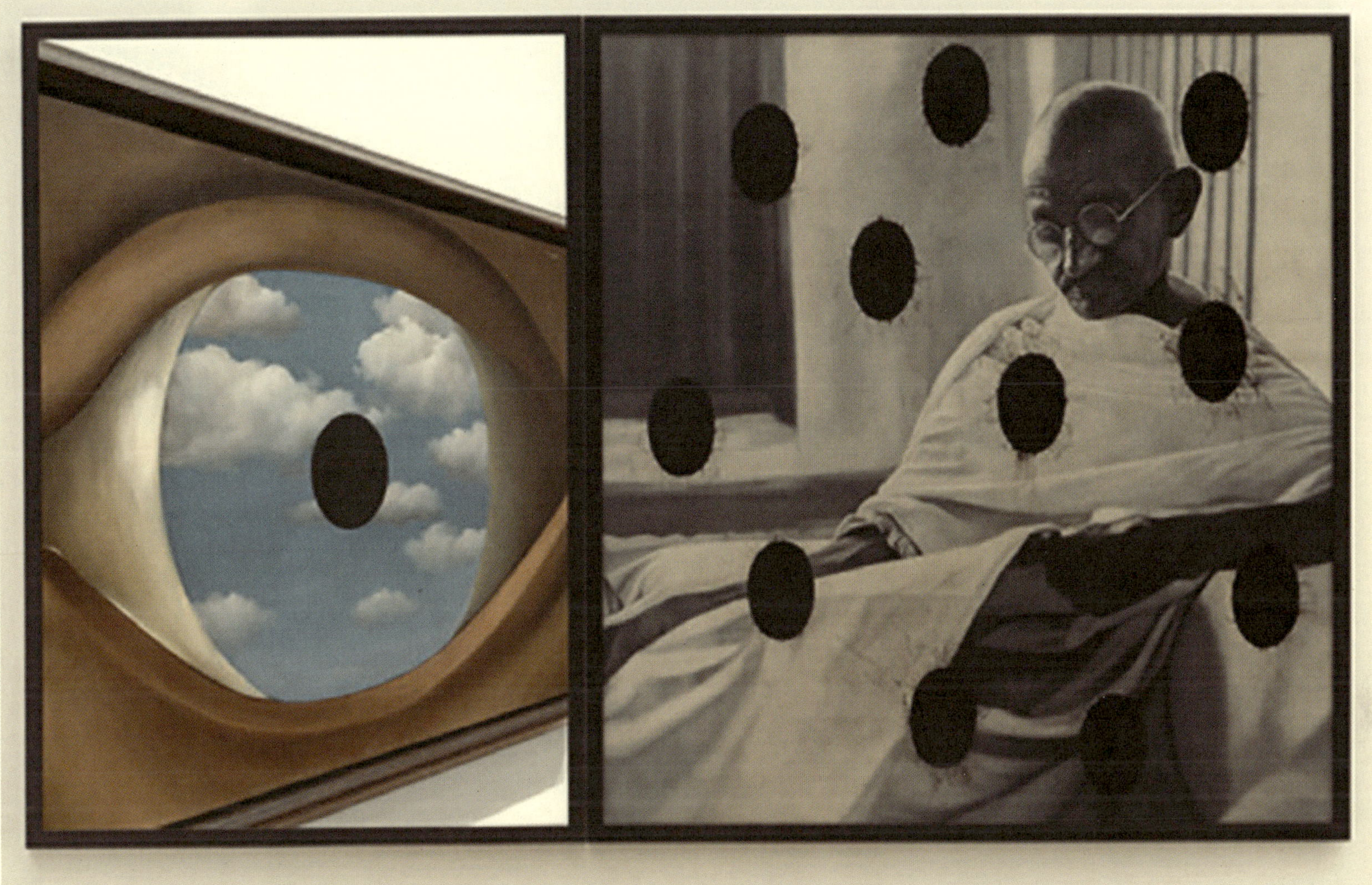

Reading a Newspaper at Dandi, 1930
2018
Right panel : Archival digital print on hahnemuehle rag paper, 36 x 26 inches.
Left panel : Oil on canvas, 36 x 36 inches
Collection : Atul Dodiya, Mumbai

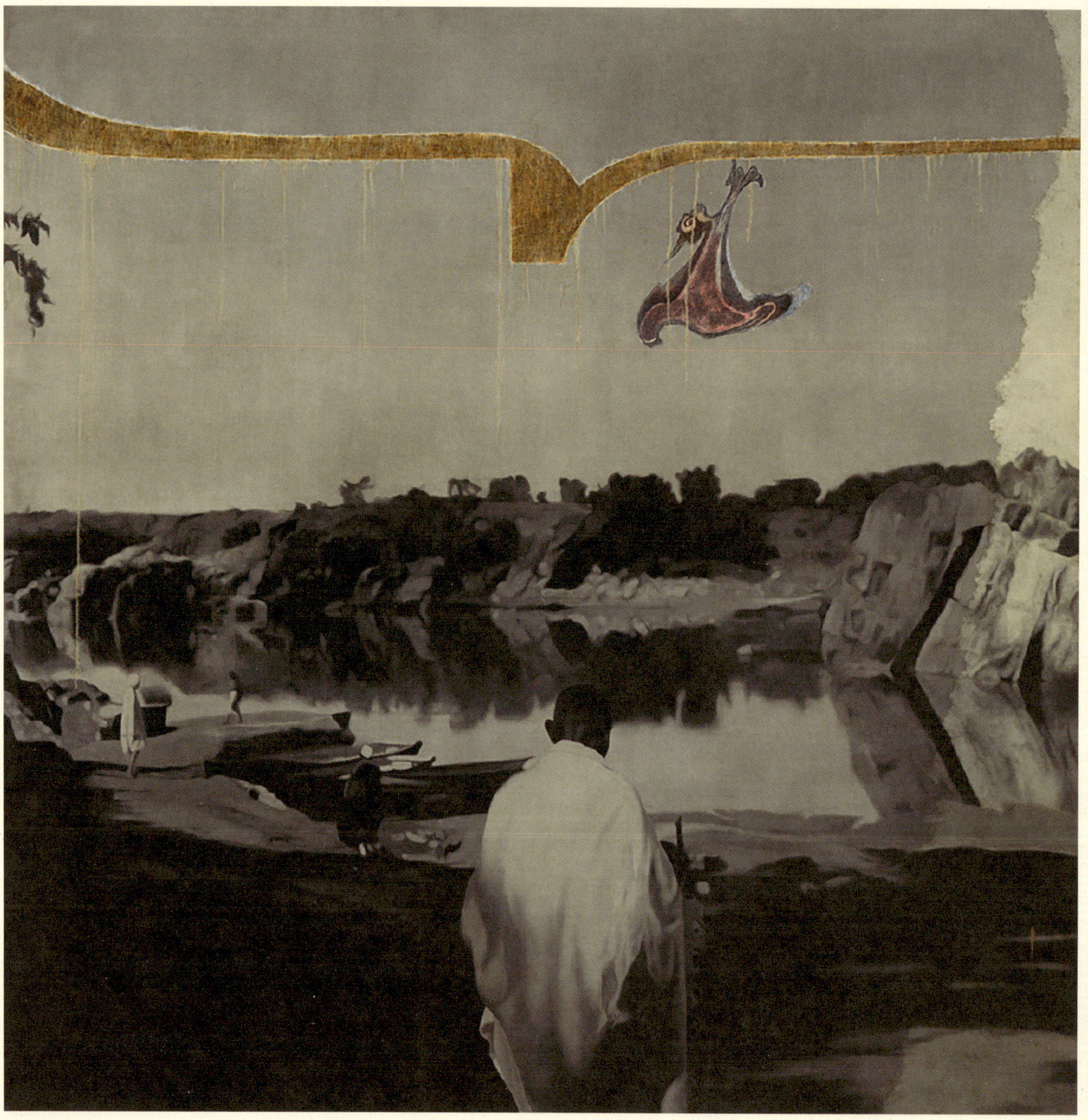

On dusk we met
We ride on dew
Till we glide to a new
Dimension of light

Visit to the marble rocks at Jabalpur, 1941
2016
Oil on canvas
72 x 72 inches
Collection: Chemould Prescott Road, Mumbai

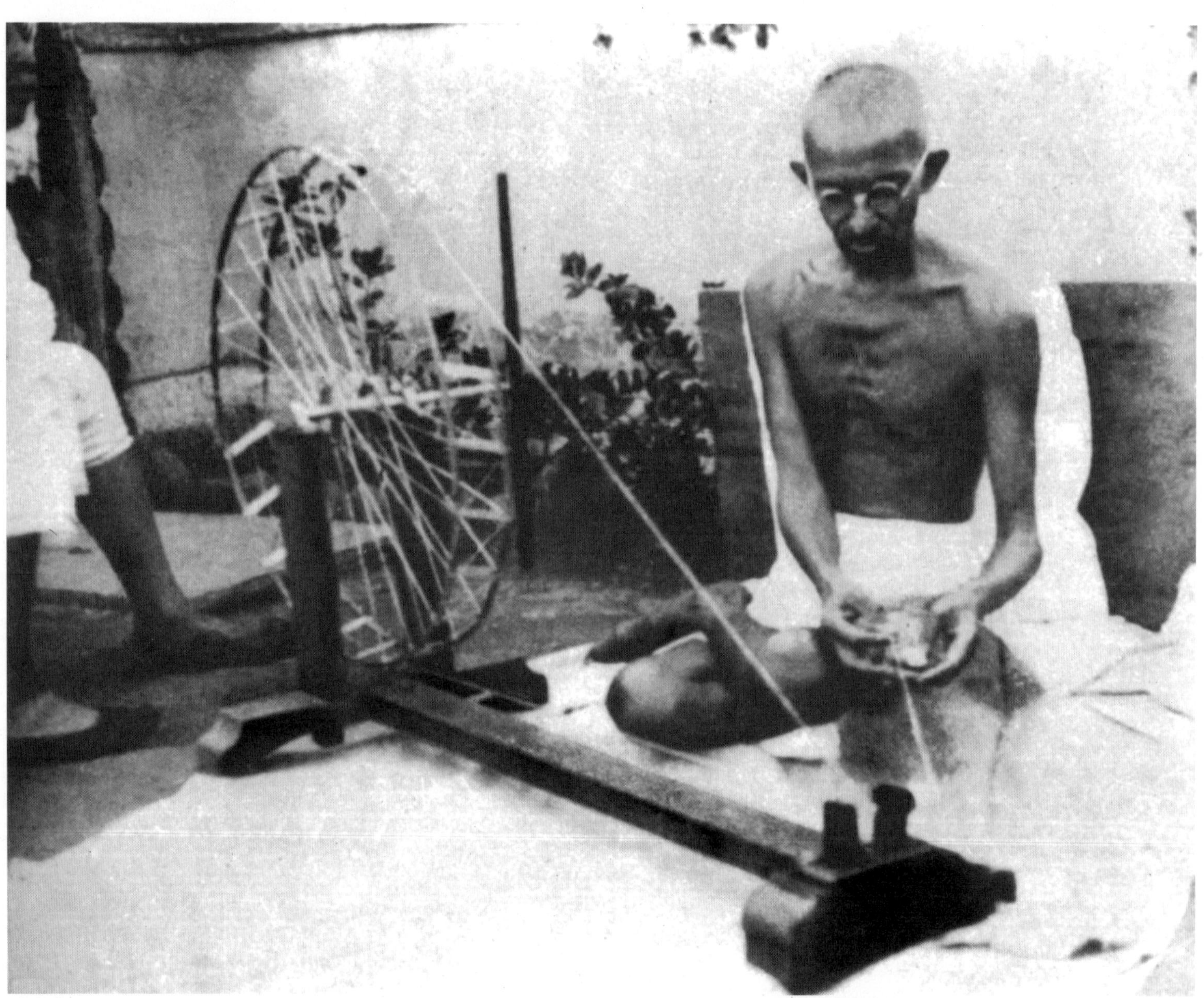

Mahatma Gandhi // National Gandhi Museum Archives

TIMELINE

1869
Born Mohandas Karamchand Gandhi in Porbandar, Gujarat, to father Karamchand and mother Putlibai

1881
Starts high school at Rajkot, Gujarat

1882
Marriage to Kasturbai, daughter of Gokuldas Makanji

1884–85
Takes to meat-eating in secret, but abandons the habit after about an year to avoid deceiving his parents

1887
Passes matriculation examination
Joins Samaldas College at Bhavnagar, Kathiawar, but gives up studies at the close of first term

1888
Harilal, their first son is born
Gandhi sails to Southampton, England
Reaches London
Enrols at the Inner Temple, Inn of Court
Reaches London
Lives on vegetarian diet
Takes lessons in dancing and music for a short while, considering them necessary parts of a gentleman's etiquette

1889
Reads books on simple living and decides to reduce his expenses by half
Studies religious literature
Reads the Bhagwad Gita for the first time and is deeply impacted

1890
Cultivates contacts with the vegetarian movement in London
Passes London Matriculation
Joins the Vegetarian Society

1891
Is called to the Bar in Bombay
Sails for India
Applies for admission to Bombay High Court

1892
Manilal, their second son is born
Struggles with legal practice at Rajkot and in Bombay
He later settles down at Rajkot as a legal draftsman

1893
Reaches Durban, South Africa, being engaged by a firm for legal work
Refuses to remove his turban as commanded by the judge, leaves the court calling it a sign of disrespect
Experiences colour discrimination in various forms, including being expelled from a train's first class carriage at Pietermartizburg Station
Decides to stay back and fight racial prejudice

1894
Founds the Natal Indian Congress
Enrols as the first Indian Advocate of the Supreme Court of Natal
Acquaints himself with the Bible, the Koran and Tolstoy's *The Kingdom of God is Within You*

1895
Devotes himself deeper to the Indian cause in South Africa
Issues *The Indian Franchise: An Appeal to Every Briton in South Africa*

1896
Returns to India and starts voicing on behalf of South African Indians
Writes, issues and tours (Bombay, Poona, Madras, Calcutta) with *The Green Pamphlet at Rajkot* to voice grievances of Indians in South Africa
Sails for South Africa with Kasturbai and their two sons

1897
Ramdas, their third son is born
Continues communicating with British and Indian public men regarding discriminatory laws

1898–99
Continues voicing against restrictions on Indians' trading rights
Establishes the Indian Ambulance Corp during the Boer War, providing stretchers and hospital assistance funded by the Indian community

1900
Their fourth son Devadas is born and Gandhi assists Kasturbai in the delivery
Sends a draft resolution on the state of South African Indians to Dadabhai Naoroji (one of the founding members of the Indian National Congress) for an upcoming Congress session

1901
Sails for India
Moves resolution on South Africa at a Congress session

1902
Visits Rangoon
Stays for a month with friend and guide Gopala Krishna Gokhale in Calcutta
Returns to Rajkot, starts practice
Moves to Bombay and sets up practice there
Is called to South Africa to champion the Indians' cause against anti-Asiatic legislation in Transvaal
Arrives in Durban and leads a delegation to the Chamberlain

1903
Enrolled as Attorney of the Supreme Court of Transvaal
Founds Transvaal British Indian Association
Sends regular updates to Dadabhai Naoroji
The first edition of *Indian Opinion* is published and later goes on to play a pivotal role in mobilizing the freedom movement

1904
Establishes the Phoenix Settlement near Durban
Organizes hospital and health services during an outbreak of plague in Johannesburg
Writes an array of articles on diet and well-being later translated and published as the *Guide to Health*

1905
Opposes the Bengal partition
Supports the boycott of British goods

1906
Takes the vow of Brahmcharya (abstinence; rightful movement towards the divine)
Satyagraha dawns at the Empire Theatre, Johannesburg where people take a pledge with God as their witness, to oppose the Black Act
Leaves for England as member of the Indian delegation to present the Indians' case to the Colonial Secretary
Returns to South Africa

1907

The Asiatic Registration Act is passed in the Transvaal Parliament amidst protests by Indians
Meets General Smuts at Pretoria and informs him of resolutions adopted at mass meetings
Pledges opposition to the "Black Act" in *Indian Opinion*
Writes to Smuts criticizing the Asiatic Registration Act, suggesting amendments. This is followed by passive resistance, picketing of permit offices
Gandhi defends passive resisters in court
Smuts decides to prosecute Gandhi

1908

Adopts "satyagraha" (insistence on the truth) instead of "passive resistance"
Gets a two-month prison sentence for refusal to register and failure to leave Transvaal
Signs agreement on voluntary registration with General Smuts, is released from prison
Near fatal attack on his life by Pathans who see his move as a betrayal of the Indian interest
Passive resistance and burning of registration certificates by Indians resumes
Gandhi is arrested for entry into Transvaal without permit and is sent to rigorous imprisonment for two months

1909

Writes to the press calling on Indians to prepare for the final phase of struggle
Arrested and released on two occasions upon failing to produce his registration certificate
Leaves for England as member of the Indian Delegation
Works tirelessly to educate British leaders and the people to move Imperial authorities
Writes to Leo Tolstoy about the Passive Resistance movement
Leaves for South Africa and pens the book *Hind Swaraj* on board the Kildonan Castle

1910

Corresponds with Tolstoy about the grave importance of passive resistance for humanity at large
Founds Tolstoy Farm in Transvaal
Vows to turn away from milk and begins experiments in fruitarian diet

1911

Constant insistence with General Smuts leads to a "provisional settlement" and his promise of repealing the Asiatic Registration and Immigrants' Restrictions Act
Invites Gopala Krishna Gokhale to South Africa

1912

Accompanies Gokhale on a tour of South Africa, Laurenco Marques, Mozambique and Zanzibar
Gives up European dressing and milk and restricts himself to a diet of fresh and dried fruit

1913

Indicates his return to India in *Indian Opinion*
Passive resistance resumes
Kasturba joins the passive resistance struggle, is arrested and sentenced to prison for three months
Kasturba released, Gandhi too released unconditionally

1914

Indian Relief Act passed (it abolished the compulsory £3 tax levied on those Indians in South Africa who hadn't renewed their indentures. It also recognized the validity of Indian marriages.)
Gandhi sails to London to meet Gokhale
Sails for India

1915

Upon reaching India, Gandhi is awarded the Kaisar-e-Hind-medal for his Ambulance Corp initiative during the Boer War
Founds the Satyagraha Ashram (later known as Sabarmati Ashram after the name of the river) in Ahmedabad
First Harijan family joins the Ashram
Is elected vice president of the Gujarat Sabha

1915–16

Tours India and Burma, travelling third class on the railways
Lectures at Benares Hindu University
Meets Jawaharlal Nehru for the first time at Lucknow Congress

1917

Travels to Champaran in Bihar to investigate the condition of the indigo farmers
Delivers a statement in the court about disobedience of prohibitary orders
Sabarmati Ashram is established
Presides over the first Gujarat Political Conference, Godhara
Mahadev Desai joined as his secretary

1918

Takes up the cause of textile labourers and becomes the arbiter between mill owners and mill hands in Ahmedabad and fasts to secure an amicable settlement of the dispute
Addresses a public meeting of 5000 peasants at Nadiad, Gujarat, and advises them to not pay land revenue

1919

Pledges Satyagraha against the Rowlett Act
National hartal (strike) and Satyagraha movement against the Rowlett Act

Arrested at Palval Station on way to Delhi for refusal to comply with order not to enter Punjab
Jallianwala Bagh massacre occurs in Amritsar, Punjab
Gandhi declares a three-day fast in Ahmedabad
After massive outbreaks of violence across the country, Gandhi suspends Satyagraha
First issue of the Gujarati monthly *Navjivan*, edited by Gandhi is published
First issue of the English weekly *Young India*, edited by Gandhi is published

1920
Returns honours bestowed by the Government
The Gujarat Vidyapith is established in Ahmedabad

1921
Leads the campaign for a complete boycott of foreign cloth
Is invested with complete powers of the Congress in Ahmedabad

1922
Notifies the viceroy of his intention to launch Satyagraha in Bardoli, Gujarat
Policemen are killed in the Chauri Chaura incident
Gandhi fasts for five days and abandons the Satyagraha movement
Is charged with sedition over articles appearing in *Young India*
Sentenced to prison for six years

1924
Is operated for appendicitis at Sassoon Hospital in Poona and is released from prison unconditionally thereafter
Begins a twenty one day fast in Delhi for communal harmony
Presides over the Belgaum Congress

1925
Establishes the All-India Spinners' Association
Madeleine Slade joins the Ashram, is named Miraben by Gandhi
Parts of his autobiography *The Story of My Experiments with Truth* begin appearing in *Young India*

1927
Gandhi visits Ceylon, erstwhile Sri Lanka

1928
Boycott of Simon Commission
Moves Congress in favour of India's independence if Dominion Status not granted by 1929

1929
Viceroy Lord Irwin announces the Round Table Conference
The idea of purna swaraj or complete independence is adopted at the Lahore Congress

1930
Gandhi writes to the viceroy about an intention to break the Salt Law if the Congress demands remain unheeded
The Dandi March begins from the Sabarmati Ashram to initiate the Salt Satyagraha
Breaks the Salt Law by a gesture of picking up a handful of salt from the shore
Gandhi is arrested without trial and sent to the Yeravda Prison in Poona

1931
Gandhi is unconditionally released from prison
The Gandhi-Irwin pact is signed
Leaves for London as Congress's sole representative for the second Round Table Conference
Meets Romain Rolland
Meets Mussolini

1932
Gandhi is arrested without trial and sent to Yeravda prison
Commences "fast unto death" in jail to secure abolition of separate electorates for Harijans in Communal Award
The Poona Pact is signed
Breaks fast on Government of India's acceptance of his demand
regarding Harijans

1933
Founds *Harijan*, a weekly paper in English and Hindi
Resolves to go on a twenty-one-day fast for purification
Declares his intention to offer individual Satyagraha
Nationwide Harijan tour commences

1934
Announces decision to retire from politics to engage in development of village industries, Harijan service and education through indigenous crafts and skills
Inaugurates All-India Village Industries Association

1936
Makes Sevagram in Gujarat his headquarters

1939
Commences "fast unto death" at Rajkot to secure the promise made to reform administration and ends it on the viceroy's intervention

1941
Relieved from his service to the Congress at his own request

1942
Gandhi appeals to the British Government to quit India

1944
Kasturba dies
Gandhi continues talks with Mohammad Ali Jinnah regarding Pakistan

1945-46
Tours Bengal and Assam
The Noakhali massacre occurs

1947
Gandhi tours riot affected areas in Bihar
Urges for amicable settlement between India and Pakistan

1948
Begins a fast for communal harmony while in Delhi, at great detriment to his health
A bomb explosion shakes up a prayer meeting but Gandhi urges people to not pay heed to the violence
Is made prey to bullets aimed at his chest on way to his daily prayer meeting

THE GREATEST MAN OF THE DAY

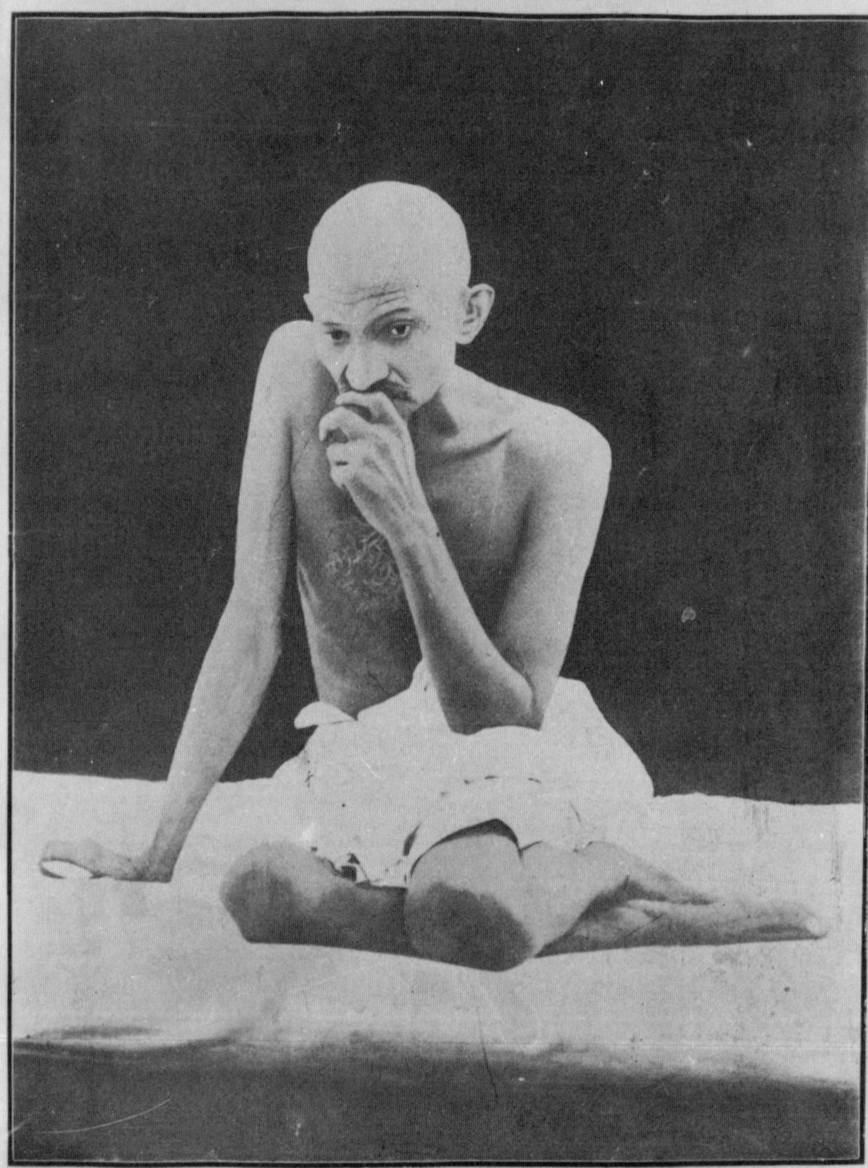

L. K. BHATT
ALLAHABAD

MAHATMA GANDHI

The Indian Press, Ltd., Allahabad.

GLOSSARY

Adi – First, foremost.

Adi yogi – The very first yogi, this refers to Lord Shiva.

Ahimsa – Non-violence. A pivotal value and tool Mahatma Gandhi urged all Indians to inculcate in the fight for freedom.

Ananta – Endless, eternal, infinitely expanding.

Apsara – Nymph.

Ashram – A sanctuary, a hermitage.

Asteya – Non-stealing.

Avatar – A form of incarnation.

Brahmacharya – Rightful movement towards the divine. Also contextualized as abstinence.

Champaran – A district in Bihar, India, where Mahatma Gandhi sowed the seeds of the independence movement in 1917 by standing up for indigo farmers who were forced to grow indigo in return of little or no payment from the British.

Channapatna – A city in Karnataka known for its wooden toys. The technique of handcrafting wooden artifacts in Channapatna uses traditional lacquer and natural dyes.

Dandi – A village in the Navsari District of Gujarat, India. Mahatma Gandhi marched from his ashram in Sabarmati to Dandi to initiate the salt satyagraha.

Dashavatar – This refers to the ten avataras Lord Vishnu is believed to have been incarnated as. Matsya, Kurma, Varaha and Narsimha are a few.

Devnagri – Literally translated as the town of gods, Devnagri generally refers to the script which forms the basis of Sanskrit, Hindi and many modern Indian languages.

Dwarka – Literally translated as "gateway", in mythology it refers to the birthplace of Lord Krishna.

Harijan – People of God. Mahatma Gandhi coined this term for people called untouchable under the Hindu caste system.

Indigo – A tropical plant from which a dye of the same colour is obtained.

Jamdani – Literally, a holder for flowers. A discontinuous weft technique of weaving where motifs are inlaid into the fabric by adding a denser thread to fine warp threads by hand.

Kantilo – An indigenous craft technique from a place with the same name in Odisha, India. The technique employs hand-crafting pieces in bell metal, an alloy of copper and tin.

Kauravas – Descendants of the Kuru dynasty and one of the main protagonists in the epic Mahabharat.

Khadi – Originating from the word "kati" which means hand-spinning, khadi refers to hand spun cloth where fibres of cotton, wool or silk are woven by hand into fabric on a spinning wheel or a loom.

Lingam – A symbol.

Lithograph – "Litho" refers to stone and "graphy" to any form of writing, drawing, painting or recording. A lithograph is a stone plate carrying works of art or writing.

Longpi – A village in Manipur, India. Also a traditional style of pottery from the region that uses black serpentite stone and weathered rock.

Loom – A structured apparatus, usually wooden, used for weaving yarn or thread to create fabric.

Magic Bus – A charity founded in Mumbai by Matthew Spacie in 1999. It enables children and young adults to complete higher education in order to delay their age of marriage, to find jobs and to move out of the spiral of economic poverty.

Mahabharat – An epic tale of the battle between the Kauravas and Pandavas on the fields of Kurukshetra. The tale is in the form of poetry, authored by Ved Vyasa around the 400 BCE. It comprises nearly 100,000 couplets.

Maharshi – Great sage.

Mahatma – "Maha" means great and "atma" signifies the soul. Mahatma is usually a title accorded to and associated with saints, great leaders and sages who impact the world with their thoughts and messages.

Manthan – Churning. Often refers to the mythical churning of the cosmic sea as narrated in ancient Indian texts like the Bhagwad and Vishnu Puranas.

Manu – The archetypal first man, considered the progenitor of mankind.

Moksha – Eternal liberation.

Mudra- A symbolic gesture involving the hands or entire body with deep significance in spiritual sciences and classical dance forms.

Neel – Indigo; the colour blue.

Pallu – The end of a sari which drapes and hangs freely over the shoulder. More often than not, it is characterized by special motifs, prints or embroidery that set it apart from the rest of the fabric of the sari.

Pandavas – Descendants of the Pandu dynasty and one of the main protagonists in the epic Mahabharat.

Santati – A continuum. It can also imply seed, generation, posterity.

Sari – A garment traditionally comprising six to nine yards of fabric that drapes around the body without involving any stitching. In Sanskrit it translates as a strip of cloth.

Satya – The truth.

Satyagraha – Insistence on truth. The term became popular as a movement when Mahatma Gandhi started the Dandi march to initiate an urging in people to understand their own truth, their wealth, their resources.

Seshnarayana/ Sheshnarayana – "Shesha" referes to a mythical, divine serpent and "Narayana" is one who resides in water. This term is used to denote the form of Lord Vishnu resting on the cosmic ocean, protected and upheld by the divine serpent.

Shakunta – A kind of bird, sometimes alluded to the Indian vulture, sometimes to the blue jay.

Shanti – Absolute peace. Stillness of being.

Swadesi/ Swadeshi – Of one's own country. Gandhi turned this into a movement by inspiring people to boycott all British goods and to harness the powers of their indigenous industry and resources.

Vaahana – Vehicle. Commonly it is a mythical animal or bird that accompanies gods and goddesses in mythology.

Veena – A classical stringed instrument.

Warp – The foundation threads on a loom over and under which other threads are passed to create cloth. Also, a twist.

Weft – Threads that go over and under the warp to weave and create cloth.

Yama – Code of living, mostly referring to one's social responsibilities and way of being. It includes values like truth, non-violence and non-accumulation.

ACKNOWLEDGEMENTS

Lavina Baldota
For her seamless helming of *Santati* from concept to curation and execution. And for her impeccable translation of verses into Hindi.

Abheraj Baldota Foundation
For being the central pillar behind the exhibition and staying true to the Gandhian values that lie at the core of the Foundation.

Kishore Jhunjhunwala
For his most inspiring life story, for lending his experience, expertise and rarest collection and their images to *Santati*.

Tina Motwani
For her incisive and poetic photography of the exhibition.

Vijendra Bhardwaj
For being the vision behind the design, flow and spirit of this book.

Meena Rajasekaran
For her careful and diligent fine-tuning throughout the design process.

National Gallery of Modern Art (NGMA)
Indira Gandhi Centre for the Arts (IGNCA)
Raja Ravi Varma Heritage Foundation
National Gandhi Museum and Library, New Delhi
Mani Bhawan, Mumbai
White Media Marketing
Sir JJ School of Art, Mumbai
Museum of Art and Photography (MAP), Bengaluru
Ministry of Culture
Ministry of Textiles

PHOTOGRAPH CREDITS

Photographs from National Gandhi Museum Archives

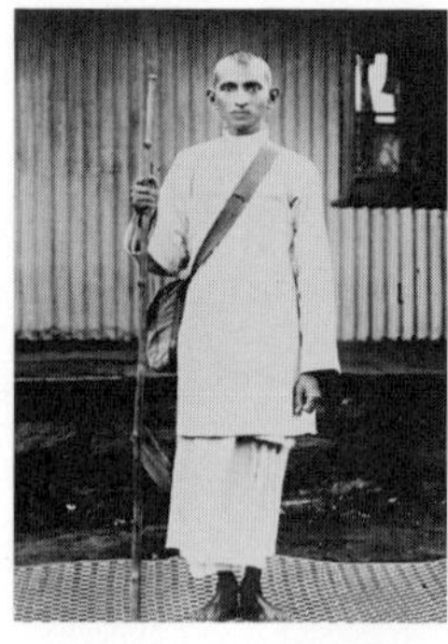

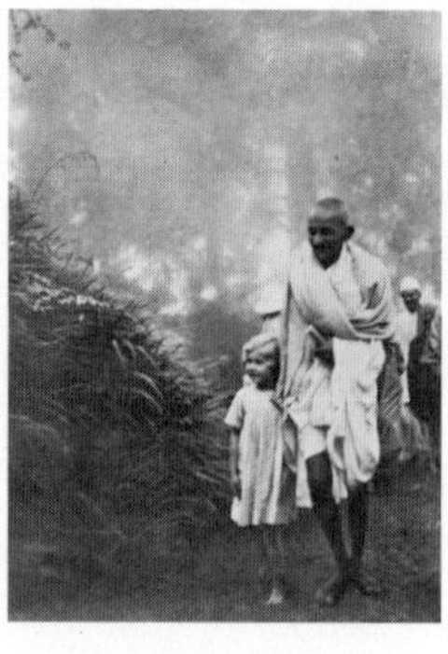

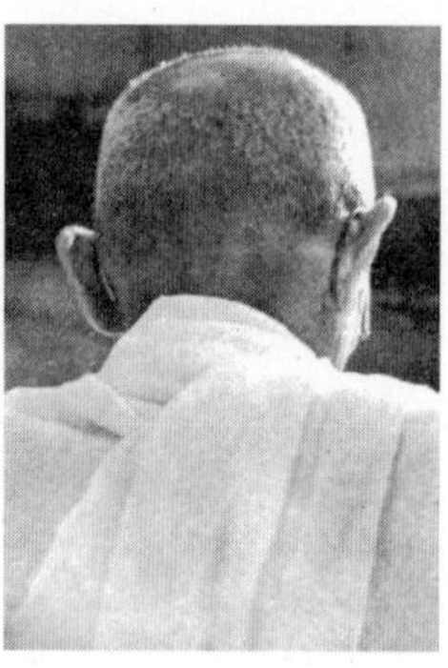

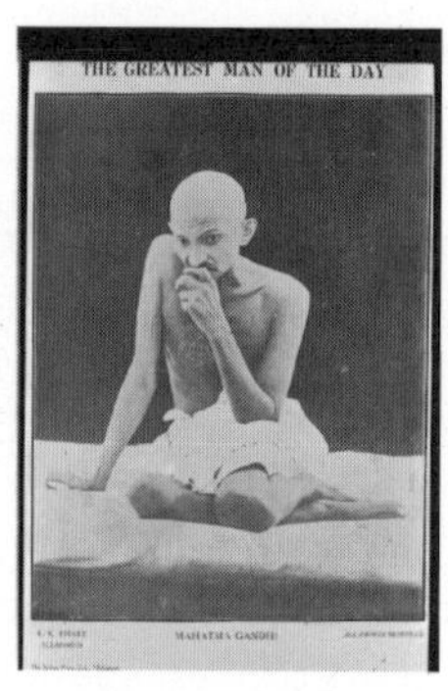

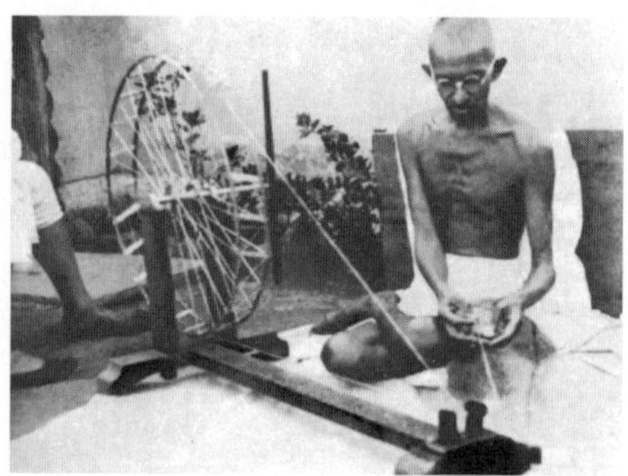

Photographs by Tina Motwani

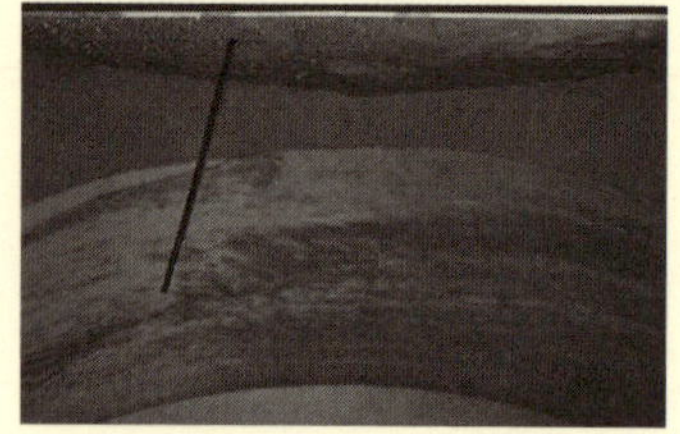

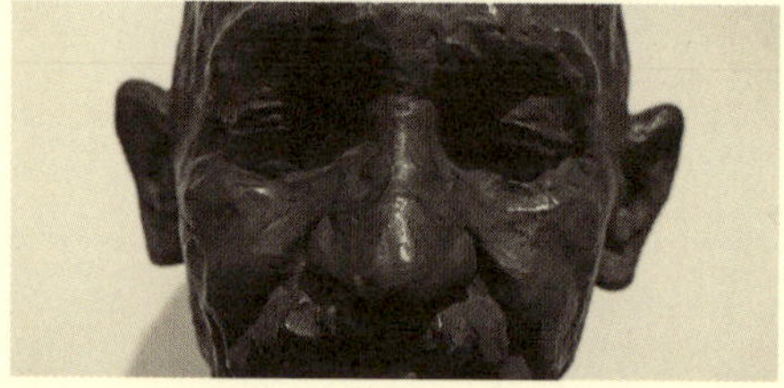

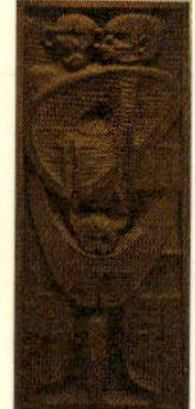

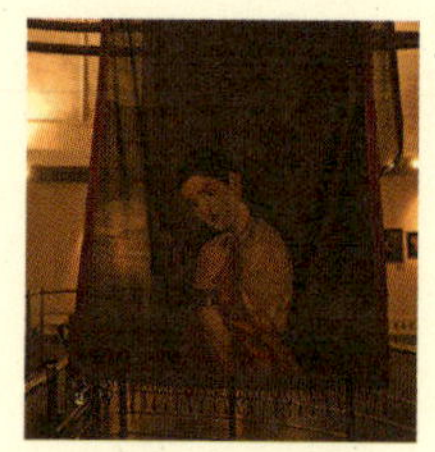

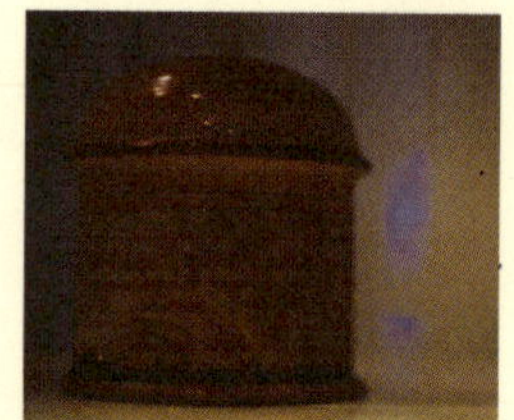

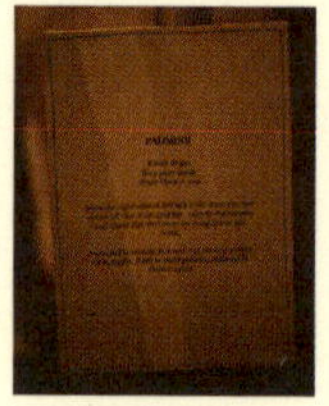

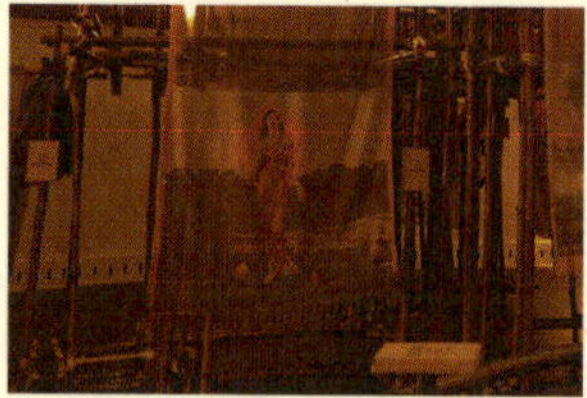

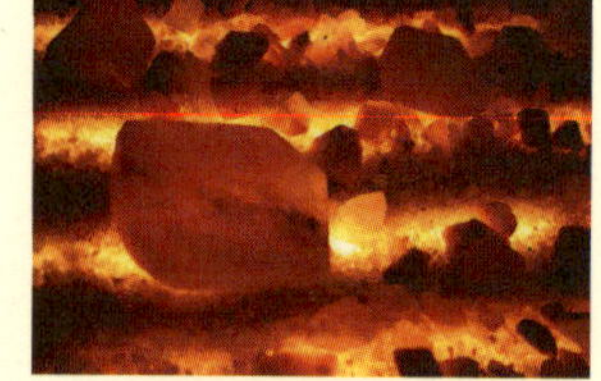

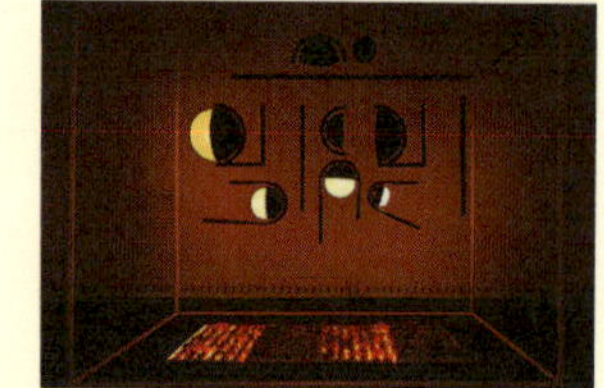

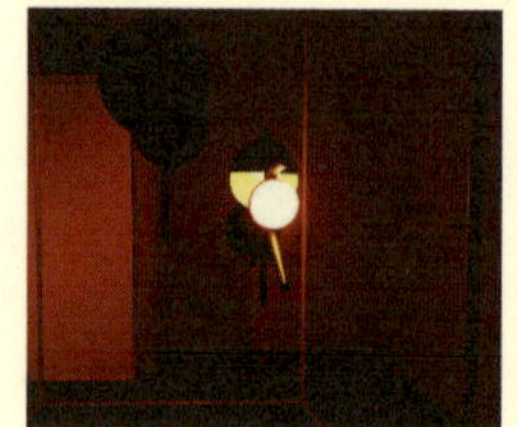

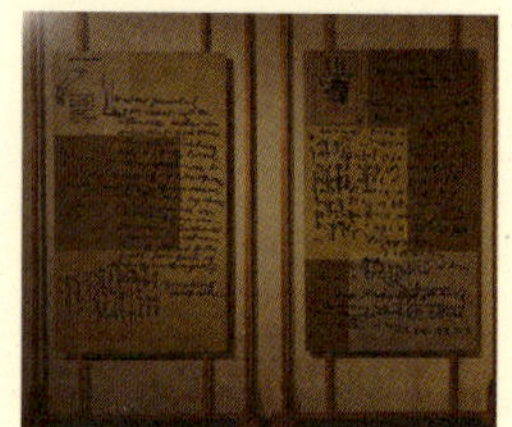

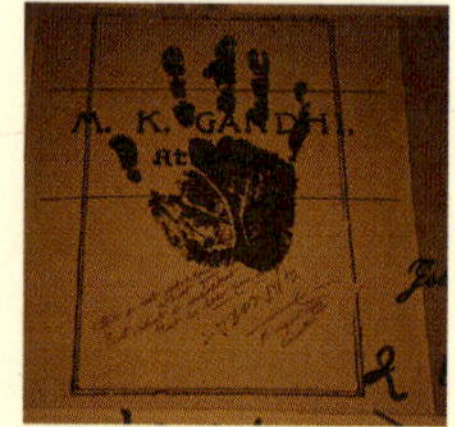

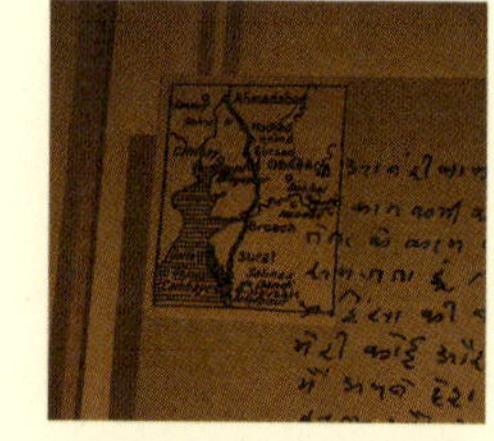

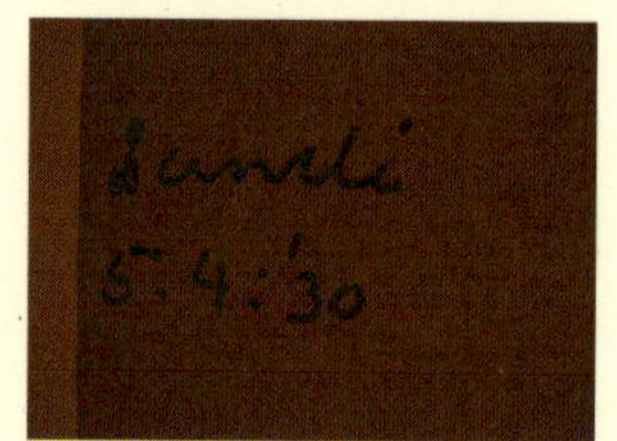

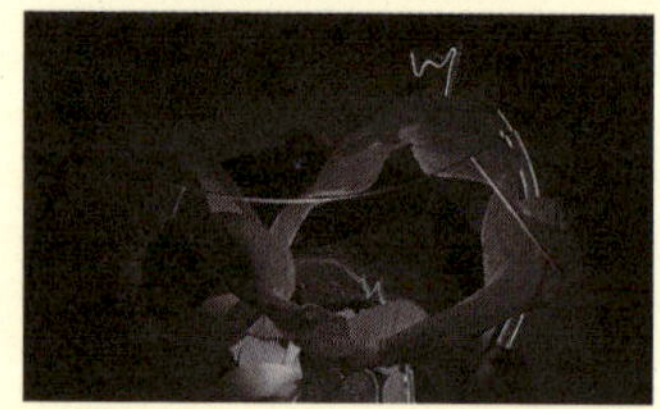

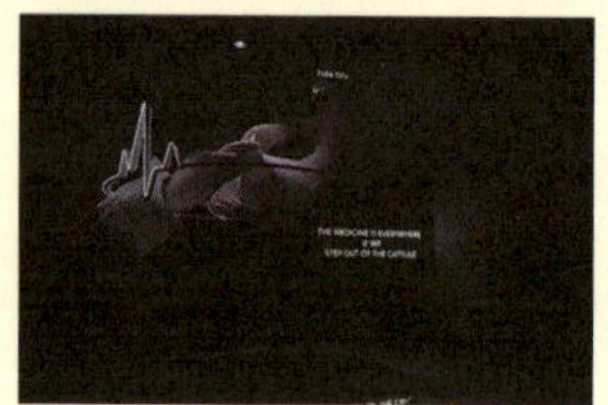

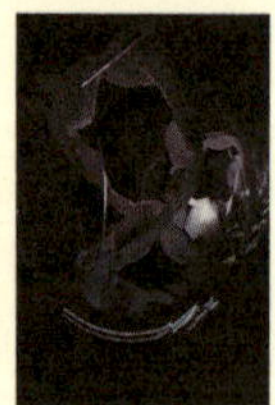

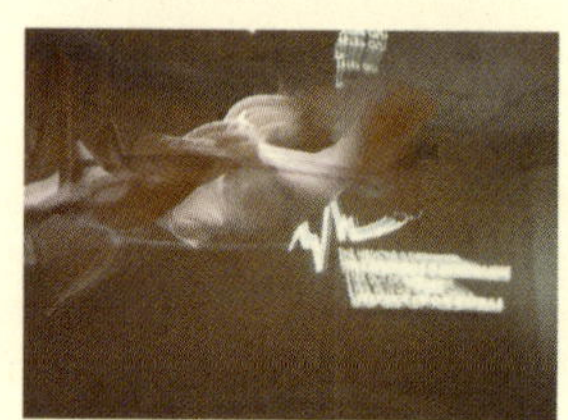

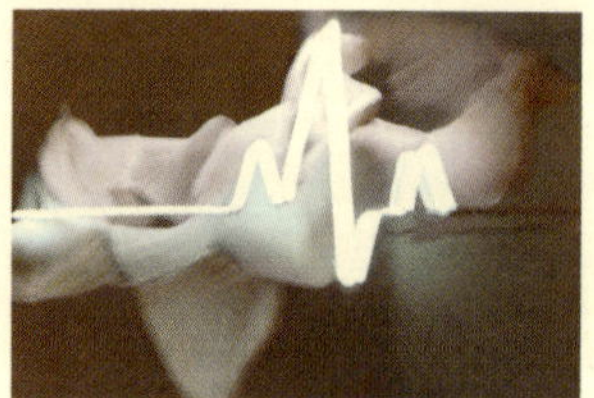

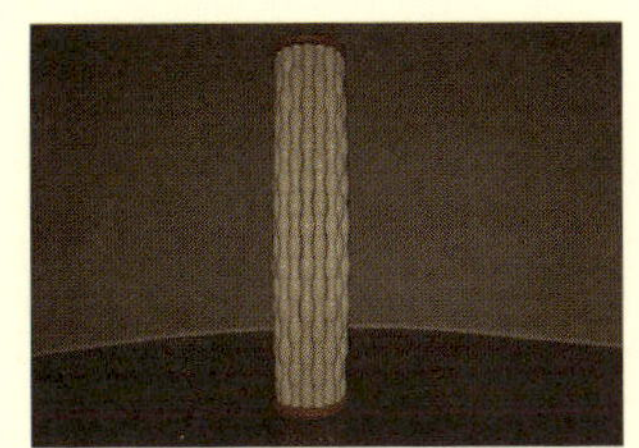
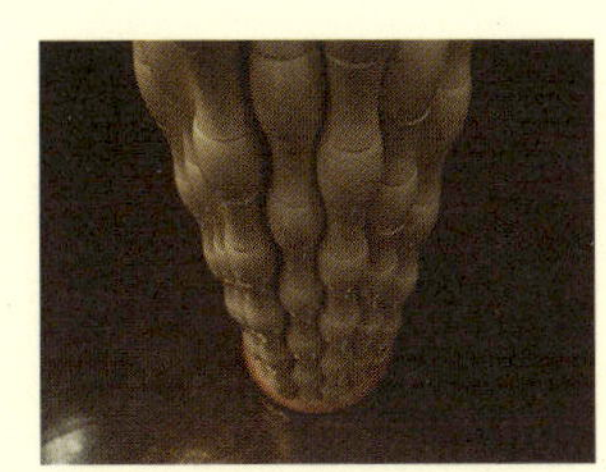
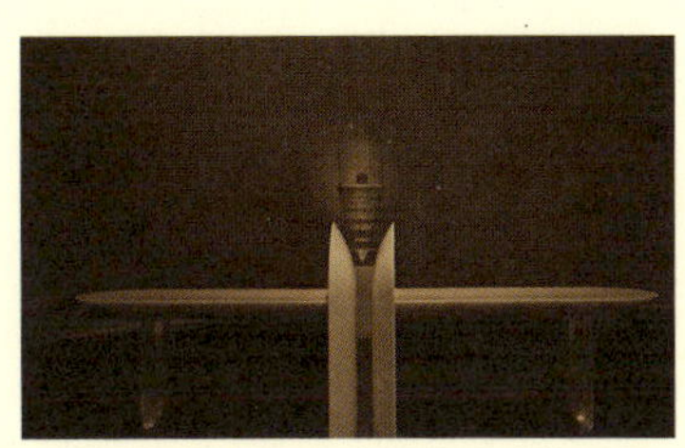
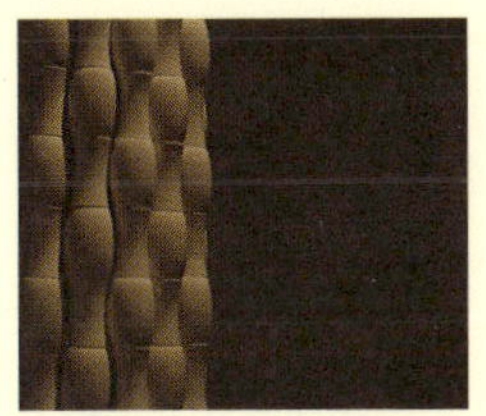
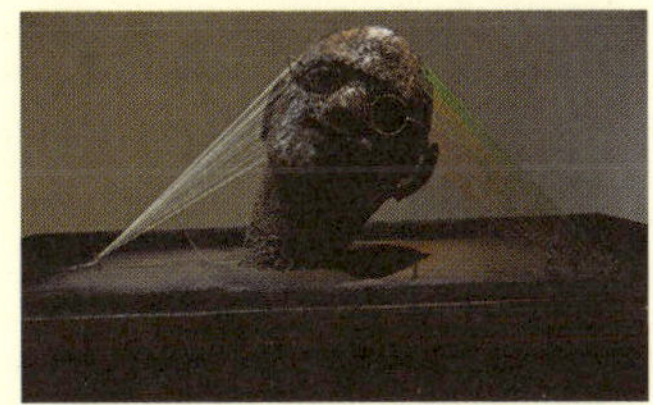
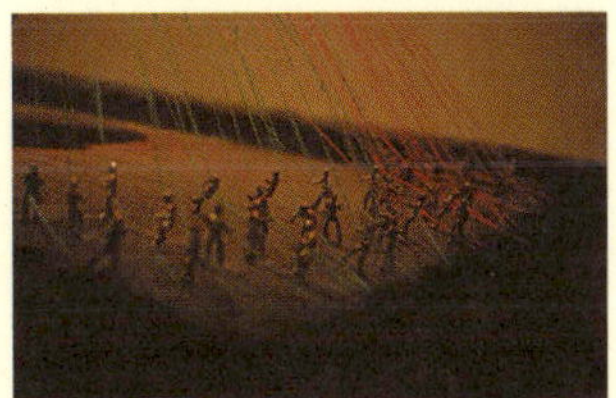
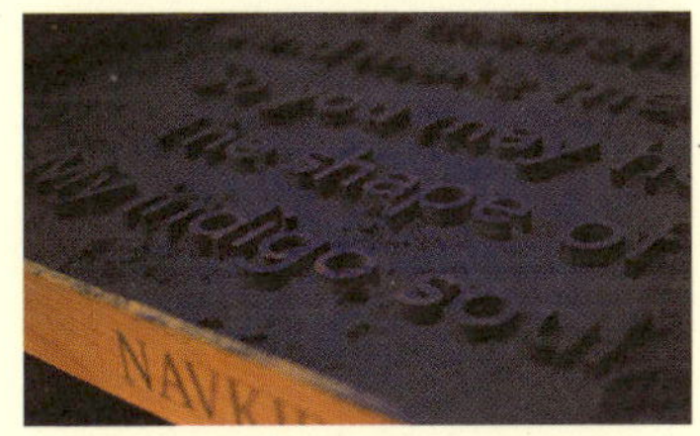
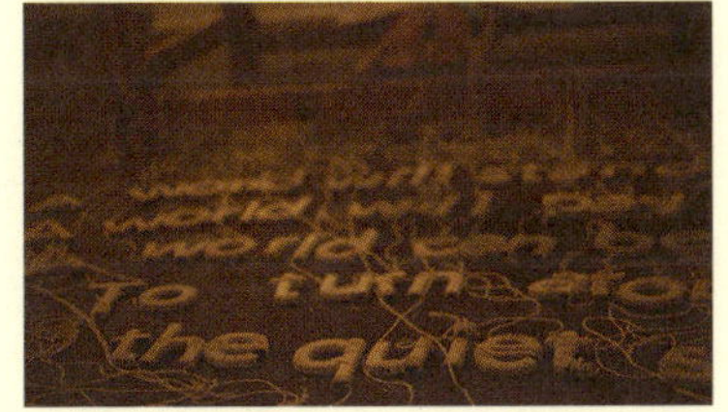
the quiet
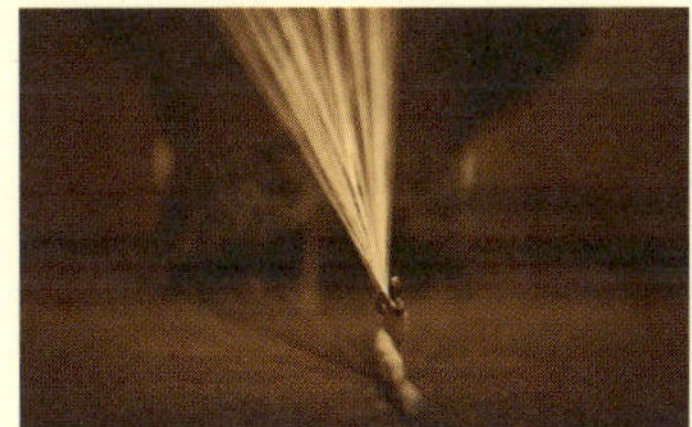
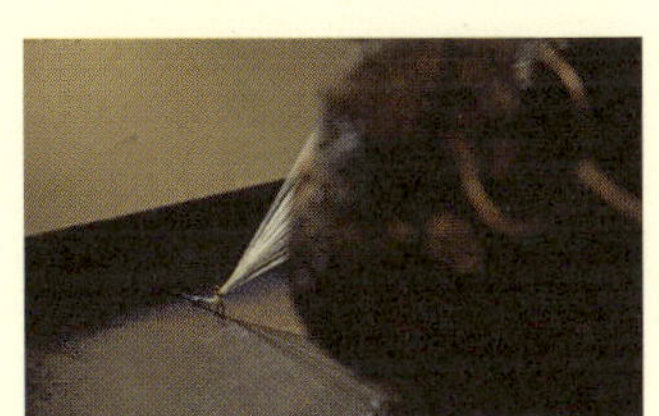

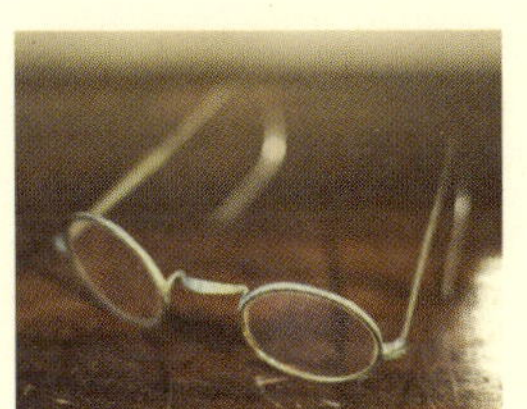
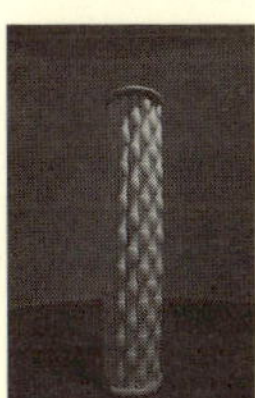

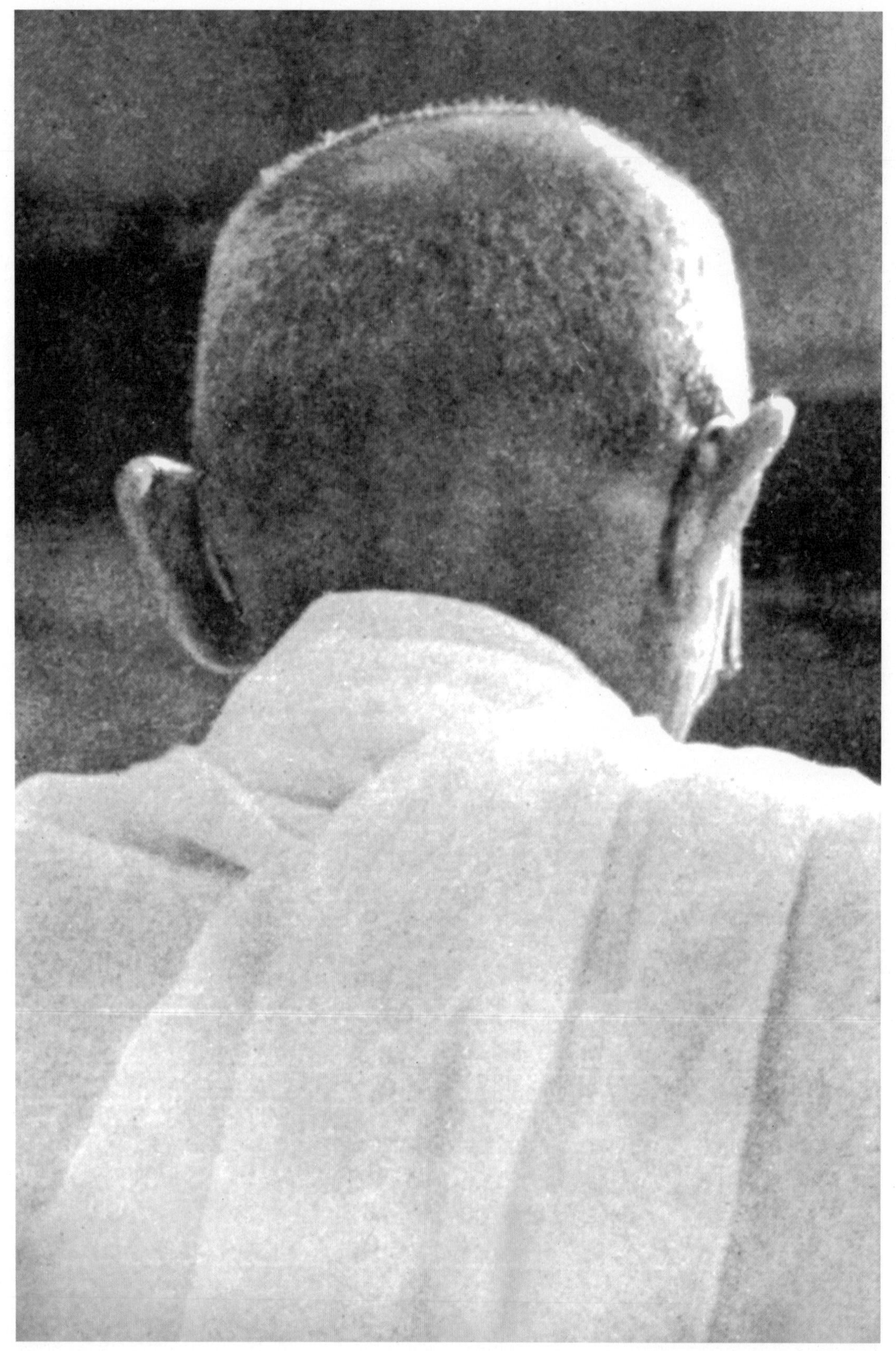

अहिंसासत्यास्तेयब्रह्मचर्यापरिग्रहा यमाः॥

Patanjali Yogsutra 2.30

Ahimsa (non-violence), Satya (truth), Asteya (non-stealing), Brahmcharya (rightful movement towards the divine), Aparigraha (non-accumulation). These five principles form the *yama* (codes of living) limb of the eight limbs of yog described in most ancient texts. If Mahatma Gandhi's life be viewed as a centre of the wheel, these principles form the very spokes around which all his actions and messages revolved.

Reflecting on how sharply precise and poetically rounded his messages continue to remain 150 years after he was born, *Santati* is a tribute to Mahatma Gandhi. Then, Now, Next.

Opposite: **Mahatma Gandhi** // National Gandhi Museum Archives

“The odd thing about assassins, Dr King, is that they think they’ve killed you.”

Mahatma Gandhi